SOCIAL CHANGE AND PUBLIC ADMINISTRATION IN INDIA

SOCIAL CHANGE AND PUBLIC ADMINISTRATION IN INDIA

Edited by
S.N. Singh
K.K. Srivastava
S.S. Chauhan

KALPAZ

ISBN: 978-93-5128-199-3
Price: ₹ 1220/-

First Published 2016

Published by

Kalpaz Publications
C-30, Satyawati Nagar,
Delhi - 110052
E-mail: kalpaz@hotmail.com Ph.: 9212142040

Printed at : G. Print Process, Delhi

Cataloging in Publication Data--DK

Courtesy: D.K. Agencies (P) Ltd. <docinfo@dkagencies.com>

Social change and public administration in India / edited by S.N. Singh, K.K. Srivastava, S.S. Chauhan.

pages cm

Papers presented at a National Seminar on Social Change and Policy Issues with particular Focus on SC/ST organised by Institute for Applied Research and Development, Lucknow with financial support from the Indian Council of Social Science Research, New Delhi.

Includes bibliographical references.

ISBN 9789351282006 (hardback)

1. Social change--India--Congresses. 2. Public administration--India--Congresses. I. Singh, S. N. (Surya Narain), 1941- editor. II. Srivastava, K. K., editor. III. Chauhan, S. S., editor. IV. Institute for Applied Research & Development (Lucknow, India), organizer. V. Indian Council of Social Science Research, sponsoring body.

HN683.5.S65 2016 DDC 303.40954 23

Contents

Preface

It is a historical fact that India persisted with a social order with an elaborate hierarchical system in which we also find an inherent inequality of various nature. However, after independence a conscious effort was made to change that social order as the framers of the Constitution of modern India believed that such a system was not in consonance with a democratic political system. Hence, we now have the Constitution of India that provided for a socialist, secular, democratic Republic for the future governance of the country. The new political system attempted to base itself on the principles of freedom and equality. It is a matter of fact that inequality of various kinds prevailed and persisted in the earlier social order while the founding fathers wanted to change it into a system wherein freedom, equality and fraternity should get primacy over inequality and reduce the gap between the rich and the poor and remove the hierarchical barrier.

There is no denying the fact that in the last six decades or so of our planned development several efforts have been made by the successive governments to address the issues concerning social change and social justice. Special programmes were designed for the underprivileged sections of our society, particularly the Scheduled Castes and Scheduled Tribes and women. However, there are serious doubts being expressed in the concerned circles about the positive impact of these efforts and their success. It is often alleged that little change can be seen so far as the question of social justice is concerned or the same making any substantial, visible impact in our contemporary social order. In view of the questions raised and doubts expressed about various governmental and non-governmental efforts in this sphere, it was thought pertinent to have the issue rationally debated. In view of this, therefore, the Institute for Applied Research and Development, Lucknow, organised a national seminar on Social Change and Policy Issues with particular Focus on SC/ST with financial support from the Indian Council of Social Science Research, New Delhi. The national seminar was well attended by imminent scholars and budding social scientists. The issue was extensively debated and papers presented. The present book is the result of the same and an attempt to get the papers a wider circulation and reach. It is hoped that the book would be able to generate interest in the concerned circles about the problem being faced in contemporary India.

S.N. Singh
K.K. Srivastava
S.S. Chauhan

Acknowledgements

Any activity of such a dimension needs cooperation and support from individuals as well as institutions to make it successful venture. We, therefore, take this opportunity to express our grateful thanks to those whose help and support made this effort a success. Our thanks are due first of all to the Indian Council of Social Science Research, New Delhi for providing the financial support to organise the said national seminar as without this it would not have been possible to organise the seminar on that scale.

We are thankful to the then Vice Chancellor of University of Lucknow, Professor S.B. Nimse for inaugurating the national seminar and also provide support to the academic activities of the Institute. We express our thanks to Professor K. Kishore, Professor Manoj Dixit, Dr N.L. Bharti, Dr Vaishali Saxena from the Department of Public Administration, Lucknow University for their continuous encouragement and cooperation not only in this particular Seminar but also in other academic activities of the Institute. We would also like to thank Professor S.K. Singh of the Department of Public Administration, Lucknow University, Professor I.D. Mishra from Gorakhpur University and Professor B.K. Tewari from Lucknow University for their active interest and interaction in the activities of the Institute for all these years. We are grateful to our contributors who have enriched the deliberations with their thoughts. We thank Dr A.K. Singh of RCUES, Lucknow for his support in our venture. We thank Sri Pramod Kumar for getting the manuscript computer typed in record time. In the end we express our thanks to the publisher for getting the book see the light of the day.

S.N. Singh
K.K. Srivastava
S.S. Chauhan

List of Contributors

I.D. Mishra: Former Professor and Head, Department of Political Science D.D.U. Gorakhpur University, Gorakhpur and Ex Senior Fellow, ICSSR, New Delhi.

P.N. Gautam: Retired Professor, Department of Public Administration, H.P.U., Shimla, Gautam Kuteer, Sanjauli, Shimla, 171006.

Harbans Pathak: Director, Punjab School of Public Administration and Formerly Professor and Head, Deptt. of Public Administration, Punjabi University, Patiala.

S.K. Singh: Former Professor of Public Administration Lucknow University and Professor of Public Management, Ethiopian, Civil Service University, Addis Ababa, Ethiopia.

R.K. Prabhakar: Associate Professor (Retd.), M.D. University, Rohtak.

A.K. Singh: Assistant Director, R.C.U.E.S., Lucknow University, Lucknow.

Vaishai Saxena: Asst. Professor, Department of Pub. Admn., University of Lucknow, Lucknow.

Nandita Kaushal: Assistant Professor, Department of Pub. Admn., University of Lucknow, Lucknow.

K.K. Srivastava: Faculty, Department of Pub. Admn., University of Lucknow, Lucknow.

S.S. Chauhan: Faculty Member, Department of Pub. Admn., University of Lucknow.

Nimish Gupta: Associate Professor, Amity Business School, Lucknow.

Mridul Srivastava: Assistant Registrar and Faculty in Criminology, Dr Ram Manohar Lohiya National Law University, Lucknow.

Preeti Dwivedi: Assistant Professor (Sociology), Mahila Mahavidyalaya (PG) College, Kidwai Nagar, Kanpur.

Devi Prasad Srivastava: PDF JNV University, Jodhpur.

Saurabh Chandra: UGC-NET (Public Administration), ORCID iD: http://orcid.org/0000-0002-3343-3676,E-Mail: schandra.info1@gmail.com, Phone No. +91-8009074196

Abha Singh: Asstt. Professor, Narmada College of Science and Commerce, Bharuch, Gujarat

Chinmayee Chaturvedi: Asst. Professor, D.S. College, Meerut.

Shilpi Mishra: Senior Research Fellow, Department of Public Administration, University of Lucknow, Lucknow.

Ram Prasad Pal: Assistant Professor, Department of Public Administration and Development Management, Dilla University, Dilla, Ethiopia.

L.K. Kundan: अध्यक्ष, स्नातकोत्तर राजनीति विज्ञान विभाग, रांची कॉलेज, रांची, झारखण्ड।

N.L. Bharti: एसोसिएट प्रोफेसर, लोक प्रशासन विभाग, लखनऊ विश्वविद्यालय, लखनऊ।

Gopal Prasad: उपाचार्य, राजनीति विज्ञान विभाग, दीनदयाल उपाध्याय गोरखपुर विश्वविद्यालय, गोरखपुर, उ.प्र.।

Meena Rahul: शोध छात्रा, राजनीति विज्ञान विभाग, प्रताप विश्वविद्यालय, जयपुर, राजस्थान।

Nagendra Kumar: प्रवक्ता, राजनीति विज्ञान, इण्टर कॉलेज, विशुनपुरकलां, देवरिया, उ.प्र.।

Ram Baran: पोस्ट डाक्टोरल फेलो, लोक प्रशासन, विभाग, लखनऊ विश्वविद्यालय।

Ajay Kumar: समाजशास्त्र विभाग, अम्बेडकर अध्ययन विद्यापीठ (समाज विज्ञान), बी0बी0ए0यू0 (केन्द्रीय विश्वविद्यालय), लखनऊ।

Arvind Kumar Patel: एम0ए0, एम0फिल प्रवक्ता, सांई डिग्री कालेज, फतेहपुर, बांराबंकी, उ0प्र0।

Deepti Srivastava: सीनियर रिसर्च फेलो, लोक प्रशासन विभाग, लखनऊ विश्वविद्यालय, लखनऊ।

Noor Fatima Ansari: शोध छात्रा, लोक प्रशासन विभाग, लखनऊ विश्वविद्यालय, लखनऊ।

A.K. Upadhyay: सहायक प्राध्यापक समाजशास्त्र, शास. महर्षि अरविंद महा.वि., गोहद।

Introduction

Social change in India remains an eternal quest. There is no denying the fact India is an ancient society with traditional hierarchies based on the principles of "Karma" which later developed into a rigid caste system. Such a social system persisted for more than five thousand years of recorded history. The post-independence India, however, opted for deliberate departure from its historical past. Traditionally India has been a hierarchical social order comprising of different class/caste categories which we now term them as 'general', SC, ST, Backward and OBC. Under each category we have different caste groups and sub-groups occupying different social status in the overall social hierarchy. The new India, however, opted for a different social order based on freedom and equality. It consciously planned for egalitarian social order. To give shape and meaning alongwith a statutory state, the Constitution of India in its Preamble clearly indicated that it shall be a 'democratic, socialist, secular, republic'. It was a conscious effort on the part of the policy planners to effect social change through various means including policy interventions.

The special concern for social change also was pertinent to attain social justice for the vast majority of people living in abject poverty. Social justice in our Socialist Republic is socio-economic revolution in the current miasmic milieu. And in contemporary India, the human condition is so poignant that governments have been constrained to profess and promise revolutionary change.[1] Socio-economic inequality has often led to serious disbalance in the overall national growth map. It has often led to law and order problem in various situations. A study conducted in the villages of all five regions of Uttar Pradesh suggested that economic causes are at the root of the caste conflicts in the State. The study makes the startling revelation that Zamindari abolition has led to disparities in the land holding and its concentration in the hands of big land holders.[2] Although the abolition of zamindari system was contemplated to help the re-distribution of land and establish a more egalitarian distribution of land in the rural areas. It however, could not achieve that and resulted into a concentration of land in the hands of big land holders. The change expected through this measure could hardly be achieved.

Social Change through Planned Approach

The post-independence period marks a different and definite era in the history of the country towards planned development through which the country anticipated to enforce change in various sectors. The First Five Year Plan was launched in 1951 with a view to achieve the goals set forth towards socio-economic upliftment. As a matter of fact the effort is on since then. It may be noted that the First Five Year Plan claimed that the central objectives of planning in India at present stage is to initiate a process of development which will raise living standards and open out to the people new opportunities for a richer and more varied life.[3] The successive plans also aimed at a similar effort. But the manner in which this purpose has been translated into specific objective varied from plan to plan. However, in a broad sense, the basic objectives of planning in India can be grouped under four heads: growth, modernisation, self-reliance and social justice.[4] This has persisted as a major goal in the decades that followed.

In the initial years in order to achieve the goals set forth in the First Five Year Plan, a new approach through Community Development Programme was launched in the country. The Community Development Programme was a participative development approach. It was anticipated that people should be involved in the planning process at the lower level. For the purpose a new unit in the name of Block was created to fulfill that objective. It was a programme started in the year 1952 to register development in the rural areas which ought to bring socio-economic change. Participation of various sections of rural society particularly the Scheduled Castes and Scheduled Tribes was expected to bring socio-economic change in the rural areas. This experiment of community development could not succeed. Consequently, we had the Balwantrai Committee set up in 1957 to suggest measures to enlist people's participation in the planning process at the district level and below to ensure development through people's participation. After the recommendations of Balwantrai Mehta Committee Report were accepted, the Panchayati Raj system was introduced in the country for the purpose. It was a three tier structure of rural local bodies in which participation of various sections of the population was ensured, particularly women, SCs and STs. This system continued for some decades to empower people in self-governing process and ensure development of the area. Through Panchayati Raj we were able to register some social and economic change in rural India.

Apart from these efforts of organisational changes in the rural sector to register change in the social and economic sphere, the Government of India made efforts through a number of programmes to bring social change. This was initiated through several programmes which improved the weaker sections economically. More specifically the Integrated Rural Development Programme launched through the Sixth Five Year Plan in the 80's was considered to be the direct attack on poverty. We had seen that the question of poverty and unemployment were the biggest challenges towards changing rural India. In order to remove poverty and generate resources in rural areas, IRDP was launched. It was expected that this programme would bring substantial change in the poverty scenario and bring about positive changes in the socio-economic sphere. It may be noted that

IRDP could bring some change, but it could not be much effective in breaking the poverty scenario to any considerable degree. Even the then Prime Minister, Rajiv Gandhi commented that only 15 paisa of a rupee reaches to the targeted group, and this explains the contemporary scenario.

During the post-Sixth Plan period too, a number of policy initiatives can be seen to bring about socio-economic change in the rural areas. It was alleged that inspite of the efforts made by the Government of India through various centrally sponsored schemes towards economic empowerment of the rural populace, not much improvement could be effected in that sector. The panchayati raj institutions did involve people in the electoral and organisational process, but that too lacked the will to change the traditional social structure, process and behaviour. The weaker sections including the SCs and STs remained largely unaffected by the general ethos of participation and development. This called for a new approach to bring about the needed change.

In this context we can very well note the historic step in the form of 73rd and 74th Constitutional Amendment Acts of the 90's which brought about a new concept in the democratic decentralisation framework. One can identify the provision of the Acts which made reservation for Scheduled Castes and Scheduled Tribes in the three tier structure. Since the panchayati raj bodies were guaranteed the constitutional status, this provision of reservation for these social groups reached meaningful proportion. It can be noted here that the rural India resisted the earlier attempts towards socio-economic changes for various reasons. These Acts anticipated to bring about new thought towards making socio-economic changes effective and realistic. States were subsequently obliged to make amendments to the law governing these institutions. It is now more than two decades since these reforms were introduced. Hence it is time to look as to how far these reforms have been able to make a dent in the traditional social order. It has to be seen as to how far it has been able to change the social hierarchical structure to empower the weaker section of the population living in the rural areas.

Issue Areas and the Challenges

We have noted earlier that ours has been a hierarchical and heterogeneous social order for centuries. The post-independence India deliberately and consciously wanted to be different and establish an egalitarian social order based on freedom and equality of social and economic nature. It decried differentiation on the basis of caste, colour, creed or sex. It ascribed for a new social order wherein social nature would be fairly achieved. In order to achieve these objectives several policy interventions have been introduced in the system. We have partly touched upon some of them. Let us identify some of the issue areas and challenges that are still there in our socio-political system adversely affecting the realisation of social change process.

There appears to be a relationship between the issue of social change and economic empowerment. In this context land reform has been an issue for a long time. It has been more symbolic than substantive. Implemented by State Governments, politically dependent upon large land holders, reforms in most States had little impact on redistribution of land to help the landless or the marginal land holders. Economically they remained largely unaffected. This affected the process of social change desired by the powers that be. In rural India land and caste, both play an important role in socio-economic upliftment. Both serve as an intermediate variable so far as the planning and development is concerned. During all these decades we find that the caste has had a predominant role in our socio-political process which affected the economic attainments. Lack of proper implementation of the plans often is linked to non-economic factors wherein the caste does have a role to play.

One can identify changes in the urban social structure wherein the role of caste is changing. Due to the impact of modern forces of Indian society it is slowly being transformed from feudal to capitalist system. Therefore, the stratification based on class is gradually emerging. The main cause for the geneses of new classes is based on the disintegration of caste control. This phenomenon however, can be seen in the urban centres, though rural India is still waiting for such changes to take shape. It is alleged that caste system prevents the mobility of the people from one occupation to another. But the new class system has encouraged social mobility. Further, legal compulsion has also encouraged social mobility and social change. An excellent example of social change by legal compulsion is provided by the abolition of untouchability by law in India. We therefore, tried several explanations and views which touché upon the question of social change.

The issue connected with social change has been noted in the field of socio-political as well as administrative system. The issue is not only connected with policy intervention of social change but also the manner in which these policies were implemented. Over the years we find that several policies and programmes were formulated by the Government of India to bring about social change, but their faulty implementation hampered the process. This needs to be addressed so that further policies and programmes do not suffer the same fate.

These are some of the issues and challenges that need to be addressed and debated. In view of the importance of the theme we proposed the seminar to discuss the theme and suggest measures for improvement. The theme is quite broad, but we identified the following sub-themes for the participants in order to help their thought process. The proposed sub-themes were as under:

(a) Historical and Constitutional Perspective

(b) Problem areas in effecting Social Change

(c) Structured and Administrative changes needed

(d) Policy Issues – Formulation and Implementation

(e) Changes needed in Contemporary Scenario

The above sub-themes were only suggestive to help the participants to organise and facilitate the debate. The national seminar, thus, discussed several issues connected with social change in India. We now present the papers contributed by eminent academician and bright research scholar so that the theme could get a wider circulation and coverage.

We now briefly present the proceedings of the said national seminar to provide an idea about the deliberation and the recommendation of the Seminar.

The Seminar was inaugurated by Professor (Dr) S.B. Nimse, the Vice-Chancellor of the University. Professor D.P. Singh, former Head of the Department of Public Administration and UGC member was the Guest of Honour. A large number of scholars and academicians from different parts of the country participated in this Seminar. A Souvenir containing the Abstract of the paper and a brief history of the Institute was released by the Vice-Chancellor on the occasion.

At the very outset, Professor S.N. Singh, Director of the Seminar welcomed the guests and dignitaries. He also briefed the audience about the activities and achievements of the institute. Further, he dwelt upon the theme of the Seminar. Guest of Honour Professor D.P. Singh, spoke about the genesis of the department of Public Administration. The introductory remarks about the Seminar were given by Professor Kumkum Kishore, Head of the Public Administration department. Professor Kishore underlined the four features namely, difficulties, problem areas, challenges and approach concerning social change.

While inaugurating the Seminar Professor S.B. Nimse, Vice-Chancellor of the University, emphasised upon the fact that social changes are always reflected in terms of economic changes. He further pointed out that economic growth is not compatible in terms of social development. To him, the schemes and programmes of the government could not benefit the tribals because of corruption and accountability.

The first technical session was Chaired and Co-chaired by Professor Harbans Pathak from Patiala and Professor S.K. Singh from Lucknow respectively. In this session, the first paper entitled "Tribal Development in Himachal Pradesh: A Lesson in Inclusive Development" was presented by

Professor P.N. Gautam of H.P. University, Shimla. In his scholarly presentation, Professor Gautam highlighted the positive developments of tribals of Himachal Pradesh which to him north-eastern states facing turmoil can learn a lesson. It was followed by another brilliant presentation by Professor Anil Dutta Mishra of New Delhi on "Naxalism in Tribal Area: Policy Issues and Challenges". He reviewed, Naxalism as a development issue. Further, he opined that Naxalism is nothing but a product of capitalist mode of production combined with corruption, unethical practices and corporate greed. While rejecting the violent means adopted by naxalites to achieve their desired goals, he suggested that goal should take rapid and massive development programmes to win the heart of the people. After that both the presentations were thrown open for discussion in which several participants offered valuable comments and their observations. The technical session came to end with the vote of thanks by Professor S.N. Singh to the chairman and Co-chairman as well as the participants.

The Second Technical Session was Chaired by Professor P.N. Gautam from Simla while the Co-chairman was Professor L.K. Kundan from Ranchi. In this session the first scholarly presentation was made by Professor Harbans Pathak on the topic entitled "Reservation Policy: Need for Transformation". To begin with, the scholar, discussed the Constitutional provisions dealing with reservation policy. He particularly focused his attention on the ill effect of the present dual system of education at school level to the disadvantage of weaker sections of society. While expressing his anguish with the existing caste-based reservation, advocated for its transformation to economic-based reservation. The next presentation was made by Professor S.C. Arora on "Review of Welfare measures for Depressed Classes". In this presentation, a humble effort has been made to discuss the various measures taken by the government since independence for the upliftment of depressed classes which failed to bring desired results. The reasons responsible for this were identified, consequences highlighted and remedial measures were suggested. It was followed by an open discussion on both the presentations in which many participants made academically sound interventions to make the session lively. The hallmark of the session was the heated discussion on some of the issues.

The third and last technical session of the day was Chaired by Professor S.C. Arora from Rohtak and Professor A.D. Mishra from Delhi was the Co-chairman. In this session three papers were presented. The first presentation was made by Professor L.K. Kundan on "दलित चेतना और सामाजिक परिवर्तन :अतीत एवं वर्तमान के आइने में नक्सल आन्दोलन". In his fine exposition Professor Kundan has traced the background of the Reservation and highlighted the role of Dr B.R. Ambedkar. He lamented that despite Constitutional provisions Dalits are subjected to various types of atrocities and this gave rise to Naxalism in Bihar. While condemning violence based Naxal movement the learned scholar pleaded for remedial measures. The second presentation was made by Professor R.K. Prabhakar from Rohtak on the issue of "Social Change and Problem Areas: An Overview". In his exhaustive exposition Dr Prabhakar first dwelt upon the concept of Social Change and then focused the attention of the house on some burning problem areas pertaining to Social Change such as political instability, falling ethical and professional standards as well as financial constraints. He pleaded that 'Sarvodaya' should be the basis of our state to ensure all-round development of all. The third paper entitled "Social Change through Education and Entrepreneurship" was presented by Professor S.M. Abbas from Ranchi. In his scholarly presentation, Professor Abbas that stated though tribes existed in various parts of the country right from the very beginning yet real attention to their problem was given by Government of India after independence. Since then the government has formulated various policies and programmes for their welfare with a view to check discrimination and un-human behaviour. The hall mark of the session remained the paucity of time so it was decided to put off the discussion on these scholarly presentations for the next day.

The fourth technical session was chaired and Co-chaired by Professor I.D. Mishra, former Professor and Head of Political Science, Gorakhpur University and Professor S.M. Abbas from Ranchi respectively. The first presentation in this session was made by Professor Gopal Prasad from Sagar on the topic entitled "आरक्षण सामाजिक सुधार कार्यक्रम है, गरीबी उन्मूलन नही". In his brilliant presentation Professor Gopal stated that tribals have suffered and are suffering from various types of atrocities. He rightly pointed out that leaders are mainly responsible for not raising the voice to protect their interests. Dr Gopal also favoured continuation of caste-based reservation policy until new one is formulated in this regard. The next presentation was made by Dr N.L. Bharti from the Department of Public Administration, University of Lucknow on the topic entitled "सामाजिक परिवर्तन एवं कल्याणकारी राजनीतिः उत्तर प्रदेश के सन्दर्भ में". In his presentation, Dr Bharti pointed out that there has been a positive change in the mindset of upper castes towards downtrodden which needs to be highlighted and there should be no politics in this regard. He strongly favoured the policy of reservation. The third presentation was made by Dr Abhinav Sharma entitled "Social Policy and Scheduled Tribes in India: Contextualising the Role of Civil Servants". In his beautiful presentation, Dr Sharma focused upon the role of civil servants in the implementation of social policy meant for Scheduled Tribes in India. He touched upon the various dimensions of this aspect. The last paper in this session was presented by Deepti Srivastava, a young scholar on the topic entitled "स्वतन्त्रता परवर्ती भारत में जनजातीय समुदायों की स्थिति का अवलोकन". In her presentation she stated that though various steps have been taken by government the welfare of tribals yet the results have not been desirable.

After that the presentation session was open for discussion in which lively discussion took place.

The last session was in the form of Open House Session. It was chaired by Professor R.K. Prabhakar from Rohtak. In this session, the large number of young scholars came forward to raise their queries to satisfy their curiosity. What transpired in the session is quite clear to anybody and need not to be repeated.

The papers which could not be presented were taken as read and form the part of this volume. This in brief is the report of the national Seminar conducted by the Institute with financial support from the ICSSR. The present book is the result of that effort.

References

1. Aiyer, V.R. Krishna; Some Half Hidden Aspects of Indian Social Justice, Eastern Book Company, Lucknow, pp. 5-6.
2. Shrimali, Dr P.D.; Agrarian Change and Tensions, Reported in Financial Express, New Delhi, May 15, 1982.
3. The First Five Year Plan, Planning Commission, Govt. of India, New Delhi, p. 7.
4. The Sixth Five Year Plan, Planning Commission, Govt. of India, New Delhi.

1

Dialogue with Hobbes' Leviathan on Social Change: Some Precepts and Perceptions

I.D. Mishra

"By MANNERS, I mean not here decency of behaviour; as how one man should salute another, or how a man should wash his mouth, or pick his teeth before company, and such other points of small morals; but those qualities of mankind that concern their living together in peace and unity."[1]

These are the words of Hobbes in Leviathan. These exclaim his anxieties. He regrets for life and liberty at stake in England and is delighted by a way out to end it.

Why do these words of Hobbes haunt in our mind? Are these words equally significant for Indian society? Hobbes' Leviathan a great classic of seventeenth century, yet relevant for twenty-first century world! It was written in British context of that time, but is contextualised here for India's Social change! A big contrast difficult to put Leviathan and present India at a point where Leviathan is looking to English and Indian both having the same nature. Why to limit Leviathan's scope to these people, and not to the people of the world? And this limitation disappears when we look into the nature of human beings in general. Hobbes is referable here. To quote him, "I put for a general inclination of all mankind a perpetual and restless desire of power after power that ceaseth only in death."[2] It speaks that the nature of man is one and the same everywhere and in every time. It is beyond time and space and thus we cannot put it between the dividing lines of past, present and future. Does it mean the infinitum quality of human nature? Does it never change? Then a fallacy arises—the fallacy of infinitum human nature. But Hobbes says that nothing is infinite, instead everything is finite. It raises a query to understand the contradiction between man and his nature. The contradiction exists between mortality and immortality. Man is mortal but his nature is immortal. When an individual is born he/she is caged into death, awaiting to embrace its target—but the human nature remains still beyond its purview. Then the question is how to determine the identity of human being and the quality of human nature, if the two have different identities.

The puzzles of contradictions do not end here. Whether human being without human nature is matter and human nature without human being is an essence of human being? If we accept it, it means that human nature is inherent in human being. It is the quality of human being. It depends on human being. Can we say it a dependent variable? As a colour, like red, black, green etc. is invisible till a noun is there to accept it, for example, a red pencil or a green pen and the like. In each case here noun is qualified by some adjective. According to this analogy human nature is an adjective. An adjective qualifies a noun. An adjective appears as long as its noun exists, but disappears soon after its noun becomes non-existent. It means an adjective and its noun co-exist and co-terminates together.

The above two perceptions of human nature are contrary to each-other. One is immortal and eternal where as another is temporal—co-existent and co-terminus with the death of an individual. Does it mean that human nature has one meaning at one place and another meaning at another place?

This contradiction is resolved by itself if we look at Hobbes' Leviathan. At one place it is universalisation of human nature beyond time and space. At another place it is particularisation of human nature which is within time and space. From the first we derive the notion of man and his nature and from the second we derive the consequence of human nature in practice. First is the theoretical foundation of human nature and the second is the test of the hypothesis of theoretical foundation and to see whether it purports to the conceptual foundation of the theory.

Within the above two lines of argument, we would explore the explanation for Indian social change, albeit 'Leviathan' would remain as a theoretical source for exploration. To start with 'Leviathan' as a source of argument, the first question is to understand what is human nature? How does it make the restless situation, conflict and war, and absence of peace everywhere? Did Hobbes mean human nature-quarreling and quarreling all the time! Ambitious, selfish, envious, prejudiced and thus nasty! Everyone is at war with every one! But this all changes with the making of a covenant–a constitution of organised society with 'commonwealth' as the supreme political master to prevent all nuisances which destroy peace and harmony and thus custodian of individual's peace and social harmony.

The history of human being in India, by the standard of human nature, from time immemorial, Vedic civilisation; ancient and medieval civilisation to the era of national movement does not support the generalisation and universalisation of human nature as 'quarrelsome, brutish and nasty'. The Vedic civilisation, although some may ask for recorded history as evidence, is qualitative human par excellence. It signals a message: 'Man is man, enduring and eternal.' The eternity is the essence of 'soul' (Aatma–a state of supreme consciousness, invisible but realisable, un-permutable and indestructible by any power and force, see Geeta), It is not only the part and parcel of human being but the nucleus of living and non-living being. Some would say it fanatic, other may call it philosophy, and philosophy of spirituality, and some by some other description. But we ask a question. Do these not constitute the part of history? Whether history is merely concrete evidence-written and recorded. It would then deprive history of being called as 'complete whole'. Such history would always be incomplete one. An incomplete history would never narrate the complete truth—the truth of causes and consequences or the reasons and results. A history that is lifeless which is unable to tell itself. It would require then some agent/spokes person to narrate it. Then what is the guarantee that narration/ description would be free from bias. A spokesperson, however, guided by reason and inspired by spirituality may be free from prejudices and partiality. The biased content may be filtered by one's rational and spiritual approach. It may be at least reduced to the minimum unaffecting the structural and substantial contents of the events. History of human life in Vedic and ancient India bears the testimony of these qualities. It speaks about the human mind engaged in holistic perspective of the cosmos by experiencing through engaging their sense organs. It is neither fanatic nor mythical, albeit the course of life as practiced and experienced by the seers and sages. It propounds the theory of human nature as 'kind, reciprocal, helpful, rational and humane.' It loves the cosmos and its beings, and teaches about these by inculcating a sense of respect for these. In broad sense it is non-violence–teaching, learning and realising the self of non-violence everywhere and anywhere reflecting 'Aatma'—un-pervasive, undeterred, silent and enlightened.

Our eyes are turned from these realities to the reality of conflict and war. The history of the mankind began to be lettered around conflict and war and the human nature was depicted on these bases. Hobbes penned down human nature on biological-instinctual behaviour of man as selfish, ambitious and quarreling but graded these as brutish and nasty. It means Hobbes considered such behaviour as animal behaves and not as human behaviour. Human behaviour in relation to the 'other' under Commonwealth is protective and peaceful. It protects individuals from war and violence and thus provides every one the opportunity to exercise one's freedom of thought and action under a common bond of social relationship that prohibits individuals and their groups to resort to violence for the fulfillment of their petty interests against the interests of the society as a whole which in Hobbes's term is 'Commonwealth.' Even the Absolute King has no power to violate his obligations to protect their rights to life, liberty and peaceful living. Thus, this great philosopher of the seventeenth century abandoned the pre-Commonwealth individual's animalistic behaviour as human nature as it lacked human and social worth.

There is rationale in Hobbes's thinking. His rationalism has propounded a philosophy of society and social relations.[3] It is however not imaginative based on hypothetical human nature but is based on the psychology of individual's behaviour, i.e. stimuli and response. Thus, there is content of psychology in his Leviathan. It is based on his concept of senses–the original that makes its sub-original by stimuli that pressures on the senses to perceive and to react and respond accordingly including imagination, reason etc. In fact, Hobbes co-relates human behaviour with automation of machine and thus propounds machination as the basic principle. It forwards a mechanical theory of man, society and state behind which lie sensual objects as motivation and response. Then there is one remarkable point to note. Individual's behaviour in the State of Nature is without reason as its basis. Although the beauty of his arguments is logistic but without a bench mark independent and apparent role of reason as the key arbiter of conflicts and disputes for peaceful living. On the other hand, individual's behaviour after the covenant is reason based. But how does he take a U-turn from senses to reason is curious to understand. Reason is also an expression of the images of the external stimuli in the senses as remnants of the past memory. This means reason is remnant of sensual images. One can support it from a distance, but not exactly the same. Modern science also supports the development of mind in newly born child not immediately as it comes in to life being but gradually in due course of physical-sensual development. But there is contradictory theory as well, occupying which will take another debate away from the present context.

In present context we are confronted here with another dilemma. The dilemma is whether reason springs from fear or fear germinates in to the background of reason in absentia. The background of this dilemma is Hobbes' hypothesis itself, in the assertion that 'his mother gave birth to twins-himself and fear.' This is the fear of insecurity. How does one feel that he is unsecured? It is reason that alerts about insecurity and enables to think the way one may be secured. It activates reason already inherent to come to rescue by covenant in which everyone is involved. It means reason is not born in fear but exists prior to fear as custodian of one's life and liberty.

Our purpose is not here to launch a debate between fear and reason but to say that reason can deactivate the stimuli of fear by diagnosing and understanding the cause and devising the remedies.

Against this background we would attempt to understand the Indian human nature and the social change influenced and determined by it. The fear of insecurity under British Empire led to national movement in sequence of events one after another–violent and non-violent both. There was repression and use of coercive force by the British Government against India's reasonable demands. Although Hobbes' fear is also in the background of movement, but there was reason as co-planner and decision-maker what action had to be taken against the British brutal authority. 'Dialogue and persuasion' as their first priority were practiced times and often. It was demand for justice and human rights. It was demand for liberty, equal treatment, self-government and participation in the system. The question is why did Indians prefer these methods. Why did not they resort to violence in response to their ill treatment and genuine demands? It reflected their Vedic nature of peace and non-violence. The prominent freedom fighters and their followers appear to have inherited the Vedic human nature. We do not include here the Muslim freedom fighters whose legacy of human nature might have different source than the sources of ancient Indian scriptures. But then one thing is there that they co-shared the movement with others. Thus, India as a whole followed human path for liberation and turned to accept and follow the other paths only after they (the British) were resistant to their liberal human approach. Even at the crucial moment they did not surrender to their cruelty.

What we want to submit here is to generalise the Indian human nature as Vedic except the Muslim invaders who settled here and the British rulers who were cunning to their interests and their fulfillment by hook or by crook. The latter one of course proved what Hobbes had said about human nature in the State of Nature as ambitious, selfish, quarreling, brutish and nasty. On these lines of argument we find two types of human nature—one that is ambitious, brutish and nasty, another one that is close to humanness, just and genuine. The former is close to animal behaviour, and the latter is an expression of human behaviour. An ambition to power is prone to become 'cunning like fox and brave like lion'. This is Machiavellian theory of grabbing power and the power seeker behaves like an individual in the Hobbes' State of Nature.

In democracy like us we see the power seekers behaving like what can harm the social relations—caste-politics, religion and communal politics, language politics, regional politics, hatred and violence politics and all that which finally disturb the social equilibrium. Political parties and their leaders are custodian of these techniques, sharply being used in these years especially during general elections. It is badly affecting the people and society and their relations. We can easily see the difference in human behaviour between the pre- and post-independent India, especially in these years, analogous to that of human nature as that of Hobbes' State of Nature–a condition in which society and social relations do not exist.

After independence, we framed our constitution-'Sovereign, Socialist, Secular and Democratic Republic'–a type of Hobbes' covenant, with a difference of owning the social and political responsibilities by themselves. These responsibilities were constitutionally framed and shouldered upon by the people themselves. People elect representatives, and representatives form the government to work on behalf of the people and their agenda. It means there is no option before the government except the people option, i.e. every action of the government should bear people's interest as mandatory. At the same time it is also mandatory for the people to be abide by their commitment framed and institutionalised in the covenant, i.e. Constitution of India. Thus, moral obligations become institutionalised and legalised and become mandatory for people and their government. Both people and the government know the intrinsic worth of the obligations, the public good as their inherent qualities. Public good as collective good includes everyone within its fold. One obeys it not because of the fear of punishment but because of one's intrinsic worth of goodness as human being and being the equal sharer of collective/social good. Goodness manifests with 'otherness'. Otherness is a criterion of knowing and adjudging goodness. It propounds a concept that goodness without otherness is unsustainable. The 'otherness' in fact, is essential qualities of goodness and the central reason of the birth of human society. From friendship to family to association to society as a whole is bond of relationships by accepting 'otherness' as good to human society.

Now how good is defined and how it becomes perversion by dragging goodness to narrower boundary from group interest to individual interest. Caste groups, religious-communal groups, political parties and all other groups working in their own interests down seize goodness to petty interests. It excludes 'otherness' of the rest except their own. It reverses the nature of human being as being 'good' to that of Hobbes' State of Nature where everyone is 'selfish', 'ambitious' 'quarreling' and at war with everyone. Can social relations remain cordial in this situation? How can a system of government like above one be called a genuine democracy?

Now look at the Indian democracy and examine whether the charges are justifiable. We would take two/three examples from the recent practices of Indian democracy for evaluation. Elections to the 14th Lok Sabha in May 2014 and State Assembly elections thereafter reveal Indian democracy customised by above parochial icons which weaken the social relations into narrow group relations where social/public good become mythical and not real. Does it not look the Nature of man as selfish as Hobbes has presumed in the State of nature, contrary to what India projects the human nature in ancient time? We have seen the pre-poll campaigns in April-May, 2014 where campaigners in general indulged in abusing contenders. Personal attack was a common feature, besides the party attack. They used different cards, viz., OBC cards, Dalit cards, communal cards, and so many innumerable cards to win the elections. The forthcoming elections in Bihar scheduled for Oct.-Nov. 2015 is the one of the worst campaigning examples in terms of abusing practices and telling lie campaigns. Are the parties and their contenders concerned about making rifts in social relations for merely fulfilling their petty interests and ambitions? What do we expect from such practices by power aspirants? Are their behaviour worthy of being titled them as leader? Have their behaviour and role strengthened social relations? Can we say such changes as caste oriented change? Will such changes (strengthening caste pockets) help democracy to achieve justice—liberty, equality and fraternity? The meaning of freedom is misunderstood and misused. Equality as an objective of democracy has been replaced by inequality. Inequality at every level is making a leap forward. Leaders are unequally upward in comparison to the people at the grass-root level. They want to be distinguished in terms of powers and positions. In order to achieve distinctions they adopt all means–both ethical and unethical. They shout for justice, but they practice injustice. These are the questions the Indian Society at large is concerned about. Injustice has become vocal shield weapon to defend justice. They shout and propagate justice, and in practice they use it as an instrument of expanding their influence in public domain. Since democracy is at hand for consideration, see the parties' boss, their supremo and their democratic character! They have crossed the limit of intolerance. The highest public body, the Parliament–the chief spokesperson of the People of India–is unable to speak the voice of the people. Not merely shouting and walk-out, but rambunctious behaviour of vested interests in the House is becoming the practice of the day. Parliament is a place for dialogue and to sort out way to resolve the issues. This requires peaceful atmosphere and tolerance to listen to others' views. Even if you do not like any bill/resolution as if opposed to party's ideology-policy, programmes and principles, you can request for sufficient time for deliberation by reasoned arguments acceptable by the Parliament. And in case the ruling party (parties) does not agree to your reasons, the Parliamentary Rules and traditions allow you to put your note of dissent. This much an opposition can do/or utmost to walk out silently, instead ransacking the whole House and its business. What does it speak about the future of parliamentary democracy in the twenty-first century India? Can Hobbes' Leviathan grade such behaviour better than man in the State of Nature? Is it not that such behaviour is more dangerous than the Hobbes man in the State of Nature? The reason is simple. After the Covenant is made, people are expected to abide by its obligations except in situations when the king fails to obey its obligations–the obligations to protect the terms and conditions of the covenant. But in India's case the Parliament is helpless in such situations except silently watching its gradual decline. The supreme law making constitutional authority is unable to enact laws because of the misuse of privileges and immunities by its members themselves. And even the Supreme Court cannot check it even by the use of its much criticised judicial-over activism. Then what is method left to prevent disruptions of the Parliament? Is it revolution? If yes, then revolutionising the social system to educate the people and upgrade their consciousness against such leaders /representatives to make them feel that you are not leaders but enemy of public interest.

One can imagine the time wasted and public money spent for no business of the House during disruptions and logjam sessions of the House. Is it democracy or no democracy, or between the two, is reserved for judgment by one's own experience. However, it is worthy of being benefitted by the wisdoms and philosophical classics like

Leviathan in delivering judgment than judgment delivered in darkness which are fumbled, vague and confused. The point in consideration is 'liberty', the foremost principle of democracy.

"By liberty is understood, according to the proper signification of the word, the absence of external impediments; which impediments may oft take away part of a man's power to do what he would, but cannot hinder him from using the power left him according as his judgment and reason shall dictate to him."[4]

Two things are obvious from the above precepts of liberty. First, it is absence of restraints, without which he cannot express the best of him. It is not the freedom from 'self-restraints' to hinder others, rather the restraints of obligations under the covenant, i.e. the Constitution of liberal democracy that defines freedom and its obligation. Second, it is freedom of judgment dictated by reason. Thus, reason occupies the command to dictate. Hobbes does not mean the arbitrary use of command for its own sake, but the command that derives its authority from reason of the covenant.

One fundamental issue comes in between the line of argument is the relation between the liberty and law. Sometimes we misinterpret it and take law in our hands as liberty. At both levels of democratic institutions and grass-root level, we find most often its misinterpretation and frequent use. For preliminary guidance, we again quote Hobbes.

"A law of nature, lex naturalis, is a precept, or general rule, found out by reason, by which a man is forbidden to do that which is destructive of his life, or taketh away the means of preserving the same, and to omit that by which he thinketh it may be best preserved. For though they that speak of this subject use to confound jus and lex, right and law, yet they ought to be distinguished, because right consisteth in liberty to do, or to forbear; whereas law determineth and bindeth to one of them: so that law and right differ as much as obligation and liberty, which in one and the same matter are inconsistent."[5]

Thus, liberty is the liberty of life and its expression, where as law is binding and to be followed. It is denial of the arbitrary use of liberty. Any changing society and social relations cannot uphold democracy and democratic relations without observing the above natural principles.

Another important part of democracy is justice. How does democracy work for social justice is equally important to understand. But before coming to this point, we would like to look in to Leviathan. In fact, his perception of justice was a head of his time. Let us see what does he say about it. We can divide it in to ordinary meaning of justice and extraordinary meaning of justice. Justice in ordinary sense of the term is meant for students as learner as well as for every individual and extra-ordinary is conceptual, complex and philosophical. We would limit our discussion to the ordinary meaning as it is meant for everyone from school-going students to a common man.

Accordingly, "justice is the constant will of giving to every man his own....... So that the nature of justice consisteth in keeping of valid covenants, but the validity of covenants begins not but with the constitution of a civil power sufficient to compel men to keep them: and then it is also that propriety begins."[6]

"Justice therefore, that is to say, keeping of covenant, is a rule of reason by which we are forbidden to do anything destructive to our life, and consequently a law of nature."[7]

Hobbes here is obvious that security to life and liberty is possible when everyone gives one's own possession to the covenant and keeping the words of the covenant accumulated by every one's giving. Significantly obedience to constitution and its laws is a clear message if justice is secured for everyone. This is what the law of reason is significantly highlighted in relation to justice. To elaborate further who is just and unjust he says:

'The names of just and unjust when they are attributed to men, signify one thing, and when they are attributed to actions, another. When they are attributed to men, they signify conformity, or inconformity of manners, to reason. But when they are attributed to action they signify the conformity, or inconformity to reason, not of manners, or manner of life, but of particular actions. A just man therefore is he that taketh all the care he can that his actions may be all just; and an unjust man is he that neglecteth it".[8]

Hobbes' justice is distinctly marked as a complete category of political-social justice based on his wide concept of natural law. However, he wisely makes a distinction between his concept of justice and other values either associated with or in the background of justice. For example, righteousness, moral aptitudes, virtues, kindness, feeling of togetherness, helpfulness, sharing common responsibility, accommodative urge, pardoning guilty of the past, i.e. to be freedom from revengeful attitude, looking forward to the good, etc. are conceptually different from justice, which however cannot be deleted from its jurisdictions of use.

Thus, his justice is peaceful condition under commonwealth to which everyone is bound by commitment to obey. His justice is realised by obeying the covenants. Indeed, Hobbes lays down the foundation of political–legal justice in relation to individual and state that guarantees peaceful social relations.

A question arises: Whether Social justice in India is constitutional Sophia interpreted and misinterpreted according to one's preference. Its misinterpretation of the objectives and spirit of the Constitution is a major cause of social conflicts and social aberration. If the objective is confined to the narrow interest, it is misinterpreted. Such interests are the interests of groups (caste or other groups) which have created dissatisfactions and conflicts in other groups who consider themselves deprived of such benefits. This has become the phenomenon of the day in Indian politics–some support and other protest. If the support and protest of narrow interests are supposed to be the criterion of people-empowerment and mark of social change, it would be a state of social conflict and social log-jam—aberration in social relations, promotion of social injustice and democratic perversion.

Can we not take lessons from the seventeenth century philosopher, though much criticised and misunderstood by the aspirants and champions of democracy, who propounded the theory of peace and tranquility both on practico-psychological and rational grounds. If democracy is the best form of government by modern-liberal standard, it demands peace and security to function and deliver its best.

References

1. Thomas Hobbes, Leviathan, ch. xi, of The Difference of Manners; reference used from the following source here and there after where Hobbes has been quoted https://ebooks.adelaide.edu.au/h/hobbes/thomas/h68l/chapter15.html
2. *Ibid*, ch xi; of Difference of Manners.
3. Warrender, Leo straus and Oakeshott are classical thinkers who have examined Hobbes from these angles. For details see Howard Warrender, The Political Philosophy of Hobbes; His Theory of Obligation; Leo Strauss, The political philosophy of Hobbes, Michael Oakeshott, Rationalism in Politics.
4. *Ibid*, ch xiv, Of the First and Second Natural Law, and of Contracts.
5. *Ibid*
6. *Ibid*, ch. xv, of the other laws of Nature.
7. *Ibid* ch. xv; of other Laws of Nature.
8. *Ibid*.

2

Tribal Development in Himachal Pradesh: Inclusive Development Approach Goes Awry

P.N. Gautam

Himachal Pradesh situated in the north-west of India is a wholly mountainous region in the lap of the Himalayas ranging from 350 metres to 6975 metres above mean sea level. It is surrounded by Jammu and Kashmir in the north, Tibet on the north/north-east, Uttarakhand in the east/south east, Haryana in south and Punjab in south-west. Tribal area constitutes 76-21 per cent of the total area of the state whereas the tribal population according the 2001 census is only four per cent of the total population of the state. Density of population per square kilometer is only seven. Tribal population is concentrated in the districts of Kinnaur, Lahaul-Spiti and Bharmour and Pangi sub-divisions of the Pradesh. 45.58 per cent of the ST population in the state was dispersed outside the tribal areas and tribal pockets as per 2001 census. The tribal areas of the state are remotely located in the outer-Himalayas beyond high mountain passes where habitation is at an average altitude of 10,000 ft. above the mean sea-level. Because of heavy snowfall during winters, Lahaul and Pangi especially get cut off from the rest of the Pradesh for varying periods ranging from three to six months. Air service is then the only means of communication left for mobility and transport. The HP Tribal Development, therefore, has been running helicopter service to various places like Stingri, Killar, Ajog, Saach, Udaipur, Barring, Tngret, Sissu, Rawa, Tandi (DIET), Jispa, Tindi and Chokhang in Lahul and Pangi valley. The helicopter service in other parts of the tribal areas is also being operated as per local requirements and demands.

Himachal Pradesh was formed on 15th April, 1948. However, rapid tribal development started from the Fifth Five Year Plan onwards when a new strategy, i.e. tribal sub-plan approach was adopted. The basic purpose of this strategy was to have separate and identifiable physical and financial programmes for tribes and the tribal areas. The allocations so worked out in the tribal sub-plan were non-divertible to other areas. For this purpose, the tribal areas were divided into two categories: (i) the area having more than 50 per cent tribal population, and (ii) areas which have dispersed tribal population. In the case of the former, an area specific development approach was adopted, whereas in case of the latter, a family-based approach of development was considered suitable. In pursuance of this policy, all areas with more than 50 per cent tribal population were placed under tribal sub-plan. The areas identified as tribal under tribal sub-plan in Himachal Pradesh were divided for administrative purposes into following five separate regions: (1) The entire district of Kinnaur; (2) Spiti sub-division; (3) Lahaul subdivision; (4) Pangi sub-division; and (5) Bharmour sub-division. These areas hitherto had been identified as Tribal Development Blocks. To further minimise the bottlenecks, single line administration approach was adopted. Every district officer posted in tribal areas was put under the direct control of the Deputy Commissioner. To ensure people's participation, a Tribal Advisory Council was constituted in 1978, the recommendations of which were to be considered while formulating policies for tribal development. In order to make implementation of the sub-plan effective, financial powers have been decentralised and special powers to various officers connected with the implementation of ITD Programmes have been delegated to heads of the departments, controlling officers, disbursing officers, etc. All these efforts were intended to achieve the objectives as outlined in the tribal sub-plan, and as such are, indeed, praiseworthy.

Problems of the tribal people and areas of Himachal Pradesh were typically as those of the central India and north-east. They suffered inaccessibility, poor infrastructure, illiteracy, lack of technical skills, etc. However, the governments in Himachal Pradesh treated their tribal people with sincerity, care and respect. They were provided with the special quota in education, employment and promotions. Almost all the students got scholarships for school education, higher education and technical education. Their total literacy rate, for better than that of all-India level, according to 2001 census is, 70.37 (81.00 – Male, 62.28 –Female) vis-à-vis 76.50 (85.00 – Male, 67.00 Female) that of the whole of Himachal Pradesh speaks a lot about the indicators of socio-economic development in the Pradesh. No wonder, now the tribal people are working not only at the lower and middle level of state civil services but at the higher level in the state and all-India services. These people are also working in the central civil services throughout the country. After Independence, two of the civil servants rose to the position of the Chief Secretary in the Pradesh, many of them have been deputy commissioners, superintendents of police, and at very senior positions. In politics also, they were Speakers and Deputy Speakers of H. P. Vidhan Sabha, ministers of cabinet ranks, state-ministers and deputy chairpersons of many state corporations. Their economic position is quite good. They are in a position to sell their horticultural produce, like hop, kuth, chilgoza, dry fruits, apples, and also their wollen shawls and tweeds at highly reasonable prices in their fairs as well as through their co-operative societies. They have technical institutes as well as colleges in their tribal areas. However, many rich tribal people send their children to cities like Shimla, Dharmshala, Chandigarh, Dehradun and even New Delhi. In the early years of development, government employees from non-tribal areas went in very high numbers to man various government departments. They were provided with very high compensatory allowance and choice posting after serving in the tribal areas. This was very much alluring to them. So many of the government employees opted for the service in the tribal areas and thereby made big bucks in an honest way. There were cases of sexual exploitation of women by the non-tribal government employees. But these were by mutual consent. No rape case was reported. Some of these relations culminated into marriages between the tribal women and non-tribal government employees. Tribal women as such were not insulted as happened in other tribal areas of the country. Tribal people enjoy rights over their forests and forest produce. They can distil wine after paying some small license fee. So they distil wine from their grapes and naturally, no hooch tragedy has been reported so far. Tribal people here are honest, hardworking and sincere. Due to cold climatic conditions, they drink daily but are seldom drunk. Their women, beautiful and sturdy, enjoy greater freedom in the choice of their spouse, but cannot inherit property as per their traditional tribal laws. Indian law of inheritance does not apply to the tribal people.

From the above story, it is clear that various governments in Himachal Pradesh have dealt with the tribal development in a very sagacious and sincere way. Results of this approach are for every one to see. No agitation armed or otherwise, has been there in the state. Tribal people, their women and children, live a life of dignity and equality throughout the Pradesh. North-eastern states and central states where we find lot of bloodshed, violence and alienation can certainly learn a lesson in inclusive development from Himachal Pradesh.

However, the above wise, useful and effective inclusive development approach of various governments in Himachal Pradesh went wrong with the state policy of constructing various hydro-power projects in the highly fragile and seismic zone quite near to the international border with Tibet. The state government has started constructing big dams in order to exploit the hydro-electricity potential in the tribal areas of the Pradesh. This has disturbed the ecological balance of the highly fragile and seismic zone. Healthy, happy, guileless and frolicsome people of the area are now getting the diseases caused by environmental pollution. Outside labour and officials, working for the construction of the dams have a little knowledge and respect for local culture and traditions pose a great danger for the culture and demography of the tribal areas. Recent natural tragedies caused by landslides in Kinnaur district of Himachal Pradesh and the adjacent areas of Kedar Nath and Badri Nath in Uttrakhand where the similar dam construction activity is going on to exploit the hydro-electricity potential are serious pointers of the wrong and myopic state policies of Himachal Pradesh and Uttarakhand. Impact of these policies for the tribal people will be degradation of their ecology, pollution of their environment, distortion of their demography and culture in the name of development and adding some money to the state exchequers. Tribal people of the Pradesh are thus, going to be the sufferers as their brethren have been in the central states of Andhra Pradesh, Madhya Pradesh, Chhatisgarh, Jharkhand, Odisha, and seven sisters of North-eastern India. This is a serious pointer to a great tragedy which is going to fall on our tribal people. In the real sense, the exploitation of hydro-electricity potential of the tribal areas in this manner will lead to the exploitation of the tribal people.

In his study, Kinnaur: Unfolding Exotic Himalayan Land, O.C. Handa has observed: "With the coming of large national and multinational companies, the fragile natural resources of Kinnaur have been ruthlessly exploited on the pretext of 'scientific harnessing'. This attractive term may befool human beings, but cannot dupe the nature. The pernicious fallouts of the mega projects are now becoming manifest day in and day out: the environment of Kinnaur has suffered wholesale transformation. Symbiotic and complementary imperatives of development, that were envisaged during the earlier Plans, have been discarded to encourage mega projects and to placate big companies at the cost of environmental degradation and public health."[1] Handa has also discussed the harmful effect of the outsiders who have established their business on the arrival of mega projects in Kinnaur district. About these immigrants he says, "Many of the have been pursuing different private trade and business activities and some of them are well-set and established at various places. To make their stay secure in this district, they even established clandestine links and relationship with the local people."[2] He has then rightly warned, "If the situation goes unchecked, not only it may disturb the ethno-historical continuity of Kinnaur, but may also cause demographic imbalance and create various other complex problems."[3]

Let us discuss the reaction of the people in detail over the state policy. The tribals in the Hangran Valley in Kinnaur District have threatened to intensify their stir if the state government failed to accede to their demands for no hydro power projects in their areas. Strongly condemning the construction of the dams, the Hangran Sangarsh Samiti president Shanta Kumar told the Hindustan Times that despite the area being fragile, falling in seismic zone IV and close to border (3-4 kms aerial distance), the governments had planned three projects in the area.[4] He further added, in January 1975, a major earthquake had hit Kinnaur district with a magnitude of 6.8 on Richter scale causing major damage. The government is constructing three projects, namely, Khotang 130 MW, Chango Yangthang 180 MW, and

Yangthang-Khab 261 MW on the Spiti river without maintaining the riparian distance of five km. as suggested by Shulka Committee report. The above three projects are being constructed at the riparian distance of about one km. between two projects. Thus, this construction is in violation of the recommendations of the Shukla Committee report on hydro power projects. The recommendations suggest of declaration of some areas as "protected zones" under the Environment Protection Act 1986, to help maintain ecological balance.[5] It may be mentioned here that, a committee headed by Abhay Shukla, then Additional Secretary Forests, Government of Himachal Pradesh, constituted by the Himachal Pradesh High Court in 2009 to examine environmental fallout submitted its report to the Court in August 2010. Its findings were worrisome. It recommended: "No power projects should be constructed above 7000-ft that is in the Alpine Zone especially above snowline area and these three power projects fall above 9000-ft in the snowline area."[6]

The Shukla Committee indicted the Hyderabad-based Nuziveedu Seeds Company executing the 100 MW Tidong-1 project in Kinnaur district for felling large number of trees, including endangered species. As against the approval granted for felling of 1,261 trees, the Company had already felled 1,851 trees. As per the revised assessment of the Forest Department, destruction of another 4,815 trees was inevitable if the construction of the surge shaft road was allowed any further. More importantly, out of 2,803 trees were the chilgoza pine trees which are already nearing extinction. The Company had prepared a false detailed project report on the basis of which forest clearance was granted to the project.[7] Again it is a sad commentary that the state government decided to contest the Shukla Committee report in respect of big projects. Environmentalist, on the other hand, want its recommendations to be applied to all hydro-electric projects, including small ones, which are causing more damage and creating serious problems for the local people. In fact, environmental fallout of the projects on small streams was much more as the people were entirely dependent upon them for drinking water, irrigation and other needs.[8]

Environmental effect on Kinnaur district has been further highlighted by a former IFS officer, R S Negi, convener of Him Lok Jagriti Manch, Kinnaur, "Experience from other hydro-electric projects in the state, especially in Kinnaur, reveals that local natural water resources get disturbed and then dry up as a result of tunnelling activity for hydro projects. Companies care least about people in the effected areas as their sole objective is to earn profit." He has further added, "Construction of projects in the Alpine areas is dangerous for the fragile ecology and would have adverse impact on the environment. The entire Satluj basin area should be declared as eco-sensitive zone."

After Kinnaur, another tribal district Lahul and Spiti is set to witness major hydro-power activities in coming years as projects for producing 1,859 MW electricity are already under investigation. On this environment activist Guman Singh, coordinator Himalaya Niti Abhiyan has remarked, "Heavy devastation in Kinnaur district has aggravated manifold due to unscientific construction and muck disposal by hydro-power projects, building of roads and other construction activity in the region. Building dams on Satluj and ongoing heavy construction has essentially impacted local climate and aggravated erratic weather".

It is a sad commentary that in Himachal Pradesh also the rights of indigenous peoples were violated by the state government. The tribals were greatly affected by the development projects in the state. The tribals were denied compensation after their lands were acquired for development projects. In 1982-83, the Border Road Organisation acquired land in Madgram village in Lahul and Spiti district for construction of the Sansari Nallah-Killar-

Throt road. However, the local tribal people who have parted with their land have not received compensation so far. The tribals had informed the matter to the National Commission for Scheduled Tribes which directed the concerned authority for payment of the land compensation amounting to Rs 7,16,81,292.[9] Further, a vast area of forest lands has been grabbed by non-tribals in Chandra and Bhaga valleys in land locked tribal district of Lahul and Spiti. The forest lands were grabbed to grow potatoes and peas under the nose of district administration. As on 13 September, 2010, the district administration claimed to have cleared encroachments of about 3000 bighas of land from the possession of land grabbers in an anti-encroachment drive in Darcha and Sissu areas. However, the tribals alleged that the administration failed to take any action against the violators.[10]

In a recent study entitled "Assessing the impact of hydroelectric project construction on the rivers of district Chamba of Himachal Pradesh in the northwest Himalaya, India" by Haresh Kumar Sharma (Department of Social Work, Punjabi University, Patiala) and Pawan Kumar Rana (Department of Botany, Punjabi University, Patiala) have rightly pointed out, "What has been over-looked is that a large number of projects are sanctioned but what affects local livelihood of remotely located poor and tribal communities and fragile biodiversity ecosystems in numerous ways is overlooked by government. In several places, these rivers and streams support the traditional irrigation channels and watermills. In many villages of the study area the streams even supply drinking water to the inhabitants."[11] After pointing out the environmental, social and cultural effects of these hydroelectric projects they have concluded: "Hydroelectric Projects can cause several problems, even though they burn no fuel. By building dams on rivers may permanently alter river systems and wildlife habitats. Fishes and other river fauna no longer be able to swim upstream.

Also no doubt hydropower projects have made an important contribution to the human but such developments had significant impact on local livelihood and the environment. The local issues must be taken into consideration. The policies should be framed by accurate examination of local sites so that proportionate balance between biotic and its component of the environment can be maintained and the potential capacity of rivers can be utilised properly."[12]

Above analysis of the tribal development policy and its implementation in Himachal Pradesh clearly shows that the inclusive development policy followed by various state governments has gone awry now. The state which earlier adopted very sagacious and pragmatic approach for the inclusive development of the tribal people of the Pradesh has now adopted anti-tribal and any environmental approach for the economic development of the state. It is high time the state governments should retrace their steps, follow the recommendations of the Shukla Committee Report in letter and spirit. The governments should understand that the Avay Shukla Committee was a vey senior officer of the state and this one man committee was constituted at the behest of the High Court of Himachal Pradesh. We need to save the water resources on which the tribal people depend. We need to preserve the fragile Himalayan ecology. We need to save the endangered species of trees. We need to protect the loose strata to save the soil from the land slides to check environmental degradation. We need to recover the forest land from greedy non-tribals, and give that back to the people who are the real owners of the land. We need to ensure that the tribals get the proper compensation for the land acquired by different central or state government agencies for development projects. The government should wake up before it gets very late. The government should not test the patient of the tribals who are otherwise very peaceful, docile and disciplined. It has to be borne in mind that these tribals live in very sensitive border areas of the country and they should be given the importance they deserve.

References

1. O.C. Handa, *Kinnaur: Unfolding Exotic Himalayan Land,* New Delhi, Indus Publishing Company, 2009, p. 308.
2. *Ibid,* p. 309.
3. *Ibid,* pp. 309-310.
4. Hindustan Times, Shimla, May 26, 2014, Bhawani Negi, Tribes in HP's Hangran Valley Oppose 3 hydro projects.
5. *Ibid,* Bhawani Negi.
6. *Ibid,* Bhawani Negi.
7. Kinnaur project endangering chilgoza trees, *The Tribune,* 30 August, 2010.
8. Shukla Committee Report, Apply recommendations to all hydel projects: Environmentalists, *The Tribune,* 13 September, 2010.
9. Land Compensation: Dhumal urges Centre to intervene, *The Tribune,* 4 September, 2010.
10. Forest land grabbed in Lahul and Spiti, *The Tribune,* 14 August, 2010.
11. Haresh Kumar Sharma and Pawan Kumar Rana, *International Journal of Social Sciences,* Vol. 3 (2), 21-25 February, 2014, p. 21
12. *Ibid,* p. 24.

3

Reservation Policy: Need for Transformation

Harbans Pathak

The people of India adopted, enacted and gave to themselves a Constitution for securing to all its citizens: "Justice: Social, economic and political): equality of status and of opportunity and fraternity, assuring unity and integrity of the nation". The question that arises is whether it is possible to evolve a policy of reservation within the parameters of these objectives. In the absence of justice and equality of opportunity to all citizens, it becomes necessary to make special provisions for the advancement of socially and educationally backward classes of citizens as laid down in Article 15(4) and Article 16(4) which for making provisions for reservation of posts in favour of backward classes of citizens which in the opinion of States is not adequately represented in the services under the State. The implication of the provision in these Articles is that for adequate provision for representation in services, reservation will have to be made for seats in professional and other colleges without which adequate representation in services will not be possible.

Basics of Reservation

Unfortunately, the criterion for reservation has been based on castes. This has generated agitations to castes not included in the list of backward classes. Now the so-called minorities are also clamouring for reservation. Such agitations have given birth to caste and communal leaders. The net result is that our country now has only caste, communal and regional leaders and there are no national leaders. The appeasement of these petty leaders has thrown to the winds the real interest of the nation. The unity and integrity of the country is in jeopardy. This obviously negates the fundamental duties of all citizens laid down in Article 51(A) Part (c). "To promote harmony of spirit of common brotherhood amongst all the people of India transcending, religious linguistic, regional and sectional diversities".

Opening a New Pandora's Box

The UPA-2 government has done itself yet another disservice by including the Jats in the category of other backward classes (OBCs) at a time of the Lok Sabha Election (2014). This was something the cabinet was able to do on its own through an administrative order. But when legislation was required to be brought in through ordinance. It decided to drop the idea because President Pranab Mukherjee was reportedly opposed to it at this stage. Neither of the two cases showed the government in a good light.

Congress and Caste

There were even differences in the Congress party itself. Janardan Dwivedi along with other influential leaders kicked up a political storm by demanding an end to caste-based quota. These leaders were snubbed in view of Sonia Gandhi's backing up quota on caste basis. Sonia Gandhi President of Congress and UPA Chairperson said that the Congress Party was the champion of reservation. Such a course is an article of faith with Congress. The party had also started a dialogue on affirmative action for SCs and STs in private sector; launched scholarships and policies to encourage SCs and STs; introduced bills in Parliament for reservations in promotions to strengthen reservation. This she felt is essential to deal with discrimination imposed by centuries of subjugation and oppression. The empowerment of SCs, STs and OBCs has been an article of faith with Congress. The reservation system was introduced by Congress, strengthened by Congress and will be continued and championed by Congress.

Looked at from one point of view the inclusion of Jats in the OBC category is not surprising because the Congress leadership had supported such a step and inability to grant them OBC status would have lowered the image of government in the eyes of the community spread over nine states. The Congress leadership probably could not see, through as such as act will lead such demands from many other communities. All OBCs are not at par economically or politically. Relatively weak OBCs may feel threatened because they will have to complete with the Jats on an equal footing and loose out in the process. So the policy of UPA-2 and Congress Party has opened a Pandora Box for all times to come to decide the rational basis of reservation.

Such a short sighted move was seen as the UPA playing politics over reservations. The States of Haryana, Punjab and Bihar etc. equally became interested to woo Jat Community in reservations in view of elections to Lok Sabha in 2014. They forget that Jats having 8.5 crore members spread in nine states will be benefitted by such narrow decisions. But is what required is their children get good competitive schooling so as to reach the elite academic institutions to claim their share of reservation. This is equally true of other categories of poor people who lag behind because of poor health, lack of nutritious food and absence of quality education.

The Punjab Cabinet in March 2014, also decided to include Jats in the backward classes category. With this Jats will be 69th community to be included in this category. Bihar Chief Minister Nitish Kumar has divided the Dalits to create a category of "Mahadalits" for political survival. The centre had already decided to extend OBC status to Jats of Haryana, Rajasthan, Himachal Pradesh, Uttar Pradesh, Madhya Pradesh, Bihar, Gujarat, Uttarakhand and Delhi. All such decisions were taken for poll rush (Lok Sabha Elections, 2014).

Need for Transformation: Meritocracy is the only way forward

Political parties should not shy away from discussing ways of ending caste reservations. This issue merit further discussion so as to evolve rational criteria with a long-term perspective. The caste quota issue has been divisive and destructive to society as a whole, often spilling over into violence in the streets. The Gujjar-Meena Violence of years ago is a case in point. A much better answer is economic empowerment, skill development and education. But these are tough and lengthy ways of ushering in an egalitarian society.

It would be a healthy trend in our democracy if we could discuss these issues in a rational fashion. Increasingly, in urban areas people do not want to be known by their caste identity. They want to be known for their merit and achievements. It sounds utopian at the moment. Let us hope after the Lok Sabha elections of 2014, national leadership should emerge and national political parties should be seeking to build transformation of such a policy.

4

Social Change and Policy Issues With Special Reference to Scheduled Castes and Scheduled Tribes in India

S.K. Singh

The Concept

According to Wikipedia "Social change" refers to an alteration in the social order of a society which may include changes in its **nature, institutions, behaviours, or relations**. It may also refer to the notion of **social progress** or **socio-cultural evolution including paradigm shift** in the socio-economic structure. Accordingly, it may also include Social Revolution.

According to Encyclopaedia Britainica, "Social Change" means the alteration of the mechanism within the social structure characterised by changes in cultural symbols, rules of behaviour, social organisations and value system. Broadly speaking, Social Change is any change in social relations and thus is ever present in any given society. The specific meaning depends on the social entity being studied.

The Sociologists borrowed the models of "Social Change" from other academic disciplines. In the latter part of nineteenth century, in the wake of EVOLUTION becoming dominant model of sociological change, Social change also underwent Evolutionary cast that still persists.

Other sociological models treated analogically the Social Change and the Technological Progress of the West. In the mid twentieth century, the Anthropologists borrowed Linguistic theory of Structuralism to elaborate an approach to social change known as Structural Functionalism. Various Theories and Schools propounded thereafter emphasise different aspects of Change.

Social Change in broadest sense is any change in social relations and thus is ever present in any society. Sometimes a distinction is made between process of change within the social structure and the process that modifies it which is called Societal Change. Its Specific meaning depends primarily in the first place, on the social entity being considered. Changes in a small group may be important at that group level, but quite insignificant at larger group level or society level. Secondly, observation depends on the time span of the entity under consideration. Most short-term changes are negligible in the long run. The small scale short-term changes are the characteristics of human societies.

Biologically human species have the universal potential for Social Change which is rooted in their flexibility and adaptability on one hand and their enormous capacity to learn, symbolise and create on the other. The human's constitution makes possible the changes that are not genetically determined.

Historical Development

Various historical periods and their cultures have seen the development of several ideas on Social Change, the most basic being: 1. Decline or Degeneration or in religious terms fall from the Original Grace Status, 2. Cyclic Change — a pattern of subsequent and recurring phases of growth and decline and 3. Continuous Progress.

These ideas were predominantly prevalent in Greek and Roman period which characterised the Western Social Thought. The concept of Progress became most important since Enlightenment Movement of seventeenth and eighteenth century, Further Anne Robert Jaques Turgot and Marques de Condorce in France and Adam Smith and John Miller in Scotland advanced the theories of Knowledge and Technology. Progress remained the key idea in the nineteenth century theories of Social Evolution and Evolutionism. It was the common core shared by most influential theories of the century. Evolutionism implied that the humans progress along one line of development which is inevitably predetermined which was subsequently disputed and discarded.

August Comte advanced the Law of Three Stages (where human societies progress from a Theological Stage dominated by religion through a Metaphysical Stage where abstract speculative thinking dominates onward to a Positivist Stage where empirically based scientific theories prevail). The most encompassing theory of social evolution was developed by Herbert Spencer linking it to biological evolution where biological organism and human societies follow the same universal natural evolutionary law. Evolutionary theory also dominated the new field of Social and Cultural Anthropology in the latter half of the nineteenth century. Sir Edward Burnett Taylor and Lewis Henry Morgan classified contemporary societies on evolutionary scale. Taylor postulated Evolutionary Religious ideas from Animism through Polytheism to Monotheism and Morgan ranked societies from SAVAGE through BARBARIAN to CIVILISED and further classified them as per their level of technology or subsistence source.

Karl Marx and Engels too were highly influenced by Evolutionary ideas. To Marx social development was a dialectical process: the transition from one stage to another took place through a revolutionary transformation preceded by increased deterioration of society and intensified class struggle. He was also influenced by Romanticism which was opposed to progress. Emile Durkheim and Max Weber at the end of nineteenth century supported the idea of Progress. Durkheim regarded increasing division of labour as a basic process rooted in Modern Individualism, while Weber rejected Evolutionism and argued that development of Western societies was unique historically.

The work of Durkheim, Weber and others at the turn of the century marked the transition from the Evolutionism to more static theories as Evolutionary theories were criticised and refuted on empirical grounds and deterministic and parochial nature. In the first half of the twentieth century the theories of Cyclic Change gained prominence. These included Wilfredo Pareto's Circulation of Elites, Oswald Spengler's and Orland Toynbee's Life Cycle of Civilisation and Pitrim Sorakin's Cycle of Change.

Interest in Social Change faded away from 1920s to 1950s as Functionalism emphasising interdependent social system became dominant paradigm and social development got substituted for it. The study of Long-term Social Change got revived in 1950s and continued to develop in 1960s and 1970s. Its revived interest was sparked by the attention of the scholars to explain the gaps between rich and poor countries. Western Sociologists and Economists developed Modernisation or Westernisation theory in this regard which was criticised for its unidirectional and parochial approach. The dominance of rich nations over the poor was further explained by Dependency Theory. World Capitalist System of Immanual Walterstien was attacked for failure to explain the fall of USSR and subsequent movements to Democracy and Third World economic developments.

Neo-evolutionist theories of Ralf Linton, Leslie A. White, Julien S. Steward, Marshal D. Sahlin and Elman Roger argued for social evolution as long-term development that is pattered and cumulative. Much attention was paid to variations between societies and their relations of influence called Acculturation. Further Social Evolution was not considered as predetermined or inevitable and also not equated with progress.

Social Change Patterns

All theories of Social Change assume its course to be patterned to some extent. The traditional ideas of Social Change in this regard i.e. Decline, Cyclic, and Progress have definitely influenced modern theories, yet they fail to make explicit distinction between Decline and Progress. In fact, the characteristics of Decline and Progress cannot be derived scientifically from empirical observation alone. Scientific and normative study of Social Change exhibits two basic patterns: Cyclic and Uni-directional, which is determined by the time span.

Cyclic Change: Much of social life is organised in the cycle of day, week, month and year in a time span. These cycles of time span changes may be regarded as conditions necessary for structural stability. Other changes are less predictable. Long-term Cyclic Changes emerge on the basis of birth, growth, decline and death of civilisations. Toynbee and Spengler conceived the world history in this way.

Uni-directional change: This change continues more or less in the same direction, is cumulative implying growth or increase. The direction of change could be of decrease or a combination of growth and decrease. Another change could be a shift from one pole to other of the continuum e.g. Religious to Secular. Simple one directional change is linear when degree of change is constant over time. The other is exponential growth where percentage of growth is constant over time and the change accelerates it accordingly. A pattern of long-term growth may also conform to three Stages Curve. (Here the change is slow enough to be imperceptible in the first phase, next phase witnesses its acceleration, and in the third phase its rate slackens till it reaches the optimum)

Combined Pattern of Change –Cyclic and One or Uni-directional Change may be observed simultaneously because of the nature of the two. These patterns cannot be applied easily to social reality as they are approximation of it at best. The transformation of medieval society into Western nations of twentieth century may be taken as several interconnected long-term one directional changes.

Factors Responsible for Social Change

The causal relationship between two or more processes leading to Determinism or Reductionism may be explained as responsible factors for social change. Certain scientific explanations may be given to different social changes. They may result from scientific or technological forces like industrial revolution which created a new social class, the urban proletariat, and the demographic changes inducing population boom. Besides, the Social Change can also evolve from the contact with other societies creating diffusion, from changes in Eco-system resulting in the loss of natural resources or outbreak of epidemic or diseases, from change or shift in societal Ideology resulting in the change and alteration of the form of government and the nature of STATE and from Social Movements which result in the shaping of the organisations and institutions and their working.

Social Change Mechanism

Causal explanations of Social Change are limited in scope in reference to the study of initial conditions or basic processes. More general and theoretical way of its explanation is to construct a model of recurring mechanism of Social Change. Such mechanisms incorporated in different theoretical models include the following:

The mechanism for Uni-directional or One Directional social change is Accumulation à Selection à -and Differentiation. Human knowledge is essentially cumulative. Since human beings are innovative, they add to existing knowledge by replacing less adequate and less appropriate ideas and practices with better ones. This leads to expansion of collective knowledge and capacities through specialisation and differentiation.

The mechanism for Curvelinear and Cyclic Change implies Saturation and Exhaustion. The models of one directional change assume that change in a particular direction induces further change in that very direction while that of cyclic change assume that it creates conditions for change in another direction, sometimes even in opposite direction. The shorter term cyclic change is explained by comparable mechanisms.

Mechanism of Conflict, Competition, and Cooperation-Group conflict has generally been considered a basic mechanism of Social Change especially of the sudden and radical transformations identified as Revolutions. The Marxists particularly depict social life in a capitalist society as a permanent struggle between the ruling class and the dominant working class striving for radical changes. This class struggle results in a Social Change. Ralph Dahrendorf explains it as a conflict model. The notion of conflict becomes more relevant to explain social change if it is broad-based to include competition between rival groups. Competition stimulates introduction and diffusion of innovation in reference to power enhancing. Additionally, completion may lead to growth in size and complexity of the entity. The classic example of this process as first suggested by Adam Smith is the tendency in capitalism towards Collusion and establishment of monopolies when small firms are driven out of competitive market. Another example suggested by

Nobert Eliasis Western European Nation States born out of competitive struggle.

Tension and Adaptation –Social Change in Structural Functionalism is regarded as an adaptive response to social tensions within the social system. When some part of the integrated social system undergoes certain change owing to a variety of reasons, a tension is created between this part and the rest of the parts, this tension is resolved by the adaptive changes of the other parts of the system.

Diffusion of Innovation –Quite a few changes result from the innovations that are adopted in society like technological inventions, scientific knowledge, new beliefs etc. Here diffusion is not automatic but selective and adoption is wilful. Many innovations tend to follow a pattern of diffusion from higher to lower status group. After diffusion takes place, innovation no longer remains the symbol of distinction which motivates people of the same group to look to something new again and innovate afresh.

Planning and Change

Planning implies institutionalisation of change but its institutionalisation certainly does not imply planning. The Social Change may occur from goal directed large scale social planning, which is mostly short-term and the goals are not fully realised. Even when the set targets are achieved, the unforeseen consequences do happen which are beyond control. The wider goals and longer time span makes it more difficult to achieve the targets and avoid unforeseen results as it happened in Communist and Totalitarian states. The institutionalisation of planning may result from goal fixation by organisational authority. Many unplanned social changes in modern societies are institutionalised as they originate in the independent research organisations, their R and D divisions, NGO's and universities, but their effects and repercussions however are not controlled. It is the state intervention in the planned social change through its instrumentalities and agencies which is very crucial. The unplanned social change occurs over a long period of time owing to the factors and forces mentioned above which may be furthered in a planned manner by the state if the Government of the day desires so. Social changes of planned nature with state intervention as a vehicle to move takes quite long to make a tangible impact. The social perceptions and moorings are very hard to change, which consequently leads to very slow pace of change.

Social Change in relation to Scheduled Castes and Scheduled Tribes in India has been quite perceptible during the functioning of the democratic polity. The Constitutional Provisions make an elaborate arrangement to uplift these castes and usher in substantial change in their social status —be it the Reservation Policy or Abolition of Un-touchability in the country. Other legislative enactments did play their contributory role in their emancipation in a substantial manner. The social welfare measures, the affirmative action, and the programmes and schemes launched periodically by the central and state governments have definitely ameliorated their lot to a great extent. As a cumulative result of all the above, the S. Cs. And S. Ts. In the country have undergone quite a tangible change in their social and economic status. Now, India can safely boast of Dalit Millionaires, Chief Justices, Chief Ministers, Ministers in the Union and State Governments, Corporate Honchoes, Social Reformers, and Political Thinkers. The social change in them has occurred over the decades of proactive policies pursued vigorously by the successive Governments both at the Centre and Stares.

Not bemoaning the myopia of different political parties at the national and state/regional levels, the social and economic status of the S.Cs. and S.Ts still has not reached its desired place. A number of obvious reasons can be advanced for this dismal state of affairs. The singular illustration of the practice of Untouchability despite being abolished more than six decades ago is being observed in some way or the other within the four corners of the country. It is not the Hindu community alone which is the culprit, the other religious communities as well, have to blame for this menace.

The caste-ridden Indian society has not fully accepted the well-meaning welfare measures and programmes for the upliftment of SCs and STs. The Khap Panchayats/Kangaroo Courts have been reported to have ordered the honour killing or even rape of the young couples or girls when they dared to have strayed beyond the bounded matrimony. All this happens in the full knowledge of the administration which remains a mute spectator to the perpetration of such crimes. Even the political leaders look the other way, in some cases they become, reportedly, a party, ceremoniously.

Such examples abound and perpetrators roam freely without any fear of law of the State. This necessitates a fresh thinking as to what has gone wrong at the level of policy planning and its implementation. Further, the practice/ implementation has to be reassessed in terms of so-called failures/drawbacks in the light of the above. It is really quite Herculean to examine and review all the policy planning, its framework and implementation, therefore some examples are attempted hereunder.

The reservation policy of the Government of India based on caste system has come under attack from all quarters. During its operation till date, quite a few serious issues have been raised in various fora. The foremost opposition to the implementation of the policy emanates from the criticism that the continued reservations to the SCs and STs have definitely made them complacent and non-competitive in nature. It has been well documented by research studies. This does no good to the castes who enjoy the benefits of the Reservation and also to the society at large. The repetitive benefits which sometimes become cumulative do more harm than good to these castes. The benefits so accruing have created classes among the castes and more menacingly within the same caste affecting their inter-personal and inter-caste relations adversely. Some remedy to exclude the well offs in these castes from the purview of the reservations applied seems inadequate and ineffective. Hence, there is pressing need to streamline and review the existing provisions.

The welfare programmes and schemes launched over the years by the centre and states target the desired segment of population in the earmarked sector. The selection of the beneficiaries always has been marred in controversies. The implementing agency or the local body responsible for the selection is blamed for this impropriety and bias. It also results in one influential family garnering most of the benefits under the scheme. It is therefore necessary to find and operationalise a fool proof mechanism to select the most deserving person.

There is a mad scramble to be included in the reserved castes by a large no. of castes in the country to reap the benefits of reservation. There have been agitations, some of them violent as well, and court cases in this regard. In the absence of predominantly clear cut policy this trend is gaining momentum which will turn self-defeating in course of time.

Policy issues in social change emerge only when the state mounted efforts for it get bogged down, ill planned and ill implemented, have disastrous impact on society and its fundamental institutions or even fail to attain stated goals. These issues may be in the domain of decision making in respect of what changes? Where to change? what is the time span?, which sector?, what intervention? and so and so forth.

All the legislative measures taken so far, the policies and programmes implemented (reservations, affirmative actions and social security measures) have thrown some policy issues to be urgently addressed by the state. It is now high time to introspect, ponder and deliberate to delineate the most suitable policies to be made and implemented in right earnest for the betterment of the SC's and ST's specially for the "last man in the row" which certainly means "Antyodaya" taking into account the issues discussed above.

References

1. Social Change by William Form in Encyclopaedia Britanica.
2. Social Change in the Wikipedia, the Free Encyclopaedia.
3. Leonard A. Jason, "Principles of Social Change", Oxford University Press, 2015, U.S.A.
4. J.S. McCue, "Technology and Social Change".
5. S.K. Singh, "Dalit Women: The Status and Issues" New Royal Book Company, Lucknow, 2009.
6. The Constitution of India, Eastern Book Company, 2014.
7. Government of India—Untouchability Offences Act 1955.
8. The Times of India, Lucknow.
9. The India Today, New Delhi.
10. "Social Change Defined" in Cliffs Notes—www.cliffsnotes.com science sociology.
11. "Social Change" in Sociology Guide—www.sociology guide.com social change.
12. "Essays on Social Change" www.your article library.com/sociology/essays on social change.

5

Social Change and Problem Areas – An Indian Overview

R.K. Prabhakar

Social change has always been one of the significant areas of study and research especially for sociologists, anthropologists, economists, political and administrative classes, planners etc. Social change is a very wide concept and is universal and all pervasive phenomena. Briefly put, it may mean any significant alteration, modification or transformation which takes place in the life pattern of people, their social relationship and social interaction. It hardly leaves any sphere of life untouched, be it cultural, economic or political.

Social change invariably becomes the driving force for social reforms for further improvement of multiple natures. Social change is continuous, complex and non-uniform in character. Its pace may be slow, moderate and at times rapid too. There are two broad categories of social change viz. unplanned and planned ones. Unplanned changes are invariably caused by sudden or sporadic factors such as natural calamities (earthquakes, landslides, floods etc.), social, economic or political upheavals/resolutions and such other forces. Such unplanned changes generally result in disequilibrium, malfunctioning and maladjustments in social organisations and institutions.

Planned changes are those which are the outcome of deliberate, conscious and disciplined efforts to bring improvement in social organisations and social life with a view to take purposive decisions to benefit the people in one way or the other. In today's democratic system of governance, government and its structures/agencies, besides some non-governmental organisations are mainly responsible for fruitful planned changes. The policies and programmes are finally shaped and reshaped by the government, of course, with the aid and advice of professional civil services whose basic job is to administer them as efficiently, effectively and objectively as possible. We may now focus our attention on Indian situation.

At the time of attaining independence in 1947, the state of affairs of our social, economic and political life was quite pathetic needing immediate and urgent actions and changes by our newly formed government. But that needed political and administrative sagacity, time, resources (men, money and material) perseverance and patience of undying nature. After attaining independence we got our own Constitution after a good deal of thinking and deliberations. Our Constitution framers were guided by noble ideas of social equality, social justice and human dignity.

In post-independent India, planned changes in social, economic and political fields became indispensable vis-à-vis the conditions prevailing in pre-independent India to enable our people to realise the benefits of such changes and feel the pulse of hard won freedom. Indian Government from the very beginning engaged itself head on to tackle the innumerable challenge and problems of diversified nature to meet its constitutional obligations and responsibilities originating right from the Preamble and running to the last page of the Constitution.

Besides meeting these constitutional obligations, the government is expected to pay attention to moral and humane aspects of its duties. Reducing inequalities of income and wealth and providing opportunities to all irrespective of caste, colour or creed etc. richer life full of facilities and comforts call for planned and sustained policies, programmes, laws and their implementation on the part of the government. The Central and State governments aim to provide policies of social, economic and political nature to ensure a social order where there is equality of status and opportunities, away from any kind of discrimination and exploitation.

Indian society is diverse and heterogeneous in nature. The government policies and actions have to face problems and challenges of varied types in balancing the social change and growth in national interest. The main problem areas taken up in this presentation are: (a) traditional way of thinking and desire for stability/status quo (b) political uncertainty/instability (c) falling ethical and professional standards in politics and administration and (d) financial constraints. These aforesaid factors put hurdles in the way, disturb the process of general development and pace of indispensable and purposeful societal changes. It may be befitting to touch upon these factors briefly.

Traditional Life and Thinking

It may be appropriate to recollect briefly the social life at the time of independence. The traditional way of life of our people particularly rural and uneducated immediately after getting freedom is quite pronounced as it has many condemnable social evils. Let us admit that these have their presence even in today's life in a noticeable proportions. There is hardly a point in repeating them in details except to mention the ills of rigid caste system and untouchability, exploitation of the underprivileged by privileged ones, poor social mobility, deplorable condition of women and children especially the female child, demonic system of dowry, rapes, black magic, child marriages, animal and at times human sacrifices....... and so on. The list is very long that puts our heads down in shame. It is now widely admitted and accepted that such a traditional life and approach need to be changed for the better from every human angle. But it is also true that change is resisted be it social, economic or political in the initial stages. Such resistances generally come from those whose power privileges; status/position or interests are adversely affected or threatened. These are a few reasons that people want stability as the change/s is/are very likely to disturb the existing equilibrium. This makes the people apprehensive about the future.

Political Instability/uncertainty

Another hurdle in the way of progressive changes. Modifications in a modern democratic set-up is the political uncertainty and instability. Suffice it to say that policies, plans and programmes are framed by the ruling political party in a parliamentary system of government. In case of a coalition government, the political parties joining the government became decision-makers in that respect. A single party government as we know provides a stable system of governance which from any angle is preferred so far as the overall development of a nation is concerned.

Straightway coming to the present Indian political scenario, an established fact is that in today's democratic system of governance in India, one party rule/dominance particularly at the Centre has lost its grounds about two decades back. Coalition government is, in fact, another name of political uncertainty and instability. Larger the number of coalition partners, the greater would be the scope of political upheavals. By the very nature of coalition politics and governance, tussle of power amongst constituents, political pressures, bargaining, compromises and alliances are obvious.

Such approaches and factors generally overshadow the national interest and result invariably in unprincipled decisions and actions, promotion of petty interest, self-aggrandisement, unjust and unholy alliances, leg-pulling, administrative instability, inefficient and poor governance to cite a few. How can a developing country like India or for that matter any nation can afford to confront such negative developments being enemies of good governance.

Much can still be said about coalition politics and its inherent ills. Suffice is to express that in the long run such situation/s the overall growth and national development is likely to be slow, lopsided, short sighted giving impetus to merely vote-catching devise and so on.

Falling Ethical and Professional Standards

Further, falling ethical and professional standards in politics and administration in our democratic system of governance are not only causing worries but also eroding the credibility of the very system. The deeds, actions and public behaviour of political and administrative actors in the present situation many a time do not fully justify the spirits of national service and development, objectivity, probity and a genuine concern for the poor and masses. Theoretically we confine politics' role in policy determining and leave administration to implement the policies. But in actual practice their roles have mixed up a great deal. According to La Palombra "policy and administration can never be separated."[1]

With the passage of time, unfortunately degradation of values and character slowly made its entry in the society. It did not spare anyone including the leaders of all shades. The best is not coming out of the performance of political and administrative leaders because of number of factors like poor educational and social background, parochial outlook and considerations, selfish ends, poor ethical and professional standards, inappropriate conduct, (highhandedness, corruption, nepotism etc.) misuse of government machinery and discretionary powers, entry of criminals and anti-social elements in political system and nexus between politicians and mafia and many more such evils. Of late, brow-beating of civil servants by political masters and bulldosing their way even by ignoring the well-intentioned advice of the professional civil servants have added serious problems to good governance and as a consequence, planned and fruitful societal changes/improvements get a back seat. Public administrators are threatened of inconvenient postings and disciplinary action just to make them fall in line and submit to even unprincipled and undue dictates of the political bosses. This is one of the reasons to suck up to them for plump postings and at times out of turn promotions. In the process the bureaucrats become unethical and perform against the established professional standards. Ultimately the national interest suffers and common man's and underprivileged's dreams of purposive changes and prospective future are jolted.

Financial Constraints

Financial resources are the backbone of plans/projects of social, economic or political nature for effecting changes fruitfully and bringing positive results. They need to be utilised very intelligently and purposefully for the national good keeping in mind their limited quantity. The basic premise in this regard is to get the maximum national good out of minimum expenditure. Budget is passed every year for implementing plans, programmes, scheme beneficial for the masses. But in fact we are in a sorry state of affairs in this concern. Scams, violation of budgetary provisions, wasteful expenditure, reports of Comptroller and Auditor-General and Financial Committees of the Parliament, media reporting, academics and scholars' comments make one to believe that wrongs done or got done seem to be a tip of the iceberg. No country howsoever financially sound can afford to be callous or inefficient in vast expanding activities of varied nature requiring the efficient and economical expenditure. It is extremely horrifying to note such big financial losses, irregularities and the benefits of the huge public expenditure not reaching the beneficiaries especially the poor ones in desirable proportions. Poor deliverance of the benefits of the schemes like employment, urban and rural housing, water supply, old age pension etc. serves an eye opener and leaves much to be desired. Reckless public expenditure without political and administrative responsibility wrecks the credibility and goodwill of the governance. Passing of the buck in this regard is another boon for real defaulters. It may not be wrong to express that our financial resources and their rightful and honest utilisation falls far below the expectation of a common man.

Remedies

When our leaders and people are aware of the ills and lacunae in the system and wish to bring about planned changes/improvements for the benefit of all, it becomes easier to think about the remedies.

It is now widely admitted and accepted that traditional approach to solve issues needs to change for the better. It is true that planned, progressive and purposive changes are resisted in initial stages but it is also true the resistances to changes become weak and neglected with the passage of time. Change in policies, programmes of social, economic and political in nature starts gaining acceptance. This becomes possible because of number of factors like global trends of modernisation, old customs, folkways and mores giving way to new values and progressive mode of life, spread of education, increasing general awareness, impact of social reformers' movements, NGOs positive contribution in different fields, growing influence of scientific and rational way of thinking, governments' reformative policies and their implementation, media's objective and constructive role in highlighting social evils and promoting communal harmony and social and economic equality and people getting motivated and influenced in the right direction and so on.

Though our traditional way of thinking and caste system have become reasonable liberal especially in cities' and amongst educated people yet it needs to give way to more open thinking and actions to promote sense of equality and feeling of oneness. Special reservations to Scheduled Castes, Scheduled Tribes and Other Backward Classes guaranteed in the Constitution and laws and their wholehearted appreciation and acceptance by all are steps in the right direction. Let such sections of the society make fullest and sincere efforts to avail such opportunities to carve a prospective career for themselves and contribute to national growth and development like any other citizen.

One of the significant needs of the hour is to ensure, promote and consolidate political stability which is a must for providing a sound base for well-directed and beneficial policies and plans by a government for meaningful social change. Political parties, their leaders and members badly need to follow ethics and professional standards and perform in the national interest rising above sectarian considerations. This equally applies to the bureaucrats/civil servants. In fact, these are the two types of actors people look up to for good governance in today's democratic systems of administration.

It is assumed that greater the chance of political stability in a democratic system of governance, the greater would be the possibility of national growth and development in different areas of our social life. In India, the number of political parties is increasing particularly at state/regional levels causing a concern for having stable government. Let the political parties/leaders themselves realise the inherent danger of an unstable government. Let them ponder about not becoming an instrument or pawn in boosting the number of political parties unnecessarily due to very selfish and personal reasons, narrow and sectarian considerations. Political parties and their leaders stand for national services for providing maximum good and welfare to the people. An idea is put across whether we need to limit the number of political parties joining a coalition government with a view to ensure political stability. And secondly, whether there has to be a minimum number of seats with a political party vis-à-vis the total number of seats in the Lok Sabha (State Assembly in case of States) to be qualified to join a coalition government. Let there be a national debate at various fora to thrash these points threadbare to identify the pros and coins before reaching a conclusion/consensus.

Further, cleansing of politics and administration in our country is urgently required to make it really people oriented and change oriented. Political and administrative reforms need to stress on depoliticising the civil services and decriminalising politics. Let political masters and civil servants follow norms of ethics and morality, do sincere heart-searching in their personal and professional life and honestly pledge to work for national interest. They are expected to exhibit their outstanding qualities like foresight, commitment for achieving national goals, probity, objectivity, spirit for just compromises, welcoming healthy and constructive criticism and ready for socially relevant and beneficial changes. Sincere actions would speak louder than merely doing formality in performing their official duty. They need to understand that a "a public office is not a job, it is an opportunity to do something for the people"[2] (Franklin Knight Lane). "Good government only happens when the people working in it do their jobs, and do them well"[3] (Metthew Lesko). Let good governance; its main contributors being political masters and civil servants, ensure and convince the people especially the underprivileged of its human face and sincerity to serve them.

National financial resources being scare have to be so planned, budgeted and utilised as bring the maximum good for the country and its masses. Not a penny could be allowed to be misused, misappropriated and mis-accounted in any country especially in India and such other countries. Let everybody especially political bosses and bureaucrats involved in the process of the governance very sincerely think and act as if country's money is their own and as if they are spending it from their own pocket. Let them not misguide and befool common man in the name of welfare schemes and fill their own purses. Indulgence in scams, corruption, misuse of public money, direct/indirect hand in the creation of black money and so on need an iron hand to sternly deal with defaulters to set an example for others. Apart from government machinery, the media, opinion leaders and the NGOs can play very useful and supportive role in creating a public opinion which stands firmly for exposing and socially boycotting such blacksheep and unpatriotic people. By doing so, the society may cause a great deal of embarrassment and bring them in disrepute; a life which becomes worse than a hell. Let them listen to the voice of their conscience which is a true and unfailing guide.

It may be expressed that changes of various nature have been taking place throughout the world. Care has to be taken to give a planned, proper and purposive direction to such changes as may be beneficial to every section of the society with special care of the downtrodden and underprivileged. In our country there have been constitutional and legal provisions to enrich the lives of such strata of society socially, politically and economically.

Having Sarvodaya Society has to be the 'mool mantra' of our state and the government to ensure alround development of, all means all. Mother India is mother to every Indian irrespective of caste, colour or creed. Rather underprivileged such as scheduled castes, scheduled tribes and other backward classes of the society need 'her' special care and protection.

References

1. Joesph La Palombra, "Bureaucracy and Political Development: Notes Queries and Dilemmas" in Joseph La Palombra (ed) Bureaucracy and Political Development, New Jersey, Princeton University Press, 1963, p. 51.
2. The Times of India, New Delhi, August 8, 2013, p. 10.
3. *Ibid.*, p. 12.

6

Educational Empowerment of Scheduled Castes through Coaching and Allied Scheme in India

A.K. Singh

Abstract

Educational empowerment of the weaker sections has been the priority of government for their mainstreaming in development and governance. Scheduled Castes, Scheduled Tribes, OBCs and Minorities are included in the weaker sections of the society. In order to provide them due share in educational institutions and government services, reservations has been given to them besides introducing educational and economic empowerment programmes and schemes for their overall empowerment and development. Government of India under the Ministry of Social Justice and Empowerment, Ministry of Tribal Affairs and Ministry of Minority Affairs, has launched educational development schemes such as pre-metric scholarship, post-metric scholarship, top class education scheme, Rajiv Gandhi National Fellowship Scheme, Overseas Scholarship Scheme, Book Bank Scheme, Babu Jagjivan Ram Chhatravas Yojana, Coaching and Allied Services Scheme etc. for the weaker sections including the students of Scheduled Castes, Scheduled Tribes, Minorities and OBCs. Coaching and Allied Services Scheme for the weaker sections including SC and OBC students has been launched by the Ministry of Social Justice and Empowerment, Government of India for providing coaching and allied services for preparation of competitive examinations. The scheme has no doubt impacted on the educational empowerment of SC and OBC students besides their overall preparation and success in competitive examinations however; constraints and drawbacks in effective implementation of the scheme are reported. In view of the above, the present paper purports to examine the functioning and performance of central sector scheme and suggesting a roadmap for effective functioning of the scheme and achieving desired results.

Introduction

Indian society has been exposed to various socio-economic changes and legal initiatives over the last five decades. The constitutional provisions of democratic governance and the policy of positive discrimination have affected the social fabric and economic structure of Indian Society. However, it is highly stratified with many glaring inequalities among the different social groups. Despite protective measures, Scheduled Castes still suffers from the stigma of inferiority and low socio-economic status. They suffered both from overall rural poverty and backwardness. Importantly, the progress and prosperity of a nation is judged from the socio-economic status of its population especially of the weaker sections of the society who suffer from abject poverty, hunger, disease, unemployment, exploitation etc. as well as disadvantage groups like women, children, Scheduled Castes, Scheduled Tribes etc. It is the prime importance that such segment of society mostly living in remote, backward and rural areas should receive serious and earnest attention of policy-makers, planners, social welfare administrators, social activities and academicians, so that the downtrodden section of the society can also live decent life ensured by the special provisions in the Constitution of India.

Indian society is highly stratified. This stratification has resulted into glaring inequalities among different social groups. This age-old social stratification is the result of the prevailing caste system, which has segregated the Dalits (SCs, STs and the OBCs) from the rest of the society to such an extent that they had been denied in the past even the basic human needs and the rights that are required to ensure one's bare existence. The caste system has created and sustained an unequal opportunity structure, which is an anathema to the egalitarian principles, which are the basis of a modern democratic society. What is worse, it intensifies and perpetuates the sufferings and servitude of the disadvantaged groups by reducing their access to developmental benefits. Importantly, the SCs came to be placed at the lowest rungs of the hierarchical caste order from where there was no scope for upward mobility. Moreover, religious injunctions blunt even the limited scope for resistance. Thus, the power and privilege accorded to the upper castes in the 'Varna' social order, in course of time, resulted in the appropriation of wealth and resources. Since wealth, power and resources were under their disposal, they could have more resources and these resources could be converted into power and power ensured acquisition of resources. In the ultimate analysis, the resources, wealth, power, position, privileges, higher status, authority, education, employment, services, land and labour got concentrated in the hands of upper castes.

The Scheduled Castes population, according to 2011 Census, was 16.66 crores constituting 16 per cent of the total population of India. In terms of absolute numbers,

Scheduled Castes are primarily concentrated in Uttar Pradesh (3.51 crores), West Bengal (1.9 crores), Andhra Pradesh (1.3 crores) Tamil Nadu (1.2 crores), and Bihar (1.2 crores). These States, together, account for 54.54 per cent of the total Scheduled Castes population of the country. Punjab occupies first position in terms of percentage of Scheduled Castes to the State population (28.85 per cent) followed by Himachal Pradesh (24.72 per cent), West Bengal (23.02 per cent), Rajasthan (17.29 per cent) and Madhya Pradesh (14.55 per cent). For development of persons belonging to socially disadvantaged group the Ministry is implementing programmes for economic development, educational development and social empowerment.

Education is the most powerful instrument for empowering the socially disadvantaged groups. Due to poor educational standards, career guidance and counselling, the disadvantaged could not avail the benefits of reservation policy in terms of getting admissions in technical, management and professional courses through appearing in competitive examinations as well as achieving higher posts of government services. In order to empowering weaker sections including Scheduled Castes and OBCs, the Coaching and Allied Scheme for SC/ST students was introduced in 1960-61 for improving the knowledge and aptitude amongst SC/ST students by providing special coaching to them through Pre-Examination Training Centres and thus for preparing them to compete with others in the Civil Services and other competitive examinations. Ministry of Social Justice and Empowerment, Government of India has launched a Central Sector scheme of Coaching and Allied Services for students preparing competitive examinations. The scheme is being implemented by the Ministry in association with NGOs, academic institutions such as universities, colleges and institutions. The scheme was common for both SC and ST students up to 2000 and it is, now exclusively for SC students.

Present paper is based on a major study conducted under the auspices of Ministry of Social Justice and Empowerment,

Government of India by Pt. G. B. Pant Institute of Studies in Rural Development, Lucknow during 2012. The study is confined to Uttar Pradesh, Rajasthan, Madhya Pradesh, Manipur, and Delhi. Overall 20 SC coaching centres in five states were selected. From each institution at least 50 students from coaching centre were selected. Thus, 20 centres and 1000 students were randomly selected for interview.

Implementation of Coaching and Allied Scheme

During the year 2007-08 to 2011-12, expenditure under the Coaching and Allied Scheme for weaker sections including SC and OBC, expenditure has increased 78.0 per cent while budget estimates increased by 71.23 per cent during the years of 2007-08 to 2012-13. The revised budget estimates also increased by 42.86 per cent during the corresponding period (Table 6.1)

Table 6.1: Allocation and Expenditure under Coaching and Allied Schemes for Weaker Sections Including SCs and OBCs (Rs. Crores)

Years	*Budget Estimates*	*Revised Estimates*	*Expenditure*	*No. of Beneficiaries*
2007-08	7.00	7.00	3.91	--
2008-09	8.00	6.00	4.00	3403
2009-10	8.00	6.00	2.79	3013
2010-11	10.00	14.00	9.43	2489
2011-12	10.00	10.00	6.96	--
2012-13	12.00	--	--	--

Source: Annual Report, 2010-11.

During 2008-09 to 2009-10, numbers of beneficiaries under the free coaching for SC and OBC students were reported to be 6416 while Rs 1622.33 lakh were spent under the scheme during 2008-09 to 2010-11. As on 31st March, 2011, 840 million students get benefits under the scheme. The largest number of beneficiaries was reported to be in the state of Andhra Pradesh followed by Delhi, Maharashtra, Rajasthan,

Haryana, Uttar Pradesh, Kerala and Madhya Pradesh (Table 6.2).

Table 6.2: State-wise Central Assistance Released and Beneficiaries Covered Under Free Coaching for SC and OBC Students

State/UT	*2008-09*		*2009-10*		*2010-11 as on 31.03.11*	
	Expenditure (Rs In Lakhs)	*Beneficiaries*	*Expenditure (Rs In Lakhs)*	*Beneficiaries*	*Expenditure (Rs In Lakhs)*	*Beneficiaries*
Madhya Pradesh	30.9	190	1.28	30	23.40	160
Rajasthan	24.48	360	12.19	130	39.53	340
Uttar Pradesh	17.97	290	18.24	300	24.34	260
Manipur	6.78	100	2.21	30	0	0
New Delhi	29.01	340	5.63	60	168.75	1840
Total	**399.98**	**3403**	**279.33**	**3013**	**943.02**	**8400**

Source: Annual Report, 2010-11.

Enrollment and Success Rate

Gender-wise enrollment in coaching centres is shown in Table 6.3. Female students constituted only 16.84 per cent in government-run coaching centres and 9.52 per cent in non-government-run coaching centres. The representation of female students in government-run coaching centres was reported high in the courses of LIC (30.02 per cent) followed by NDA (24.68 per cent) and IAS (18.99 per cent) while it was found low in other public/private sector services (6.63 per cent) and PCS examination (12.83 per cent). Similarly, women representation in non-government-run coaching centres was reported significant in PCS examinations (17.39 per cent) and very low in Railway services

(4.80 per cent). Thus, it is imperative to encourage female students for their enrollment in coaching centres.

Table 6.3: Gender-wise Enrollment

Name of Examinations	*Government*		*Non-Government*	
	Total	*Female*	*Total*	*Female*
IAS	1053	200 (18.99)	1130	121 (10.71)
PCS	1099	141 (12.83)	983	171 (17.39)
Lower Subordinate	843	113 (13.40)	945	49 (5.18)
Banking Services	820	135 (16.46)	930	83 (8.92)
Railway Services	745	110 (14.76)	895	43 (4.80)
NDA Services	782	193 (24.60)	918	73 (7.95)
LIC	573	172 (30.02)	805	85 (10.56
Other Public/ Private Sector Services	664	44 (6.67)	789	79 (10.01)
Total	**6579**	**1100 (16.84)**	**7395**	**704 (9.52)**

(Figures in brackets means percentage)

Source: Field Survey.

Majority of the students were found belonging to the Scheduled Castes and Scheduled Tribes Groups. The representation of Scheduled Caste Students was reported significantly high in case of LIC examination, followed by Lower Subordinate examination and banking services. The representation of ST students was recorded high in IAS examination and other public/private sector examinations. Only 10 per cent students were OBC communities (Table 6.4).

Table 6.4: Social Group-wise Distribution of Enrolment in Government-Run Coaching Centres

Name of Examinations	*Total*	*SC*	*ST*	*OBC*	*Others*
IAS	1053	568 (53.94)	370 (35.14)	115 (10.92)	--
PCS	1099	653 (59.42)	240 (21.84)	200 (18.19)	6 (0.55)
Lower Subordinate	843	612 (72.59)	204 (24.26)	24 (2.85)	3 (0.36)
Banking Services	820	581 (70.85)	162 (19.76)	75 (9.15)	2 (0.24)
Railway Services	745	495 (69.49)	66 (8.86)	79 (10.60)	5 (0.67)
NDA Services	782	550 (70.33)	86 (10.99)	45 (5.75)	1 (0.13)
LIC	573	464 (80.94)	36 (6.28)	72 (12.56)	1 (0.17)
Other Public/ Private Sector Services	664	388 (58.43)	205 (30.87)	70 (10.54)	1 (0.16)
Total	**6579**	**4311 (65.53)**	**1569 (23.85)**	**680 (10.33)**	**76 (1.16)**

(Figures in brackets means percentage)
Source: Field Survey.

Most of the students in the non-government-run coaching centres were found belonging to Scheduled Caste (62.07 per cent) and Scheduled Tribes (32.06 per cent). The representation of Scheduled Caste students was reported higher in case of LIC followed by banking services and other public/private sector services. Similarly, the representation of Scheduled Tribes was reported high in NDA services followed by Railway services and IAS examination.

Success rate of coaching institutions is shown in Table 5. During the year 2008-09 to 2010-11, 6316 students were coached in government-run coaching centres while 7395 students were provided coaching in non-government-run coaching centres during the corresponding period. Out of the coached students, 612 students in government-run coaching centres and 452 students from non-government-run coaching centres could get success. Thus, the success rate was reported 9.69 per cent for government-run coaching centres and only 6.11 per cent in non-government-run coaching centres. The success rate for government-run coaching centres was found significant in the examinations

Table 6.5: Success Rate of Coaching Institutions

Name of Examinations	*No. of Students Coached (2008-09 to 2010-11)*		*No. of Students Succeeded (2008-09 to 2010-11)*	
	Government	*Non-Government*	*Government*	*Non-Government*
IAS	783	1090	44 (5.62)	68 (6.24)
PCS	1106	983	62 (5.62)	66 (6.71)
Lower Subordinate	843	945	75 (8.89)	60 (6.35)
Banking Services	820	930	88 (10.73)	35 (3.76)
Railway Services	745	895	73 (9.70)	65 (7.26)
NDA Services	782	918	81 (10.36)	43 (4.68)
LIC	573	805	86 (15.01)	55 (6.83)
Other Public/ Private Sector Services	664	789	103 (15.51)	60 (7.60)
Total	**6316**	**7395**	**612 (9.69)**	**452 (6.11)**

(Figures in brackets means percentage)

Source: Field Survey.

of other public/private sector services (15.51 per cent) followed by LIC (15.01 per cent), NDA (10.36 per cent) and banking services (10.73 per cent). However, success rate was found low in IAS and PCS examinations. Similarly, the success rate for non-government-run coaching centres was reported significant in Railway examinations (7.26 per cent) followed by other public/private sector services (7.60 per cent) and low in banking services (3.76 per cent).

Poor background of students, lack of interest and lack of competitive reading materials as well as lack of subject experts are some of the important reasons for low success rate. However, higher success requires for commitment and accountability of the faculty and staff besides providing coaching to the students. Lack of reading materials for competitive examinations may be procured through internet search, consulting good libraries and academic centres besides translating into Hindi and other vernacular language for proper understanding by the students. However, this will requires additional efforts and resources.

The coaching centres have adequate infrastructure such as classrooms, administrative block, toilets, etc. besides library and common room with facility of TV and entertainment. However, mess facility was not found satisfactory. Most of the coaching centres were of the view that discontinuation of stipend under the scheme will affect the enrollment and success rate for competitive examinations. They were also of the view that present amount of stipend is not sufficient. Though, majority of the enrolled students are belonging to Scheduled Castes and Scheduled Tribes however, female representation in coaching centres was reported to be very low. The overall success rate has been found highly dissatisfactory as only a few students could get success in the competitive examinations. Thus, it is imperative to focus more on preparation of students for competitive examinations so that success rate may be enhanced.

Impact of Coaching and Allied Scheme

Most of the respondents admitted that there has been positive impact of coaching and allied services scheme on the existing body of knowledge and confidence level. About 82.7 per cent respondents belonging to government institutions reported that their confidence level has increased after attending the coaching classes. This was found significantly high in Uttar Pradesh followed by Madhya Pradesh and New Delhi. Similarly, the proportion of respondents from non-government institutions, accepting that their confidence level has increased, was reported significantly high in Manipur followed by Madhya Pradesh and Rajasthan. About 17.2 per cent respondents from government institutions and 14.8 per cent of respondents from non-government institutions reported that their existing body of knowledge has substantially increased. Interestingly, majority of the respondents reported that their existing body of knowledge has increased to the greater extent after attending the coaching classes. This was also found more pronouncing in Manipur, Uttar Pradesh and Rajasthan in non-government institutions (Table 6.6).

Most of the respondents were found satisfied with the teaching methods in coaching institutions. However, the proportion of respondents who were found satisfied with the teaching methods was found significantly high in non-government institutions as compared to government institutions. Only 34.9 per cent respondents from government institutions and 61.9 per cent respondents from non-government institutions were found fully satisfied with teaching methods while 14.2 per cent respondents from government institutions and 2.2 per cent respondents in non-government institutions were found somewhat satisfied with teaching methods in coaching institutions (Table 6.7).

The respondents were asked regarding their satisfaction about the availability of quality of resource literature in the library. Most of the respondents were found satisfied with

Table 6.6: Impact of Coaching on Knowledge

State	*Increased confidence level*		*Increased existing body of knowledge substantially*		*Increased existing body of knowledge to the greater extent*		*No improvement in knowledge base*		*Total*	
	Govt.	*Non-Govt.*	*Govt.*	*Non-Govt.*	*Govt.*	*Non-Govt.*	*Govt.*	*Non-Govt.*	*Govt.*	*Non-Govt.*
Uttar Pradesh	86	82	14	13	0	5	0	0	100	100
	86.0%	82.0%	14.0%	13.0%	0.0%	5.0%	0.0%	0.0%	100%	100%
Madhya Pradesh	46	123	9	22	0	0	0	0	55	145
	83.6%	84.8%	0.0%	15.1%	0.0%	0.0%	0.0%	0.0%	100%	100%
New Delhi	36	119	12	33	0	0	0	0	48	152
	75.0%	78.2%	25.0%	21.7%	0.0%	0.0%	0.0%	0.0%	100%	100%
Manipur	0	171	0	20	0	9	0	0	0	200
	0.0%	85.5%	0.0%	10.0%	0.0%	4.5%	0.0%	0.0%	100%	100%
Rajasthan	0	168	0	30	0	2	0	0	0	200
	0.0%	84.0%	0.0%	15.0%	0.0%	1.0%	0.0%	0.0%	100%	100%
Total	168	663	35	118	0	16	0	0	203	797
	82.7%	83.1%	17.2%	14.8%	0.0%	2.9%	0.0%	0.0%	100%	100%

Source: Field Survey.

Table 6.7: Satisfaction with Teaching Methods

State	*Fully satisfied*		*Satisfied*		*Somewhat satisfied*		*Do not satisfied*		*Total*	
	Govt.	*Non-Govt.*	*Govt.*	*Non-Govt.*	*Govt.*	*Non-Govt.*	*Govt.*	*Non-Govt.*	*Govt.*	*Non-Govt.*
Uttar Pradesh	22	20	69	74	9	6	0	0	100	100
	22.0%	20.0%	69.0%	74.0%	9.0%	6.0%	0.0%	0.0%	100%	100%
Madhya Pradesh	26	85	29	56	0	4	0	0	55	145
	47.2%	58.6%	52.7%	38.6%	0.0%	7.2%	0.0%	0.0%	100%	100%
New Delhi	23	89	5	55	20	8	0	0	48	152
	47.9%	58.5%	10.4%	36.1%	41.6%	16.6%	0.0%	0.0%	100%	100%
Manipur	0	142	0	58	0	0	0	0	0	200
	0.0%	71.0%	0.0%	29.0%	0.0%	0.0%	0.0%	0.0%	100%	100%
Rajasthan	0	158	0	42	0	0	0	0	0	200
	0.0%	79.0%	0.0%	21.0%	0.0%	0.0%	0.0%	0.0%	100%	100%
Total	71	494	103	285	29	18	0	0	203	797
	34.9%	61.9%	50.7%	35.7%	14.2%	2.2%	0.0%	0.0%	100%	100%

Source: Field Survey.

Table 6.8: Satisfaction with Availability of Quality of Stock in Library

State	*Very satisfied*		*Satisfied*		*Somewhat satisfied*		*Do not satisfied*		*Total*	
	Govt.	*Non-Govt.*	*Govt.*	*Non-Govt.*	*Govt.*	*Non-Govt.*	*Govt.*	*Non-Govt.*	*Govt.*	*Non-Govt.*
Uttar Pradesh	15	11	75	61	10	28	0	0	100	100
	15.0%	11.0%	75.0%	61.0%	10.0%	28.0%	0.0%	0.0%	100%	100%
Madhya Pradesh	29	113	16	22	10	10	0	0	55	145
	52.7%	77.9%	29.0%	15.1%	18.1%	6.8%	0.0%	0.0%	100%	100%
New Delhi	18	112	19	40	11	0	0	0	48	152
	37.5%	73.6%	39.5%	26.3%	22.9%	0.0%	0.0%	0.0%	100%	100%
Manipur	0	117	0	48	0	35	0	0	0	200
	0.0%	58.5%	0.0%	24.0%	0.0%	17.5%	0.0%	0.0%	100%	100%
Rajasthan	0	119	0	81	0	0	0	0	0	200
	0.0%	59.5%	0.0%	40.5%	0.0%	0.0%	0.0%	0.0%	100%	100%
Total	62	472	110	252	31	73	0	0	203	797
	30.5%	59.2%	54.1%	31.6%	15.2%	9.1%	0.0%	0.0%	100%	100%

the quality of stock in the library however, the proportion of respondents who were found satisfied with the quality of stock in library was reported slightly high in case of government institutions as compared to non-government institutions. Again, the proportion of respondents who were satisfied with the availability of quality of stock in library was reported significantly high in Uttar Pradesh followed by Madhya Pradesh and New Delhi (Table 6.8).

More than half of the respondents were found very satisfied and about 22 per cent respondents were found satisfied with the availability of quality stock in library. About 13 per cent respondents were found dissatisfied with the availability of stock in library. This was found more pronouncing in New Delhi (18.5 per cent) and Madhya Pradesh (14.4 per cent) (Table 6.9).

Table 6.9: Satisfaction of Scheduled Caste Respondents with Availability of Quality of Stock in Library

State	*Very satisfied*	*Satisfied*	*Somewhat satisfied*	*Do not satisfied*	*Total*
Uttar Pradesh	117	33	16	21	187
	62.6%	17.6%	8.6%	11.2%	100.0%
Madhya Pradesh	103	66	4	29	202
	51.0%	32.7%	2.0%	14.4%	100.0%
New Delhi	112	22	20	35	189
	59.3%	11.6%	10.6%	18.5%	100.0%
Manipur	96	53	37	18	204
	47.1%	26.0%	18.1%	8.8%	100.0%
Rajasthan	92	42	43	21	198
	46.5%	21.2%	21.7%	10.6%	100.0%
Total	**520**	**216**	**120**	**124**	**980**
	53.1%	**22.0%**	**12.2%**	**12.7%**	**100.0%**

Source: Field Survey.

The respondents were further asked about their satisfaction with the quality of teaching in coaching institutions. About 97.3 per cent respondents were found satisfied with the quality of teaching in non-government institutions. This was found significantly high in Manipur, Rajasthan and New Delhi. Interestingly, about 10.9 per cent respondents from non-government institutions and 31.5 per cent respondents from government institutions were found very satisfied with the quality of teaching in coaching institutions (Table 6.10).

The aspirants were asked regarding the general use of stipend. The respondents from the government-run institutions reported that they use stipend mainly for local conveyance and purchasing of books/reading materials, food intake and lodging and accommodation. The respondents from the non-government institutions reported that they use stipend mainly for local conveyance, food intake and purchase of books/reading materials. There have been marked variations in the general use of stipend across the states and type of coaching institutions. The respondents were asked that whether the present amount of stipend is sufficient. About 74.9 per cent of respondents from government-run institutions and 69.4 per cent respondents from non-government run institutions reported that the present amount of stipend is sufficient however, about 30.5 per cent of respondents from government-run institutions and 23.9 per cent from non-government-run institutions respondents reported that present amount of stipend is not sufficient (Table 6.11).

The Scheduled Castes respondents were asked that whether present amount of stipend is sufficient. About 55 per cent respondents reported that present amount of stipend is sufficient. This was found more pronouncing in Rajasthan followed by Manipur. More than one-fourth respondents reported that present amount of stipend is not sufficient at all (Table 6.12).

Table 6.10: Satisfaction with the Quality of Teaching

State	*Very satisfied*		*Satisfied*		*Somewhat satisfied*		*Do not satisfied*		*Total*	
	Govt.	*Non-Govt.*	*Govt.*	*Non-Govt.*	*Govt.*	*Non-Govt.*	*Govt.*	*Non-Govt.*	*Govt.*	*Non-Govt.*
Uttar Pradesh	16	19	74	75	10	06	00	00	100	100
	16.0%	19.0%	74.0%	75.0%	10%	6.0%	0.0%	0.0%	100%	100%
Madhya Pradesh	19	21	18	116	18	8	0	0	55	145
	34.5%	14.4%	32.7%	80.0%	32.7%	5.5%	0.0%	0.0%	100%	100%
New Delhi	29	18	19	134	0	0	0	0	48	152
	60.4%	11.8%	39.5%	88.1%	0.0%	0.0%	0.0%	0.0%	100%	100%
Manipur	0	11	0	189	0	0	0	0	0	200
	0.0%	5.5%	0.0%	94.5%	0.0%	0.0%	0.0%	0.0%	0.0%	100%
Rajasthan	0	18	0	182	0	0	0	0	0	200
	0.0%	9.0%	0.0%	91.0%	0.0%	0.0%	0.0%	0.0%	100%	100%
Total	64	87	111	696	28	14	0	0	203	797
	31.5%	10.9%	54.6%	97.3%	13.7%	1.7%	0.0%	0.0%	100%	100%

Source: Field Survey.

Table 6.11: Whether Present Amount of Stipend is Sufficient?

State	*Yes*		*No*		*Not at all*		*Total*	
	Govt.	*Non-Govt.*	*Govt.*	*Non-Govt.*	*Govt.*	*Non-Govt.*	*Govt.*	*Non-Govt.*
Uttar Pradesh	75	69	25	31	0	0	100	100
	75.0%	69.0%	25.0%	31.0%	0.0%	0.0%	100.0%	100.0%
Madhya Pradesh	39	129	16	16	0	0	55	145
	70.9%	88.9%	29.0%	11.0%	0.0%	0.0%	100.0%	100.0%
New Delhi	27	117	21	35	0	0	48	152
	56.2%	76.9%	43.7%	23.0%	0.0%	0.0%	100.0%	100.0%
Manipur	0	133	0	63	0	4	0	200
	0.0%	66.5%	0.0%	31.5%	0.0%	2.0%	0.0%	100.0%
Rajasthan	0	149	0	46	0	5	0	200
	0.0%	74.5%	0.0%	23.0%	0.0%	2.5%	100.0%	100.0%
Total	141	597	62	191	0	9	203	797
	69.4%	74.9%	30.5%	23.9%	0.0%	1.0%	100.0%	100.0%

Source: Field Survey.

Table 6.12: Adequacy of Present Amount of Stipend

State	*Yes*	*No*	*Not at all*	*Total*
Uttar Pradesh	103	22	62	187
	55.1%	11.8%	33.2%	100.0%
Madhya Pradesh	112	32	58	202
	55.4%	15.8%	28.7%	100.0%
New Delhi	97	42	50	189
	51.3%	22.2%	26.5%	100.0%
Manipur	117	44	43	204
	57.4%	21.6%	21.1%	100.0%
Rajasthan	114	42	42	198
	57.6%	21.2%	21.2%	100.0%
Total	543	182	255	980
	55.4%	18.6%	26.0%	100.0%

Source: Field Survey.

The aspirants were asked that whether the discontinuing of stipend will affect the quality of learning and success. About 88.1 per cent of respondents from government-run institutions were found strongly agree on this view point while about 12.1 per cent respondents from non-government run institutions were found agree on this view point. All the respondents reported that discontinuation of stipend will affect the quality of learning and success. About 87 per cent respondents were found strongly agree on the view point that discontinuation of stipend will affect the quality of learning and success.

The aspirants were asked that whether minimum bar of 50 per cent in qualifying examinations is justified. About 48.2 per cent respondents in case of government institutions and 25.0 per cent respondents in non-government institutions were found agree on this view point and about 69.5 per cent from non-government institutions and 29.0 per cent from government institutions respondents were strongly agree in the opinion for minimum bar of 50 per cent in qualifying examinations. While only 22.6 per cent respondents from government-run institutions were found somewhat agree on this view point (Table 6.13).

All the surveyed aspirants reported that they are availing hostel facility. They reported that they are availing the hostel facility for well preparation for their examination and enjoying the conducive academic environment and infrastructural facilities such as library, accommodation, etc. Living in hostel also ensures closer interaction and discussion among the peers and disturbance-free environment for carrying out the study (Table 6.14).

Most of the respondents reported that they are living in hostel on twin sharing basis. This was found more pronouncing in case of non-government-run institutions as compared to government-run institutions. Again, the proportion of respondents belonging to non-government-run institutions living in hostel on twin sharing basis was reported significantly high in Manipur, New Delhi, Madhya Pradesh and Rajasthan while the proportion of respondents from the government institutions was recorded high in Madhya Pradesh followed by New Delhi and Uttar Pradesh. Interestingly, about 45.2 per cent respondents from the government-run institutions were found living in hostel with single occupancy. This was found significantly high in Uttar Pradesh followed by New Delhi and Madhya Pradesh. The proportion of respondents living in hostel on single occupancy was recorded high in Uttar Pradesh in case of non-government-run institutions.

The level of satisfaction of aspirants availing hostel facilities is shown in Table 6.15. About 62.8 per cent from non-government-run institutions and 40.3 per cent from government institutions were very much satisfied with hostel facilities being provided to them this was found more pronouncing in the state of Madhya Pradesh and New Delhi in non-government run institutions. While only 36.4 per cent of respondents from government-run institutions were found satisfied this was seen highest in the state of Uttar Pradesh and only 17.1 per cent of respondents were satisfied from non-government institutions and only 23.1 and 19.9 per cent of respondents from government and non-government

Table 6.13: Whether Minimum Bar of 50 Per Cent in Qualifying Exam is Justified?

State	Strongly agree		Agree		Somewhat agree		Do not agree		Total	
	Govt.	Non-Govt.	Govt.	Non-Govt.	Govt.	Non-Govt.	Govt.	Non-Govt.	Govt.	Non-Govt.
Uttar Pradesh	20	23	67	65	13	12	0	0	100	100
	20.0%	23.0%	67.0%	65.0%	13.0%	12.0%	0.0%	0.0%	100%	100%
Madhya Pradesh	19	118	18	27	18	0	0	0	55	145
	34.5%	81.3%	32.7%	18.6%	32.7%	0.0%	0.0%	0.0%	100%	100%
New Delhi	20	76	13	45	15	31	0	0	48	152
	41.6%	50.0%	27.0%	29.6%	31.2%	20.3%	0.0%	0.0%	100%	100%
Manipur	0	158	0	42	0	0	0	0	0	200
	0.0%	79.0%	0.0%	21.0%	0.0%	0.0%	0.0%	0.0%	0.0%	100%
Rajasthan	0	179	0	21	0	0	0	0	0	200
	0.0%	89.5%	0.0%	10.5%	0.0%	0.0%	0.0%	0.0%	100%	100%
Total	59	554	98	200	46	43	0	0	203	797
	29.0%	69.5%	48.2%	25.0%	22.6%	5.3%	0.0%	0.0%	100%	100%

Source: Field Survey.

Table 6.14: Availing Hostel Facility

State	*Yes*		*No*		*Total*	
	Govt.	*Non-Govt.*	*Govt.*	*Non-Govt.*	*Govt.*	*Non-Govt.*
Uttar Pradesh	98	1	2	99	100	100
	98.0%	1.0%	2.0%	99.0%	100.0%	100.0%
Madhya Pradesh	12	0	43	145	55	145
	21.8%	0.0%	29.6%	100.0%	100.0%	100.0%
New Delhi	46	132	2	20	48	152
	95.8%	86.8%	4.1%	13.1%	100.0%	100.0%
Manipur	0	125	0	75	0	200
	0.0%	62.5%	0.0%	37.5%	0.0%	100.0%
Rajasthan	0	185	0	15	0	200
	0.0%	92.5%	0.0%	7.5%	0.0%	100.0%
Total	156	443	47	354	203	797
	76.8%	55.5%	23.1%	44.4%	100.0%	100.0%

Source: Field Survey.

institutions were somewhat satisfied with hostel facilities of the institutions.

The level of satisfaction regarding mess facility is shown in Table 6.16 about 57.1 per cent respondents from government-run institutions and 65.2 per cent respondents from non-government-run institutions were found satisfied with the mess facility. The satisfaction level was reported significantly high in Madhya Pradesh followed by New Delhi and Uttar Pradesh while it was found low in Manipur and Rajasthan. Only 14.7 per cent respondents in case of government-run institutions and 12.9 per cent respondents from non-government-run institutions were found very satisfied with mess facility. About 28 per cent respondents from government-run institutions and 21.8 per cent respondents from non-government-run institutions reported that they are somewhat satisfied with the mess facility.

The above analysis simply demonstrates that most of the aspirants are from the low age group and males. A significant proportion of respondents were found married while majority of the respondents admitted that they have migrated from smaller towns and cities to avail the better education facilities. Only a negligible proportion of respondents were found pursuing academic programmes from university/college. Majority of the respondents were found satisfied with the teaching methods, availability of quality of stock in library, quality teaching of faculty members, hostel facilities and mess facilities. Most of the respondents were agreed on the view point that minimum bar of 50 per cent in qualifying examination is justified while almost all the respondents were in favour of continuing the stipend for quality learning and higher rate of success, however one-third respondents were found dissatisfied with the current amount of stipend being provided under the scheme.

Recommendations

- Proper and adequate hostel facilities are to be made available to all SC and OBC students enrolled for various programmes in coaching centres. The enrolled students should be provided proper and regular mess

Table 6.15: Satisfaction Regarding Hostel Facilities

State	*Very Satisfied*		*Satisfied*		*Somewhat Satisfied*		*Dissatisfied*		*Total*	
	Govt.	*Non-Govt.*	*Govt.*	*Non-Govt.*	*Govt.*	*Non-Govt.*	*Govt.*	*Non-Govt.*	*Govt.*	*Non-Govt.*
Uttar Pradesh	5	09	65	34	30	57	0	0	100	100
	5.0%	9.0%	65.0%	34.0%	30.0%	57.0%	0.0%	0.0%	100%	100%
Madhya Pradesh	38	139	9	6	8	0	0	0	55	145
	69.0%	95.6%	18.0%	4.1%	14.5%	0.0%	0.0%	0.0%	100%	100%
New Delhi	39	136	0	16	9	0	0	0	48	152
	81.2%	89.4%	0.0%	33.3%	5.9%	0.0%	0.0%	0.0%	100%	100%
Manipur	0	119	0	29	0	52	0	0	0	200
	0.0%	59.5%	0.0%	14.5%	0.0%	26.0%	0.0%	0.0%	0.0%	100%
Rajasthan	0	98	0	52	0	50	0	0	0	200
	0.0%	49.0%	0.0%	26.0%	0.0%	25.0%	0.0%	0.0%	0.0%	100%
Total	82	501	74	137	47	159	0	0	203	797
	40.3%	62.8%	36.4%	17.1%	23.1%	19.9%	0.0%	0.0%	100%	100%

Source: Field Survey.

Table 6.16: Level of Satisfaction Regarding Mess Facility

State	*Very Satisfied*		*Satisfied*		*Somewhat Satisfied*		*Dissatisfied*		*Total*	
	Govt.	*Non-Govt.*	*Govt.*	*Non-Govt.*	*Govt.*	*Non-Govt.*	*Govt.*	*Non-Govt.*	*Govt.*	*Non-Govt.*
Uttar Pradesh	4	7	64	73	32	20	0	0	100	100
	4.0%	7.0%	64.0%	73.0%	32.0%	20.0%	0.0%	0.0%	100%	100%
Madhya Pradesh	16	26	39	119	0	0	0	0	55	145
	29.0%	17.9%	70.9%	82.0%	0.0%	0.0%	0.0%	0.0%	100%	100%
New Delhi	10	22	13	111	25	19	0	0	48	152
	20.8%	14.4%	27.0%	73.0%	52.0%	12.5%	0.0%	0.0%	100%	100%
Manipur	0	19	0	128	0	53	0	0	0	200
	0.0%	9.5%	0.0%	64.0%	0.0%	26.5%	0.0%	0.0%	0.0%	100%
Rajasthan	0	29	0	89	0	82	0	0	0	200
	0.0%	14.5%	0.0%	44.5%	0.0%	41.0%	0.0%	0.0%	0.0%	100%
Total	30	103	116	520	57	174	0	0	203	797
	14.7%	12.9%	57.1%	65.2%	28.0%	21.8%	0.0%	0.0%	100%	100%

Source: Field Survey.

facility besides providing library with quality resource stock –books, journals and other periodicals. The internet facility should also be made available in the library and computer centre so that students may get quality resource literature through downloading from various websites and digital libraries.

- The amount of stipend for coaching and allied scheme should be increased substantially to meet the basic requirements and give a sense of equality. Moreover the students should be provided loans for pursuing programmes in the coaching.
- The coaching centres should be provided funds for combined classes such SCs, STs, OBCs and Minorities. This will require special provision for releasing funds and resources are to be pooled from Ministry of Tribal Affairs, Ministry of Minority Affairs, and Ministry of Social Justice and Empowerment. Moreover such centres may also approach to state government for availing funds for maintenance of coaching centres. Thus, combined classes will provide equal opportunity for mainstreaming of SC, ST, OBC and Minority students with other castes and classes. The coaching centres should be allowed to enroll non-reserved category students on professional basis so that they may hire quality teachers, upgrade teaching methods, enrich the library stock and improve the infrastructural facilities through mobilising resources.
- The coaching centres should be provided funds timely; however recommendation of state level officials may be kept in mind while releasing the second installment by the Central Government. The delay in releasing of second installment of coaching centres and quality of coaching and other services may be deteriorated.
- The coaching centres should be allowed to diversify in the programmes and civil services, provincial civil services, state level entrance examination, etc. should be included in the coaching classes. Importantly, the coaching for civil services and provincial civil services may be started at the state headquarter while such programme may be discouraged to initiate in the backward district because in such areas quality faculty

is not available. However, other competitive examinations coaching may be provided to such centres. Again, coaching centres should ensure the availability on quality teaching through contract classes and capsule classes by renounced faculty members may take a series of schedules in the centre at one stretch.

- Universities and well established institutes of learning, education and research including NGO's may be promoted to start the coaching centres because they have plenty of experienced, qualified and competent faculties well equipped and enriched libraries, hostel and other infrastructural facilities.
- All the universities and deemed universities should establish a separate section of SCs, STs, OBCs and Minority for facilitating and providing career guidance to them. Importantly, these centres should be established till for individual career counselling, up-gradation of skills, motivation and mobilisation of aspirants for various services and competitive examinations.
- The coaching centres should appoint core faculty while library should be enriched. It is also suggested that photostat version of high priced, quality and rare books may be arranged through issuing such books from well established libraries and be kept in the Centres for consultation of students.
- Accountability should be enforced in terms of success rate of the various programmes. The preferences should be given to professional institutions having required facilities.
- Girls from SCs and OBCs should be given preference in admission in such coaching centres. They should be provided social security, separate toilet facility, and hostel and individual career guidance so that they may join the mainstream and avail the reservation benefits.
- In all the coaching schemes whether through NGO's or through state organisations or through universities or private education institutions, the rate of remuneration for teachers should be high enough to attract competent teachers. The rates followed by

successful coaching organisation should be used as a good indicator for fixing the rates.

- In order to have quality faculty and resource persons, the coaching centres should invite resources persons from various national level academic institutions as guest faculty while the coaching centres should allocate substantial amount for honorarium to the guest faculty for delivering such special classes to their students. The students should be given more exposure related academic inputs rather than theoretical inputs.
- It is suggested that Knowledge Manager/Information Officer may be appointed on contractual basis in each coaching centre who should be given the responsibility of developing quality resource literature for various competitive examinations through internet search, consulting books, periodicals, journals and also translating into vernacular languages for easy understanding of the enrolled students.
- Performance indicators for monitoring the overall success of the coaching centres should be evolved and those coaching centres who are unable to get the minimum qualifying marks in terms of success rate, the support under the scheme should be withdrawn by the government. Besides, the coaching centres should insist on enrollment of students for specific examinations only and the enrolled students should be discouraged for appearing various competitive examinations as it affects their concentration on one particular examination.

7

ICT as an Instrument for Social Change

Vaishali Saxena

"Brother and sister the youth of India have completely transformed the identity of India in the world. Earlier, in what manner did the world know our country? Till only 25-30 years back, if not more, there were many people in the world who thought that India was a country of snake charmers, it was a country which practiced in black magic. The real identity of India had not reached the world, but my dear brothers and sisters, our youngsters, 20-22-23 years old youngsters have mesmerised the whole world with their skills in computers. Our young I.T. professionals have given a new path of making a new identity of India. If our country has this strength, can we think something about the country? Our dreams is, therefore, of "Digital India". When I talk of "Digital India", I don't speak of the elite, it is for the poor people. You can imagine what a quality education the children in village will get, if all the villages of India are connected with Broadband connectivity and if we are able to give long distance education to the schools in every remote corner of the villages. If we create a network of telemedicine in the places where there is a shortage of doctors, we can have a clear guideline of the way in which health facilities have to be provided to the poor people living in those areas. The citizens of India have mobile phones in their hands, they have mobile connectivity, but can we walk in the direction of mobile governance? We have to move in a direction where every poor person is able to operate his bank account from his mobile, is able to demand various things from the government, can submit application, can conduct all this business, while on the move, through mobile governance and if this to be done, we have to move towards: digital India and if we have to move towards digital India then we have a dream. Today, we are bringing in these televisions, mobile phones, i-pads, and all these electronic goods. If we move ahead with the dream of digital India to manufacture electronic goods and become self-reliant at least there, how big can be the benefit for the treasury; therefore, e-governance is what we need to take this idea of digital India forward. E-governance is easy governance, effective governance and also economic governance. E-governance paves the way for the good governance. There was a time when we used to say that the railways provided connectivity to the country. That was it. I say that today it is IT that has the potential to connect each and every citizen of the country and that is why we want to realise the mantra of unity with the help of digital India. (Sri Narendra Modi, 2014)

At the wake of revolution of information technology, change is visible in every nook and corner of the world. Various systems and subsystems and processes are influenced by its spill over effect. This technological revolution is such powerful mechanism to have potential to reach to every citizen conveniently and expediently. So to realise the goals of governance, ICT is playing transformative role. People and places which are otherwise placed remotely may be approached very conveniently through a click of mouse or through pressing a button of mobile phone. Connectivity potential of the technology had led to revolutionary changes in social, economic, political, fields and sub-fields. Government is no exception. Government with all its fields and dimensions are now under this influence, be it emergence of good governance or e-governance.

We have stepped up in a new millennium with new hope and a new horizon. The distinctive feature of the present is characterised with fundamental changes in the mode and technology of communication. It has also brought changes in the governance per se. To ensure results in the non-performing bureaucratic style of governance, good governance is conceptualised with the features of participatory, transparency, accountability, and responsibility....... It has been hypothesised that good governance will bring efficiency and effectiveness in the administration and governance. Good governance is heavily relying on information technology to establish good governance. Hence, at any layer of the government, desirability and adoption for e-governance is a must.

Among others, special attention has been placed to the use of ICT in the government. According to Roger W. O. Okot-uma (2000), e-governance seeks to realise processes and structures for harnessing the potential of information and communication technologies at various levels of governance. Hence, emerged e-governance, as most powerful instrument to establish good governance. 17, October 2000, government passed the Information technology Act ana has recognised E-Commerce and E-Governance. Year 2001 was also declared as good governance year by the GOI.

Percentage Distribution of Rural Poor by Social Class (1993-94)

Scheduled Tribes	57.6
Scheduled Castes	27.6
Other Backward Classes	14.8

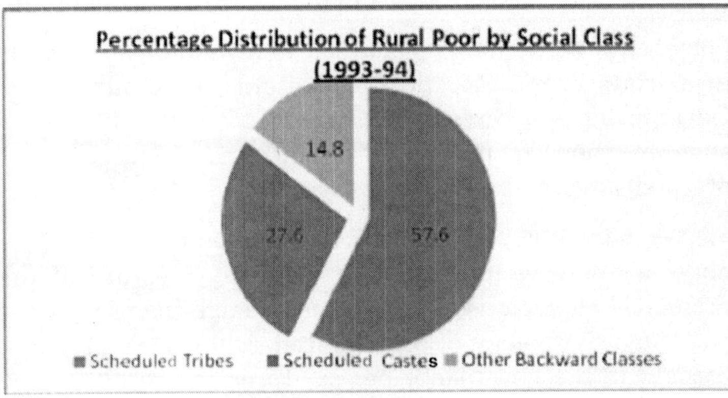

Percentage Distribution of Rural Poor by Social Class (1999-2000)

Scheduled Tribes	17.5
Scheduled Castes	27.3
Other Backward Classes	36.3
Other Castes	18.9

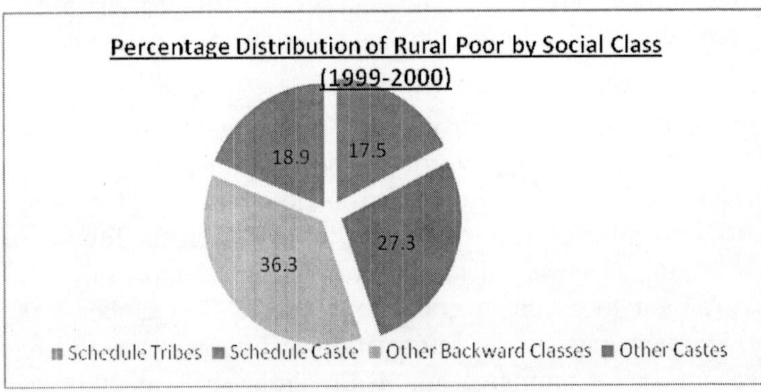

Source: Based on unit level record for 50th and 55th round.

In India, the population is uneven in terms of gender, caste, religion, education, employment etc. so the development. Various pockets of the population is still denied of basic amenities and a decent life (Kaushik, 2007).

Table 7.1: Incidence of Poverty by Social Group (in per cent)

Category	*Very Poor*		*Poor*	
	1993-94	*1999-00*	*1993-94*	*1999-00*
Caste	*Rural*			
Scheduled Tribes	22.1	17.0	50.2	40.2
Scheduled Castes	21.7	11.5	48.3	38.3
Other Backward Castes	NA	11.5	NA	38.3
Caste	*Urban*			
Scheduled Tribe	24.0	17.5	43.0	37.5
Scheduled Castes	26.1	16.4	50.9	39.1
Other Backward Castes	NA	10.7	NA	30.2

Notes : Very Poor denotes all those persons whose per capita total expenditure is less than 75 per cent of State Specific Poverty Line and Poor denotes all those persons whose per capita total expenditure is less than State Specific Poverty Line.

Source: Radhakrishna and Roy, 2005b.

For example, among the Social groups, the Scheduled Castes (SCs) constituted 27.6 per cent of the rural poor in 1993-94, the Scheduled Tribes (STs) 14.8 per cent. While the share of SCs marginally came down from 1993-94 to 1999-00, that of STs has gone up by nearly three percentage points (see Figures 7.1 and 7.2). The SCs are primarily concentrated in Uttar Pradesh, Madhya Pradesh, Bihar and West Bengal, while the tribal are concentrated in the Central Tribal Belt comprising Jharkhand, Andhra Pradesh, Chhattisgarh, Odisha, Madhya Pradesh, Gujarat and Maharashtra. The inclusion of the two better-off states, namely, Gujarat and Maharashtra in the list is indicative of deep disparities across population groups within the better-off states. Table 7.1 shows the incidence of poverty level by social group for all India.

Poverty among the scheduled castes and scheduled tribes population has also been found to be severe in Category 1 states. In the rural areas of Odisha, 73.9 per cent of the scheduled tribes population is poor, when the average poverty ratio among the scheduled tribes population at the national level is around 45.8 per cent. Considered together, these three groups of population (SC, ST and OBC) constitute about 77.5 per cent of the total population in these three states as compared to 63.4 per cent at the national level. The concentration of economically and socially backward population, therefore, could explain the persistence of perennial poverty in these three states.

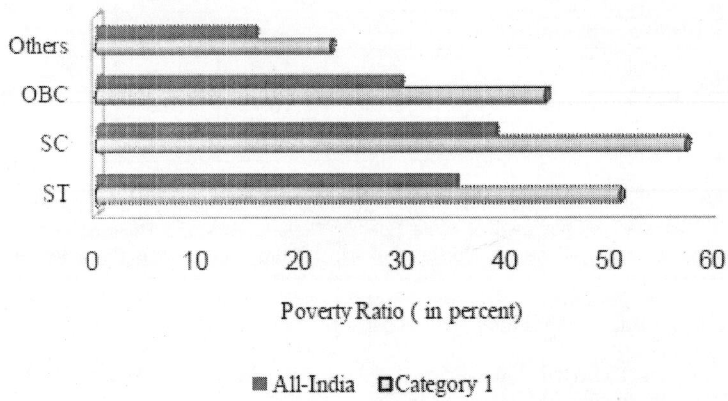

Fig. 7.1 Poverty Ratio by Social Class in Urban Areas.

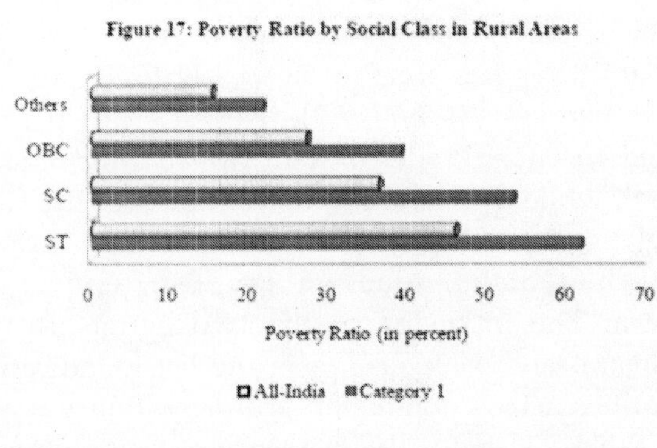

Fig. 7.2 Poverty Ratio by Social Class in Rural Areas

Source: Based on unit level record on NSS consumer expenditure for 55th Round.

India Social Development Report (CSD, 2006), there is a clear disparity in mortality across region, gender, social class, religion and between the poorest and richest quintile. The rural population, females, STs and SCs and Muslims are relatively worse off in terms of health status as evinced by the mortality rates among infants and under-5 per 1000 live births.

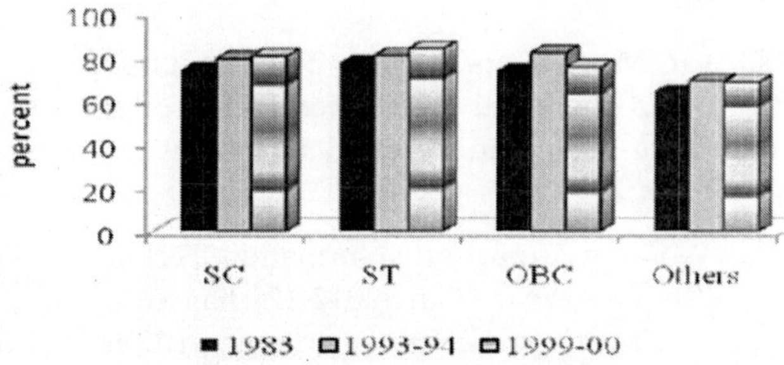

Fig. 7.3 Percentage of Rural Population below Recommended Caloric Intake by Social Group.

Source: Estimated from unit level record on consumption expenditure for 38th, 50th and 55th rounds of NSS respectively.

Lots of statistical data and various analysis indicates that disparities in development are still prevalent not only in post-independent India but also in post-reform period. Inclusive development remains a challenge for the governance.

Role of ICT

ICT is playing a key role in India's development. The potential of ICT in transforming socio-economic development of the nation can be viewed from two vulnerable groups is quite possible through capacity building and perspectives First, is its transformative-cum-empowerment role.

Empowerment of these by creating opportunities for employment. All over the globe IT sector is at boom and there exist plethora of job opportunities in this sector. In this direction, government has launched many training and capacity building programmes successfully to these targets groups. IT for Masses is one such programme of the government under the department.

IT FOR MASSES

Background

"IT for Masses" is a Plan Scheme of Deit. It was introduced in the Tenth Five Year Plan, continued in the Eleventh Five Year Plan, retained in the Twelfth Five Year Plan.

The Working Group on Information Technology Sector for Twelfth Five Year Plan (2012-17) has considered and recommended continuance of the scheme in 12th Plan under 'e-Inclusion' as thrust area.

From 2013-14 onwards, IT for Masses Programme will be merged with Manpower Development Scheme of the Department.

Objective

Initiate/promote activities in ICT for focus groups and areas for inclusive growth of IT sector.

Source: Outcome Budget 2012-13 of Deit

Strategy

The components of e-Inclusion are:

- Using ICT for Capacity Building.
- IT infrastructure creation primarily at schools/colleges.
- Development of entrepreneurial skills in the identified target group.

- Development of electronic products, software tools and e-services.
- Creation of e-Inclusion centres for development and deployment of IT products and solutions for differently-abled persons.
- Conducting studies and advocacy of e-Inclusion initiatives.
- Content creation in Indian languages.
- Develop appropriate systems and software for applications in areas like health, education, training and governance, which will facilitate inclusive development.

Source: Report of the Working Group on IT Sector for Twelfth Five Year Plan (2012-17).

Towards achieving these objectives project proposals are initiated in the following areas:

- Training
- Infrastructure Development
- Capacity Building

Target Groups

- SC
- ST
- Gender
- Minorities
- Differently-abled
- Senior citizens

Source: Report of the Working Group on IT Sector for Twelfth Five Year Plan (2012-17).

Target Areas

To achieve greater equity and inclusivity, there is a need to concentrate efforts in selected geographical areas, comprising of:

- North East Region.
- Blocks and Districts having more than 40 per cent SC/ST population.
- Backward Districts.

Source: Report of the Working Group on IT Sector for Twelfth Five Year Plan (2012-17).

Allocation and Expenditure

Year	*GBS Approved (B.E.) (Rupees in Crore)*	*GBS Approved (R.E.) (Rupees in Crore)*	*Actual Expenditure (Rupees in Crore)*
2007-08 to 2011-12	55.94	58.29	43.20

Twelfth Plan Allocation and Expenditure

	GBS Approved (B.E.) (Rupees in Crore)	*GBS Approved (R.E.) (Rupees in Crore)*	*Actual Expenditure (Rupees in Crore)*
2012-13	16.94	7.06	7.02

Note: From 2013-14 onwards, IT for Masses Programme will be merged with Manpower Development Scheme of the Department.

Eleventh Plan –Achievements

Year	Number of on-going projects	Number of projects completed	Number of beneficiaries - Completed projects
2007-08 to 2011-12	22 (Spill over to 12th Plan)	38	2,95,468

Twelfth Plan –Achievements

Year	Number of on-going projects	Number of projects completed	Number of beneficiaries - Completed projects
2012-13	20	43	3,05,912

Projects have been Implemented in 25 States and 2 UTs

Uttar Pradesh, Kerala, West Bengal, Assam, Tripura, Mizoram, Karnataka, Andhra Pradesh, Rajasthan, Tamil Nadu, Himachal Pradesh, Madhya Pradesh, Sikkim, Manipur, Meghalaya, Nagaland, Odisha, Chhattisgarh, Gujarat, Jharkhand, Bihar, Goa, Jammu and Kashmir, Haryana, Maharashtra, Delhi and Chandigarh.

Project Implementing Agencies (On-going Projects)

- Centre for Development of Advance Computing (C-DAC).
- National Institute of Electronics and Information Technology (NIELIT – formerly DOEACC).
- Haryana State Electronics Development Corporation Limited (HARTRON), Haryana.
- Karnataka State Electronics Development Corporation Ltd. (KEONICS), Karnataka.

- Tripura State Council for Science and Technology, Tripura.
- Raj COMP, Rajasthan.
- Indira Gandhi National Tribal University (IGNTU), Madhya Pradesh.
- North Orissa University, Odisha.

The role of National Institute of Electronics is highly appreciated in this direction.

The institute design and provide training to these target groups. Given below is some details of such programmes/ projects undertaken by the Institute:

Projects undertaken during 2012-2013

S.No.	*Project Title*	*Project Objective*
1.	Training and Certification of 600 SC students in job oriented courses in Information Technology.	Providing free training to 600 candidates belonging to SC population so as to make them eligible for appearing for Public Service examination.
2.	Skill Enhancement of 150 ST candidates of Ladakh region of J&K State for Employment as Computer Hardware & Networking Professional.	To produce industry ready hardware professionals to Repair, maintain and service IT hardware equipments such as Desktop, PCs Loptop, UPS, and Printers etc and produce computer networking professionals who can establish and maintain different kinds of computer networking.
3.	Skill Enhancement of 500 SC candidates of Jammu & Sambha region of J&K State for Employment as Computer Hardware & Networking Professionals.	To produce industry ready hardware professionals to Repair, maintain and service IT hardware equipments such as Desktop, PCs Laptop, UPS, and Printers etc and produce computer networking professionals who can establish and maintain different kinds of computer networking.
4.	Training of 1st batch of SC/ST job seekers in Computer Hardware Maintenance CHM -O level.	To provide job-oriented training to SC/ST candidates sponsored by DGE&T, M/o Labour and Employment.

contd...

contd...

S.No.	*Project Title*	*Project Objective*
5.	Training of 5th batch of SC/ST Job seekers in DOEACC 'O' level	To provide job-oriented training to SC/ST candidates sponsored by DGE&T, M/o Labour & Employment.
6.	Setting up Intranet of NIELIT and Smart Virtual Class Rooms at NIELIT Centres for quality training to students in remote areas.	Setting up of a MPLS network of NIELIT to carry out multicasting, videoconferencing, video streaming and virtual classroom sessions with the help of ERNET connecting all the NIELIT Centres in the country with the focus to improve the quality of education to students from remote/rural part of the country, passing out of the Centres of NIELIT and its accredited centres.
7.	Capacity Building in WSN Security and Training in J&K State.	To develop lab facility for capacity building in Training and Research & Development in the area of Wireless Sensor Network Security. The facility thus developed will be useful in particular for students and professionals pursuing their academic and research interests in wireless sensor networks with emphasis on security, in J&K State.
8.	Capacity Building in the areas of Electronic Product Design and Production Technologies by Aurangabad and Chennai Centres jointly with CDAC Hyderabad.	To develop Human Resource at various levels including Certificate, Diploma, Post Graduate, and Research Professionals with adequate competence levels in the area of Electronic Product Design and Production Technologies.
9.	Training of SC&ST students in Capacity Building for e-Governance Applications at NIELIT Imphal Centre	To train SC/ST students of Manipur in IT & e-governance Applications in 5-locations of Manipur so that either they can be employed or start their own business.

Ongoing Projects

S.No.	*Project Title*	*Project Objective*
1.	Capacity Building for improving the IT literacy and employability of SC candidates in IECT area in UP and Bihar (at Gorakhpur, Patna, Allahabad, Gonda and Fatehpur).	To create a pool of 2140 skilled persons encompassing SC population in the area of IECT (DOEACC 'O' level, Advance Diploma in Hardware, Networking and Information Security (ADHNS) – 1 yr, Computer Application and Office.
2.	Capacity Building for improving the IT literacy and employability of ST candidates in IECT area in Jharkhand (at Jamshedpur, West Singhbhum).	To create a pool of 880 skilled persons encompassing ST population in the area of IECT (DOEACC 'O' level, Advance Diploma in Hardware, Networking and Information Security (ADHNS) - yr, Computer Application and Office Practices (CAOP)- 3 months).
3.	Capacity Building for improving the Employability of Women in ICT Area at Cuttack and Puri in Odisha..	To provide training to 1380 women candidates in Elementary Computer Education (i.e. Computer Application and Office Practices and DOEACC 'O' Level) for improving the self-employability opportunities of women.
4.	Training of Graduate/ Undergraduate Women and SC/ST candidates for various job-oriented courses at NIELIT Centre Chandigarh and its branches at Shimla, Lucknow and Delhi and Monitoring and Impact Assessment for IT for Masses Programme at EP Division, Deit, New Delhi.	To increase employability of women candidates by imparting professional IT Training (A total of 760 candidates to be trained).
5.A	Training Programme on IT Skill, to improve employability of the Rural Youth belonging to SC/ST, Minority community and Women.	To train a total of 48000 SC/ST/Minority/Women Candidates in IT Skills to make them employable.
5.B.	Training Programme on Electronics Equipment Repair and Maintenance to improve employability of the Rural Youth Belonging to SC/ST, Minority community and Women.	To train 32400 SC/ST/Minority/Women Candidates in Electronics Equipment Repair and Maintenance Courses to make them employable.
5.C.	Training Programme on ITES - BPO (Customer Care and Banking) to improve employability of the Rural Youth Belonging to SC/ST, Minority community and Women.	To train a total of 9000 SC/ST/Minority/Women candidates to make them employable.

Second, ICT as e-governance is facilitating various characteristics of good governance like transparency, accessibility. The UNESCO definition is: "E-governance is the public sector's use of information and communication technologies with the aim of improving information and service delivery, encouraging citizen participation in the decision-making process and making government more accountable, transparent and effective. E-governance involves new styles of leadership, new ways of debating and deciding policy and investment, new ways of accessing education, new ways of listening to citizens and new ways of organising and delivering information and services. E-governance is a generally considered as a wider concept than e-government, since it can bring about a change in the way citizens relate to governments and to each other. E-governance can bring fourth new concepts of citizenship, both in terms of citizen needs and responsibilities. Its objective is to engage, enable and empower the citizen."

Although, India's status of e-governance is still at rudimentary stage. As per the report recently (2012) released by the United Nations department of Economics and Social Affairs on e-governance Development at World level, India ranks 124 out of 190 nations in using e-governance practices with index of 0.383 in comparison to the world index 0.497. Infrastructure index is 0.110, in comparison to the world index of 0.326 and e-participation index is 0.184 in comparison to 0.268. But continuous efforts are being done in this direction to promote e-citizenship skills in these target groups.

E-governance projects are well suited to such normative shaping of skills and knowledge. Learning to be an e-citizen entails becoming familiar with technique of on-line searching information, protocol for digitally interacting and legal regulation of software use. The cultivation of these skills often referred as digital literacy–not only point citizen towards particular view of governance but governed the process of being governed. Digital literacy is kind of regulatory project intended to cultivate the citizenry capable of responsible digital interaction. In this context of e-governance, it includes knowing which level of governance one should address in relation to particular problems; being able to navigate through the bureaucratic departments and agency remits; behaving in a civilised way; and having appropriate (i.e. well managed) expectations about outcomes. From the perspective of governmentality, none of these skills are politically neutral. Government websites tend to dull and solomn, design in ways that impress upon users the seriousness of their purpose and their distance from fun and frivolity. The politics of the governance should be made more explicit. The democratic process could be made to feel more like pleasure.

References

1. Narendra Modi, excerpt from his speech on 15, August 2014.
2. Okot-Uma R., Electronic Governance: Reinventing Good Governance, Common Wealth Secretariate, London, 2002, p. 5.
3. http://mospi.nic.in/mospi_nsso_rept_pubn.htm>.
4. Kaushik Ranjan Bandhopadhayay, Poverty Alleviation and Pro-Poor Growth in India, Asian Institute of Transport Development, New Delhi, 2007, pp. 20-30.
5. Radhakrishna, R. and Shovan Ray, 'Poverty in India: Dimensions and Character'.
6. Chapter 3 in R. Radhakrishna and Kirit Parikh (ed.), *India Development Report 2004-05, 2005b*, (New Delhi: Oxford University Press).
7. www.mhrd.gov.in
8. www.neilit.gov.in/projects.aspx#content
9. Stephen Coleman, (2008).
10. Stephen Coleman, Digital Government (*ed.* Chen, Brandt, Gregg...), Springer, USA, 2008, pp. 9-17.

8

An Insight into Health and Nutrition Status of Adolescent Girls in India

Nandita Kaushal

Introduction

Adolescence is a period following the onset of puberty. It is a transitional stage between childhood and adulthood. It is a stage when physical and mental transition takes place from immaturity of childhood to maturity of adulthood. It is usually regarded to be occurring between the ages 10 and 19. As adolescents of today will be the responsible adult population of tomorrow so their health and nutritional status assumes significance.

Adolescence is a period of rapid growth: up to 45 per cent of skeletal growth and 15 to 25 per cent of adult height is achieved during adolescence. During the growth spurt of adolescence, up to 37 per cent of total bone mass may be accumulated. Nutrition influences growth and development throughout infancy, childhood, and adolescence; it is, however, during the period of adolescence that nutrient needs are the greatest.[1] According to the World Health Organisation (WHO) more than 1.75 billion population of the world is young, aged between 10 and 24 years. Adolescents are regarded as healthy group but a large number of adolescents die prematurely for reasons like accidents, suicide, violence, pregnancy-related complications and other illnesses that can be prevented or treated. Besides, the occurrence of several serious diseases in adulthood has their beginnings during adolescence. For instance use of tobacco and alcohol, sexually transmitted infections, poor eating and exercise habits result in illnesses or premature deaths later in life. It has been reported by WHO that one-third of new sexually transmitted disease cases, more than half the new HIV infections, and one-third of all births are among youth. While the five leading causes of death, illness and disability among young men are depression, traffic accidents, alcohol use, war and schizophrenia; in young women they are depression, obstructed labour, suicide, chlamydia, and iron deficiency anaemia.[2]

India has one of the fastest growing youth populations in the world. The absolute number of adolescent (10-19 years) population was 177.7 million in 1991, 225.1 million in 2001, and 253.2 million in 2011. The proportion of adolescent (10-19 years) population in total population was 21.2 per cent in 1991, 21.9 per cent in 2001, and 20.9 per cent in 2011. Uttar Pradesh (24.5 per cent), Nagaland (24.2 per cent), Arunachal Pradesh (24.2 per cent), Meghalaya (23.9 per cent), and Rajasthan (22.9 per cent) are top five states of India having highest percentage of adolescents (10-19) years to total population as per Census 2011.

Girls below 19 years of age comprise one-quarter of India's population. A large number of girls are out of school so they are not able to receive services from school-based health programmes. Due to gender discrimination within families girls are at a disadvantage when it comes to matters like education, healthcare, nutrition and employment. Girls have little avenues for a bright future and they are caught in the cycles of early marriage, pregnancy and child bearing. Despite an improvement in the socio-economic perspective of the country sex ratio in the country is not at all satisfactory. Sex ratio has declined from 972 females per 1000 males in 1901 to 940 females to 1000 males in 2011.

Health and Nutritional Status of Adolescent Girls

In patriarchal society like India gender discrimination starts from the stage of pregnancy and continues throughout the life of a female. Gender discrimination perpetuates age-old inequities. Inadequate attention paid to health and nutrition of young and adolescent girls has far-reaching ramifications. Gender affects health outcomes through male and female differences in roles, access, and power; and sex differentially affects the health of women and men because of biologically determined physiological and genetic differences that manifest in differences in needs and vulnerabilities. Gender-based inequalities translate into greater value being placed on the health and survival of males than of females. In India, examples of health and population indicators that are driven by gender differences in the perceived worth of males and females include sex ratios at birth, infant and child mortality by sex, and low ages at marriage for women. Further, at the household level, disempowerment of women results in their lowered access to resources such as education, employment, and income, and limits their power over decision-making and freedom of movement.[3]

Undue preference given to sons in Indian society is responsible for gender-based distribution of food in households and access to quality healthcare. Girls are often at a disadvantage in terms like that they are more likely to receive less and that also poor quality food. Less attention is paid to their preventive health and in case of illness they are less likely to receive quality and timely medical treatment. Girls face a number to hurdles to access healthcare facilities like getting permission to go, getting money needed for treatment, distance to the health facility, having to take transport, finding someone to go with them, concern that there they may not be a female health provider and no drugs in a health centre. Under-nutrition and limited access to healthcare reduces their chances of leading a healthy life style.

All these coupled with poverty and food insecurity reduce the dietary intake of adolescent girls. In households, particularly in poorer ones, there is as such no concept of balanced diet. Girls are more prone to have such food which is far below the recommended dietary intake.

Girls themselves tend to neglect their health and nutritional issues due to excessive burden of household responsibilities. The intra-household distribution of labour is affected by gender concerns. Adolescent girls have major share of economic, procreative, and family responsibilities. These put pressures on them with regard to time and energy. The socialisation of girls is such that since birth this feeling is deeply engrained in their mind that their status is subordinate in society. All these are responsible for neglect of health and nutrition of adolescent girls. Adolescent girls face the problem of early marriage, unwanted pregnancy, illegal and unsafe abortions, sexually transmitted diseases, sexual exploitation and violence, poor health and malnutrition.

The specific reasons responsible for poor health and nutrition status of adolescent girls can be summed up as gender discrimination; poverty; insecurities relating to regular income, food, shelter; lack of access to health information and services; difficult and unsafe physical and social environments; inadequate interventions; weak public health services and infrastructure. The vicious cycle of poverty affects the well-being of girls in a way that it contributes to low intake of food and nutrients and which results in under-nutrition, stunted development of children, small body size of adults, impaired productivity, low earning capacity and all these perpetuate poverty.

Adolescent girls have specific nutritional requirements commensurate with the adolescent growth spurt. A large number of adolescent girls are malnourished. The main nutritional issues of adolescent girls are under-nutrition, protein energy malnutrition and associated deficiencies; iron deficiency anaemia and other micronutrient deficiencies like vitamins, folic acid, zinc, copper, selenium, iodine ; early pregnancy; and inadequate or unhealthy diet and lifestyle.

According to *National Family Health Survey –3 (2005-06)* the prevalence of low birth weight is nearly 30 per cent. About 55 per cent of preschool children are underweight and 50 per cent stunted. Micro-nutrient deficiencies, mainly iron deficiency anaemia (70 per cent in women and children), iodine deficiency disorders, and vitamin A deficiency continue to be public health problems. B-vitamins deficiencies are common.[4] A large proportion of girls have body mass index (BMI) below 18.5 indicating chronic nutritional deficiency. Nutritional problems exist in every state of the country but they are more pronounced in several states of central and eastern India. The proportion of girls who are undernourished is highest in Bihar, Chhattisgarh, Madhya Pradesh, and Odisha. Women who are undernourished themselves are much more likely to have undernourished children.

Malnutrition and under-nutrition have serious long-term consequences for adolescent girls. Their cognitive, emotional, motor, sensory, and social developments as well as sexual maturation are retarded. The puberty period of girls is affected and there is delay in the onset of menarche. Malnutrition increases the risks associated with adolescent pregnancy. Physical stunting and short stature of girls are often associated with small pelvis. Small pelvis is a high risk factor for obstructed labour which is a major cause of maternal health. The probability of low birth weight is increased which, in turn, increases the probability of neonatal deaths due to infections and asphyxia. As malnutrition has an adverse effect on height and body mass so the work capacity and endurance of girls are reduced.

Malnutrition reduces immunity of the body. The chances of diseases like malaria, measles, diarrhoea, pneumonia and perinatal disorders are highly increased and these at times prove to be fatal. Various types of body infections and diseases reduce appetite, impair absorption, and lead to catabolic losses of precious nutrients from the body. Malnutrition not only causes human suffering but is a leading contributor to morbidity, disability, mortality, loss of national productivity and medical expenses.

Children born with low birth weight remain stunted. Their learning capacity and ability to fight infections are impaired. Intrauterine malnutrition and consequent low birth weight epigenetically predispose to higher body fat and lower muscle mass. In later life they are suspectible to life-style related chronic diseases like diabetes, hypertension, and dyslipidaemia.[5]

Iron deficiency anaemia is the most common nutritional deficiency and continues to remain a major nutritional problem in adolescent girls. Due to onset of menarche girls have high requirement of iron. Adolescent girls and women in the reproductive age group are more vulnerable to iron deficiency mainly because they lose iron through monthly menstrual and their diets are often deficient in iron. Iron deficiency has significant health consequences like delayed physical and mental development, negative behavioural consequences, weakened physical performance, reduced physical work capacity, decreased productivity and increased mortality. Maternal short stature and anaemia are associated with an increased risk of maternal mortality and death of mother at the time of delivery. Anaemia is one of the main causes of poor pregnancy and it increases the risk of low birth weight, premature birth, still birth and neonatal infection. Children of anaemic mothers are at a higher risk of suffering from hypertension and heart diseases. Iron deficiency affects cognitive function in adolescents which may affect their performance in schools.

Iron deficiency is related to vitamin A status. Many studies suggest a direct interaction between vitamin A status and the utilisation of dietary and stored iron for hemoglobin formation. Vitamin A deficiency may contribute to the aetiology of iron deficiency anaemia. Thus, marginal vitamin A status may compromise iron metabolism. This is of particular concern in adolescent pregnancy.[6]

Iodine is an essential trace element for life and its deficiency has long-lasting effects on the survival and intellectual attainments of adolescent girls. Its deficiency results in hypothyroidism and intellectual disability. As level of iodine affects mental development so adolescent girls suffering from its deficiency have neural impairment, learning disability and have low motivation to perform.

Calcium requirements for skeletal development are greater in adolescent girls as maximum bone mass is acquired during this period. The risk of osteoporosis in adulthood is largely determined by calcium deposited during adolescence. Deficiency of calcium increases the risk of bone fracture and high post-menopausal bone loss.

Marriage of girls at a young age is a serious problem of Indian society. Early marriage has long-lasting repercussions for the health of girls.

According to WHO:

- About 16 million girls aged 15 to 19 years and two million girls under the age of 15 give birth every year.

- Almost all adolescent births – about 95 per cent – occur in low–and middle-income countries. Within countries, adolescent births are more likely to occur among poor, less educated and rural populations.
- An estimated three million girls aged 15-19 undergo unsafe abortions every year.
- In low–and middle-income countries, complications from pregnancy and childbirth are a leading cause of death among girls aged 15-19 years.
- Stillbirths and newborn deaths are 50 per cent higher among infants of adolescent mothers than among infants of women aged 20-29 years.
- Infants of adolescent mothers are more likely to have low birth weight.[7]

India has the highest absolute number of child brides in the world. A large number of young girls are married before their 15th birthday. Some child brides are as young as eight or nine years. Millions of girls under the age of 18 are married off every year with little or no say in the matter. As per *National Family Health Survey (NFHS-3) (2005-06)* 47.4 per cent of women age 20-24 (29.3 per cent in urban and 56.2 per cent in rural areas) were married by age 18. Of these women an overwhelming 76.5 per cent had received no education. 16 per cent of women age 15-19 (8.7 per cent in urban and 19.1 per cent in rural areas) were already mothers or pregnant at the time of survey. 19.8 years (20.9 years in urban and 19.3 years in rural areas) was the median age at first birth for women age 25-49. A large number of child marriages take place every year in Bihar, Jharkhand Rajasthan, Andhra Pradesh, Madhya Pradesh, Chhattisgarh, Uttar Pradesh and West Bengal. A majority of girl children are not able to experience the changes taking place during adolescence as they shift from childhood to adulthood and soon become pregnant adult.

Early marriage leads to early child bearing. Several reasons are responsible for adolescent births. These include pressure on girls to marry and bear children at an early age, limited educational and employment prospects, restricted access to contraceptives, lack of comprehensive and correct sexuality education, forced sexual encounter, and sexual violence.

Pregnant adolescents have greater chances of unsafe abortion which are likely to lead to lifelong health problems and maternal health. Adolescent births have serious health consequences for both the girls and their infants particularly in areas which have weak health systems. Complications from pregnancy and childbirth are the leading cause of death among girls aged 15-19 years. Infants born to adolescent mothers have 50 per cent more chances of stillbirths and newborn deaths as compared to the infants born to adult mothers. These infants are more likely to have low birth weight which has serious long-term implications for their health and development.

Even though health indicators have improved over a period of time yet India lags behind. The situation is grimmer for adolescent girls due to widespread gender discrimination. A change is visible in outlook towards girls but still a large number of girls in rural areas and in slums in urban areas are in a disadvantageous situation.

Hurdles on the way to Improve the Health and Nutrition Status of Adolescent Girls

There are number of hurdles on the way to improve the health and nutrition status of adolescent girls in India. The significant ones are:

- Insufficient emphasis on core public health functions.
- Inadequate accountability mechanisms.
- Lack of sufficient incentives for good performance.

- Ineffective monitoring and impact evaluation.
- Lack of effective and meaningful partnership with private and voluntary sectors.
- Scarcity of human and material resources.
- Weak public health system.
- Lack of enabling environment for adolescents to seek healthcare services, particularly reproductive health services.
- Unsatisfactory performance of school health programmes.
- Lack of inter-sectoral coordination.

Suggestions

- A life cycle approach should be adopted for adolescent girls which comprises their education, health and empowerment.
- An authentic database regarding health and nutritional status of adolescent girls should be developed.
- There should be nutrition security for adolescent girls including physical, economic and social access to balanced diet, clean drinking water, safe environment and healthcare.
- An integrated and holistic approach should be developed and made use of.
- Effective partnership should be fostered between public sector, private sector, voluntary sector and civil society.
- Measures related to women's empowerment should be vigorously implemented. Timely interventions should be taken. Women should be made aware about their rights by organising awareness campaigns.
- Interventions are required at health facility and population levels. Interventions at the district level

can include measures like monitoring nutrition, identifying population groups at risk of nutrition problems, updating nutrition policies and protocols, and providing resources and tools to implement nutrition activities.

- Adolescent girls should be provided intermittent iron and folic acid supplementation to improve their iron status and haemoglobin concentrations and reduce the risk of anaemia. Salt fortified with adequate iodine should be distributed.
- Gender sensitive strategies should be developed to address the rights and needs of adolescent girls. A behavioural change communication strategy should be adopted and implemented.
- Social marketing and educational campaigns should be conducted regularly.
- There should be adequate facilities at primary and community health centres.
- Health service providers should be equipped with knowledge and skills, particularly in counselling and communication, to effectively implement adolescent health and nutrition programmes.

Conclusion

Adolescent girls of today will be responsible adults of tomorrow so it is important to pay attention to their well-being and save their lives. Adequate and timely interventions which promote health practices during adolescence are required so that adolescents are protected from risks and a new generation of productive adults emerges who can contribute to the progress of their communities.

Notes

1. World Health Organisation, 2005: Nutrition in Adolescence – Issues and Challenges for the Health Sector, http://whqlibdoc.who.int/publications/2005/9241593660

2. World Health Organisation, 2005: Nutrition in Adolescence – Issues and Challenges for the Health Sector, http://whqlibdoc.who.int/publications/2005/9241593660_
3. Ministry of Health and Family Welfare, Government of India, and International Institute for Population Sciences, Mumbai: National Family Health Survey (NFHS-3) India 2005-06: Gender Equality and Women's Empowerment In India.
4. Indian National Science Academy, New Delhi, Report of Symposium on Nutrition Security for India, Issues and Way Forward, 2009, http://typo3.fao.org/fileadmin/user_upload/fsn/docs/Symposium-Report-Nutrition-Security-India.pdf
5. Indian National Science Academy, New Delhi, Report of Symposium on Nutrition Security for India, Issues and Way Forward, 2009, http://typo3.fao.org/fileadmin/user_upload/fsn/docs/Symposium-Report-Nutrition-Security-India.pdf
6. World Health Organisation, Nutrition in Adolescence – Issues and Challenges for the Health Sector, 2005, http://whqlibdoc.who.int/publications/2005/9241593660_eng.pdf
7. World Health Organisation, Adolescent Pregnancy, Fact Sheet N 364, May 2012, http://www.who.int/mediacentre/factsheets/fs364/en/index.html

References

Indian National Science Academy, New Delhi, *Report of Symposium on Nutrition Security for India, Issues and Way Forward,* 2009.

Mehra, Sunil and Deepti Agarwal, *Adolescent Health Determinants for Pregnancy and Child Health Outcomes among the Urban Poor, Indian Pediatrics,* 2004, 41: pp. 137-145.

Ministry of Health and Family Welfare, Government of India, New Delhi, *National Health Policy 2002.*

Ministry of Health and Family Welfare, Government of India, New Delhi and International Institute for Population Sciences, Mumbai, *National Family Health Survey-3, India, Volume 1; Key Indicators for India;* and *Gender Equality and Women's Empowerment in India.*

Ministry of Human Resource Development, Department of Women and Child Development, Government of India, New Delhi, *National Nutrition Policy,* 1993.

Office of the Registrar General and Census Commissioner, India, Ministry of Home Affairs, Government of India, Age Data, Census 2011.

The Centre For Development And Population Activities (CEDPA), *Adolescent Girls in India Choose a Better Future: An Impact Assessment*, September 2001.

World Health Organisation, *Adolescent Pregnancy, Fact Sheet N 364*, May 2012; *10 Facts on Adolescent Health*, September 2008.

World Health Organisation, *Nutrition in Adolescence – Issues and Challenges for the Health Sector*, 2005.

World Health Organisation, *Essential Nutrition Actions, Improving Maternal, Newborn, Infant and Young Child Health and Nutrition*, 2013.

Web References

http://apps.who.int/iris/bitstream/10665/84409/1/9789241505550_eng.pdf accessed on 14.12.2013

http://typo3.fao.org/fileadmin/user_upload/fsn/docs/Symposium-Report-Nutrition-Security-India.pdf accessed on 14.12.2013

http://wcd.nic.in/nnp.pdf accessed on 13.12.2013

http://whqlibdoc.who.int/publications/2005/9241593660_eng.pdf accessed on 13.12.2013

http://www.indianpediatrics.net/feb2004/feb-137-145.htm accessed on 13.12.2013

http://www.measuredhs.com/pubs/pdf/FRIND3/00FrontMatter00.pdf accessed on 13.12.2013

http://www.measuredhs.com/pubs/pdf/OD57/OD57.pdf accessed on 13.12.2013

http://www.who.int/features/factfiles/adolescent_health/en/index.html accessed on 13.12.2013

http://www.who.int/mediacentre/factsheets/fs364/en/index.html accessed on 13.12.2013

http://www.who.int/topics/adolescent_health/en/accessed on 13.12.2013

9

Social Change with Special Reference to Women

K.K. Srivastava

Prelude

"Nothing is permanent in the world except change; time and tide wait for none".

Social life is never static – it is in a state of constant transition, transformation, revival, renewal and revitalisation. Everything around us is made-up of forever moving and altering patterns of energy. In fact, every aspect of human life is subject to change. Change is the dynamic quality of human life. Change is omnipotent phenomenon; it is present everywhere and permeates into all aspects of human life. Change is ever present it is a law of nature.

Social change refers to a process which results in some difference, alteration, modification or replacement in the society. Change implies the emergence of something new, which either replaces the old or modifies it. Change is a phenomenon that affects all aspects of human life – genetic and biological geographical and environmental, physical and chemical, social, psychological, economic and political. In fact, no aspects of human life can remain unaffected by change. It is imminent and ubiquitous, permeates and influences human life in numerous ways. Here an endeavour has been made to describe changes which occurred in status of women in different periods i.e. from Ancient India to modern India.

Paradigm Shift in Status of Women

India is land of mysticism, spiritualism, myths and legends within a closed society which has been in existence for more than 5000 years.

Women Status in Ancient India

According to the ancient Hindu scriptures and their belief, women are the manifestation of energy, power, i.e. Shakti. She is responsible for creation. She is 'Prakriti', the Nature. Shakti is female, therefore, our creation and all the power in the Universe are based on this femininess, and there would be no being without this energy or power. The creative principle, the female is also Prakriti (nature) the undifferentiated "Mother of the Universe". In Hindu mythology, a woman is considered equal to men. Hindus believed that during the early stages of creation or *shristi* of Universe, Brahma, the creator, expounded himself to the size of man and woman embracing each other and then his body split into two 'Satrupa', the woman and the man. Brahma ordained that all further creation would be through twin forms of his own-self. Apart from it there is another concept 'Ardhanareeshwara" in India which illustrates how man and woman complement to each other. According to this concept, Shiva is considered the God of Gods and the Lord of the entire Universe and all its beings (Deva-Dh-Dev). Lord Shiva is known of immense inner energy of penance and austerity, knowledge and power. Lord Shiva is also called Shakti Shiva, because Shakti is his consort (Parvati) and always a part of his body. Hence, Lord Shiva is considered 'Ardhanareeshwara' (half male and half female).

Without Shakti Shiva is powerless. In ancient scriptures Lord Vishnu Ji rendered his heart for the dwelling of Mahalakshmi through woman is considered a foundation of good qualities in the heart of man. In all Indian languages good qualities like Bhakti, Shakti, Shanti, Daya, Chama, Sruti, Shradha are feminine words. In Bhagwat Gita, it is said that God is present more prominently as soon divine qualities in women – Fame, Prosperity, Speech, Ceremony, Intelligence, Fortitude and Forgiveness. The sacred institutions of Hindu way of life, portrait dual position of woman as wife and mother and the high regard given to Indian motherhood clearly defines the woman's role in the ancient society.

Women in Vedic Period

It is evident from all accountable accounts that the Vedic Society was patriarchal one and hence father was the head of the family. But women also occupied the same position as men. Reference to complete gender equality is found in all parts of Vedic literature. Women reached high standards of learning and culture and made all-round development. Rig Veda, the oldest literature work of human kind, states the status of women during that period. Women were given equal status with men in every walk of life, as in education, religious rights, and freedom of movement. The high esteem in which the wife was held during the Vedic age is evident from the fact that she was considered the better half of her husband. A man could not accomplish any social or religious duty without his wife. Women were supposed to participate in various social activities. Women made valuable contribution also in literary sphere. Some of the important Vedic poets were women. Hymns (Suktas) were also imposed by women in Rig Veda.

During this period girl children had equal opportunities of education as the boys. It was a matter of pleasure to have girl child in family. If someone wanted to devote her life to studies and remain unmarried, that was also acceptable. "Brahmvadini" meant women who pursued knowledge all through their life, while remaining unmarried. In several meaningful mantras, it is said that women of this country have given her man folk value, spiritual illumination, piety and intellectual brilliance. During the Vedic period, the position of women was honourable and exalted.

Post-Vedic Period

This era is known as Manu Samhita, Smritis, Epics and Pauranaic period. In post-Vedic period, the status of women declined. During this period Kautilya's Arthshastra and Manusmriti were written. Women were denied the right to individual freedom; they were to be under the protection of father during their childhood, husband during their youth and son during their old age. In Manusmriti defines the most important and code of conduct for women. So far position of women in the society was very low in this period. They were not allowed to move freely and were confined to the house. There was no religious life except the nuptial ceremony. Girl's education was also lacking. There was no provision right for sharing in the property. Thus, the freedom of movement, which women enjoyed during Vedic era, was steadily suppressed.

In Medieval Era

The growth of caste system and other factors led to a further social decline in the status of women. Declining nature is featured by two important factors i.e. rigidity of caste system, and restriction of women freedom. It was further strengthen due to invasion of Afghanis, Pathans, Turkis and Mughals etc. These invaders more deteriorated the position of women. During this period female infanticide and child marriages became so popular. Purdah system became a practice as a result of Muslim rule. With the arrival of Muslims, they were compelled to live in seclusion of their homes. Great epics are evident that Hindu girls had the freedom to select their husbands themselves. While in medieval period, false pride developed with regard to marital and social practice. Marriage was considered a socio-economic contract. It deprived women the freedom to marry men of their own choice. Due to attitudinal and behavioural changes of society the parents of girls found resort in early marriages. This was most prevalent feature of that time. During this period two schools of law emerged, viz. Mitakshra and Dayabhaga, the exponents of these schools being Vigneshwara and Jimutavahana. Both these schools of law considered Streedhan as the property given to girl at the time of her marriage. Mitakshara and Dayabhaga give rights to the women to give, sell or use independently her property without her husband's consent; these two schools of law also say that the husband has no right over Streedhan.

Thus, a definite pattern of inheritance of property emerged during this phase, which to some extent benefitted women.

In British Rule (Pre-independence)

The 200 years of British rule led to some positive changes and improvements in the status of women, such as eliminating inequalities between men and women in different aspects like education, social reforms and rights etc. The use of English language as a medium of instruction significantly affected the educational system and also presided a gateway to the ideology of liberalism, which enshrined the value of liberty, equal respect for individual and secularism. During the British period, there were two major movements helped in elevating the position of women in society. These movements are known as Social Reform of the nineteenth century and Nationalist Movement of the twentieth century respectively. Both these movements raised the question of equal status of women.

Social reform movements have been regarded as unfolding a process or unliking the intellectual process that went into the making of modern India. The issues, which attracted in nineteenth century social reforms, were sati, ill treatment of widows, ban on widow marriage, polygamy, child marriages, denial of property rights and education to women. The social reformers felt that the social evils could be eradicated by raising consciousness and making people sensitive to the injustice perpetuated against women. Justice

Ranade condemned these injustices against women. It was said by the early reformers that unless the womenfolk were educated, it was not possible and it will not be able to improve her position in the society.

The cause of women was first raised by Raja Ram Mohan Roy and followed by other contemporary Stalwarts and social reformers like Rabindranath Tagore, Ishwar Chandra Vidyasagar, Swami Dayanand Saraswati, Gopal Krishna Gokhale etc. supported and launched for betterment of life of women in terms of abolition of Sati Pratha through Sati Abolition Act, 1829. Ishwar Chandra Vidyasagar launched a movement for the rights of widows to re-marry and also for the education of women. As a consequence of his effort, the Widow Remarriage Act was passed by the Government in 1956. It is the Britishers who spearheaded these legal measures and establish Rule of Law. They encouraged the Christian Missionaries to start educational institutions for girls. The first school for girls by Christian Missionaries was started in 1824 in Bombay (Mumbai). Later, Swami Vivekanand, Annie Beasant and Mahatma Gandhi took interest in the social and political rights of women. Swami Vivekanand quoted women as "Shakti". If you do not raise the women who are living embodiments of Divine Mother, don't think that you have any other way to rise.

Under the leadership of Mahatma Gandhi presided necessary impetus towards restoration of women's rights and status. According to him, "if she is weak in striking, she is strong in suffering". He described women as the embodiment of sacrifice and *ahinsa*. A mass participation under Gandhi Ji's leadership gained momentum to give sense of equality of women with men. A special organisation to awaken and educate women in rural areas was the contribution of Gandhi Ji to the women cause. Women's education has gained tremendous importance. Gandhi Ji also worked hard to remove major social evils that existed in the society during national movement period. He strongly opposed child marriages and supported widow re-marriage. Gandhi Ji was one of the first crusaders to fight against the practice of Devdasi system, which was the practice of religious prostitution of women. Gandhi Ji induced to other organisations which is led by different pioneer women like Annie Besent, Lady Tata, etc. few upliftment of women and equal rights in political, economic, social spheres.

Post Independence

The Constitution of India adopted in 1950 is progressive not only in granting equality to women, but also in empowering the State to adopt measures of affirmative discrimination in favour of women. The Constitution further imposes a fundamental duty on every citizen to abstain from practices of derogatory to the dignity of women. Yet, the Hindu Code Bill, which proposed equal inheritance for women, prohibited polygamy, and liberalised divorce and custody rights; was vehemently opposed by influential Congressmen including the First President of free India, Dr Rajendra Prasad. However, the Government of India enacted certain laws to improve the status of women. Independent India continued the process of enacting legislative measures to raise the legal status of women the preamble of the Constitution of India resolved to secure to all citizens, social, economic and political justice, liberty of thought, expression, belief, faith and worship, equality of status and opportunities, dignity of the individual and unity of the nation. Indian women are entitled to these rights first as Indian men are.

The Constitution of India guarantees to all Indian Women.

- Equality before the law. Article 14.
- No discrimination by the State as the grounds only religion, race, caste, sex, place of birth on any of these. Article 15(1).
- Special provisions to be made by the State in favour of women and children. Article 15(3).
- Equality of opportunity for all citizens in matter relating to employment or appointment to any office under the State. Article 16.

- State policy to be directed to securing for men and women equally, the right to an adequate means of livelihood. Article 39(9)
- Equal pay for equal work for both men and women. Article 39(d)
- Provisions to be made by the State for securing just and humane conditions of work and for maternity relief. Article 42
- To promote harmony and to renounce practices derogatory to the dignity of women. Article 51 A(c)

Women in the Five Year National Plans

- In the 1950s women were mainly looked at the recipients of welfare.
- In the 1960s, women's education started to receive priority, along with measures to improve maternal and child health and nutrition services.
- There was a marked shift in the 1970s from welfare to Development, recognising women as participants in the process of development.
- In the 1980s, we adopted a multi-disciplinary approach, with special thrust on three core sectors – Health, Education and Employment.
- In the early 1990s, the emphasis was on training and skill development programmes to make women economically independent and self-reliant.
- In the Ninth Plan, which runs from 1997 to 2002, the paradigm shift from Development to Empowerment of Women.
- The Tenth Five Year Plan (2002-2007) has empowerment of women as a focus and also views development of children as the most desirable societal investment with a rights based approach to the development.

- In the Eleventh Five Year Plan (2007-12) women are recognised not just as equal citizens but as agents of economic and social growth. The approach to gender equally is based as the recognition on that intervention in favour of women must be multi-pronged and they are: Provide women with basic entitlements, address the reality of globalisation and its impact on women prioritising economic empowerment, ensure an environment free from all forms of violence against women (VAW), physical, economic, social, psychological, ensure participation and adequate representation of women at the highest policy levels, particularly in Parliament and State Assemblies, and, strengthen existing institutional mechanisms and create new ones for gender mainstream and effective policy implementation.

Country has made more legislations and plans for women empowerment. It requires actions in the form of implementation and executions. An eminent jurist V.R. Krishna Iyer said, "The Constitutional provisions are weapons, not victories. Law has to be activated".

The fact remains that the current scenario of insecurity, vulnerability and denial of equality as well as dignity to women and men, stands in direct contrast with the urges and aspirations which emerge from the ground.

Indian National Council for Women has made following suggestions to bridge the gap between theory and practices:

A. Empowerment should be viewed as two-fold process. Constructive activities re-organise women's role system to be accompanied by effective interventions leading to the community internalising the idea of women's empowerment for its better future.

B. Providing economic and political strength to women through collective activities should be given the necessary focus. Clubbing of women's issues should be avoided.

C. The need for women to have social space like "Shakti Sabha", "Mahila Mandal" etc. within the community set-up through local bodies should be given due recognition. Development of leadership among women for advancement of community is also necessary.

D. Communication within the women's organisation and the community at large has to be fostered.

The plight of women is distressing and their conditions in society are deplorable, notwithstanding the fact that there have been some improvements in the lives of negligible section of women. This empowerment has been because of the measures taken for amelioration of their lot by the governments, voluntary organisations and social groups. But there still remains a lot to be done to ensure meaningful, peaceful and secured life for the women folk of our country.

References

- Government of India, Department of Social Welfare, Ministry of Education and Social Welfare, Towards Equality, Report of the Committee on the Status of Women in India, 1974.
- Government of India, Planning Commission, Five Year Plans.
- Government of India, Ministry of Women and Child Development – A National Policy for the Empowerment of Women, 2001.
- Social Change and Planning – Pearson.
- India Social Development Report, 2006.
- India Social Development Report, 2012.
- Empowering Women – Arun Kumar.
- Empowerment of Destitute Women Through Swadhar Homes – K.K. Srivastava.

10

Scheduled Castes and Scheduled Tribes Education and Welfare

S.S. Chauhan

Indian society has been exposed to various socio-economic changes and legal initiatives over the last six decades. The constitutional provisions of democratic governance and the policy of positive discrimination have affected the social fabric and economic structure of Indian society. However, it is highly stratified with many glaring inequalities among the different social groups. Despite protective measures, Scheduled Castes still suffers from the stigma of inferiority and low socio-economic status. They suffered both from overall rural poverty and backwardness. Importantly, the progress and prosperity of a nation is judged from the socio-economic status of its population especially of the weaker sections of the society who suffer from abject poverty, hunger, disease, unemployment, exploitation etc, as well as disadvantage groups like women, children, Scheduled Castes, Scheduled Tribes etc. It is the prime importance that such segment of society mostly living in remote, backward and rural areas should receive serious and earnest attention of policy-makers, planners, social welfare administrators, social activities and academicians, so that the downtrodden section of the society can also live decent life ensured by the special provisions in the Constitution of India.

The Indian Constitution is committed to the equality of citizens. The Directive Principles of the State Policy is also to promote with special care the educational and economic interests of the weaker sections of the people, and, in particular, of the SCs/STs. To achieve 'Equality' with many facets, special provisions have been made in the Constitution of India. Article 46 of the Constitution states that, "The State shall promote, with special care, the educational and economic interests of the weaker sections of the people, and, in particular of the Scheduled Castes and Scheduled Tribes, and shall protect them from social injustice and all forms of social exploitation. Articles 15(4), 15(5), 16(4), 16(4A), 16 (4B), 164(1) proviso, 275(1) first proviso, 243D, 243T, 330, 332, 335, 338 to 342 and the entire Fifth and Sixth Schedules of the Constitution deal with special provisions for implementation of the objectives set forth in Article 46.

The National Policy on Education (NPE) 1986 modified in 1992 gives special emphasis on the removal of disparities and equalising educational opportunity by attending to the specific needs of those who have been denied equality so far. The Eleventh Plan had given highest priority on education as a central instrument for achieving rapid and inclusive growth. The Twelfth Plan has stressed upon the need of faster and more inclusive development.

Scheduled Caste Sub-Plan and Tribal Sub-Plan (SCSP and TSP)

The Ministry of Human Resource Development has Constituted a National Monitoring Committee (NMC) for Education of SCs, STs and Persons with Disabilities to advise the Government on all matters pertaining to education and its pursuit for SCs, STs and Persons with Disabilities. A Task Force constituted by the Planning Commission to (a) review the operational guidelines in implementing SCSP and TSP and (b) suggest remedial measures for an effective and meaningful implementation of SCSP and TSP, has kept the Department of Higher Education under Category III for earmarking of funds 15-16.2 per cent and 7.50 per cent for SCSP and TSP respectively. Department of School Education and Literacy has been kept under Category IV for earmarking of funds more than 16.2 per cent and 10.70 per cent for SCSP and TSP respectively. The Planning Commission has accepted the recommendations of this Task Force on differentiated Ministry/Department-wise earmarking of Plan funds under SCSP and TSP. The guideline of SCSP/TSP has been prepared circulated to all the Centrally Funded Higher Educational Institutes. The progress of implementation of SCSP/TSP is also being reviewed by Standing Committee of NMC.

A number of initiatives are being taken by this Ministry both at school and higher education levels. Special emphasis is laid on education of children belonging to disadvantaged groups and simultaneously to provide greater opportunities for access to quality education at all level by taking several legislative measures and also investing in infrastructure and faculty, promoting academic reforms, improving governance and institutional restructuring.

The initiatives of the Ministry of Human Resource Development may be divided into two categories (A) Programmes/Schemes formulated exclusively to provide interventions for these groups and (B) Programmes/Schemes which have significant bearing on educational development of SCs and STs.

Programmes/Schemes exclusively for SCs/STs

(i) Rajiv Gandhi National Fellowships for SC/ST: This Scheme is funded by the Ministry of Social Justice and Empowerment and Ministry of Tribal Affairs and implemented by the UGC. The objective of this scheme is to provide fellowships in the form of financial assistance to unemployed students belonging to SC/ST to pursue higher studies leading to M.Phil and Ph.D Degrees (full time) in Sciences, Humanities and Social Sciences and Engineering and Technology in Indian Universities/Institutions/Colleges approved under Section 2 (f) and 12 (B) of the UGC Act.

(ii) Post-Graduate Scholarships for Students belonging to SCs/STs: The objective of this scheme is to provide financial assistance to 1000 SC/ST candidates to pursue postgraduate level studies in Professional subjects at recognised Indian Universities/Institutions/Colleges.

(iii) Post-Doctoral Fellowships for SC/ST: The objective of this Scheme is to provide an opportunity to SC/ST candidates to undertake advanced studies and Post Doctoral research in Science, Engineering and Technology, Humanities and Social Sciences in recognised Indian Universities/ Institutions/Colleges.

(iv) Remedial Coaching for SC/ST/OBC (non-creamy layer) and Minorities: In order to enable students belonging to SC/ST/OBC (non-creamy layer)/Minority communities, who need remedial coaching to come up to the Level necessary for pursuing higher studies efficiently and to reduce their failure and drop-out rate, the UGC provides financial assistance for conducting special classes outside the regular time table.

(v) Coaching for NET/SET for SC/ST/OBC (non-creamy layer) and Minorities: The main objective of the scheme is to prepare SC /ST candidates and candidates from Minority communities for appearing in NET or SLET, so that sufficient numbers of candidates become available for selection of Lecturers in the University system from these groups.

(vi) Establishment of Residential Coaching Academics of SC/ST/Minorities and Women: The basic objective of this coaching scheme is to prepare students belonging to SC/ST/OBC (non-creamy layer) and Minority communities to get gainful employment in Group 'A', 'B' or 'C' Central services, State services or equivalent positions in the private sector. The coaching under the scheme is oriented for particular examinations conducted for selection to services, such as the IAS, State Public Services, Bank recruitment, etc.

(vii) Establishment of Equal Opportunity Cells for SC/ ST/OBC/Minorities: To make colleges and universities more responsive to the needs and constraints of the disadvantaged social groups, the UGC establishes the EOC to oversee the effective implementation of policies and programmes of these groups.

(viii) Opening of Centres for Studies in Social Exclusion and Inclusive Policy: The key objectives of opening of these Centres include conceptualising discrimination, exclusion and inclusion based on caste/ethnicity and religion; developing understanding of the nature and dynamics of discrimination and exclusion; developing an understanding of discrimination at an empirical level; formulating policies for protecting the rights of these groups and eradicating the problem of exclusion and discrimination.

Initiatives having significant bearing on educational development of SCs & STs	*Progress*
School Education	
Sarva Shiksha Abhiyan: Implemented in partnership with State Governments to cover the entire country to open new schools in those habitations which do not have schooling facilities and strengthen existing school infrastructure (i) Opening of Primary Schools (ii) Opening of Upper Primary Schools	2.07 lakhs primary schools of which 1135 were sanctioned in the year 2013-14 and 1.59 lakhs upper primary schools have been sanctioned in a radius of 3 km, including 220 sanctioned in 2013-14.
Kasturba Gandhi Balika Vidyalaya: KGBVs are residential upper primary schools for girls from SC, ST, OBC and Muslim communities. KGBVs provide for a minimum reservation of 75 per cent seats for girls from SC/ST/OBC and minority communities and 25 per cent to girls from families that live below the poverty line.	3609 KGBVs were sanctioned. Out of which 3602 are operational enrolling 3.48 lakh girls out of which 30.46 per cent are from SC category, 24.67 per cent from ST Category and 31.29 per cent from OBC Category.
Opening of Model Schools: The scheme aims to provide quality education to talented rural children through setting up of 6,000 model schools, out of which 3,500 are to be set up in as many educationally backward blocks (EBBs) through State/UT Governments, as benchmark of excellence at block level at the rate of one school per block.	2166 Model Schools, including 241, 2013-14 have been sanctioned.
Construction & Running of Girls' Hostel for Students of Secondary and Higher Secondary Schools: The Scheme envisages construction of a hostel with the capacity of 100 girls in each of about 3479 Educationally Backward Blocks (EBBs) in the country.	As on 31 March, 2014, 137 hostels in SCCD were approved by PAB and 7249.56 lakh has been released for construction of 132 hostels in SCCD. Similarly 429 hostels in STCD were approved by PAB and 12923.67 lakh has been released for construction hostels in STCD of 277 hostels in STCD.

contd...

contd...

Initiatives having significant bearing on educational development of SCs & STs	*Progress*
National Means-cum-Merit Scholarship Scheme: The objective of this Scheme is to award scholarships to meritorious students of economically weaker sections to arrest their drop out at class VIII and encourage them to continue the study at secondary stage.	In 2013-14, 12.06 crore and 4.29 crore were incurred under SCSP and TSP in this Scheme.
National Scheme of Incentive to Girls for Secondary Education: The Scheme has been started in May, 2008 to establish an enabling environment to reduce the drop outs and to promote the enrolment of girls children belonging mainly to SC/ST communities in secondary schools.	18.69 lakh girls have benefitted from the Scheme up to March, 2014 since its launch.
The Right of Children to Free and Compulsory Education **(RTE) Act, 2009:** Section 12(1) (c) of the Act inter alia, provides that a specified category school and a private unaided school shall admit in class I to the extent of at least twenty-five per cent of the strength of that class, children belonging to weaker sections and disadvantaged group in the neighbourhood and provides for free and compulsory elementary education till its completion. It further states that this provision shall apply for admission to the pre-school stage where the school imparts pre-school education. The definition of 'child belonging to disadvantaged group' includes a child belonging to SC/ST and now also, children with special needs.	Corresponding enrollment is 4.04 crore and 2.17 crore respectively during 2012-13 in Elementary Education.

<table>
<tr><td>Initiatives having significant bearing on educational development of SCs & STs</td><td>Progress</td></tr>
<tr><td colspan="2">Higher Education</td></tr>
<tr><td>Central Educational Institutions (Reservation in Admission) Act, 2006: The Act provides 15 per cent, 7.5 per cent and 27 per cent reservation in admission of the students belonging to the SCs, STs and OBCs, in certain Central Educational Institutions established, maintained or aided by the Central Government, and for matters connected therewith or incidental thereto. The Central Universities are following the reservation policy of Government of India. However, the State Universities including their affiliated/constituent Colleges and other institutes are following the norms of percentage of reservation of SCs/STs as prescribed by the respective State Governments.</td><td>
<table>
<tr><td rowspan="2">CFHEI</td><td colspan="2">Share for Year 2010-11</td></tr>
<tr><td>SC%</td><td>ST%</td></tr>
<tr><td>Central University</td><td>4.64</td><td>3.36</td></tr>
<tr><td>IGNOU</td><td>7.09</td><td>5.72</td></tr>
<tr><td>IIT</td><td>12.87</td><td>4.95</td></tr>
<tr><td>NIT</td><td>13.08</td><td>6.12</td></tr>
<tr><td>IIM</td><td>7.83</td><td>3.46</td></tr>
<tr><td>IISER, IIIT</td><td>11.07</td><td>3.56</td></tr>
</table>
Source: All India Survey on Higher Education (AISHE), 2010-11.</td></tr>
</table>

contd...

contd...

Initiatives having significant bearing on educational development of SCs & STs	*Progress*
Sub-Mission on Polytechnics: Sub-Mission on Polytechnics includes four components namely (i) setting up of new Polytechnics (ii) Strengthening of existing 500 Polytechnics (iii) Community Development through Polytechnics and (iv) Constructions of Women Hostels in Polytechnics.	291 Districts have been provided partial financial assistance of ` 2113.69 crores till 31.03.2014. Major beneficiaries of these Polytechnics are from weaker sections like SC/ST/OBC.
Scheme of Community Development through Polytechnics (CDTP): This Scheme aims at providing non formal, short term, employment oriented skill development programmes, through AICTE approved Polytechnics, to various sections of the community, particularly the rural, unorganised and disadvantaged sections of the society, to enable them to obtain gainful self/wage employment. No fees are charged from the trainees under this Scheme and there is no restriction of age and qualification.	Major beneficiaries of these Polytechnics are from weaker sections like SC/ST/OBC.
Setting up of Model Degree Colleges in backward districts	37 Model Degree Colleges have been sanctioned in 20 Universities in 8 States. Major beneficiaries of these Colleges are from weaker sections like SC/ST/OBC.
Colleges with relatively higher proportion of SC/ST & Minorities: The Scheme aims to encourage access of students Belonging to SC/ST/ Minority/OBCs.	Financial assistance to 3028 institutes has been provided.

In addition to above, several other general programmes/ schemes have also lay emphasis on education development of students belonging to SCs and STs which mainly includes 'National Programme of Mid-Day Meal in Schools', 'Opening of Jan Shikshan Sansthans', 'Rashtriya Madhyamik Shiksha Abhiyan', 'Opening of Jawahar Navodaya Vidyalayas and Kendriya Vidyalayas', 'Vocational Education at Secondary Education Level', 'Mahila Samakhya Programme', 'Consturciton of Women's Hostel in Polytechnics and Colleges', 'Central Sector Scheme of Scholarship for College and University Students', 'Special scholarship Scheme for Jammu and Kashmir', 'Interest Subsidy on Educational Loans', 'AICTE's Tuition Fee Waiver Scheme', AICTE's Post Graduate Scholarship for GATE qualified ME/M.Tech students', etc. Further, the IITs and NITs also made special provisions like exemption/concession in payment of tuition fees; travelling allowance from residence to Institute to join the program; free mess facilities, pocket allowance; preparatory courses, conduct of special programmes for training in communication skills, presentations and placements; special evening classes in subjects and specialisations; etc. for SC/ST students.

National Monitoring Committee for Education of Scheduled Castes, Scheduled Tribes and Persons with Disabilities

The Ministry of Human Resource Development has constituted a "National Monitoring Committee for Education of SCs, STs and Persons with Disabilities" to advise the government on all matters pertaining to education and its pursuit for SCs, STs and Persons with Disabilities. In addition, the Committee will review the functioning of various schemes launched by the Ministry for the purpose of promoting SCs, STs and Persons with Disabilities in education. The composition of the Committee includes some Members of Parliament, Education Ministers and Education Secretaries of State Governments with concentration of SC/ST population. The Committee also includes the academics, activists and administrators connected with SCs, STs and Persons with Disabilities. In pursuant of decision taken in the First meeting of the National Monitoring Committee, held on 27 June, 2012, a Standing Committee and following Six Task Forces have been constituted:

(i) Task Force for Educational Development of SCs.

(ii) Task Force for Educational Development of STs.

(iii) Task Force for Educational Development of PwDs.

(iv) Task Force to promote and develop quality faculty from SCs, STs and PwDs.

(v) Task Force for promotion of vocational education and skill development amongst PwDs.

(vi) Task Force to promote educational opportunities and welfare of students from North East Region belonging to SCs, STs and PwDs.

All the six Task Forces have been submitted their final reports and recommendations of these Task Forces have been circulated to the concerned Ministries and all the Bureau Heads of this Ministry for comments/views.

Regulations on Prevention of Discrimination and Establishment of Ombudsman

Universities and colleges have their own grievance redressal mechanism to address the complaints of all students including the grievances pertaining to SC/ST students. However, UGC has also framed two important regulations namely, UGC (Promotion of Equity in Higher Education Institutions) Regulations, 2012 and UGC (Establishment of Mechanisms for Grievance Redressal), Regulations, 2012 to ensure the implementation of Constitutional provisions relating to the SCs and STs and to check the incidents of discrimination and harassment against the students of these communities. These regulations have already been sent for publication in the official Gazette.

The All India Council for Technical Education (Establishment of Mechanism for Grievance Redressal) Regulations, 2012, provide for establishment of a grievance redressal committee in each technical institutions approved by the AICTE; and appointment of Ombudsman, by the Technological Universities for the purpose of redressal of grievances of the students, parents and others.

The Indian Institutes of Technology have Disciplinary Action Committees to take immediate action if any complaint of caste-biased discrimination is received. They also have student mentors in various Departments who help them in their academic and other problems by providing proper guidance and also bring to the notice of concerned authorities about their problems for timely address. In addition, there are Student Tutors who help them to cope up with their academic problems. Further, following the recommendations made by the Council of IITs in its 39th meeting held on 28.01.2009, a Standing Committee comprising chairpersons of Board of Governors of IIT Delhi, IIT Guwahati and IIT Roorkee was constituted on 16.06.2009 to look into the grievances of students and employees of IITs. It was also decided that the committee will take up those representations made by the students and employees which are referred to it by Secretary, IIT Council in MHRD and have already been considered by the Board of Governors of IITs. The committee submits its report to the Secretary, IIT Council. The Appellate Committee also looks into specific complaints, if any, from SC/ST Students and employees. Further, the Ministry, from time to time is issuing strong advisory letters to all Centrally Funded Educational Institutions to emphasise that officials/ faculty members should desist from any act of discrimination against students on grounds of their social origin.

References

1. Agarwal, Pawan (2006), Higher Education in India, The Need for a Change, ICRIER, Working Paper No. 179.
2. FICCI (2013), Higher Education in India: Vision 2030, Ernest and Young and FICCI, New Delhi.
3. Annual Report (2013-14) Ministry of Human Resources Development, Government of India, New Delhi.
4. Annual Report (2014-15) Ministry of Social Justice and Empowerment, Government of India, New Delhi.

11

An Evaluation of Free Coaching and Allied Scheme for the Candidates belonging to Minority Communities in India

Nimish Gupta

The well-being of people is unquestionably the ultimate objective of all development efforts of a country and the basic quest of human endeavour is always to seek a better quality of life. The quality of life of citizens of a nation can be effectively improved only by raising the standards of living of the people on the margin and in countryside. Social empowerment is very fundamental in achieving this goal. The institution of democracy provides a strong foundation for harmonising social and economic objectives. Thus, within the broad democratic framework there are great opportunities for synergising the economic development programmes to help achieve the better quality of life in the shortest possible span of time.

India, the largest democracy in the world, pledges to secure all its citizens equality of opportunity. The supreme law of the country prohibits discrimination on ground of religion, race, caste, sex or place of birth. The Constitution makes provision for protecting the interests of minorities. However, the experiences have not been very encouraging. The plight of a good part of people, including the minorities, is not worth appreciable. The 'trickle down' effect of economic development has not worked satisfactorily and the benefits of growth have not reached equitably to all sections of the society.

India is a land of diversity and of different religions with Hindus is in majority. According to the 2001 census, religious minority population has reported to be 19.5 per cent of the total population of country. However, most of them are reported to be Muslims. India is a secular republic and the constitution guarantees equal rights to all its citizens without any discrimination. The Indian constitution provides many legal safeguards to the minority community and special provisions are made for their social and economic growth. Despite these, minorities in India face all types of inequity in the public sphere. Even the violence and human right violations of the minority community in India is a common phenomenon. In this context, the note of UN Special Reporter on Freedom and Religious Belief Ms. Asma Jahangir, is pertinent when she praised India's secularism, human right activism, and strong legal protection for religious minorities at the national level but also made the point that due to the federal structure of Indian state the implementation of law varies from states to states. She said, "organised groups claiming roots in religious ideologies have unleashed an all-pervasive fear of mob violence in many parts of the country". Asma Jahangir, was making special reference to the violence in Odisha, where Hindu fundamentalists attacked Christian and tribal communities. The violence in Khandamal region of Odisha continued for a long period, despite massive protest by activists and secular organisations.

As per census 2011, minorities (Muslims, Christians, Sikhs, Buddhists, Parsis and Jains) constitute a little less than one–fifth (about 18.5 per cent) of the total population of the country, and among minorities, Muslims account for more than two-thirds (about 71.36 per cent). As regards concentration of minorities, it is found that Muslims are mainly concentrated in Jammu and Kashmir, Lakshdweep, Assam, West Bengal, Uttar Pradesh, Bihar and Kerala. The Christians are mainly inhabited in Nagaland, Mizoram, Goa, Manipur and Kerala. Most of the Sikhs are found in Punjab, Chandigarh, Haryana, Delhi and Jammu and Kashmir. Buddhists are concentrated mainly in Sikkim, Arunachal Pradesh and Maharashtra. Majority of the Jains are living in Maharashtra, Delhi, Rajasthan and Madhya Pradesh. The Parsis are confined mainly to Maharashtra. However, people belonging to these communities are found everywhere across the country.

Amongst the minorities in India, Muslim is the largest community but still far behind the benefits of development. This is true that every common citizen of the country is derived from the gains of economic growth but the quotient of this deprivation is more amongst the Muslim community. This came into light when Sachar Committee report on the condition of minority community was placed in the parliament. Some of the glaring findings of the report are as follows.

- In the field of literacy the Committee has found that the rate among Muslims is very much below than the national average. The gap between Muslims and the general average is greater in urban areas and women. 25 per cent of children of Muslim parents in the 6–14 year age group have either never attended school or have dropped out.

- Muslim parents are not averse to mainstream education or to send their children to affordable government schools. The access to government schools for children of Muslim parents is limited.

- Bidi workers, tailors and mechanics need to be provided with social safety nets and social security. The participation of Muslims in the professional and managerial cadre is low.
- The average amount of bank loan disbursed to the Muslims is two-third of the amount disbursed to other minorities. In some cases it is half. The Reserve Bank of India's efforts to extend banking and credit facilities under the Prime Minister's 15–point programme of 1983 has mainly benefited other minorities marginalising Muslims.
- There is a clear and significant inverse association between the proportion of the Muslim population and the availability of educational infrastructure in small villages. Muslim concentration villages are not well served with pucca approach roads and local bus stops.
- The presence of Muslims has been found to be only three per cent in the IAS, 1.8 per cent in the IFS and four per cent in the IPS.
- Muslim community has a representation of only 4.5 per cent in Indian Railways while 98.7 per cent of them are positioned at lower levels. Representation of Muslims is very low in the Universities and in Banks. Their share in police constables is only six per cent, in health 4.4 per cent, in transport 6.5 per cent.
- For the Maulana Azad Education Foundation to be effective the corpus fund needs to be increased to 1000 crores. Total allocation in the four years 2002 to 2006 for Madarsa Modernisation Scheme is 106 crores. The information regarding the Scheme has not adequately percolated down. Even if the share of Muslims in elected bodies is low they and other underrepresented segments can be involved in the decision making process through innovative mechanisms.

- Most of the variables indicate that Muslim–OBCs are significantly deprived in comparison to Hindu–OBCs. The work participation rate (WPR) shows the presence of a sharp difference between Hindu–OBCs (67 per cent) and the Muslims. The share of Muslim–OBCs in government/PSU jobs is much lower than Hindu–OBCs.

The scheme of Free Coaching and Allied Assistance aims to empower the minority communities, which are relatively disadvantaged section of society, by assisting them as well as those institutions working for them, towards enhancing their skills and capabilities to make them employable in industries, services and business sectors in addition to the government sector. It has the built–in resilience to adapt itself to the market dynamics on a continuous basis so that the target groups are not deprived of the professional acumen demanded by the changing/emerging market needs and opportunities for employment at domestic as well as international levels.

Separate schemes for providing coaching to students belonging to scheduled caste, minority communities and backward classes were being implemented from Sixth Five Year Plan. These separate schemes were amalgamated with effect from September, 2001 into a combined Scheme of Coaching and Allied Assistance for Weaker Sections including Scheduled Castes, Other Backward Classes and Minorities. However, after the creation of Ministry of Minority Affairs, a new scheme called "Free Coaching and Allied Assistance" for candidates belonging to the minority communities is being implemented by this Ministry. The scheme has to be made more comprehensive keeping in view the emerging trends of employment in the era of economic reforms, liberalisation and globalisation.

The socio-economic status of minorities in general in the country is not satisfactory. A large number of minorities specially Muslims are the victim of low literacy, low enrollment in educational institutions and high drop-outs. Although there are large number of minority institutions engaged in imparting education, training and professional skills, most of them are engaged in promoting traditions, customs and religion. They have largely failed to modernise their educational curriculum and system. Most of the people from the minority communities (particularly Muslims) are found engaged in unorganised sector of economy and a large number of them are doing their own petty business.

Objectives of Study

The main objectives of study are as follows:

- To review the policy, programmes and schemes on empowerment of minority population in India;
- To study the functioning and performance of free coaching and allied scheme in the selected areas and also to assess the level of awareness of major stakeholders regarding the scheme;
- To study the modus operandi of the scheme in terms of eligibility criteria, selection process, stipend/ scholarship, disbursement, etc.;
- To examine the socio-economic profile of the beneficiaries and their parents and also to assess the impact of the scheme on academic achievement and selection in competitive examinations;
- To examine the problems, constraints and challenges in effective implementation of the scheme;
- To suggest the policy measures for effective implementation of the scheme and also for empowering minority in India.

Research Methodology

The present paper is based on a empirical study and based on primary data. The study was conducted by HIIT,

Lucknow and was funded by Ministry of Minority Affairs, Govt. of India. The author acted as consultant. Besides collection and analysis of primary data, secondary data and pertinent literature has been compiled from published and documented sources. The main sources of secondary data and pertinent literature include the publications and documents of state governments, Central Government and non-governmental organisations. Academic institutions such as universities, colleges, research institutes and various departments of government and non-government have been consulted for collection of secondary data and literature. Department of Minority Affairs of respective states, District Social Welfare Departments of respective districts and other concerned departments have been approached for collection of relevant information.

Sample Area

S. No.	*Unit of Coverage*	*Number*
1.	Zone	6
2.	States	12
3.	Districts	24
4.	Beneficiaries	2880
5.	Head of Coaching Institutions	60
6.	Faculty Members	201
7.	State and District Level Officials	48

Representative random sampling procedure has been used from the identified districts and coaching institutions for interview of beneficiary students and faculty members. The field survey has been conducted in the states of Andhra Pradesh, Bihar, Haryana, Jammu and Kashmir, Madhya Pradesh, Maharashtra, Manipur, Mizoram, Rajasthan, Tamil Nadu, Uttar Pradesh and West Bengal. The field survey has been conducted with the help of structured interview schedules. Interview schedules for head of the coaching institutions, faculty members, beneficiary students and state and district level officials were developed keeping in view the relevant research points, questions and scales of view perception pertaining to ecological background of inmates, infrastructure facilities, support services, training, eligibility criteria, selection process, disbursement of stipend/ scholarship, academic environment, imparting education and coaching, convergence of schemes and programmes, socio-cultural, economic, educational and ecological profile, undertaking coaching classes, success rate in competitive examinations, etc. of beneficiaries.

Scope of the Study

Present study has been conducted in the national perspective with the representation of 12 states across the all geographical regions of India. The study has covered all major stakeholders including the beneficiary students, faculty members, and head of the institutions. The sample of the study is also large enough to draw the conclusions and results.

Conclusion and Policy Recommendations

Weaker sections including Scheduled Castes, Scheduled Tribes, OBCs and minority communities. In India present a significant degree of cultural and ethnic diversity. They differ in their socio-economic levels of development as well as in their behavioural patterns. Moreover their situation in India poses peculiar problems of development, not encountered in other areas the peculiarities can be broadly sum them as geographical, demographic, socio-culture and exploitative. The representation of SC's, ST's, OBCs and minorities in government services, particularly in premier services has been reported to be low despite positive discrimination and reservation provision. This is because of the fact that their share in enrollment in higher education sector is low and they are poor in fundamental knowledge and entrepreneurship. Therefore central government as well as state government have implemented educational empowerment programmes and schemes for SC's, ST's,

OBCs, and Minorities. These mainly includes pre-metric scholarship, post-matric scholarship, hostel facility, special education development programme, Ashram schools, book bank schemes, up-gradation of merit and coaching and allied services scheme. These schemes and programmes have no doubt impacted positively on educational development of SC's, ST's, OBCs and minorities but effective implementation for such programmes and schemes could not be ensured. Against this backdrop, present study purports to review the performance of coaching and allied services scheme for the candidates belonging to minority communities in various states of India and suggesting policy measures for effective functioning of the scheme.

Main Findings of the Study

- Free Coaching and Allied Scheme for the candidates belonging to minority communities has been launched by the Ministry of Minority Affairs, Government of India during 2006–2007. During the period of 2007–08 to 2013–14, Rs 76.17 crores were allocated under the scheme however, a large segment of allocated fund was not released by the Ministry due to several factors. The Ministry has achieved the maximum target for providing training and coaching to the candidates belonging to the minority communities. Overall 34,000 candidates were provided training and coaching under the scheme in the corresponding period.
- The infrastructure, library resources, human resources, amenities and basic facilities in the coaching institutions were found somewhat adequate however; there is vast scope for improvement in order to ensure quality learning and teaching. Most of the coaching institutions are functioning in the rented buildings. Though, availability of computers has been reported high in majority of the states however, internet access is limited both for faculty and candidates belonging to

minority communities. Coaching institutions located in Andhra Pradesh, Haryana, Maharashtra, Rajasthan, Uttar Pradesh and West Bengal reported that they are providing hostel and mess facilities to the enrolled students. Though, most of the states reported that they have adequate number of faculty members however, they are getting consolidated salary.

- During last three years, the total enrollment in coaching institutions was recorded 9899 candidates belonging to minority communities. Out of total enrolled candidates, 28.79 per cent candidates were female while majority of the candidates were male. The proportion of female candidates was recorded high for the entrance examination for technical/professional courses. Out of total enrolled students, 83.49 per cent students were from belonging to Muslim community. The proportion of female candidates was recorded high in the state of Andhra Pradesh followed by Mizoram and Madhya Pradesh. About nine per cent candidates were found belonging to Christian community while about five per cent candidates were Buddhists/Parsis. Thus, only two per cent candidates were Sikhs.

- Most of the coaching institutions reported that they are providing support services in terms of handouts, conducting tests and providing assignments to the students. The average duration of class has been reported to be 1.5 to two hours. The duration of course has also been reported to be four to six months.

- The expenditure pattern of grants received so far demonstrates that most of the coaching institutions are using the grant mainly for providing honorarium to the faculty and stipend to the students. Other expenses include wages and salaries of the staff and maintenance of coaching institutions.

- The success rate for the last three years in the coaching institutions shows that about half of the enrolled candidates were succeeded. The success rate has been reported high among the Sikh students followed by Muslim students. Again, success rate has been reported high for the coaching/training for job in private sectors and low for Group–C services. Success rate has been reported high in the states of Haryana followed by Maharashtra, Andhra Pradesh, Rajasthan and West Bengal. Success rate among female candidates has been recorded significantly high (64.67 per cent) as compared to male candidates (44.33 per cent).

- All the coaching institutions reported that the present amount of stipend is not sufficient. They have suggested the ideal amount of stipend Rs. 3417 for local candidates and Rs. 4542 for outstation candidates. They were also of the view that discontinuation of stipend will adversely affect the enrollment and success rate as well as discourage the candidates belonging to minority communities.

- Most of the faculty members were found belonging to middle age group and males. About one-fourth faculty members were working on permanent basis while others are getting honorarium on lecture basis. About half of the faculty members were postgraduates and doctorates while less than one-fourth faculty members were graduates. They are undertaking about 20 classes per week. Thus, academic stress has been reported significantly high among the faculty members.

- Faculty members revealed that they are regularly distributing handouts to the students besides conducting tests on regular basis. All the faculty members were found satisfied with the batch of students. They were of the view that discontinuation of stipend will adversely affect the scheme in terms of enrollment and success rate. They also reported that present amount of stipend is not sufficient.

- Most of the students were found belonging to urban areas and the proportion of candidates coming from rural areas constituted 18.3 per cent. This shows that the proper publicity of the scheme could not be ensured as awareness about the scheme in rural and backward areas is low as students coming from rural and semi–urban areas are very low.

- Majority of the students were found belonging to the age group of 16–22 years while about one-fourth students were found belonging to the age group of 23–28 years. Only one-third students were females. This was found more pronouncing in Andhra Pradesh followed by Mizoram, Tamil Nadu and Manipur. About three-fourth students were found belonging to Muslim community while 16 per cent students were Christians. More than half of the students were localites.

- More than half of the students were found enrolled for coaching/training for jobs in private sectors while less than one-third students were enrolled for entrance examination for technical/professional courses. The enrollment for Group–A, B and C services constituted about 15 per cent. There was no enrollment for remedial coaching/tuition and coaching for recruitment.

- Majority of the students were found satisfied and fully satisfied with the teaching method, quality of stock in library and quality of teaching of teachers.

- Overall less than two-fifth students succeeded in their examinations. The success rate was recorded high for the entrance examination for technical/professional courses. Again, success rate has been found high among Muslim candidates and low among Buddhists/Parsis. Success rate has been found significantly high among female candidates as compared to male candidates. Success rate has been reported high in the state of Andhra Pradesh followed by Rajasthan, Jammu and Kashmir, Haryana and Uttar Pradesh.

- Most of the students reported that free coaching and allied scheme has quality impact on them as it has increased their confidence level and existing body of knowledge. Most of the students were of the view that the discontinuation of stipend will discourage them.
- The ranking of factors demonstrates that significant segment of students are not found satisfied with the location of coaching/training centres, quality of teaching, availability of public conveyance to coaching institutions, availability of qualified and experienced faculty, placement services, availability of hostel facility in the locality of coaching institutions, usefulness of reading materials, stock of library resources, adequacy of infrastructure services, organising of guest lectures, duration of library services and institutional efforts for placement.

Policy Recommendations

- Proper and adequate hostel facilities are to be made available to minority students enrolled for various programmes in coaching institutions. The enrolled students should be provided proper and regular mess facility besides providing library with quality resource stock – books, journals and other periodicals. The internet facility should also be made available in the library and computer centre so that students may get quality resource literature through downloading from various websites and digital libraries.
- As head of the institutions, faculty members and candidates reported that present amount of stipend is not sufficient, the amount of stipend for coaching and allied scheme should be increased substantially to meet the basic requirements and give a sense of equality.
- The coaching institutions may be provided funds for combined classes such SCs, STs, OBCs and Minorities.

This will require special provision for releasing funds and resources are to be pooled from Ministry of Tribal Affairs, Ministry of Minority Affairs, and Ministry of Social Justice and Empowerment. Moreover, such institutions may also approach to state government for availing funds for maintenance of coaching institutions. Thus, combined classes will provide equal opportunity for mainstreaming of SC, ST, OBC and Minority students with other castes and classes. The coaching institutions should be allowed to enroll non–reserved category students on professional basis so that they may hire quality teachers, upgrade teaching methods, enrich the library stock and improve the infrastructural facilities through mobilising resources.

- The coaching institutions should be provided funds timely; however recommendation of state level officials may be kept in mind while releasing the second installment by the Central Government. The delay in releasing of second installment of coaching centres and quality of coaching and other services may be deteriorated.

- The coaching institutions should be allowed to diversify in the programmes and civil services, provincial civil services, state level entrance examination, etc. should be included in the coaching classes. Importantly, the coaching for civil services and provincial civil services may be started at the state headquarter while such programme may be discouraged to initiate in the backward district because in such areas quality faculty is not available. However, other competitive examinations coaching may be provided to such centres. Again, coaching centres should ensure the availability on quality teaching through contract classes and capsule classes by renounced faculty members may take a series of schedules in the centre at one stretch.

- Universities and well established institutes of learning, education and research including NGO's may be promoted to start the coaching institutions because they have plenty of experienced, qualified and competent faculties well equipped and enriched libraries, hostel and other infrastructural facilities.
- All the universities and deemed universities should establish a separate section of SCs, STs, OBCs and Minority for facilitating and providing career guidance to them. Importantly, these centres should be established till for individual career counselling, up–gradation of skills, motivation and mobilisation of aspirants for various services and competitive examinations.
- The coaching institutions should appoint core faculty while library should be enriched. It is also suggested that photostat version of high priced, quality and rare books may be arranged through issuing such books from well-established libraries and be kept in the institutions for consultation of students.
- Accountability should be enforced in terms of success rate of the various programmes. The preferences should be given to professional institutions having required facilities.
- Girls from minority communities should be given preference in admission in such coaching institutions. They should be provided social security, separate toilet facility, and hostel and individual career guidance so that they may join the mainstream and avail the reservation benefits.
- In all the coaching schemes whether through NGO's or through state organisations or through universities or private education institutions, the rate of remuneration for teachers should be high enough to attract competent teachers. The rates followed by

successful coaching organisation should be used as a good indicator for fixing the rates.

- In order to have quality faculty and resource persons, the coaching institutions should invite resources persons from various national level academic institutions as guest faculty while the coaching institutions should allocate substantial amount for honorarium to the guest faculty for delivering such special classes to their students. The students should be given more exposure related academic inputs rather than theoretical inputs.

- It is suggested that Knowledge Manager/Information Officer may be appointed on contractual basis in each coaching institution who should be given the responsibility of developing quality resource literature for various competitive examinations through internet search, consulting books, periodicals, journals and also translating into vernacular languages for easy understanding of the enrolled students.

- Performance indicators for monitoring the overall success of the coaching institutions should be evolved and those coaching centres who are unable to get the minimum qualifying marks in terms of success rate, the support under the scheme should be withdrawn by the government. Besides, the coaching institutions should insist on enrollment of students for specific examinations only and the enrolled students should be discouraged for appearing various competitive examinations as it affects their concentration on one particular examination.

- It is imperative to review the selection criteria of coaching institutions as some of the good coaching institutions are not willing to apply under the scheme to the Ministry as they are required to get recommendation from the concerned state.

The Ministry may also adopt a judicious thinking to consider the proposals recommended by the state government under the scheme. As per the concentration of minority population and educational backwardness, the quota for the states may be fixed up by the Ministry while approving the proposals. The Ministry may also consider proposals from the coaching institutions coming directly without recommendation of the concerned states. The good coaching institutions may be empanelled for a longer period so that effective implementation of the scheme may be ensured.

- The Ministry may evolve criteria and indicators for evaluation of the performance of the coaching institutions. On the basis of grading system, the coaching institutions may be sorted out for allotment of the number of seats under the scheme. The coaching institution should also evolve criteria and indicators for evaluation of the performance of faculty members and selection of candidates in order to attract the quality faculty and good batch of students.
- It may be recommended that Ministry should directly transfer the amount of stipend to the students enrolled under the scheme as there is no timely disbursement of stipend to the students. Delay in disbursement of stipend to the students creates a lot of confusion and misunderstanding among the students and coaching institutions besides affecting the enrollment, retention, quality of learning and success rate.
- It is suggested that reading materials should be developed by the coaching institutions in consultation with academic experts. The reading materials in proper shape (modules, papers, monographs and reports) should be provided time to time to the students so that they may go through the reading materials in advance and participate effectively in the discussions and deliberations in classrooms. The coaching

institutions may approach to the academic experts for developing a feedback form for the assessment of the faculty.

- Coaching institutions should emphasise on institutional efforts for placement services. The data bank for private and corporate sectors may be prepared in advance where students may be placed besides compiling and display of information on competitive examinations and various career opportunities.
- MIS must be developed for tracking the enrollment, retention, attendance and success for the various courses in coaching institutions. The MIS should be linked with concerned state governments and the Ministry. The physical and financial performance may be provided on monthly basis on a prescribed format both through electronic and printed forms.
- The coaching institutions may adopt biometric attendance system for ensuring good attendance in the classes. This will also ensure quality learning, understanding and higher success rate.
- It is suggested that proper publicity and awareness creation about the scheme should be ensured both at the Ministry level and in the states so that candidates from backward and remote areas may be made aware about the scheme and they may avail the benefits under the scheme.

12

Civil Society: Participation in Governance and Social Change

Mridul Srivastava and Preeti Dwivedi

Civil Society and Governance

Society intervention; outcome of the intervention and; implication of the intervention for governance is a big question to be answered by the system in order to understand the system of governance and its role in the social change process.

- Under which context and in relation to which issues do civil society interventions influence the state to be responsive towards the disadvantaged sections?
- How does the state create an environment, as well as conditions for the initiatives of civil society?
- How does the nature of interface of civil society with governance vary at different levels of the state and at different layers of the state institutions?
- How does the state respond to civil society and how the response of the state affects civil society?

- What kind of strategies, approaches and leadership in civil society combine to bring about an impact on governance?
- What kind of alliance and partnership develop between civil society and other players during the intervention and how that influences and enhances the quality of governance?
- What kind of human, institutional, material, and information resources do civil society players need in order to effectively influence governance?
- What type of civil society leadership is crucial in assuring the legitimacy and sustainability of civil society's actions aimed at influencing governance?
- What are the immediate and long-term results of this intervention and what implications do they have for governance?
- How do conflicts and fragmentation within civil society affect the governance?
- Under what kind of political and ideological environment civil society activities can be legitimately and effectively pursued in relation to effective governance?

Conceptual Framework

Civil Society

Though the term has existed since early times, civil society as an intellectual concept gained clarity and lucidity with the advent of modernity in the western world during the seventeenth century. As may intellectual construct, civil society concept evolved with developments in other spheres such as, economy, polity and knowledge. Many events like the growth of the institutions of private property, spread of urbanisation, replacement of the despotic state by the liberal state etc., contributed immensely to the meaning of the term 'civil society'. However, it is the rise of capitalism that led to a clearer distinction between political and non-political and thus prepared ground for the emergence of civil society as a separate domain, to be seen independent from, yet vis-à-vis the state.[1]

The early modern theorists like Hobbes and Locke (Social Contract School) in their writings on the origin of the State, treated civil and political society interchangeably and a direct contrast to the state of nature which was their imaginary construct to describe absolute lawlessness and chaos. The civil/political society was rule bound-putting limitations on individual rights, and bound by civility-mutual respect for other's rights. Both civil and political society was indistinguishable from and reinforced each other. However, these theorists, by putting limitations on the state in the exercise of power and granting autonomy to certain individual rights gave emphasis on the autonomy of the individual in matters related to private property, somehow made a distinction, even if it was not clear, between political and non-political spheres of human existence.

It was Hegel, writing in a different tradition from the liberals, who first clearly distinguished civil society as an intermediate stage between family and the state. The domain of civil society, according to Hegel, was characterised by individuals striving for the fulfillment of their private needs, and the resultant tension and conflict. He, therefore, treated civil society as a transitional stage that needs to be transcended.[2] He saw the possibility of resolving the conflict with in the existing framework of society-state relationship. It was Marx, who rejected the existing framework of society-state in capitalism as capable of resolving the tensions generated in the civil society sphere. He looked at civil society itself to find a force from within, to replace the existing framework.

Since then the concept 'civil society' has been bestowed with many meanings and has undergone many revisions. Some theories of civil society describe it as a 'space' independent of the state. For Seligman, civil society is an ethical ideal which holds the public and the private in a balance.[3] For Tocqueville and more recently for Putnam, civil society is a network of associations and applications which safeguard democratic space between the state and the family.[4]

The second meaning of civil society has arisen from the challenges posed by citizens to communist regimes in Eastern Europe. As citizens began to protest against authoritarian these movements began to represent the aspirations of collective forces of individuals. The thrust of these movements was to democratise the state and fundamental freedoms and liberties for their citizens. In such a formulation, civil society began to be equated with the process of democratisation in political structures and system.

A third approach to the notion of civil society has its roots in the growing universal acceptance of free market and private enterprise as engines of economic development. Public Sector (the state and its institutions) and Private Sector (the for-profit business enterprises) have been undergoing realignments and shifts in their roles and relative contributions to societal development. As questions about the role of the state in economic development began to be raised, there evolved a growing demand for liberating economic activities from the clutches of state hegemony. In this formulation, non-state actors included for-profit private enterprises, just as it included not-for-profit civil society actions. Third Sector (assuming that the state is the first and for-profit business is the second) formation is now being reconceptualised as civil society.

In this paper civil society is defined as the sum of individual and collective initiatives directed towards the pursuit of common public good. This definition of civil society acknowledges the presence of individual initiatives in different cultures. Individual action, howsoever limited and small, contributes to the well-being of society as a whole. This has been reinforced through various religious and spiritual traditions in different societies in different periods and spiritual traditions in different societies in different periods of history. Collective initiatives take on different forms in different periods of history. In today's context, they take on a variety of associational forms based on the nature of association between citizens and their families. Today, traditional associational basis of caste, ethnicity and community are being replaced with more contemporary affiliations based on neighbourhood, profession, class and work place.[5]

This approach to public good, therefore, implies differences, conflicts and contestations in the very meaning of public good. Not only among different classes, but also among the socially and economically disadvantaged groups the nature of public good varies. As result, civil society becomes the space where establishment of common public good is process of struggle between different sections of society.

This approach to understanding civil society, therefore, makes it amply obvious that this is not a virtuous concept promoting good and happiness for all. There are differences and conflicts within civil society, there are inequalities and hegemonic forces operating in the functioning of civil society. This is true at the local and national level just as it is happening in the international arena.

With growing disenchantment of ordinary people with institutions of the government, with declining capacity of these institutions to respond to diverse interests and expectations of their population, with increasing gap in the policies of governments and their practical elaboration, with growing distance with and alienation of the poor and the marginalised from the elite-dominated institutions of government, with continued persistence of problems of poverty, exclusion and marginalisation in many countries of the world, and with growing importance of national and transnational private business interests, the concept of government has now begun to be changed to the concept of governance. In its elementary meaning however, governance, is equated with the functioning of the state and consequently good governance is equated with efficient functioning of the state and its institutions and promotion of equity and social justice.[6]

It is World Bank first brought the concept "good governance" into development discourse in recent years. The Bank's experience of failure of its economic policies in African countries led the Bank to attribute the failure to "bad governance" i.e. administrative inefficiency, corruption, lack of transparency, etc., in the countries. The conceptualisation of "bad governance" then led to the conceptualisation of "good governance" which include parameters like administrative efficiency, rule of law, accountability and transparency. The Bank however, did not associate "good governance" with any particular political regime. This association between "good governance" and democracy is vigorously pushed into the development discourse by the bilateral aid agencies by making aid conditional to promotion of regular election, promotion of human rights and rule of law.

In this paper governance is defined as the joint responsibility of the state, market, and citizens to mobilise public resources and promote public decision-making towards the advancement of common public good.

Good governance, therefore, will entail not only reform of the public services, efficiency and cost effectiveness of public agencies but also ensure participation of the poor, the marginalised and the under-represented. Following points need emphasis for elaborating the elements of good governance:

- universal protection of human rights.
- promotion of equity and equality of opportunity;
- rule of law that is implemented in a non-discriminatory manner;
- efficient, impartial and quick judicial system;
- transparency in functioning of public agencies and officials (right to information);
- accountability of decisions made about public issues and public resources by public leaders and officials;
- devolutions of resources and decision-making power to local levels and bodies in rural and urban areas;
- Participation and inclusion of all citizens in debating public policies and choices.

Main Areas of Governance

The agenda of good governance is vast. The range of issues of governance from local to national level could be myriad. In order to have a focus, we have concentrated on three dimensions of governance:

1. *Public policy*
2. *Accountability.*

1. *Public Policy*

Civil society organisations, nevertheless, have been interrogating and putting pressure on the state to broaden the scope of making public policy exercise to include the interests of the marginalised which are absent in the current policy provisions. At the same time there is an effort towards the implementation of the existing policies and resistance to the policies which are perceived as oppressive. It is believed that many social movements and civil organisations focusing on the issues of environment, gender, health etc., have brought the affected people to the forefront and have pressurised the government to register their opinion. As a result, the top down approach in policy formulation and implementation is influenced from the bottom-up.

2. *Accountability*

The question of accountability like all governance issues is a reflection of the deviation of democratic developmental state from its set procedures and goals. The constitutional granting of democratic rights, promotion of equality, delivery by public institutions, promotion of collective good-in short the responsibility for creation of an environment in which citizens exercise their democratic rights and enhance their life chances by availing the benefits of development endeavours was assumed by the state with much alacrity the opening decades of independence. Needless to say this requires the elected representatives and public officials and institutions to be accountable to the citizens. But despite the democratic form of governance and the constitutional granting of rights, the non-accountability of the state to its citizens, which the state depicts by either observing silence or by continuing it in action, has generated a feeling of discontent among the people towards the state and its agencies. This feeling of discontent has manifested in the contemporary times in the form of collective action in the public sphere.

Civil Society Structure

1. Traditional Associations

Such associations existed around a social unit either defined by a tribe, ethnicity or caste. Associations of this variety undertook a wide range of functions in the lives of those citizens. Besides mediating inter-family relations, such associations developed elaborate systems, norms and procedures for governing the use and protection of natural resources (Tandon, 1996). In the course of state expansion in the past five decades, many of these associations have declined or disintegrated as their legitimacy and resource base was undermined by various state agencies and procedures. Forces of modernisation and capitalist penetration have further weakened such associations. In several tribal areas, such associations still exist[7] PRIA, 1991,

Voluntary Development Organisations in India: A study of History, Roles and Future Challenges, New Delhi

The recent constitutional support to tribal self-rule in local bodies (Panchayats) provides both recognition and support to such associations. Several important struggles to protect and advance customary rights of tribals over natural resources in different parts of the country have been led by such associations.

2. Religious Associations

Religion has always been a way of defining life in India. Over the centuries, new sects and religions were born and incorporated into Indian life. Buddhism, Jainism, Sikhism and many other variations challenged Hinduism. Judaism, Christianity and Islam emphasised on reform and renewal. Charity, help to the needy, service to the poor and *'Daan'* (giving) have been uniformly recommended by all these religions and sects in India. Hence, civil society organisations have clear religious and spiritual inspiration and mandate. Education, heathcare, drinking water, afforestation, social welfare, etc., are numerous arenas of human action where fairly organised forms of civil society activity is carried out by religiously inspired civil society organisations.

3. Social Movements

In contemporary Indian context, a number of social movements have merged as major manifestations of civil society. These movements are of several types:

(a) The first category essentially focuses on the needs and interests of a particular group of people. Historically, Indian society oppressed the tribals (indigenous people), dalits (untouchables) and woman. In the past decade or so, social movements focusing on the interests, concerns and aspirations of tribals, dalits and women have gained ascendancy.

(b) Another form of social movements have been to (protest against a set of practices, institutions, policies or programmes. Social movements to reform social evils have specially been targeting liquor, inheritance rights of women etc.

(c) The development paradigm and programmes have resulted in mass displacements, especially of tribals and rural poor. Social movements have emerged in protest against or to prevent displacements due to development.

Various issues in the protection, preservation and regeneration of environment are triggering social movements throughout the country as well.

(d) A fourth type of social movement has focused upon governance and state accountability. Anti-corruption campaigns against government officials, civil liberties and human rights campaigns, campaigns for right to information, right to education, right to livelihood are some example of this type.

4. Membership Associations

The modern meaning of association is membership. In many modern civil society organisations, therefore, criteria and method of recruiting members, services to members and ways of securing contributing from members are clearly laid down. The degree of formality in membership and the criterion of exclusivity vary greatly across civil society organisation types. In the Indian context, the following types of membership civil society organisations can be identified:

Such membership organisations are primarily set up to represent the opinions and interest of a particular category of citizens. Depending on the strength of the number of their members, such civil society organisations attempt mass memberships and broad coverage to gain visibility, articulate collective and advance common interests. A number of civil society organisations exist as membership organisations around a particular occupation and/or profession. Lawyers, teachers, journalists, doctors, nurses, engineers, managers, all have their membership associations. This category of civil society organisations brings those organisations together which serve an intermediary function among individual citizens, and between them and macro state institutions like the bureaucracy, judiciary, legislature, police, etc. Such associations are typically formed by a group of citizens (generally middle class) to advance a larger societal cause or broader public good. The citizens forming such intermediary associations are not serving their own issues or needs but those of other or broader sections of society. Several types of intermediary organisations are active in India today.

Relationship between Civil Society and the State

Civil society shares a dual relationship with the state. On one hand, a framework of the state defines acceptable public arena for civil society action. State policy, legislation, statutes, institutions are necessary for creating a legitimate playing field for civil society. On the other hand, civil society interface with the state on issues of governance begins to challenges the boundaries of that playing field and this is the very act of influencing governance which attempts to redefine policies, laws nature of institutions. This dialectical relationship between state and civil society is exemplified in the cases discussed earlier. The nature of the state in a democratic political framework, however, makes it further complicated. In one respect, free and fair elections on a periodic basis have been the strength of Indian democracy. Within the margin of acceptable error, collective voice of voters has been the basis of electing ruling elites.

Ignoring and rejecting the interests of vast sections of Indian population by the elected political leaders has also been the character of the democratic Indian state. When civil society interacts with the issues of governance, it begins to challenge the hegemony of the ruling elites in managing the government. In a way, civil society interventions on governance issues question the legitimacy of the duly elected ruling elites. Thereby, civil society interventions on governance issues get challenged by the state as unrepresentative and not legitimate in democratic polity.[8]

As has been pointed our earlier, governance needs to be differentiated from government. Governance includes the institutions of government but goes beyond that to include institutions of civil society and in the changing context of economic liberalisation, it also includes market institutions, both national and international. Civil society attention to this challenge is a broader challenge of deepening democracy in the Indian society and good governance of all public and private institutions. Engagement on good governance agenda, therefore, can only be strengthened when it is seen to be incorporating these different aspects of good governance in the complex and diversified scenario of institutional landscape in public domain in India.

Secondly, the agenda of good governance in a democratic political framework acquires complexity as has been evident from the deliberations on civil society. Historically, civil society assertions have attempted to resist authoritarian regimes or military dictatorships. As part of the process of gaining democratic freedoms for their people, civil society contributions have been acknowledged. However, in an old democracy like India, the challenge for good governance becomes multi-faceted. On the one hand, it implies reforming institutions of the state, on the other, it implies creating a culture in the society, which is consistent with the democratic values and practices. Thus, issues of transparency, accountability, self-managing and self-governance have a societal relevance and not merely limited to government institutions. It is obvious that merely a framework of political democracy is not sufficient. It may provide necessary conditions for good governance to emerge but does not guarantee the same.

Thirdly, the defining agenda of governance is also a matter of concern in a country like India. Given the context of entrenched inequalities of Indian society where people are often invisible and lack voice, mere articulation and amplifying the concern is also a step towards affecting governance, even if no visible impact is discerned.

Fourthly, a well understood dimension of governance agenda demands its follow up, as defined initially till its logical end be it the rights of pavement dwellers for shelter or of informal workers on labour laws or running of primary schools or getting possession of titles to agricultural land. What is rarely appreciated is the evolving nature of that governance agenda. This is particularly so in a dynamic democratic polity where forces and counter-forces coalesce and governance agenda gets transformed. The case of Subarnarekha brings this out eloquently. In many protests against oppressive state policies, civil society actors have contributed to extend, elaborate and expand the governance agenda through their persistent and sustained interventions.

In the context of the poor and the marginalised, the role of civil society in governance has been primarily that of intermediation. Civil society actions have mobilised, and empowered the poor and the marginalised. By accessing authentic information nationally and internationally, civil society has contributed to the empowerment of the local communities. Intermediation has also created opportunity for the voices of the poor and the oppressed to be articulated in the language that the state agencies and officials can understand. The middle class participation in civil society associations of professional and intermediate types in support of the interests of the marginalised and the oppressed has been an interesting and potentially important phenomenon civil society interface with governance in India.[9]

Coalitions of various kinds among civil society associations are formed when they begin focusing on governance issue. This coalitions in civil society are seen as desirable to the extent that they complement each other in their approach, strategies and resources. However, these coalitions approach to influencing governance in India also highlights internal disagreements and conflicts within such coalitions. The inevitable nature of such disagreements poses the challenge of sustaining such coalitions for the explicit purpose of influencing governance without compromising the autonomy, diversity and distinctiveness of each partner in the coalition. What has been under acknowledged in the Indian context is the role of intermediary associations which have acted as an anchor to many such coalitions by providing institutional resources, linkages with different tiers of government, partnerships with academia and media as well as access to international fora. The role of such intermediary associations in contributing towards the effectiveness of civil society coalitions in engaging with governance agenda needs to be appreciated in the Indian context than has been made out so far.[10]

The durability of civil society interventions in engaging on governance agenda is the crucial issue that arises from above. Spontaneous action and nascent coalitions of civil society have asserted themselves to give voice to the excluded and the marginalised; but to sustain that voice, to bring about effective changes in policies, legislations and agencies of implementation of the same requires long-term commitment of effort and resources. In the absence of such capabilities and partnerships within civil society, many civil society interventions on governance remain sporadic and not able to engage with the governance issues in durable and long-term manner.

The institutional and financial bases of civil society, therefore, become important dimensions of attention if such durability of interventions on governance agenda has to be promoted. Bulk of the civil society actors are under-organised. Most of them are constituted around specific temporary issues. Even formally organised civil society initiatives lack institutional capabilities and financial resources at a scale needed to address the complex governance agendas as they emerge in the coming period.

The material base of many intermediary associations in the Indian context comprises of public resources drawn from various agencies, departments and programmers of the government as well as resources accessed from the community and international sources. This material base needs to be strengthened and rooted more widely in the Indian society if civil society engagement on governance has to be promoted. The conflicts of interests created by material base in international funding, on the one hand, and that derived from the government agencies, on the other, restrict the ability of civil society organisations to engage effectively on a long-term basis.

The challenges civil society actors faces in influencing governance are many. These challenges demand the broadening of sphere to include different types of formations in civil society. Particular challenges are faced in terms of linkages with religiously inspired civil society associations as well as with the traditional associational types, where there is convergence of purpose around a specific governance issue. Similarly, incorporating smaller, local, under-organised citizens' associations in such coalitions pose particular challenges in Indian context. It also necessitates incorporating differences of perception and opinion and resolving the competing and in many instances conflicting issues related to ideology and leadership. Meeting the material needs becomes particularly challenging for the unorganised civil society such social movements and community-based small groups. Thus, the strength of civil society actors to pursue the governance agenda depends on their ability and willingness to forge alliance with those who hold different opinions, strong and mutually supportive leadership and a strong material base.[11]

Notes

1. Zelhiot, Eleanor, 1970, Learning the use of Political Means: The Mahars of Maharashtra, in Kothari, Rajini (ed.), *Caste in India Politics,* Orient Longman, New Delhi.
2. Rudolph, Lloyd I and Rudolph, Susanne H., 1987, *In pursuit of Lakshmi: The Political Economy of the India State,* Chicago University Press, Chicago.
3. Seligman, Adam, 1995, The *Idea of Civil Society,* Princeton University Press, Princeton.
4. Tocqueville, Alexis de, *Democracy in America, Translated by H.Keene,* The Colonial Press, New York.
5. Haynes, J., 1997, *Democracy and Civil Society in the Third World: Politics and New Political Movements,* Polity Press, Cambridge.
6. Uphoff, Norman, 1995, Why NGOs are not a Third Sector: A Sectoral Analysis with Same Thoughts on Accountability, Sustainability and Evaluation, in Michael, Edward and Hulme, David (eds). *Non-Governmental Organisations: Performance and Accountability,* Earth Scan Publication, London.
7. PRIA, 1991, *Voluntary Development Organisations in India: A study of History, Roles and Future Challenges,* New Delhi.
8. Kohli, Atul (ed.), 1988, Interpreting India's Democracy: A State-Society Framework, *in Kohli, Atul (ed.), India's Democracy: An Analysis of Changing State-Society Relation,* Princeton University Press, NJ.
9. Naidu, Kumi and Tandon Rajesh, 1999, The Promise of Civil Society, *in Civil Society at the Millennium,* CIVICUS, Kumarin Press.
10. Bardhan, Pranab, 1988, *Dominant Proprietary Classes and India's Democracy,* in Kohli, Atul (ed.), 1988, *India's Democracy: An Analysis of Changing State-Society Relation,* Princeton University Press, NJ.
11. Ahluwalia, I.J. and Little, L.M.D. (eds.), 1998, *India's Economic Reform and Development: Essays for Manmohan Singh,* Oxford University Press, Delhi.

13

Social Change: Characteristics and Factors

Devi Prasad Srivastava

Social change refers to an alteration in the social order of a society. Social change may include changes in nature, social institutions, social behaviours, or social relations. It also refer to the notion of social progress or sociocultural evolution, the philosophical idea that society moves forward by dialectical or evolutionary means. It may refer to a paradigmatic change in the socio-economic structure, for instance a shift away from feudalism and towards capitalism. Accordingly, it may also refer to social revolution, such as the Socialist revolution presented in Marxism, or to other social movements, such as Women's suffrage or the Civil rights movement. Social change may be driven by cultural, religious, economic, scientific or technological forces. Developmental psychology can play a role in social change. Developmental psychology is essential in looking at the history of magic, religion, science, morals, law, politics, the economy, and more. Without this, instead of a rise in industrial technology and medical advances, humans could still be thinking with cave-man-like thinking.

Theories of Social Change

Change comes from two sources. One source is random or unique factors such as climate, weather, or the presence of specific groups of people. Another source is systematic factors. For example, successful development has the same general requirements, such as a stable and flexible government, enough free and available resources, and a diverse social organisation of society. So, on the whole, social change is usually a combination of systematic factors along with some random or unique factors.

There are many theories of social change. Generally, a theory of change should include elements such as structural aspects of change (like population shifts), processes and mechanisms of social change, and directions of change.

Hegelian: The classic Hegelian dialectic model of change is based on the interaction of opposing forces. Starting from a point of momentary stasis, Thesis countered by Antithesis first yields conflict, then it subsequently results in a new synthesis.

Marxist: Marxism presents a dialectical and materialist concept of history; Humankind's history is a fundamental struggle between social classes.

Kuhnian: The philosopher of science, Thomas Kuhn argues in The Structure of Scientific Revolutions with respect to the Copernican Revolution that people are likely to continue utilising an apparently unworkable paradigm until a better paradigm is commonly accepted.

Heraclitan: The Greek philosopher Heraclitus used the metaphor of a river to speak of change thus, "On those stepping into rivers staying the same other and other waters flow" (DK22B12). What Heraclitus seems to be suggesting here, later interpretations notwithstanding, is that, in order for the river to remain the river, change must constantly be taking place. Thus, one may think of the Heraclitan model as parallel to that of a living organism, which, in order to remain alive, must constantly be changing. A contemporary application of this approach is shown in the social change theory SEED-SCALE which builds off of the Complexity Theory subfield of Emergence.

Daoist: The Chinese philosophical work Dao De Jing, I.8 and II.78 uses the metaphor of water as the ideal agent of change. Water, although soft and yielding, will eventually wear away stone. Change in this model is to be natural, harmonious and steady, albeit imperceptible.

Some Major Current Social Changes

One of the most obvious changes currently occurring is the change in the relative global population distribution between countries. In the recent decades, developing countries became a larger proportion of world population, increasing from 68 per cent in 1950 to 82 per cent in 2010, while population of the developed countries has declined from 32 per cent of total world population in 1950 to 18 per cent in 2010. China and India continue to be the largest countries, followed by the US as a distant third. However, population growth throughout the world is slowing. Population growth among developed countries has been slowing since the 1950s, and is now at 0.3 per cent annual growth. Population growth among the less developed countries excluding the least developed has also been slowing, since 1960, and is now at 1.3 per cent annual growth. Population growth among the least developed countries has not really slowed, and is the highest at 2.7 per cent annual growth.

Gendered Patterns of Work and Care

In much of the developed world, changes from distinct men's and women's work to more gender equal patterns have been economically important since the mid twentieth century. Change is a process. Change denotes any alternation, difference or modification that takes place in a situation or in any object through time. It is the universal law of nature. It refers to the difference that exists between the past and the present situation. Change is an "on-going" process. No society remains completely static. Society is subject to constant changes. The term social change refers to changes taking place in human society. Basically the changes in human interactions and inter-relations, indicate social change. Society is the net-work of social relationship. Hence, social change obviously implies a change in the system of social relationship. So any difference or any modification or transformation in the established pattern of human interaction and standards of conduct amounts to change. Abolition of child marriage, inter-caste marriage, high status to Indian women is some of the important instances of social change.

Characteristics

(1) Change is Social

Social change means a change in the system of social relationship. Social relationship is understood in terms of social process, social interactions and social organisations. So in any variation of social process, social interactions and social organisations social change-takes place. In an another instance it is found that society is like an organisation, which never dies. New civilisations and societies come up by replacing old societies and thereby retaining some of its elements in its change. Thus, social change is different from individual change. Its cause and consequences are always social which make it social.

(2) Universal

Social change is universal. Because it is present in all societies and at all times. No society remains completely static. The society may be primitive or modern, rural or urban, simple or complex, agrarian or industrial, it is constantly undergoing change. The rate or the degree of change may vary from society to society from time to time but every society keeps on changing. A changeless society is an unreality.

(3) Continuous

Social change is a continuous process but not an intermittent process. Because the changes are neither stopped nor the societies are kept in museum to save them from change. It is an on-going process without any break. In the process of change every society grows and decays, where it finds renewal and accommodates itself to various changing conditions. The sources, direction, rate and forms of change may vary time to time but it is always continuous.

(4) Inevitable

Change is inevitable. It is the human nature that desires change and also it is his tendency to bring change and to oppose or accept change. Human wants are unlimited which always keep on changing. To satisfy these wants social change has become a necessity not only to him but also to the society.

(5) Temporal

Social change is temporal. Change in anything or any object or in a situation takes place through time. Time is the most important factor and social change denotes time-sequence. According to Maclver, "It is a becoming, not a being; a process, not a product". Innovation of new things, modification and renovations of the existing behaviour take time. So a social change is temporary or permanent on the basis of time. Sometimes some social changes may bring about immediate results while some others may take years to produce results. Similarly, some social changes spread rapidly and also disappear rapidly. Movements, style, fashion and cults are the examples of this type. But in the biological process of ageing short time does not cause change.

(6) Degree or rate of change is not uniform

Though social change is an ever-present phenomenon, its degree or rate or what we call the speed is not uniform. It varies from society to society and even in the same society from time to time. Sometimes the degree of change is high and sometimes low depending upon the nature of society like open and close, rural and urban and traditional and modern etc. For example, in the rural social structure the rate of change is slower because the rate of change is not governed by any universal law, whereas it is quick in the urban societies.

(7) Social Change may be planned or unplanned

Social change takes place sometimes with planning and sometimes without planning. Social change which occurs in the natural course is called the unplanned change. The unplanned changes are spontaneous, accidental or the product of sudden decision. Usually the change resulting from natural calamities like flood, drought, famines, volcanic eruption, etc. are the instances of unplanned changes. Here in this unplanned change there is no control on the degree and direction of social change. It is the inborn tendency of human beings that they desire change. So sometimes plans, programmes and projects are made effective by them to bring change in the society. This is called planned change. As it is consciously and deliberately made, there is every possibility to have control on the speed and direction of change. For example, the five years plan made by the government.

(8) Social change is multi-causal

A single factor may cause a particular change but it is always associated with a number of factors. The physical, biological, demographical, cultural, technological and many other factors interact to generate change. This is due to mutual interdependence of social phenomenon.

(9) Social change creates chain-reactions

Social change produces not a single reaction but chain-reactions as all the parts of the society are inter-related and interdependent. For example, the economic independence of women has brought changes not only in their status but also a series of changes in home, family relationship and marriages etc.

(10) Prediction is uncertain

We can see some elements for prediction in social change. But the prediction we make is uncertain. It is because of three reasons. They are:

(a) There is no inherent law of social change.

(b) The forces of social change may not remain on the scene for all times to come.

(c) The process of social change does not remain uniform.

Apart from the above characteristic features it may be said that social change can be qualitative or quantitative. It is a value free term as it does imply any sense of good or bad, desirable or undesirable. It is a concept distinct from evolution, process and development which are regarded as key concepts in the literature of social change.

Factors of Social Change

Social change takes place in all societies and in all periods of time. But here question arises why does social change takes place? The word 'Why' represents the reasons, the causes or the factors which are responsible for social change. From the discussion of the nature of social change we know that there are some potential factors responsible for bringing social change. Hence, it is multi-causal. Cause refers to a set of related factors which, taken together, are both sufficient and necessary for the production of certain effect. Here it is necessary to take up each factor by itself and to find out the way in which it affects social change. Some of these factors are shown in the following diagram:

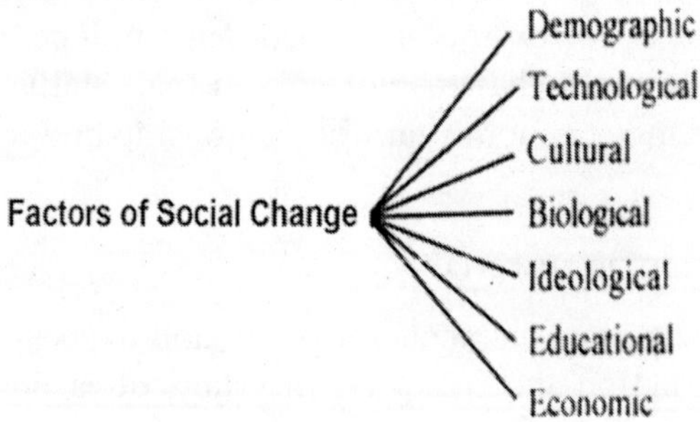

Demographic Factors:

Demography plays an important role in the process of social change. The term "demography" has been derived from two Greek words, 'Demos' and 'Graphs' meaning the "people" and to "draw" or "write" respectively. The dictionary meaning of demography is the scientific study of human population, primarily with respect to their size, structure and their development. In the study of social change, demographic factors have been viewed from two different angles. They are the qualitative and quantitative. Qualitatively speaking it refers to physical potentialities, mental abilities etc. that are determined by genetic order, though the hereditary quality of successive generation play some role in cultural determination, it cannot be ascribed the place of a deterministic cause of social change. But the demographic factor in its quantitative aspect has been playing the most decisive role in causing social change. The quantitative view of demography takes into account, the size, composition and density of human population that are determined by natural reproduction, migration and social mobility. This aspect has been acknowledged by many past as well as modern thinkers. There are three important factors that determine the rise, fall or density of population. They are:

(a) High Fertility (High Birth Rate)

(b) Low Morality (Low Death Rate)

(c) Migration

When there is high birth rate and the death rate is low, we find growth in population Let us know few points regarding the causes of high birth rate. They are given in the following table:

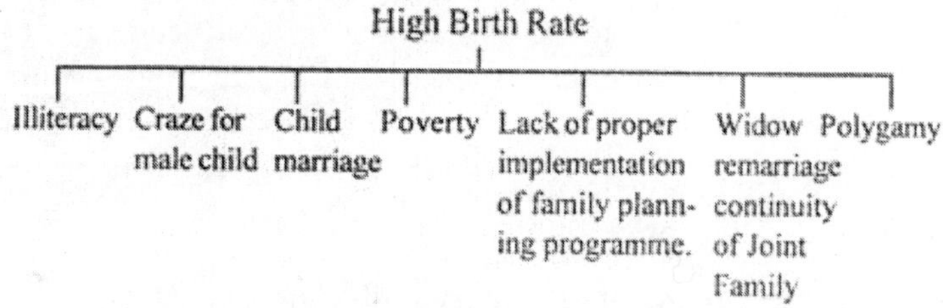

(a) From the above table it is found that population increases due to illiteracy, popularity of child marriage, widow remarriage, polygamy, craze for a male child, poverty and also because of lack of proper implementation of family planning programmes. The fall in death rate has also affected the growth of population. There are many causes of low mortality or low death rate. They are modern education and scientific knowledge to hygiene, better sanitation and therapeutic and preventive medicines, the increase of productivity which raises the standard of living, control of natural calamities, control of nutrition of mother, maternity facilities etc.

(b) Excess growth of population accelerates the process of migration. Migration refers to the process of movement of population from one place to another for considerable period of time. It plays a significant role in population growth in the history for the past 100 years or more. There are four forms of migration. They are:

   (i) **Immigration:** It refers to migration into a country.

(ii) **Emigration:** It refers to migration of a country.

(iii) **In-migration** refers to migration into a particular area.

(iv) **Out-migration** refers to movement out of a particular area. Thus, migrants who come from Bihar to Odisha are considered to be immigrants for Odisha and out-migrants for Bihar.

There are many factors contributing to the process of migration. They are:

(a) Development of transport and communication.

(b) Natural calamities like earthquake, flood, famine etc.

(c) Absence of restrictions on social mobility.

(d) Non-availability of land and vocational opportunities etc. So the changes in population have a far-reaching effect on society. It has both positive and negative effects.

Positive Effects

(a) The growth of population has a direct bearing upon the availability and utilisation of resources.

(b) More population brings about more innovations and discoveries.

(c) It encourages rapid growth in industrialisation and urbanisation.

(d) The high birth rate and an alarming growth in population also stimulates attitude towards birth, death and family life.

(e) Due to growth of population Acts are passed by the government for the control of population. For example, in India, due to rapid population growth, the government has introduced family planning programmes.

Negative Effects

(a) The growth of population has decreased the standard of living of the people in the society.

(b) The growth of population has given birth to a variety of problems like poverty, unemployment, child labour, crime, juvenile delinquency and beggary.

(c) Increase in population leads to an increase of social differentiation and division of labour.

(d) It brings destructive social conflict and disorganisation in migrants line.

(e) In the societies where the female population exceeds the male population, polygamy may flourish and on the other hand, if the number of males exceeds the females, polyandry is likely to prevail.

From the above discussion we find that demography plays a significant role in the socio-economic and political transformation of society. It certainly brings drastic changes not only in the micro-structures but also in macro-structures.

Biological Factors

Social change is a complex process. It is caused by multiple factors. All factors of social change are closely related to each other. But at the same time each individual factor brings change in society in its own way. Accordingly, biological factor plays an important role in the causation of social change. An ordinarily biological factor refers to those which are concerned with the genetic constitution of the human beings.

A biological factor includes both non-human beings such as animals, birds, herbs, insects, plants etc. and human beings. Human beings use animals, birds, plants and herbs according to the direction of his own culture. At the same time human beings protect themselves from different harmful elements.

If there is increase or decrease of these animals, birds, plants etc. it will bring a number of changes in human society.

Rapid decline of useful animals, birds and plants will also create a number of problems in human society and influences social change. Similarly, rapid increase or decrease of population also brings a number of changes in society. Different biological process like human procreation, fertility and mortality also influence the rate of change in a society. Size, density, migration, immigration etc. bring a number of changes in society.

Rapid population growth influences our environment causes poverty, food shortage and multiple health problems and thereby brings changes in society. Migration accelerate the process of urbanisation. Urbanisation creates multiple problems like slum, quality of health and life style. Increasing urbanisation and declining number of useful animal and birds affects our environment.

Similarly, the nature and quality of human beings in a society influences the rate of social change. Sociologist like Pareto opines that the biological evolution of mankind brings social changes. Elites in a society are determined by inherited biological instincts. Besides composition of population also influences social change.

Both age composition and sex composition are very closely related to social change. Number of population in the productive age group deeply influences the rate and speed of social change. If the number of child and unproductive or ageing population increases, a country faces a number of economic problems. If the number of ageing population decreases, the youths may be deprived of wisdom and experience which resulted in slow change.

Besides the process of natural selection, social selection also affects the rate and speed of social change. The process of natural selection works through twin alternatives like adaptation and annihilation. Here man is required to adapt to natural environment. But in social selection the forces created within human society and operating through human relationships creates situations that deeply affect the reproduction process and survival rates of population.

Cultural Factors

In sociology, the word 'Culture' denotes acquired behaviour which are shared by and transmitted among the members of the society. Man learns his behaviour and behaviour which is learnt is called culture. Singing, dancing, eating, playing belong to the category of culture.

It includes all that man has acquired in the mental and intellectual sphere of his individual and social life. It is the expression of our nature, in our modes of living and thinking, in our everyday intercourse, in art, in literature, in recreation and enjoyment. For the clear understanding of the term 'Culture' here, it is necessary to discuss some of the important definitions of culture.

Definitions

According to White, "Culture is a symbolic, continuous, cumulative and progressive process."

Malinowski defines culture, "as the handiwork of man and as the medium through which he achieves his end."

Maclver and Page defines, "Culture is the realm of styles, of values, of emotional attachments, of intellectual adventures."

In the words of Green, "Culture is the socially transmitted system of idealised ways in knowledge, practices and beliefs, along with the artifacts that knowledge and practice produce and maintain as they change in time."

Culture, as is defined by Tylor, refers to, "that complex whole which includes knowledge, belief, art, morals, law, customs and any other capabilities and habits acquired by man as a member of society."

From the above definitions of culture, the features of culture may be summarised below. They are:

(1) Culture is social, but not individual.

(2) Culture is idealistic.

(3) Culture is communicative.

(4) Culture is an acquired quality.

(5) Culture meets the recurring demand of mankind.

(6) Culture has the characteristics of adaptation.

(7) Culture has the quality of becoming integrated.

Culture plays a very significant role in social change. No culture even remains constant. It always keeps on changing. So it is treated as an important source or instrument of social change. The very nature of culture makes it dynamic. The terms like continuous, cumulative adoptive, transmissive etc. signify the elements of dynamism within the culture. Besides, there are host of other internal and external variables that interact upon the culture and cause changes within it.

Change in culture takes place by three important factors. They are discovery, invention and diffusion. A discovery may be a material item or a non-material item. But any discovery brings about social change only when it is widely used. An invention generates pressure for change in different parts of social life. Diffusion is the process by which cultural traits spread from one culture to another or from one part of culture to another. It is a two-way process. Because in this process one culture gives something to the other and at the same time takes something from it.

Several sociologists have highlighted the determining role of culture effecting social change. Some of the important effects are given below. They are:

(i) Culture gives speed and direction to social change: If the culture is too much conservative, then its rate of change becomes too low and vice versa. People whether accept change or not depends upon their attitudes and values which are the products of the culture.

(ii) Culture influences the direction and character of technological change: Our belief and social institutions not only correspond to the changes in technology but these determine the use to which the technological inventions will be put. It is the culture that decides the purpose to which a technical invention must be put.

(iii) Culture shapes economy and is effective towards economic growth: Culture not only gives direction to technology but it shapes the economy which is too much effective towards economic growth.

(iv) It keeps the social relationship intact: It makes people think not of their own but also of the others. By regulating the behaviour of the people and satisfying their primary drives pertaining to hunger, shelter and sex, it has been able to maintain group life.

Concept of Cultural Lag

To examine the role of cultural factors in social change, it is necessary to discuss the concept of "Cultural Lag".

W.F. Ogburn, an American sociologist introduced the concept of 'Cultural Lag' in his book "Social Change" which was published in the year 1920. The word 'lag' connotes crippled movement. Hence cultural lag means the flatering of one aspect of culture behind another. According to Ogburn there are two aspects of culture. One is the material and another one is the non-material.

(i) Material Culture: It includes those elements or things which are tangible, visible and touchable like goods, tools, machines and furnitures etc.

(ii) Non-material Culture: It includes those elements which are neither tangible nor touchable rather these are experienced by men like customs, values, ideologies, religion and behaviour pattern etc. It is found that technological innovations and discoveries stimulate the material culture to a great extent. As a result, the changes are quick in material culture. But non-material culture responds very slowly to such changes in material culture. So the material culture goes ahead leaving behind the non-material culture. This is called the "cultural lag". For example, The development in the field of industry requires a corresponding change in the system of education. The failure of education to meet the needs of modern industrial development leads to cultural lag.

Causes of Cultural Lag

What is the cause of this cultural lag?

Regarding the answer we find many factors causing cultural lag.

They are:

(1) Difference in the degrees of changeability of various elements of culture.

(2) Changes in law.

(3) Man's psychological dogmatism.

Criticisms

The theory of 'cultural lag' of Ogburn is not free from the criticisms.

(a) There is no clear-cut distinction between material and non-material culture. Again, it is not necessary that non-material culture should invariably lag behind material culture.

(b) A major defect in Ogburn's theory is that he uses the "cultural lag" for expanding all gaps in the process of social change. Maclver has suggested the use of different terms for the various types of disequilibrium and conflicts, such as technological lag, technological restraint and cultural clash etc.

(c) According to the theory of cultural lag, while one thing progresses forward, another lags. Hence this word should not be used in the context of those objects which are the encouraging as well as the restraining and are similar and possess a common standard of evaluation.

(d) Finally, Ogburn has not provided any standard or scale to measure the units of material and non-material culture. So it is difficult to find out whether one aspect of culture changes faster than the other or not.

Inspite of the above short-comings, the theory of "cultural lag" of Ogburn has been proved to be beneficial for understanding the cultural factors in bringing about social change.

Technological Factors

The technological factors also play important role in causing social change. Then what is technology? How it brings social change? In the study of sociology, technology has a wider connotation. It implies an appropriate organisation and systematic application of scientific knowledge to meet the human requirements. Technology is a product of utilisation. When the scientific knowledge is applied to the problems of life, it becomes technology. Technology is fast growing. Modern age is the "Age of Technology".

According to W.F. Ogburn, "Technology changes society by changing our environments to which we in turn adopt. This change is usually in the material environment and the adjustment that we make with these changes often modifies customs and social institution initiates a corresponding social change.

Sources of Technological Change

There are mainly two important sources of technological change. They are:

(i) Inventions.

(ii) Discovery.

(i) **Inventions:** Invention denotes creation of new ways of using existing knowledge or new ways of combining existing artifacts. A single invention in technology can produce a large scale change in society. One important example of invention is the invention of automobile.

(ii) **Discovery:** Discovery means the new way of looking at the environment. Technological innovation originates also from another source called discovery.

Example, Discovery of modern medicines is the result of discoveries in biology and partly the result of invention.

Invention and discovery are significant characteristic of our age. Apart from these two, there are three technological factors which are mainly responsible for social change.

They are:

(a) Technological Innovations.

(b) Changes in production technology.

(c) Changes in transportation and communication.

(a) Technological Innovations: The technological innovations have brought about revolutionary changes in man's idea about the world and universe. The world is no more a mysterious creation for man because even in case of the natural calamities like flood, cyclone, earthquake and drought etc. are no more being viewed as the divine punishments against man's bad deeds. No man has been able to find out their causes. As a result of which the degree of gaining control over them has increased.

(b) **Changes in production technology:** Invention of new agricultural tools and chemical measures has led to the gradual development of an agrarian system. Industrialisation has caused a number of changes in family, status of women, mode of living of people, religion and ideologies of people etc. It has also led to the growth of urban centres with new types of social organisation.

(c) **Changes in transportation and communication:** Rapid development in transportation and communication has greatly influenced the socio-cultural life. It has broken down the regional barriers. Due to transportation world wide trade and commerce has been possible and communication technology has increased national awakening. Apart from the above factors, cultural factors play significant role in bring about technological change. Customs, traditions, folkways, mores habits, conservatism etc. have resisted the technological inventions and contribute to it.

Effects of Technology

No device, technological or otherwise, whether originating within a society or borrowed from outside, obviously set up a network of effects. The status of the individual is no more ascribed rather achieved. A man is judged in what he has, not what he is. The social relation is gradually becoming superficial, temporary as well as selfish by nature. Changes in technology have resulted in some fundamental changes in social structure. The impact of technological changes may be discussed under the following broad headings.

Technology and Different Process

(a) Industrialisation: Industrialisation refers to the process by which industries have been set up. It has given birth to the factory system and replaced domestic system.

The invention of machines has led to the creation of big factories which employ thousands of people and where most of the work is performed automatically. It has created new social class and has improved the condition of women. It has affected the nature, character and the growth of economy.

(b) Urbanisation: Industrialisation has led to urbanisation. As a result of industrialisation people have started moving towards the industrial areas, the areas neither very far from the cities nor from the villages with the hope of getting employment in those industries and factories. Hence only when a large portion of inhabitants in an area comes to cities, urbanisation is said to occur. Towns like Kanpur, Jamshedpur and Ahmadabad in India owe their birth to the factories established there.

(c) Modernisation: It is a process by which adoption of the modern ways of life and values take place. It has brought about remarkable changes in social relationship and installed new ideologies in the place of traditional areas. It has changed the social structure, which adds impetus to the growth of science and technology. As a result of which the rate of change increases rapidly.

Technology and Social Life

The changes in technology have changed the whole gamut of social life. It has performally altered our modes of life and thought. The different institutions which are already changed may be discussed below one by one. They are:

(a) Caste: Due to technological changes the structure as well as the functions of caste are already changed.

(i) The ascribed status has been replaced by achieved status.

(ii) There is no restriction on food, water as well as social relationship.

(iii) Marriage under caste system is no more endogamous.

(iv) Hereditary occupational structure has been replaced by occupation based on one's own choice depending on one's own capacity, ability and talent.

(b) Joint Family: Indian traditional family which was purely of joint pattern has started changing its size, structure and functions by the impact of technology.

(i) Change in its unity and natural co-operation of its members.

(ii) Change in the control and rub of Karta.

(iii) Fragmentation of land or distribution of common property.

(iv) It has lost its importance and has started disintegrating day by day.

(c) Marriage: Marriage is an important institution which has been undergoing tremendous changes due to the impact of technology.

(i) It has lost its sanctity.

(ii) It is treated more as a civil contract than a sacred bond.

(iii) It is becoming more and more unstable.

(iv) The rate of divorce is increasing rapidly day by day.

(d) Religion: Religion has undergone the following changes:

(i) The role of superstition has been declined.

(ii) People are becoming more and more secular, rational and scientific in their outlook.

(iii) Conservative or orthodox religious activities have been replaced by simple activities.

(iv) The religious toleration among the people has been destroyed.

(e) State: State have undergone the following changes:

(i) State have become secular in nature.

(ii) There is a shift of functions from local government to the central government of the whole state.

(iii) Modern inventions have strengthened nationalism.

(iv) It has increased the size and power of bureaucracy.

References

1. Eisenstadt, SN (1973). *Tradition, Change, and Modernity.* Krieger Publishing.
2. Giddens, A (2006). Sociology. Cambridge: Polity Press.
3. Haralambos, M and Holborn, M (2004). *Sociology: Themes and Perspectives.*
4. Directory of Social Change (DSC) –Civil Society – Directory –providing news and in-depth coverage of charities, voluntary organisations and not-for-profits". Civil Society. Retrieved 6 July 2012.
5. The Directory of Social Change –IFC Wiki. Wiki.internationalfundraisingconsultancy.com. 25 June 2010. Retrieved 6 July 2012.
6. Directory of Social Change, Report and Financial Statements for the year ended 31 December 2010, Directory of Social Change, 2010, London: Harper Collins.

14

Constitutional Provisions for the Protection and Development of Scheduled Tribes in India

Saurabh Chandra

Introduction

The Scheduled Tribes (STs) is an official assignment given to a deprived and primitive community in India. The term is perceived in the Constitution of India. Article 366(25) of the Constitution of India defines Scheduled Tribes as those communities, who are scheduled in accordance with Article 342 of the Constitution. This Article says that only those communities who have been declared as such by the President through an initial public notification or through a subsequent amending Act of Parliament will be considered to be Scheduled Tribes. The list of Scheduled Tribes is State/UT specific and a community declared as a Scheduled Tribe in a State need not be so in another State/UT. The essential characteristics, first laid down by the Lokur Committee, for a community to be identified as Scheduled Tribes are –

- indications of primitive traits;
- distinctive culture;
- shyness of contact with the community at large;
- geographical isolation; and
- backwardness.

The 1991 Census figures reveal that 42.02 per cent of the Scheduled Tribes populations were main workers of whom 54.50 per cent were cultivators and 32.69 per cent agricultural labourers. Thus, about 87 per cent of the main workers from these communities were engaged in primary sector activities. The literacy rate of Scheduled Tribes is around 29.60 per cent, as against the national average of 52 per cent. More than three-quarters of Scheduled Tribes women are illiterate. These disparities are compounded by higher dropout rates in formal education resulting in disproportionately low representation in higher education. Not surprisingly, the cumulative effect has been that the proportion of Scheduled Tribes below the poverty line is substantially higher than the national average. The estimate of poverty made by Planning Commission for the year 1993-94 shows that 51.92 per cent rural and 41.4 per cent urban Scheduled Tribes were still living below the poverty line.

The framers of the Constitution took note of the fact that certain communities in the country were suffering from extreme social, educational and economic backwardness arising out of age-old practice of Untouchability and certain others on account of this primitive agricultural practices, lack of infrastructure facilities and geographical isolation, and who need special consideration for safeguarding their interests and for their accelerated socio-economic development. These communities were notified as Scheduled Tribes as per provisions contained in Clause 1 of Articles 341 and 342 of the Constitution respectively. The Constitution of India incorporates several special provisions for the promotion of educational and economic interest of Scheduled Tribes and their protection from social injustice and all forms of exploitation.

Provisions in the Constitution for the Protection and Development of Schedule Tribes in India

Established procurements are living instruments to lit the light of the lights for tribes. These are the foundation of Scheduled Tribes and also for others in reverse classes. To stroll for a handiwork individual, strolling stick is essential, similar to this to remain for the tribes' kin protected shields are vital. Protected composers made a few procurements for the advancement of tribes' kin. It was the credit of Dr B.R. Ambedkar who had confronted with a few issues from conception to death of his life on account of social indecencies rehearses.

The constitutional provisions for STs can be categorised into five categories:

(i) Educational and Cultural Rights (Articles 14, 15, 15(4), 16, 17, 29, 46 and 350.)

(ii) Social Rights (Articles 21, 21A, 23, 24, 16(4), 335)

(iii) Economic Rights (Articles 244, 244A and 275)

(iv) Political Rights (Articles 164, 330, 332, 243D and 243T, 338A, 341 and 342)

(v) Employment Rights [Articles 15(5), 16(4) and 16(4A)].

Educational and Cultural Rights [Articles 14, 15, 15(4), 16, 17, 29, 46 and 350)]

Article 14: Equality before law and equal protection law.

Article 15: Prohibition of discrimination on the ground of religion, race, caste, sex or place of birth.

Article 15(4): The State is permitted to make any special provision for the advancement of the SCs/STs.

Article 15(5): The state is empowered to make any special provision for the advancement of the SCs/STs regarding their admission to educational institutions (including STs) both in public or private, aided or unaided school by the state, except the minority educational institutions.

Article 16: Equal opportunity in matters of public employment.

Article 17: Abolition of Untouchability and prohibition of its practice.

Article 29: Protection of language, script, and culture of minorities through educational institutions including STs.

Article 46: Directive Principle of State Policy directed to the leaders in future to promote educational and economic interests of STs and protect them from social injustice and types of exploitation.

Article 350: The Constitution also gives right to every person to submit a representation for the redress of grievance to any officer or authority of the Union or a State in any of the languages used in the Union or in the States as the case may be.

Social Rights (Articles 21, 21A, 23, 24, 16(4), and 335)

Article 21: Protection of life and personal liberty (including STs).

Article 21A: Right to elementary education (Including STs).

Article 23: It prohibits the system of bonded labour in human being and forced labour.

Article 24: It prohibits employment of children below the age of 14 years in factories and hazardous employment.

Article 16(4) and Art. 335: Reservation of seats by ST in public services and in employment under the State. Under Article 335, belonging to SCs/STs can claims to services and posts.

Economic Rights (Articles 244, 244A and 275)

Article 244: Article 244 in part X of the Constitution envisages a special system of administration for certain areas designated as 'scheduled areas' and 'tribal areas'.

Article 244A: It deals with the formation of an autonomous state comprising certain tribal areas in Assam and creation of local legislature or council of ministers or both.

Article 275: The Union Government can provide the special grants for the welfare of STs.

Political Rights (Articles 164, 330, 332, 243D and 243T, 341 and 342)

Article 164: It empowers the State to establish special Ministry for welfare of the Scheduled Tribes in Bihar, Madhya Pradesh, and Orissa.

Article 330: Reservation of seats for Scheduled Castes and Scheduled Tribes in the House of the People (Lok Sabha).

Article 332: It deals with the reservation of seats for Scheduled Castes and Scheduled Tribes in the State Legislative Assembly.

Article 243D and 243T: It deals with the reservation of seats in Panchayati-raj Institutions and Municipality for SCs/STs respectively.

Article 338A: Under 89th Constitutional Amendment Act of 2003 a new Article 338A is added to form a separate National Commission for STs. The separate National Commission for STs came into existence in 2004.

Article 342: The President has the power to specify the tribes in relation to a State or Union Territory.

Employment Rights [Articles 15(4), 16(4) and 16(4A)]

Article 15(5): It provides reservations to scheduled tribes in the educational institutions.

Articles 16(4) and 16(4A): It provides reservations to scheduled tribes in the employment and promotions.

Fifth and Sixth Schedules of the Constitution

Article 244: The provisions relating to the administration and control of the Scheduled Areas and Scheduled Tribes in any state, other than Assam, Meghalaya, Tripura and Mizoram are contained in the Fifth Schedule to the Constitution (Fifth Schedule).

Articles 244 and 275: It deals with the provisions relating to the administration of tribal areas in the states of Assam, Meghalaya, Tripura and Mizoram (Sixth Schedule). These four states have been constituted as autonomous district. It provides for autonomous districts and autonomous regions. The governor is empowered to organise and reorganise the autonomous district. He can increase or decrease their areas. Each autonomous district has a district council consisting of 30 members, of whom four are nominated by the governor and the remaining 26 are elected on the basis of adult franchise. The elected members are elected for five years and nominated members hold office during the pleasure of the governor.

The National Commission for Scheduled Tribes

The National Commission for Scheduled Tribes (NCST) was established by amending Article 338 and inserting a new Article 338A in the Constitution through the Constitution (89th Amendment) Act, 2003. By this amendment, the erstwhile National Commission for Scheduled Castes and Scheduled Tribes was replaced by two separate Commissions namely: (i) the National Commission for Scheduled Castes (NCSC), and (ii) the National Commission for Scheduled Tribes (NCST) w.e.f. 19 February, 2004. Detailed background information about the historical evolution of the National Commission has been given in Chapter-1 of the first Report of the Commission for the year 2004-05 and 2005-06.

Functions of the Commission

[Under Clause (5) of Art. 338A]

To investigate and Monitor matters relating to Safeguards provided for STs under the Constitution or under other laws or under Govt. Order, to evaluate the working of such Safeguards.

To inquire into specific complaints relating to Rights and Safeguards of STs;

To participate and advise in the Planning Process relating to Socio-economic development of STs, and to evaluate the progress of their development under the Union and any State;

To submit report to the President annually and at such other times as the Commission may deem fit, upon/working of Safeguards, Measures required for effective implementation of Programmes/Schemes relating to Welfare and Socio-economic development of STs;

To discharge such other functions in relation to STs as the President may, subject to the provisions of any law made by Parliament, by rule specify;

The Commission also discharges the following other functions in relation to the protection, welfare and development and advancement of the Scheduled Tribes, namely:

1. Measures that need to be taken over conferring ownership rights in respect of minor forest produce to the Scheduled Tribes living in forest areas.
2. Measures to be taken to safeguard rights to the Tribal Communities over mineral resources, water resources etc. as per law.
3. Measures to be taken for the development of tribal and to work for move viable livelihood strategies.

4. Measures to be taken to improve the efficacy of relief and rehabilitation measures for tribal groups displaced by development projects.
5. Measures to be taken to prevent alienation of tribal people from land and to effectively rehabilitate such people in whose case alienation has already taken place.
6. Measures to be taken to elicit maximum cooperation and involvement of Tribal Communities for protecting forests and undertaking social afforestation.
7. Measures to be taken to ensure full implementation of the Provisions of Panchayats (Extension to the Scheduled Areas) Act, 1996 (40 of 1996).
8. Measures to be taken to reduce and ultimately eliminate the practice of shifting cultivation by Tribal that lead to their continuous disempowerment and degradation of land and the environment, etc.

Safeguards under Various Laws

1. The Scheduled Castes and Scheduled Tribes (Prevention of Atrocities) Act, 1989 and the Rules 1995 framed there under;
2. Bonded Labour System (Abolition) Act 1976 (in respect of Scheduled Tribes);
3. The Scheduled Castes and the Scheduled Tribes Prevention of Atrocities Act, 1989;
4. The Scheduled Castes and the Scheduled Tribes (Prevention of Atrocities) Rules, 1995;
5. The Child Labour (Prohibition and Regulation) Act, 1986;
6. States Acts and Regulations concerning alienation and restoration of land belonging to STs;
7. Forest Conservation Act, 1980;
8. Panchayati Raj (Extension to Scheduled Areas) Act, 1996;
9. Minimum Wages Act, 1948.

Constitutional Amendment Acts for Empowerment of STs

Fifty-First Constitutional Amendment Act, 1984: 51st Constitutional Amendment Act provided for the reservation of seats in the Lok Sabha for STs in Meghalaya, Arunachal Pradesh, Nagaland and Mizoram as well as in the Legislative Assemblies of Meghalaya and Nagaland.

Fifty-Seven Amendment Act, 1987: 57th Constitutional Amendment Act of 1987 provided the reserved seats for the STs in the Legislative Assemblies of the states of Arunachal Pradesh, Meghalaya, Mizoram and Nagaland.

Sixty-Fifth Amendment Act, 1990: The Act provided for the establishment of a multi-member National Commission for SCs/STs in the place of a Special Officer for SCs/STs.

Seventy-Second Amendment Act, 1992: This Act provided for reservation of seats for the STs in the Legislative Assemblies of Tripura.

Seventy-Seventh Amendment Act, 1995: The Act provided for reservation in promotions in government jobs for SCs/STs.

Eighty-Second Amendment Act, 2000: The Act provided for making of any provision in favour of the SCs/STs for relaxation in qualifying marks in any examination or lowering the standards of evaluation, for reservation in matters of promotion to the public services of the centre and the states.

Eight-Third Amendment Act, 2000: The Act provided that no reservation in Panchayats need be made for SCs in Arunachal Pradesh. The total population of the state is tribal and there are no SCs.

Ninety-Third Amendment Act, 2005: The Act empowered the state to make special provisions for the socially and educationally backward classes or the SCs or STs in educational institutions including private educational institutions (Whether aided or unaided by the state), except the minority educational institutions [(Clause (5) in Article 15]. The Supreme Court declared that reservation in private, unaided educational institutions was unconstitutional.

Conclusion

Promotion of all round development of tribal inhabiting the length and breadth of our country has received priority attention of the government. The framers of the Indian Constitution has made efforts to provide opportunity to these communities for their economic development by eradicating poverty and health problems and developing communication for removal of isolation of their habitats. The Constitution of India seeks to secure for all its citizens, among other things, social and economic justice, equality of status and opportunity and assures the dignity of the individual. The Constitution provides social, economic and political guarantees to the disadvantaged sections of people.

References

1. Census of India 2011, *Primary Census Abstract, Scheduled castes and scheduled tribes*, Office of the Registrar General and Census Commissioner, Government of India (October 28, 2013).
2. Kumar (1992), *The affirmative action debate in India, Asian Survey*, Vol. 32, No. 3, pp. 290–302
3. *National Commission for Scheduled Tribes a Handbook*, Retrieved from:http://www.ncst.nic.in/writereaddata/mainlinkFile/File413.pdf
4. *The Constitution (Scheduled Castes) Order, 1950*". lawmin.nic.in
5. *The Constitution (Scheduled Tribes)*". lawmin.nic.in
6. The National Commission for Scheduled Tribes (NCST) Website: http://www.ncst.nic.in

15

Co-operatives and Women Empowerment – A Case of Gujarat

Abha Singh

"Co-operatives, and other collective forms of economic and social enterprise, have shown themselves as distinctly beneficial to improving women's social and economic capacities."

The essence of co-operatives is 'co-operation'. Co-operation means working together. This principle is as old as when primitive societies came into existence. It is a very basic instinct of human behaviour, where people work collectively to overcome their problems and make their lives better. Around the world co-operatives contribute to their societies in different ways, but sometimes such contributions become the engine of growth and development.

Brief History of Co-operatives

The history of co-operatives can be divided into two phases; the co-operative movement before and after independence. It was the British who set up this institution. In 1899 when India faced a severe famine, the British government in 1901, appointed a Commission to suggest measures for rehabilitation of those affected. In it, setting up of co-operatives was strongly recommended. The government through the 'Co-operative Societies Act' in 1904, officially established the institute. The aim of the societies was to help the rural farmers and artisans get long-term and short-term credit facility. The institution suffered from serious defects. In 1928, due to 'Great depression', the farmers could not reply the credit as the agricultural prices fell steeply and the movement suffered immensely.

In 1933, the RBI set up which had a separate department for co-operative societies, which helped the movement to pick up gradually. With the outbreak of World War II, the prices of agricultural goods rose which helped the farmers in terms of economic gains. The co-operative movement further gained momentum with the establishment of India Co-operative Planning Committee in 1845.

The growth of co-operative movement in the post-independence era is quiet impressive. After independence, planning was adopted to give a direction to growth and development in the country. It acknowledged the role of rural development through societies a priority. The Sixth Plan transformed the primary village societies into multi-purpose societies that will generate employment and move towards poverty eradication and social justice.

Co-operatives and Rural Development

India is primarily an agrarian economy. For sustainable growth, rural economy needs to perform and develop in a sustained manner. The term 'rural development' connotes development of the rural economy. This is a comprehensive and multi-dimensional process and phenomenon which has a multiplier effect on agriculture and allied activities, rural and agro-based industries, socio-economic environment, community services and facilities and primarily the human resources in the rural areas.

Organisations like co-operatives help rural development in different ways – it improves the input allocation, reduces the transport cost and improves the bargaining power potentially. It can be rightly said that co-operatives are organisations set up to achieve economic and social benefits for its members and the group at large. It is organisation characterised by democratic principles with equitable distribution of cost and benefits.

Such organisations become more imperative and influential because they very well represent the concerns of the poor women. Women who are deprived of social and economic justice tend to find a strong representation and redressal of their concerns and issues in them and tend to gain. Co-operatives have provided rural women with enhanced employment opportunities, economic, social, physical and tenural security.

A Case of Gujarat

Gujarat is one of the most progressive states of India. It can be rightly attributed to socially and economically empowered women in the state. The natural instinct of entrepreneurship and active participation of the rural women led to social and economic empowerment. The co-operative movement in the state played a pivotal role in this achievement, women's active participation in co-operatives, not only in Gujarat (India) but worldwide is supported by international fundings agencies like UNDP and World Bank has led to their indispensible existence.

The shift in policy focus from welfare to development to empowerment and rightly heading towards inclusiveness has made them an agent of change. Co-operative societies provide social and economic inclusiveness to women. Many societies of such nature have come into existence in the state but the most successful and prominent are AMUL and SEWA.

They have made a remarkable contribution in women's empowerment in Gujarat.

AMUL-Anand Milk Union Ltd.

In the 60's the dairy sector was very much dominated by the middlemen. These people did everything possible to exploit the poor and helpless farmers. It was the enactment of the Indian Co-operative Act, 1912, which helped the dairy sector to establish itself on the lines of co-operative society. Today's dairy co-operatives owes it's origin to Sardar Patel when in 1946, under his guidance and direction the institution was established. In the Kheda district of Gujarat, the process of establishment of the institution was started. The co-operatives will directly undertake sale and processing of milk collected from members of the dairy farmers of the village.

This organised community became empowered, since majority of the participants were women and their lives was about to change for good. The government improved the quality of milch animals through two plans; Key Village Scheme (1951-56) and Intensive Cattle Development Plan (1961-66) which improved the productivity and quality of the animals. Further the absence of a stable and fair price for milk that the prices were almost stable, devoiding the farmer of any incentive to improve his product. The growth was hardly one per cent annually while the per capita availability declined by an equitable amount. This prompted many state governments to develop dairying, which included setting up of dairy plants in urban areas like Mumbai, Calcutta and Madras. These cattle colonies were set up to fulfill the excessive demand for milk of the urban areas.

It is in this background that Operation Flood (OF) was undertaken by National Dairy Development Board (NDDB) from 1970-96, which brought a remarkable transformation in the dairy development in the state and country. The OF programme was initiated by Dr Kurien, established milk co-operatives throughout the state. The objective of the programme was modernisation in techniques in the dairy industry by drastically improving the milk production, increase rural incomes and transfer the benefits to the farmer themselves and thus empowering them. Since most of the participants in this programme were women, they were the true and direct beneficiary.

Salient Features of Operation Flood and Achievements, 1970-96

Features	*Operation Flood (OF) Phase*		
	OF-I	*OF-II*	*OF-III*
Date when started	July 1, 1970	October 2, 1979	April 1, 1985
Date when concluded	March 31, 1981	March 31, 1985	March 31, 1996
Investments (Rs Crore)	116.5	277.2	1303.1
No. of Federations/ Apex Milk Unions set up	10	18	22
No. of milk sheds covered	39	136	170
No. of DCSs set up (_000)	13.3	34.5	72.5
No. of Members (lakh)	17.5	36.3	92.63
Average Milk Procurement (mkgpd)	2.56	5.78	10.99
Liquid Milk Marketing (llpd)	27.9	50.1	100.2
Processing Capacity: Rural Dairies (llpd)	35.9	87.8	180.9
Metro Dairies (llpd)	29.0	35.0	38.8
Milk Drying Capacity (MTPD)	261.0	507.5	842.0
Technical Inputs: No. of AI centres (_000)	4.9	7.5	16.8
No. of AIs done at end (lakh/ Year)	8.2	13.3	39.4
Cattle feed capacity (_000 MTPD)	1.7	3.3	4.9

Sources: (1) Dairy India 1997; (2) Quarterly and Monthly Progress Reports on Operation Flood, NDDB, Anand, 1996 as quoted in Singh (1999b:205). Mkgpd:million kg per day; llpd: lakh litre per day; MTPD: metric tone per day.

The OF programme was a success since its target were the rural poor. With the lack of employment opportunity in the rural areas, dairy proved to be a lucrative occupation. Almost 70 per cent of the small and marginal farmers are associated with this movement; and amongst these women are active participants. With low capital intensity, a short cycle of operation and steady returns proved to be the most preferred occupation for these marginal farmers particularly rural women. Even landless people find themselves engaged, who depend for fodder on the common grasing and forest land. On an average 22.5 per cent of the household income in rural areas comes from milk.

The success of OF programme which was first experimented in Anand and later replicated in the entire nation, lies in its three pronged strategy from procurement, processing and marketing of milk products. Today AMUL is a trusted brand of India in terms of quality and trust.

Women and Dairy Co-operatives

AMUL realised the potential of engaging women in this field and so from the very beginning women took care of the milch cattle. The programme has empowered them both socially and economically. In the early stages of OF, emphasis was on the training the rural women in modern animal husbandry methods and motivating them to involve themselves in governing the everyday co-operatives function. The co-operatives have been successful in increasing the social participation of women, building the managerial and leadership qualities in them. It has encouraged them to speak up against the evils of a patriarchal society, which they otherwise would not have dared to speakup. They are now socially empowered to raise issues which affects them in particular and society at large. AMUL seem to believe that if women are empowered then society at large is empowered. This is very much visible in Gujarat. Co-operatives have helped them overcome various social taboos, they have stood up collectively, in one voice against such evils. They stood up for provision of safe drinking water, safety of women, harassment or anti-liquor activism to name some, have found a collective voice through these co-operatives.

Co-operatives have empowered them economically too. They are financially independent and there is an increase in women oriented self-employment opportunities. Dairying is the most lucrative means of livelihood because they are set up in natural village environment. Women being familiar with their surrounding further adds to their advantage. Easy availability of credit has encouraged women to diversity into other activities. Co-operatives have helped in uplifting the economic status of women in the society in Gujarat. Women feel safe and have a voice and the co-operative has been the driving force.

Conclusion

Women are the backbone of our families and social structure. Co-operatives have made them economically independent, which has led to their social empowerment. Social empowerment has redefined their role, has given them a new voice, greater autonomy, mobility and new dimensions in household decision making. Co-operatives are the lowest unit but the most effective in transforming the lives of millions of women in our society. The case of Gujarat can be a lesson to replicate in the entire nation where the grassroot organisations of the co-operative can bring about a striking and visible change in the status of women and the society at large.

References

Abhinav: National Monthly Refereed Journal of Research in Commerce and Management, www.abhinavjournal.com, Volume No. 1, Issue No. 5, ISSN 2277-1166

Agricultural Refinance and Development Corporation (1976) – Report of the Committee on Integration of Co-operative Credit Institutions, (Chairman: R.K. Hazari), Bombay. Anandaram, K.S. (1996) – Shree Ganesh Co-operative Spinning Mills Ltd.: A Performing Co-operative, in Rajagopalan (ed.) Rediscovering Cooperation. Volume III, Institute of Rural Management, Anand.

16

Agricultural Policy and Poverty: A Glimpse

Chinmayee Chaturvedi

"Indian agriculture is broadly a story of success. It has done remarkably well in terms of output growth, despite weather and price shocks in the past few years. India is the first in the world in the production of milk, pulses, jute and jute-like fibres, second in rice, wheat, sugarcane, groundnut, vegetables, fruits and cotton production, and is a leading producer of spices and plantation crops as well as livestock, fisheries and poultry."

-Economic Survey 2013-14

Agriculture, in a vast, naturally diversified country as India can nothing less but be the base of the domestic economy. However, the present growth indicators of agriculture do not portray an enthusiastic scene despite a 'remarkable output growth'.[1]

Immediately after independence the most imperative need was to enhance production and productivity and so initially land reforms and at later stages green revolution were the centre of Indian agricultural policy. The implementation of land reforms was undoubtedly a long and gradual process, the success of which depended not only on administrative pragmatism but broadly on social cohesion. Since the targets of the different policies of land reforms were not possible to achieve immediately due to conventionally imbibed social outlook, the emphasis at later stages of the planning shifted to the idea of Green Revolution which without much hassles was capable of increased production and productivity.

The success of green revolution gave a new dimension to hitherto industry based development models. However, post green revolution Indian economy witnessed technological and geographical dualism without an urban bias. It created inter-and intra-regional gulf between rural areas. The present paper, divided in two sections, tries to bring out the agricultural growth scene in India. The second section attempts to look into the policy implications of this growth model, if any, adopted for agriculture sector.

I

According to the Economic Survey 2013-14, Indian agriculture has made strides and stands second in the world in the production of food grains. However, the paradoxical aspect of the growth is that it has not converged with the similar rise in GDP or per capita income in agriculture. The reason may be attributed to the not quite successful working of Lewis's model in Indian conditions despite the second plan (1956-61) that emphasised heavily on heavy industries with one of the objectives of creating employment but could not impact much the disguised employment of Indian rural masses.

Along with the policy of heavy industrialisation to provide impetus to industrial production, land reforms targeted to boost the agriculture production by redefining the land relationship. Had it overcame the political and social hurdles in implementation, the redistribution of agriculture assets to accomplish an egalitarian rural society would have materialised. However, the shackles of feudal and caste ridden society were difficult to break. Moreover, agriculture being a state subject the modus operandi for implementation had to be state specific. Thus, the success of land reforms depended precisely on the political ideology and pressure groups in the state.

In the midst of sixth decade of twentieth century green revolution was implemented as experiment in western

Uttar Pradesh, Punjab and Haryana where there were proper irrigation facilities. With the onset of new agricultural technology the productivity and production increased. The production of agriculture went up manifolds accomplishing the immediate targets of self-sufficiency in production of foodgrains. However, the use of new technique is limited to certain crops and regions till this date.

Post-liberalisation, alike other sectors agriculture also got impetus as the pattern of consumption underwent a change. The launching of several agro based industries increased the demand of cash crops. The share of agriculture in Gross Domestic Product at factor cost in the year 2010-11 and 2011-12 was 7.5 and 3.1 respectively when the GDP_{FC} for the whole country was 9.3 and 6.2. The index of agricultural production in 2013-14 was 129.2 on the basis of 2007-08 prices. This is indicative of a 'remarkable growth.'

Distribution of Number of Holdings and Area Operated in India as per Agriculture Census 2010-11[2]

Sl. No.	*Size Group*	*Number of holdings (in millions)*	*Area operated (in million ha.)*	*Average operated area per holding (ha.)*	*Percentage of holdings to total holdings*	*Percentage of area operated to total area*
1	Marginal (Below 1.00 ha.)	92.4	35.4	0.38	67.04	22.25
2	Small (1.00-2.00 ha.)	24.7	35.1	1.42	17.93	22.07
3	Semi-Medium (2.00-4.00 ha.)	13.8	37.5	2.71	10.05	23.59
4	Medium (4.00-10.00 ha.)	5.9	33.7	5.76	4.25	21.18
5	Large (Above 10.00 ha.)	1.0	17.4	17.38	0.73	10.92
All holdings		137.8	159.2	1.16	100.00	100.00

Source: 'State of Indian Agriculture 2012-13', Dept. of Agriculture and Cooperation.

As referred to in the above paragraphs the use of new technique in agriculture and the paradigm shift at the policy level led to increased growth in the production of agricultural commodities. Various government publications have been prominently emphasising the growth story of Indian agriculture in terms of yield, area and production. The statistics below is a testimony to the same.

Of the three parameters yield in case of coarse cereals and pulses has gone up despite a negative growth rate in area. Of important green revolution crops i.e. wheat and rice yield has gone down.

This growth, however, has not converged with similar remarkable achievement in per capita income in agriculture.

As can be concluded from the statistics above, of the total number of holdings in India majority are marginal holdings i.e. less than one hectare. Agriculture activities employ nearly half of the total population. According to Census 2001, 58.2 per cent people are involved in agriculture[3] and its contribution in GDP_{FC} was 13.69 per cent in 2012-13 at 2004-05 prices and 17.39 per cent at current prices in the period in the total GDP_{FC} of 94610.13 billion rupees.[4] Agriculture alone contributed 15 per cent of the total.

The contribution of agriculture in GDP though has gone down considerably since the inception of planning its significance as a major employer cannot be doubted. The total agriculture production has gone up manifolds still "reforms are urgently required to achieve greater efficiency and productivity in agriculture for sustaining growth."[5]

II

Various government policy statements and government sponsored research[6] have emphasised on the increased growth rate in agriculture production as referred in earlier section. However, they have also mentioned the decreasing per hectare yield. The two major ideological aspects in agriculture planning of land reforms and green revolution tried to change the course of its modus operendi in different ways. Where land reforms aimed at redefining the land relationship and improving the productivity it could not be

CAGRs of Area, Production, and Yield Indices of Principal Crops during 1980-81 to 1989-90, 1990-91 to 1999-2000 (Base: TE 1981-82=100), and 2000-2001 to 2011-12 (Base: TE 1993-94=100) (per cent per annum)

	1980-81 to 1989-90			*1990-91 to 1999-2000*			*2000-2001 to 2011-12*		
	Area	*Production*	*Yield*	*Area*	*Production*	*Yield*	*Area*	*Production*	*Yield*
Rice	0.41	3.62	3.19	0.68	2.02	1.34	0.00	1.78	1.78
Wheat	0.46	3.57	3.10	1.72	3.57	1.83	1.35	2.61	1.24
Coarse Cereals	-1.34	0.40	1.62	-2.12	-0.02	1.82	-0.81	3.01	3.85
Total Pulses	-0.09	1.52	1.61	-0.60	0.59	0.93	1.60	3.69	2.06
Total Oilseeds	1.51	5.20	2.43	0.86	1.63	1.15	2.12	3.36	1.22

Source: Table 8.4, Economic Survey 2012-13, p. 176.

implemented as expected. The implementation of policy of green revolution with a limited reach had undoubtedly helped in mitigating the scarcity of foodgrains but along with that the ground reality is that it has created a wide gulf among rural areas of different states. The paradigm shift post-1991 may have resulted in a better trade off for agriculture but it coincided with a slow growth rate that could not even touch the targeted four per cent.

The emphasis of the current agriculture research and policy planning is on increasing public investment, availability of credit, providing irrigation facilities, better allocation of funds supported by coordinated research and extension activities. The government documents mentions the need for a second green revolution beginning this time from eastern India. Emphasis is also on promoting a production process that is environment friendly.

With this multi-dimensional approach to the uplift of agriculture and the people involved therein and a comparative analysis of all the statistics brings about a peculiar situation where agriculture, of all the three sectors, is the largest employer and lowest contributor in the GDP. The per capita income of people involved in agriculture thus, is the minimum.[7] Further, the maximum number of operational holdings in the country are marginal i.e. the cultivators of these holdings fall below the per capita income. The conclusion precisely can safely be drawn that the majority of poor people in rural areas belong to this section. How this marginal size of the holding will be brought in the ambit of the different schemes to increase the production and enhance the living of people may be a point of concern.

The crux of the whole issue is that agriculture policy hitherto had not experienced stability in the long run. The agriculture policy, after putting land reforms on back seat, has been growth centric. The goal had been to increase production and improve the life of cultivators through different welfare schemes. Government provisioning can never be a permanent solution to any ill. However, government faced fiscal dilemma as regards agriculture policy. Thus, the consequences of trickle down through green revolution techniques have not worked wonders in Indian conditions. The huge exodus of rural population and increased urbanisation in the form of slum areas are a testimony to this. Moreover, green revolution was heavily subsidised and thus, protected. Its reach remained limited and the agriculture in its ambit was not affected by market volatility. The majority of rest of the agricultural population produced for subsistence and hardly affected by market prices.

The advent of reforms slackened the quantum of protection, though seemingly improving trade off. The farming class now has to face global competition without prior preparations. In such conditions it also cannot be made a profitable venture for small and marginal farmers who search alternative occupation. Farmers in different pockets are committing suicides. They still need protection from international competitive network.

In such a situation the emphasis of agriculture may need refurbishing so that marginal populace in rural areas suffering from low income can be included in the process of development. For this to take place Arthur Lewis's model should be remodeled in Indian conditions to incorporate non-farm sector which can have better linkages with agriculture. The strategy for non-farm sector hitherto has been a compulsion as majority of rural populace is either asset less or have meager assets. The section has not been provided impetus as a major prospective contributor in the national mainstream. A potential factor for grass root development has been neglected.

Further, agricultural policy cannot be one fit all size. There are sub-sub regional variations that need to be taken care of through a people-private researcher partnership. Agriculture can be the mainstay and a potential source of development and poverty reduction provided it is given the consideration at par with secondary and tertiary sector.

Notes

1. PLAN-WISE GROWTH RATES (per cent) BY ECONOMIC ACTIVITY (at 2004-05 prices)

Five Year Plan/ year	*Total Economy*	*Agriculture, forestry and fishing*	*Agriculture, including livestock*
7/ 1985-90	5.7	3.0	3.1
8/ 1992-97	6.5	4.8	4.9
9/ 1997-2002	5.7	2.5	2.5
10/ 2002-2007	7.6	2.4	2.5
11/ 2007-12	8.0	3.7	3.8

Source: State of Indian Agriculture 2012-13, Dept. of Agriculture and Cooperation, Ministry of Agriculture, Government of India.

2. Table 1(a) All India Report on Number and Area of Operational Holding, Agriculture Census 2010-11, Ministry of Agriculture.
3. "Agriculture, including allied activities, accounted for only 14.1 per cent of the GDP at constant (2004-5) prices in 2011-12, its role in the country's economy is much bigger with its share in total employment according to the 2001 census, continuing to be as high as 58.2 per cent." Economic Survey 2012-13, p. 173.
4. http://www.rbi.org.in/scripts/Publications View.aspx?id=15123
5. 'Agriculture and Food Management', Economic Survey 2012-13, p. 174.
6. 'Agriculture Growth in India' Department of Economic Analysis and Policy, RBI; 'State of Indian Agriculture 2012-13' Department of Agriculture and Cooperation, Ministry of Agriculture; Economic Survey, Various Issues.
7. The per capita income in agriculture in 2011-12 was Rs 73,520 if only the number of cultivators is taken. If the whole primary sector is considered along with agricultural labourers then it turns out to be Rs 42,411.

17

Educational Inequalities Among Scheduled Tribes in India

Shilpi Mishra

Introduction

In any civilisation, education is considered to be an important mechanism for development of its people, particularly in India and especially for the schedule tribes, it can be seen as panacea for all sort of problem they are facing. Since these sections of our society were traditionally and historically deprived of their basic rights necessary for their development and growth. The most basic element and mother of all solutions that is education was far away from their reach. Education is a fundamental human right and a major driver of human and economic development. It strengthens personal integrity and shapes the societies in which we live. However, with the advent of British rule, the industrial revolution in the west, modern technological growth and fast means of communication, together with some social movements led to some changes in the basic social structure of Indian society. Further, these changes were followed by the Indian national movement that led to India's Independence. After independence, when the Constitution was adopted the nation declared itself to be a welfare state with the principle of equality and justice, committed itself by constitution to the welfare of weaker sections like scheduled castes (SCs) and scheduled tribes (STs). To strengthen even more several special provision have been incorporated by the constitution for these sections in the employment and political representation through the mechanism of reservation.

India is a home to a large variety of indigenous people. The Scheduled Tribes population represents one of the most economically impoverished and marginalised groups in India. With a population of more than 10.2 crores, India has the largest tribal population in the world except perhaps in Africa. This constitutes 8.6 per cent of the total population of the country (Census of India, 2011). Today as of now when we have completed 68 years of independence and having experimented with special welfare programmes for these vulnerable sections, as an outcome of assessment it was found that still tribal people are struggling for the basic needs of life such as health, education, housing, food, security, employment, justice and equity. Even they are being deprived of social and political participation. Some of them are being dispossessed of their traditional lands as their livelihoods are being undermined. Their belief systems, cultures, languages and ways of life continue to be threatened, sometimes even to the point of extinction. Government has failed to guarantee tribal people's rights in the implementation level.

Education, is considered of utmost importance to the tribal because it paves the crucial road for total development of tribal communities and is particularly helpful to build confidence among the tribes to deal with outsiders on equal terms. Literacy and educational attainment are the only required and powerful tools for their social and economic development. Only after the full fledge education of the members belonging to tribal societies will make them able to acquire and use their rights to overcome the problems they are facing.

Profile of Tribal Literacy in India

Since independence there is continuous increase in the tribal literacy but not with pace of national average. The total literacy rate of the tribal in India is 58.96 per cent whereas it is 72.99 per cent at the national level. And on the basis of male-female percentage, the male accounts 68.53 per cent (80.89 per cent national) and female 49.35 per cent (64.64 per cent national). There is wide variation of tribal education at the State or Union Territory level, for example Lakshadweep tops with 91.7 per cent, followed by Mizoram (91.5), Nagaland (80.0), Sikkim (79.7), Tripura (79.1) and Daman and Diu (78.8). The poor performing states in India are: Andhra Pradesh (49.2), Jammu and Kashmir (50.6), Bihar (51.1) and Odisha (52.2). The female literacy of the STs in India is 49.35 per cent but yet much below the national level. States with low general and tribal literacy are also states having higher gender disparity. Accordingly, the ST female literacy rate in India varies across states and Union Territories such as from 37.3 per cent in Rajasthan to 89.5 per cent in Mizoram. Except Mizoram, Lakshadweep, Nagaland, Sikkim, Tripura, Goa, Andaman and Nicobar, Manipur, Meghalaya, Daman and Diu and Kerala, all other states and Union Territories have women literacy below the national level. (Census of India, 2011).

Tribal Literacy in India (in percentage)

Year	*Male*	*Female*	*Total*
1961	13.83	3.16	8.53
1971	17.63	4.85	11.30
1981	24.52	8.04	16.35
1991	40.65	18.19	29.60
2001	59.17	34.76	47.10
2011	68.53	49.35	58.96

Source: Registrar General of India and Annual Report 2010-11, Ministry of Tribal Affairs, Government of India.

Educational Programmes and Schemes for Scheduled Tribes: An Overview

The Central Government and State Governments after independence have taken various schemes and programmes for overall development with special reference to education of the Tribals. Few of them have been cited here:

- **Special Central Assistance and Grants Under Article 275(1) of the Constitution:** Special Central Assistance is given to States/UTs to supplement their efforts in tribal development through Tribal Sub-Plan. This assistance is basically meant for family-oriented income-generating schemes in the sectors of agriculture, horticulture, minor irrigation, soil conservation, animal husbandry, forests, education, cooperatives, fisheries, village and small scale industries and for minimum needs programme. Grants are also given to States/UTs, under the first proviso to Article 275(1) of the Constitution to meet the costs of projects for tribal development and for raising the level of administration of Scheduled Area therein on par with the rest of the State/UT. Part of the funds are utilised for setting of residential for providing quality education to tribal students.
- **Scheme of Development of Primitive Tribal Groups (PTGs):** Based on pre-agricultural level of technology, low level of literacy, declining or stagnant populations, 75 tribal communities in 17 States and one Union Territory of Andaman and Nicobar Island, have been identified and categorised as Primitive Tribal Groups (PTGs). Considering the vulnerability of these groups, a Central Sector Scheme was introduced in the year 1998-99 for the all round development of PTGs. The scheme is very flexible, and covers housing, infrastructure development, education, health, land distribution/development, agricultural development, cattle development, society security, insurance, etc.
- **Strengthening Education among Scheduled Tribe Girls in Low Literacy District:** It is a gender scheme of the Ministry. The scheme aims to bridge the gap in literacy levels between the general female population and tribal women, through facilitating 100 per cent enrollment of tribal girls in the identified Districts or Blocks, more particularly in naxal affected areas and in areas inhabited by Primitive Tribal Groups (PTGs),

and reducing drop-outs at the elementary level by creating the required ambience for education. The scheme recognises the fact that improvement of the literacy rate of tribal girls is essential to enable them to participate effectively in and benefit from, socio-economic development. The scheme covers 54 identified districts in 12 States and one Union Territory where the ST population is 25 per cent or more, and ST female literacy rate is below 35 per cent or its fractions, as per 2001 census. In addition, any other tribal block in a district, other than aforesaid 54 identified districts, which has scheduled tribes populations 25 per cent or above, and tribal female literacy rate below 35 per cent or its fractions, as per 2001 census, are also covered. The scheme also covers PTG areas and gives priority to areas affected by naxalism.

The scheme also envisages the establishment of District Education Support Agency (DESA), which would be a non-governmental organisations, for varied functions like ensuring 100 per cent enrollment, reducing drop-outs, arrangement of preventive health, education, monitoring the performance of NGOs, etc.

- **Coaching for Scheduled Tribes:** The scheduled tribes candidates coming from deprived families and disadvantaged environment find it difficult to compete with those coming from a socially and economically advantageous background. To promote a more level playing field, and give ST candidates a better chance to succeed in competitive examinations, the Ministry of Tribal Affairs supports a scheme for coaching for disadvantaged ST candidates in quality coaching institutions to enable them to successfully compete in examinations for jobs/admission to professional courses. The scheme supports free coaching to scheduled tribe students for various competitive examinations viz. Civil Services/State Civil Services/ Other Exams conducted by UPSE like CDS, NDA, etc./ professional courses like Medical, Engineering,

Business Administration/Banking/Staff Selection Commission/Railway Recruitment Boards/Insurance companies etc.

- **Post-Matric Scholarship for Scheduled Tribes Students:** The objective of the scheme is to provide financial assistance to students belonging to Scheduled Tribes pursuing Post-Matriculation recognised courses in recognised institutions. The scheme covers professional, technical as well as non-professional and non-technical courses at various levels and the scheme also includes correspondence courses including distance and continuing education. The scheme is implemented by the State Government and UT Administrations, which receive 100 per cent Central Assistance over and above the committed liability which is required to be borne by them from their own budgetary provisions.
- **Girls' and Boys' Hostels for Scheduled Tribes:** The scheme of Girls' Hostel which started in the Third Five-Year Plan with the aim of providing residential facilities to tribal girls in pursuit of education. Central assistance of 50 per cent cost of construction to the states, cent per cent to the union territories is provided under the scheme.
- **Rajiv Gandhi National Fellowship Scheme (RGNFS):** This Scheme was introduced in the year 2005–06. Under the Scheme, fellowship is provided to ST students for pursuing higher studies such as M. Phil. and Ph.D. The maximum duration of a fellowship is five years. Every year 667 fellowships are to be provided to ST students. The scheme is being implemented by University Grants Commission (UGC) on behalf of the Ministry of Tribal Affairs. Any ST student who has passed post-graduation from a UGC recognised University can apply under the scheme.
- **Establishment of Ashram School in Tribal Sub-Plan Area:** The scheme of Ashram Schools was launched in 1990–91 with the objective to extend facilities like establishment of residential schools for STs in an

environment conducive to learning in increasing the literacy rates among the tribal students and to bring them at par with other population of the country. The Scheme has been revised with effect from the financial year 2008-09. The funding for the scheme to the State is done on matching (50 : 50) basis, while cent per cent assistance is given to UTs.

- **Vocational Training in Tribal Areas:** The main aim of this scheme is to develop the skill of the tribal youth in order to enable them to gain employment/self-employment opportunities. This scheme was introduced in 1992–93 and is being implemented through the State Governments/UT Administrations, Institutions or Organisations set up by government as autonomous bodies, educational and other institutions like local bodies and cooperative societies and Non-Governmental Organisation.

- **National Overseas Scholarship Scheme for Scheduled Tribes:** The Scheme provides financial assistance to meritorious students belonging to STs for pursuing higher studies abroad in specified fields of Master level courses, Ph.D. and Post-Doctoral research programmes, in the field of Engineering, Technology and Science. The selected candidates are given cost of tuition and other educational fees charged by the foreign university etc., maintenance and other grants along with travel expenses.

- **Book Bank:** Many ST students selected in professional courses find it difficult to continue their education for want of books on their subjects, as these are often expensive. In order to reduce the dropout rate of ST students from professional institutes/universities, funds are provided for purchase of books under this scheme. The scheme is open to all ST students pursuing medical (including Indian Systems of Medicine and Homeopathy) engineering, agriculture, veterinary, polytechnic, law, chartered accountancy, business management, bio-science subjects, who are receiving Post-Matric Scholarships.

- **Scheme of Top Class Education for ST Students:** The objective of the scheme is to encourage meritorious ST students for pursuing studies at degree and post degree level in any of the selected list of institutes, in which the scholarship scheme would be operative. The Scheme has been started from 2007-08. There are 213 institutes approved under the scheme in both the government and private sectors covering the field of management, medicine, engineering, law and commercial courses. Each institute has been allocated five awards, with a ceiling of total 625 scholarships per year.

Problems and Issues-related with Tribal Education

The tribal of India are faced with a number of problems among which the following may be noted:

1. Economic factor/poverty: The tribal people are economically the poorest people of India. Majority of them live below the poverty line. The tribal economy is based on agriculture of the crudest type. Almost all the tribes whether food gatherers, hunters, fishermen, shifting cultivators, or settled agriculturalists lack adequate food to sustained the family for the whole year. Poor economic conditions accompanied by subsistence economy is a great hindrance to successful education of the tribal children. In this situation, they find it difficult to afford their children to go school; rather, they see children as an economic asset in the family and contribute to the family income by working along with the parents and with others. Boys work in the field with their parents and girls give help to their mothers at the housework and some time even girls too found to work in agricultural land to maximise profit. They have no faith in formal educational organisation. They feel no urge to educate their children. Since most of the tribal are poor, education appears to be a luxury for them.

2. Apathy of Parents: Both the tribal and non-tribal teachers find it very difficult to convince the tribal to send their children to school to adopt new ideas as they are more concerned with the present than the future and their concept of time is circular rather than longitudinal. A large section of tribal parents do not send their children to school to utilise the free education opportunities offered to them. It is practical, utilitarian and vocational aspect of education accompanied by the notion of immediate economic return appeals to the parents more than the academic discourse. In addition, there are many factors responsible for apathy of the parents towards education. These are:

- Psychological and social factors like illiteracy of the parents and their indifference to education, lack of encouragement by the community, motivation and "insecurity" of future for being educated.
- Low social interaction between students and teachers, and between teachers and parents.
- Suspicion over the sincerity of the non-tribal teachers and shortage of tribal teachers.
- The scattered population with low density and location of schools at a long distance, in consequence, has resulted in the indifferences of the parents to send their children to walk a long to reach the school.
- Parental hesitation to send the girls to co-educational institutions.

3. Apathy of children towards formal education: In many states tribal education is taught through the same book, which forms the curriculum of the non-tribal children. A tribal child who lives in an isolated and far flung place, untouched by civilisation, can hardly get interest in any information about Indian society, history, polity, geography, economy and technological development of his country. So the contents of the teaching syllabus, instead of pleasing the learners, generate indifferences within the tribal students. All these are necessary part of any curriculum but the students are far away from these real perceptions and they do not understand what they are taught. For them these information and knowledge constitutes alien and imposed portions of their thought, which have nothing to do with tribal history and tribal surroundings.

4. Superstitions and Prejudice: The tribal have their own social problems also. They are traditional and custom-bound and want to maintain their individual tribal character also. They have become the victims of Superstition, blind beliefs, do outmoded and meaningless practices, have harmful habits, like child marriage, infanticide, homicide, animal sacrifice, exchange of wives, black magic are still found among them. They believe in ghosts and spirits also and such kind of prejudices play negative role in imparting education in the tribal areas and tribal schools. Except tribal communities in north-eastern region, there is widespread feeling in the tribal community that education makes their children defiant and insolent and alienates from the rest of their society. Since some of their educated boys felt alienated and cut off their links with their families and villages after getting education and employment, a large section of tribal groups oppose the spread of education. This is further complicated when religious groups teach the students by focusing on the glory of their religion and religious values. This religiosity, in consequence, often encourages educated pupils to abrogate their ancestral village and their socio-cultural interaction with the kins as it found among Zimi Nagas in North-East.

5. Problem of suitable teacher: The competency and interest of the teachers is of prime importance in generating interest of the students towards education. The non-tribal teachers treat themselves 'civilised' and tribal as 'uncivilised' and 'savage'. So there is little appreciation of the tribal values and way of life. There is no good relationship between children and the teachers. Sometimes the teachers for their personal work use the tribal students. For a non-tribal teacher, the cultural gap plays a vital role due to the long hanging dominant ideology, and he treats tribal students differently. The ego and selfish motive of such tribal teachers have been discouraging the tribal to send their children to the educational institutions. Moreover, although there are views that the tribal teachers are best suited to non-tribal teachers, instances shows that the tribal teachers of one community looks students and parents of another community hesitantly. Some of the tribal groups, better educated and progressive in thinking have some prejudices against backward tribal e.g. the Valmiki tribes in East Godavari district of Andhra Pradesh occupies lower ritual status than Konda Reddi tribes, but are mostly educated. If a teacher from Valmiki tribe teaches Konda Reddis, the later will not prefer to give the former a house for shelter, and does not treat them equally. On the same way, Valmiki teachers feel that the Konda Reddis are lazy and superstitious.

Effective functioning of the tribal education much depends on teachers and their willingness to teach and positive attitude to live in tribal areas—close to tribal schools. However, in practice the teachers are reluctant to reside in such areas, rather they stay in nearby towns. Only in those cases teachers would like to stay if the area is inaccessible. In maximum cases teachers in the tribal areas see the appointment as 'stop-gap' arrangement. So there comes the problem of insincerity and non-commitment of interaction of the teachers with the guardians and discussion with them over the education of their children.

6. Problem of language: Language provides social, psychological and emotional expression of an individual in a society. But in the absence of knowledge on tribal dialect both students and teachers face the problem of communication and teaching-learning. It is found that tribal students are often ridiculed, humiliated and reprimanded for speaking in their own language, and are punished for failing to talk in their standard language or continuously lapsing back in the mother tongue. This also led to discourage student from active participation in class.

7. Inadequate Facilities in Educational Institutions: School buildings in the tribal areas are without basic infrastructural facilities. The schools basically have thatched roofs, dilapidated walls and non-pastoral floors.

In Ashram schools which are residential in nature, there is no space for the children to sleep. As a consequence, the classrooms turn into dormitory and vice versa. In addition to poor maintenance of the school and classrooms, inadequate teaching-learning materials such as blackboards and chalks causes problems for the teachers and students in teaching and understanding the content.

8. Wastage and Stagnation: Problem of education in the tribal areas is also the problem of wastage and stagnation. Wastage is the withdrawal or dropping out of a student before completing the prescribed period of the concerned course. A data revealed by the Eleventh Five Year Plan also indicated the high dropout of the STs at different levels of study. As per the data, at the Primary level, the dropout rate among STs was 48.9 per cent and 70.1 per cent at the Upper Primary level. It indicates the apathy of the tribal students for the existing curriculum and system and problems of teaching-learning process. When a student takes more than one year to pass a class it is considered a case of stagnation. As per the Eleventh Five Year Plan report, stagnation at the primary level was 67.3 per cent whereas it was 49.3 per cent at the Upper Primary level. School timing i.e. clash of class hour with the working hour particularly, during the harvesting period, formal education, poverty, lack of academic atmosphere, unwillingness of the teachers to convince the parents and parental apathy towards education and lack of proper medical aid, balanced diet and suitable self-employment opportunities are the major factors for which there is wastage and stagnation.

9. The Problem of Geographic Separation: The tribal of India are in a way geographically separated from the rest of population. Some of them are living in the unapproachable physical areas such as deep valleys, dense forests, hills, mountains, etc. It is difficult for them to establish relations with others, and hence, socially they are far away from the civilised world. This kind of physical isolation or seclusion has also contributed immensely for not coming in mainstream of education.

10. Cultural Problems: The tribal culture is entirely different from the way of life of the civilised people. The tribal fail to understand the civilised people, their customs and practices, beliefs and attitudes and so on. They are suspicious towards the civilised people. They are clinging tenaciously to their customs and traditions. The cultural gap between the civilised and the tribal people is coming in the way of the assimilation and integration of the tribal people into the mainstream of the national life of India.

11. Insurgency in tribal dominated Region: The final reason is the existing insurgency in tribal dominated regions. States like Jharkhand, Chhattisgarh, Bihar, West Bengal and North-East States are severely affected by Naxalism and violent insurgencies. It is no secret that the insurgents use the tribals as a shield to protect themselves and operate their own 'Governments' in these regions, which makes it exceedingly difficult for tribals to receive the benefits from government schemes and NGOs to make interventions. In Chhattisgarh, CRPF has been known to occupy schools to attack Naxalites, while Naxalites destroy schools to thwart the security forces. In the midst of the never-ending conflict between the government and Naxalites, hapless tribal children are denied their basic constitutional right of education.

12. Corruption: Corruption is a major drain on the effective use of resources for education meant for tribal students and should be drastically curbed. Corruption in education is more detrimental than corruption in other sectors because of its long-term effects. Stollen resources from education budgets mean overcrowded classrooms and crumbling schools, or no schools at all. Books and supplies are sometimes sold instead of being given out freely meant for tribal students. Embezzlement of funds allocated to purchase teaching materials or to build schools.

Teachers and lecturers are appointed through family connections, without qualifications. These are the things which further hamper the serious attempts of government to include tribal in mainstream of education.

Suggestions

Some suggestions for improvement of tribal education are as follows:

1. Proper awareness campaign should be organised to create the awareness about the importance of education. Extensive literacy campaign in the tribal dominated districts may be undertaken on a priority basis to literate the tribal.
2. The attitude of the tribal parents toward education should be improved through proper counselling and guidance. Each parent must be motivated to send their children above six years to school or teachers and parents may be legally bound to do this task. The school time table is co-opted with the agricultural and social necessities, which will facilitate the parents in economic development and educational development of the child.
3. Study books must be prepared in tribal language up to upper primary level. Tribal students must be supplied with study materials and dresses free of cost. Every school must be well-equipped with all study materials.
4. Teachers from the same tribe and from the nearby villages if possible from the same village should be appointed. Teachers must be paid regularly with free accommodation facility in school campus. Responsibility may be laid down to teachers for enrollment of all children from the age group of 6 to 14 years and not allow dropouts at any circumstances.

5. Training at intervals to the Non-tribal teachers about the tribal culture and language should be provided. All NGOs functioning in the district may be involved in the process to educate all Tribal children from 6 to 14 years. A realistic survey should be made in the tribal areas as regards how many children are not coming to schools and about the actual number of schools required.
6. Special incentives and allowance should be provided to the teachers working in tribal areas. The teachers should establish a healthy rapport with the tribal students and create a positive environment for them.
7. It is suggested to appoint more tribal teachers and female teachers in the tribal areas. The ecological, cultural, psychological characteristics of tribal children should be considered carefully by the teachers in tribal areas.
8. Higher level officials should check the functioning of schools frequently relating to the teaching methods, working hours, and attendance registers.
9. There is the need of introduction of tribal dialect in the curriculum and teaching-learning process. By developing script and vocabulary and preparing teaching and learning materials for tribal children can be a big boost for their active participation.
10. As government and different commissions have recommended that the teachers knowing tribal languages are to be posted in tribal areas should be abide strictly.

Conclusion

From the above discussion we can say despite special initiatives on tribal development by the central and the state Governments since independence, the achievement is far from satisfactory and the problem of tribal development is still a matter of concern. The problems associated with the tribal development in India are manifold, complex and inter-related. Tribal development even indicates serious challenges to policy-makers, administrators and development activists. In this context, it is imperative to bring the tribal people in India to the forefront of educational revolution and mainstream of national development. Education imparts knowledge, and knowledge self-identity and human environment will infuse a sense of confidence, courage and ability among the STs to know and overcome their problems associated with exploitation and deprivation, and avail socio-economic and political opportunities extended to them. So, in the years to come, due attention is to be paid for the overall improvement of the tribal. We need to look at the education of tribal people in a holistic manner and redefined our goals and delivery mechanism to suit the needs, cultures, values, and sensibilities of the people. Ultimately, it is not classroom transaction alone but the combined mobilisation of community, political machinery and the bureaucracy that holds the key to success in this regard.

References

1. Abdulraheem, A. (2011), Education for the Economically and Socially Disadvantaged Groups in India: An Assessment Economic Affairs, Vol. 56
2. Lal, M., Education, The Inclusive Growth Strategy for the economically and socially disadvantaged in the Society.
3. Sedwal, M. and Sangeeta, K.(2008), Education and Social Equity with special focus on Scheduled Castes and Scheduled Tribes in Elementary Education, NUEPA, New Delhi.
4. Department of Education, National Policy on Education, Ministry of Human Resource Development, Government of India, New Delhi.
5. Ministry of Tribal Affairs, Annual Report 2014-2015, Ministry of Tribal Affairs, Government of India, New Delhi.
6. Sachadeva, D.R. (2001). Social Welfare Administration in India, Kitab Mahal Pvt. Ltd., New Delhi.

18

Social Justice in India: An Overview

Ram Prasad Pal

The term 'social justice' implies several sound and eminently desirable concepts enunciated for the good of society in general, and of course it covers fair play for every section of the society, especially the weaker groups in the society. This seems unexceptionable and no one, however prejudiced or narrow minded, would object to the promotion of this ideal. The reckless flouting of the concept of social justice, and the denial of equal opportunities in life which this postulates, all reflect a tendency that is anti-national and marks totally unfair and unjustified behaviour. India is a land of diversity, a truly plural society in terms of racial multiplicity, religious discord, caste antagonism, linguistic exclusiveness, cultural segmentation and in many other ways to give a lie to the oft-quoted cliché of unity in diversity. Dr B.R. Ambedkar, the stormy petrel of amelioration of untouchables went to the extent of saying that as untouchables and Harijans, they belonged to Hindu religion but not to the Hindu society and he, together with a branch of other reformist leaders took up the cudgels on behalf of these deprived and discriminated segments of Hindus who were virtually ostracised from mainstream Hindu society.

Intellectually social justice means the acceptance of every human being not as a means but as an end. As Kant says, "Every man or woman has a worth and a dignity, which forbids his exploitation by any purposes whatever." In economic terms it means material good ought to be more equally distributed. This has been the interpretation of social justice in western civilisation from the days of the Bible to that of Marx. This means, as Mahatma Gandhi says, "We should wipe the tears from the face of the poorest of the poor in the land." In practical terms social justice means bringing together the fierce and the meek, economically rich and poor, socially and politically high and low on equal footing so far as governmental and non-governmental treatment concerned.

The spiritual dimension of social justice has been enumerated in the holy epic Bhagwadgita when it says they learned Brahmins, cows, elephants, dogs and chandals should all be treated equally.[1]

In the present context of India social justice has come to mean improving the lot of the downtrodden and weaker sections of the community, removing untouchability and the system of beggar; abolishing social evils like child-marriage, dowry, and child-labour; preventing gambling, drinking and immoral traffic; and improving the lot of the scheduled castes, the scheduled tribes and other backward class by reserving seats for them in the educational institutions, legislatures and administration.

Characteristics of Social Justice

Followings are the salient features of social justice:

1. Social justice is closely connected with some kind of material well being.[2]

2. The concept of social justice is reformative in character.[3] It calls for the revision of social order so as to have a more equitable society. Thus, while the main emphasis of legal justice is on preservation, social justice aims at reform and change.

3. While legal justice is pounced by the courts of law, social justice is initiated either by legislature or by reformers or by leaders.

4. Social justice is collectivist in nature. Here also it differs from legal justice. Legal justice is mainly concerned with the rights of individuals. But social justice is not concerned with individuals. It is concerned with a section or group or collectivity, especially, with the least advantaged.

5. Social justice does not mean equality. Sometimes it gives a call for unequal and preferential treatment. Thus, social justice demands reverse discrimination in favour of the worst off.

We start with certain provisions of the Indian Constitution, which is the fundamental law of the land. The Preamble of the Constitution itself says, "We the people of India, having solemnly resolved to constitute India into a Sovereign, Socialist and Democratic Republic and to secure to all its citizens—justice, social, economic and political..." Clearly, social justice in all its forms and to all citizens was regarded as fundamental to the set-up which our founding fathers prescribed for the country; it is mentioned on top of the other equally sound concepts, and yet this concept is being violated by countless people with amasing impunity, without fear. In fact, many of us would say that it is absurd to talk of social justice in this country, because almost, all the traditional and prevalent systems are loaded against social and economic justice. The Preamble provides for 'equality of status and of opportunity. 'In reality, neither equality of status nor of opportunity is assured.

There are distinct classes in society which stick to their privileges and refuse to share their riches and assets with others even while cores of people live in misery and perpetually groan under the burden of unfair practices, unjust policies and gross inequalities.

Provisions of Social Justice in the Indian Constitution

The Indian Constitution has many provisions for social justice. It places justice higher than the other principles of liberty, equality and fraternity. The Constitution also places social justice higher than economic and political justice. In Chapter III of Indian Constitution, which deals with fundamental rights, there are special provisions for social justice. For example, Article 15 authorises the Indian State to make special provisions for the advancement of women and children. Article 16 focuses upon the state the responsibility to make special provisions for the reservation of posts in favour of the least advantaged strata. Article 17 abolishes untouchability. Article 23 prohibits exploitation through traffic in human being, beggar and other forced labour. Article 17 abolishes untouchability. Article 24 prohibits the employment of children below the age of 14 in factories, or mines or in any other hazardous jobs.

Besides, an Articles 330 and 332 provide for reservation of seats for the least advantage section of the population in the Central parliament and state legislatures.

Corruption itself is a form of exploitation because people holding key positions extort money in the shape of bribes, gifts and services even for rendering simple services which are their duty. This process makes total nonsense of "equality of opportunity" guaranteed under the Constitution. Only those who have money can give bribes and grease the palms of greedy people. The rest have to suffer through the bureaucratic ways, especially red tape which in itself involves injustices to the countless people whose petitions or applications are kept pending for years.

Wherever we may go and whichever sphere we might study, we shall come across numerous cases where justice has been continuously denied to innocent citizens. Are all those who cause such denial not morally and legally guilty and are they not punishable under the eyes of law? And yet even the idea of hauling up highly placed offenders does not occur to the powers that be. The helpless citizen, of course, suffers in silence. The number of people in India who are suffering in silence must be legion. Almost the entire nation is suffering in silence.

Murders take place in Uttar Pradesh with impunity. The culprits of several broad daylight crimes, including murders, remain untraced. These sordid events leave their imprint on the sands of time, and the impression becomes widespread that people can commit any crime and get away with it. Where indeed is justice? Perhaps in no other democratic country would such events be allowed to happen.

The fact remains that there is a general climate of lawlessness; there seems to be no fear of the police or other officials. The police are unable to control to criminals. The foundations of social justice have been eroded. Ministers and other people holding power are apparently busy amassing wealth for themselves. They have no time to look into the people's problems. There is in large-scale misappropriation of public funds, another injustice. The result is that right before their eyes, lawless elements pose a continuing threat to the personal safety and liberty of innocent people. Is this the social justice by which our ministers swear day in and day out. The concept of social justice has been subjected to severe and searching criticisms on more grounds than one. To begin with the expression 'social justice' itself is a misnomer.[4] As a matter of fact, justice is always social. It never means a virtue that affects an individual alone.

There is no discipline, and there are hardly any morals. In the Indian context the critics of social justice point out that unequal treatment constitutes injustice to other individuals not belonging to the backward social groups but who are equally economically poor. The absence of these vital traits of character signify the absence of social and economic justice. Even within the backward groups, the benefits do not accrue to the most oppressed. As a result, only a few families of reserved castes have concerned most of benefits. The whole issue of the social justice in India, has been greatly politicised. It has become a handy weapon in the hands of politicians and political parties to form their vote-banks. There is no sign of justice or fair play in any sphere of life. It is injustice and corruption in each and every sphere of activities. The critics also point out that social justice is neither social nor justice. It is not social because instead of strengthening society, it is bent upon breaking it by generating caste-war and tensions. It is not justice because while justice aims at joining and uniting the various sections of society, it has divided society in forward and backward sections.

Therefore, the issue of social justice has given rise to serious debate in India and it is our duty as academicians to discuss it in a right direction. The issue is too important to be left only to the politicians for feathering their own nests. We hope in the coming years hold little promise of restoring social justice in the country.

References

1. *Bhagwadgita*.
2. C.J. Fredrich, *An Introduction to Political Theory*, Jaico Publishing House, Bombay, 1967, pp. 24-34.
3. D.D. Raphael, *Problems of Political Philosophy*, The MacMillan Press Ltd., London, 1976, p. 170.
4. *Ibid*, pp. 171-72.

19

दलित चेतना और सामाजिक परिवर्तनः अतीत एवं वर्तमान के आईने में नक्सली आंदोलन

लालेन्द्र कुमार कुन्दन

भारत में आरक्षण हजारों वर्ष से समाज की एक व्यवस्था रही है और यह विधिवत कानून के रूप में मान्य रहा है। इसी के तहत रामायण, महाभारत, गीता, वेद, पुराण, स्मृति, धर्मसूत्र आदि सभी ग्रन्थों में ब्राह्मण के नाम विद्या, क्षत्रिय के नाम सत्ता, वैश्य के नाम व्यापार और शूद्र के नाम गुलामी का आरक्षण रहा है। इस आरक्षण का परिणाम यह हुआ कि शूद्र भूखा, नंगा, गृह विहीन और सम्मानहीन हो गया। इससे समाज में भेद–भाव की खाई पैदा हुई और राष्ट्रीय भावना का लोप हो गया। परिणामस्वरूप भारत विदेशी आक्रमणकारियों के सामने संगठित होकर मुकाबला न कर सका और उसके सामने घुटने टेक दिये। यद्यपि पूर्व में ज्योतिबा फूले, रानाडे, शाहूजी महाराज, पेरियार ने जातिगत भेद–भाव के विरूद्ध शंखनाद किया, जिससे प्रभावित होकर अम्बेडकर ने ब्राह्मणवादी सामाजिक ढ़ांचे के खात्मे और उसकी जगह स्वतंत्रता, सामाजिक न्याय तथा समानता के आधार पर दलित वर्ग के लिए विशेष संरक्षण की जोरदार मांग की और आजाद भारत के संविधान में समानता का हक दिलाया। लेकिन इसके बावजूद सुविधाभोगी सामंत वर्ग अपने पूर्व के हक को छोड़ने

के लिए मानसिक रूप से तैयार नहीं था। दलितों के साथ मार–पीट, गाली–गलौच, उनकी बहू–बेटियों के साथ बलात्कार तथा दर्जनों नरसंहार जैसी घटनाओं से त्रस्त–पीड़ित लोग नक्सली संगठनों का दामन थामने को विवश हुए। भूमिपतियों व सामंतों की निजी सेनाओं तथा नक्सली संगठनों के मध्य जारी लम्बे संघर्ष, उनकी खेती पर लगे आर्थिक प्रतिबंध के चलते उनकी मनोवृत्ति में बदलाव स्पष्ट रूप से दृष्टिगोचर हो रहे हैं। हालांकि लोकतंत्र में हिंसा का कोई स्थान नहीं है और इसे कभी भी उचित नहीं ठहराया जा सकता। फिर भी इसमें सच्चाई है कि हिंसा–प्रतिहिंसा के कृत्य ने सामाजिक, राजनीतिक व आर्थिक मोर्चे पर ग्रामीण समाज के रूपान्तरण में महत्वपूर्ण योगदान दिया है।

भारतवर्ष में दो तीन हजार वर्ष से हिन्दुओं के धर्मशास्त्र में लिखित बातों को कानूनी दर्जा प्राप्त था और जब तक यहां से अंग्रेज नहीं गए तथा नया संविधान लागू नहीं हुआ तब तक राजाओं और न्यायालयों ने उसी शास्त्र–सम्मत कानून के अनुसार ही दण्ड आदि दिये। धर्म, जाति व ईश्वर के नाम पर उच्च जातियाँ सदियों से शत–प्रतिशत आर्थिक–सामाजिक आरक्षण भोगती रही हैं। धर्मशास्त्र आधारित आरक्षण के फलस्वरूप विद्या, धन, यश, वैभव व सत्ता मुट्ठी भर लोगों के पास सिमट कर रह गया था और बहुसंख्यक शूद्र, अशिक्षा, अंधकार, गरीबी तथा गुलामी की चक्की में पिसता रहा। जैन, बौद्ध, सिख, इस्लाम के प्रवर्तक–महावीर, गौतम, नानक, सूफी संत के अलावा कबीर, रैदास, चार्वाक आदि जैसे महापुरूष भी आये पर उनका विद्रोह इस हिन्दू व्यवस्था को हिला नहीं सका। जिस समाज की इतनी बड़ी आबादी गरीबी की रेखा से नीचे रहे, बदहाल सामाजिक जीवन जीये, अशिक्षा, कुपोषण तथा अकाल मृत्यु का शिकार हो, वह समाज, इन समुदायों को दरकिनार कर, खुद अपनी संवृद्धि और अग्रगति के विश्व में अपने यथोचित सम्मानजनक स्थान अपनी मुक्ति, अपने अधिकारों के सपने कैसे देख सकता था? फलस्वरूप भारत विदेशी हमलावरों का शिकार हुआ, क्योंकि एक तिरष्कृत बड़ी आबादी के लिए 'कोई नृप होए हमें क्या हानि' वाली बात थी और मुट्ठी भर सुविधा भोगियों ने हमलावरों के सामने घुटने टेक दिये।

भारतीय राष्ट्रीय कांग्रेस की स्थापना के बाद जहाँ एक ओर औपनिवेशिक शासन के खिलाफ संघर्ष की शुरूआत हुई, वहीं दूसरी ओर भारतीय समाज की कमजोरियों का आकलन–विश्लेषण तथा उसके निराकरण की कोशिशें भी तेज हुई। 1885 में कांग्रेस के प्रथम अधिवेशन में ही दीवान

बहादुर आर० रघुनाथ राव तथा एम० जी० रानाडे ने राजनीतिक आंदोलन और समाज सुधार आंदोलन के अंतःसंबंध पर पुरजोर ढ़ंग से विचार व्यक्त किये थे। 1886 में कांग्रेस के दूसरे अधिवेशन की अध्यक्षता करते हुए दादाभाई नौरेजी ने कहा कि निःसंदेह सामाजिक सुधार की आवश्यकता के प्रति कोई सदस्य उतना जागरूक नहीं है जितना मैं हूँ। परन्तु प्रत्येक काम के लिए उचित समय, उचित परिस्थितियों, दलों और उचित स्थान की आवश्यकता होती है। हम राजनीतिक दल के रूप में अपने राजनीतिक उद्देश्यों को अपने शासकों के समक्ष प्रस्तुत करने हेतु एकत्र हुए हैं, सामाजिक सुधार पर विवाद करने के लिए नहीं।................ अतः केवल उसी वर्ग के लोग ही अपने वर्ग में वांछित सुधारों के बारे में उचित कार्यवाही करें, जिनकी उन्हें अपेक्षा है। राष्ट्रीय कांग्रेस को केवल राष्ट्र के सामान्य हितों तक ही अपने को सीमित रखना चाहिए और अन्य वर्गों के सामाजिक सुधारों के सामंजस्य तथा अन्य मामले उन्हीं वर्गों पर छोड़ देने चाहिए। इसी आधार पर 'इंडियन नेशनल सोशल कांफ्रेन्स' नामक संस्था की बैठक मद्रास में राष्ट्रीय कांग्रेस के अधिवेशन के तुरंत बाद उसी पंडाल में बुलाई गई, जो 1895 ई० तक जारी रहा। मगर 1895 ई० में कांग्रेस के पूना अधिवेशन में सामाजिक सुधार विरोधी गुट विद्रोह कर बैठा और उसने धमकी दी कि यदि कांग्रेस ने सोशल कांफ्रेन्स को अपने पंडाल का उपयोग करने की अनुमति दी तो पंडाल फूंक दिया जाएगा।

तब भारतीय समाज की पुनर्रचना की दिशा में सर्वाधिक महत्वपूर्ण अछूत प्रश्न था। बीस प्रतिशत आबादी जो जातीय सोपान के निचले पायदान पर थी उन्हें कोई सामाजिक, राजनीतिक और धार्मिक अधिकार हासिल नहीं था। जन्म से लेकर मृत्यु तक हिन्दुओं के सभी महत्वपूर्ण कर्मकांडों में अपनी अहम भूमिका का निर्वाह करने के बावजूद वे अछूत थे, पर उनकी बहू–बेटियाँ नहीं, मंदिरों तथा स्कूलों में उनका प्रवेश वर्जित था पर कुत्ते, बिल्लियों का नहीं, कुओं तथा तालाबों से वे पानी नहीं ले सकते थे, उनके साथ गाली–गलौच तथा मार–पीट तो आम बात थी, सेवा तथा उत्पादन के वे औजार थे, फिर भी उनका उठना–बैठना, जीना–मरना सब कुछ ऊँची जातियों की मर्जी पर निर्भर था, परन्तु सन् 30 का दशक आते–आते प्रतिरोध के स्वर व्योम में गूंजायमान होने लगे और दलित प्रश्न एक सशक्त वैचारिक–राजनीतिक धारा बन चुकी थी, जिसके सशक्त प्रवक्ता अम्बेडकर थे। भारत के विभिन्न अंचलों में चले अनेक सामाजिक आंदोलनों, मालाबार में नारायण गुरू, महाराष्ट्र में ज्योतिबा फुले, महादेव

गोविन्द रानाडे, शाहूजी महाराज, मद्रास में पेरियार, रामास्वामी नायकर से प्रभावित होकर अम्बेडकर ब्राह्मणवादी सामाजिक ढांचे के खात्मे और उसकी जगह स्वतंत्रता, सामाजिक न्याय तथा समानता के आधार पर भारतीय समाज को पुनर्गठित करने की प्रक्रिया में दलित वर्ग के लिए विशेष संरक्षण तथा प्रोत्साहन के हिमायती बन गए। वे कहते थे कि "हिन्दू दलितों का उतना ही विरोधी है जितना भारतीयों के लिए यूरोपियन। यूरोपियन अभी तटस्थ हैं लेकिन हिन्दू दलितों के कठोर विरोधी हैं। जितनी जरूरत है देश की आजादी के लिए लड़ना, उससे अधिक जरूरत है सामाजिक अन्याय के लिए संघर्ष करना। बाद में जब स्वतंत्र भारत का संविधान बना तब दलितों को संवैधानिक संरक्षण प्रदान किया गया। अस्पृश्यता का अंत, शिक्षा, नौकरी तथा राजनैतिक आरक्षण, आर्थिक उत्थान आदि सुनिश्चित किये जाने के लिए अनुसूचित जाति आयोग की स्थापना की गई। लेकिन आजादी के छह दशक बाद भी उन्हें जिंदा जलाया जाता है, उनकी औरतों के साथ सामूहिक बलात्कार होता है, स्थानीय निकायों में निर्वाचित महिलाओं को (स्वतंत्रता तथा गणतंत्र दिवस) के मौके पर झंडा फहराने से रोका जाता है। बिहार में पिपरा, दनवार–बिहटा, अरवल, बेलछी, पारसबिगहा, लक्ष्मणपुर बाथे जैसे नरसंहार तो सामंती मानसिकता के दबदबे को याद बनाये रखने का काम करती हैं। न्यायालय द्वारा सबूत के अभाव में खूंखार अपराधी जेल से रिहा होकर खुलेआम सीना तानकर घूम रहे हैं। ऐसा इसलिए हो रहा है कि नीतियों व कानूनों को लागू करने का दायित्व उन्हीं लोगों के हाथों में है, जो इस अन्यायपूर्ण व्यवस्था का अंग होने की वजह से पूर्वाग्रहों से ग्रसित हैं।

ऐसी स्थिति में जहाँ सहज, स्वाभाविक जिंदगी पर इतनी पाबंदियाँ हों, वहाँ जाहिर है, जिंदगी अपना एक भूमिगत संसार रच लेती है। लेकिन अब उनके धैर्य की सीमा टूट चुकी थी और सामंतों के अतीत के दिन लद गए हैं। बिहार में जहाँ आज से कुछ साल पहले तक जो मजदूर बड़े जोतदारों का सेवक था, वह वामपंथी संगठनों की सभा में भाग लेने के बाद उन्हें मालिक कहना भी भूल गया है और उनसे जवाब–तलब करने की घृष्टता भी करने लगा है। नक्सली आंदोलन ने परम्परागत व मनुवादी व्यवस्था से ग्रस्त समाज को जबरदस्त ढंग से प्रभावित किया है और सामाजिक, राजनीतिक व आर्थिक मोर्चे पर ग्रामीण समाज के रूपान्तरण में महत्वपूर्ण योगदान दिया है। इसने मजदूरी का संघर्ष, जमीन का संघर्ष, नदी, तालाब, बाग–बगीचों पर संघर्ष तथा भ्रष्टाचार विरोधी आंदोलन जैसे

मुद्दे को अपने हाथ में लिया है। इनकी वजह से गांवों में चोरी–डकैती, छेड़खानी व बलात्कार जैसी गतिविधियों पर अंकुश लगा है। ऊँची जातियों के सामंती तेवर नरम हुए हैं और सूर्यास्त होते ही दलितों के टोले से होकर गुजरने वाले रास्ते उनके लिए बंद हो गए हैं। यह परिवर्तन भूमिपतियों व सामंतों की निजी सेनाओं तथा नक्सली संगठनों के मध्य जारी लम्बे संघर्ष, बड़े तथा क्रूर जोतदारों के कृषि–भूमि पर लगे आर्थिक नाकेबंदी, उनकी तैयार फसलों को काट लिये जाने तथा जलाये जाने, स्कूल के बंद हो जाने (पुलिस बलों के स्थायी आवास बन जाने से) तथा बेटे–बेटियों की शादियों (बारात पर हमला होने का खतरा) रूक जाने की वजह से हुआ।

बहरहाल, नक्सल प्रभावित क्षेत्रों में इस आंदोलन के फलस्वरूप आये जातीय व वर्गीय जागरूकता का आलम यह है कि हाल में सम्पन्न हुए स्थानीय निकायों के चुनाव में दलितों ने अपनी महत्वपूर्ण भागीदारी सुनिश्चित की है। संघर्ष के इलाकों में बड़ी संख्या में मजदूर, किसान खासकर युवकों की नयी पीढ़ी अंधविश्वासों से कमोवेश मुक्त हुई है। पहले जहाँ गांवों में या तो पौराणिक कथाओं या डाकू सरदारों के कारनामों पर आधारित नाटक खेले जाते थे, वहीं आज 'इन्कलाब', 'खून का बदला खून', 'रोटी और इन्साफ', 'जंजीरें तोड़ दो', 'कारवां दिल्ली जाएगा' आदि का मंचन हो रहा है। आज से कुछ वर्ष पूर्व तक बिहार के गांवों में जो हिंसक माहौल विद्यमान था, सामाजिक तनाव था तो इसके पीछे मजदूरों, दलितों का उग्र होना नहीं है, वरन् यह इस बात का परिचायक है कि वे अपने अधिकारों, विशेषाधिकारों के प्रति पहले से ज्यादा सचेत व जागरूक हुए हैं और अब वह गूंगा–बहरा बनकर बैठे रहने को विवश नहीं है। हालांकि यह पूरी तरह सच है कि पूरा नक्सली आंदोलन घृणा पर आधारित नकारात्मक आंदोलन है, जो सम्पन्न और बर्बर किसानों की प्रतिक्रिया में चल रहा है। लेकिन यह भी सच है कि जो जातियां सामाजिक सोपान में निचले पायदान पर खड़ी थी, उनकी पहचान का संकट अब खत्म हो गया है और वे सीना तानकर खड़ी होने लगी हैं तथा सत्ता में वाजिब हिस्सेदारी लेकर निर्णय–प्रक्रिया को प्रभावित करने की स्थिति में आ गयी है।

इन उपलब्धियों के बावजूद इस तथ्य से इंकार नहीं किया जा सकता कि मामला चाहे हत्या का हो, आगलग्गी का हो, बलात्कार का हो, सर्वत्र गरीब–गरीब से टकरा रहा है, गरीब ही निशाना बन रहा है, अमीर–अमीर

से कहीं भी नहीं टकरा रहा है और वह इस अराजक स्थिति के बीच भी सुरक्षित है। वस्तुतः नक्सली वारदातों के शिकार जितना गरीब व मध्य वर्ग के लोग हो रहे हैं, उतने सामंत व पूंजीपति नहीं। मेहनतकश जनता के प्रति यह साजिशाना हरकत बंद होना चाहिए अन्यथा निर्धनता के बजाय संघर्ष के इलाके के सारे गरीब समाप्त हो जायेंगे। ऐसी स्थिति में दलितों तथा वंचितों को भी चाहिए कि वे सरकार द्वारा घोषित स्वयं के कानूनों को ही लागू करने के लिए दबाव डालें तथा कोई ऐसा हिंसक रास्ता अख्तियार नहीं करें, जिससे शासन को वंचित करने पर दमन ढाने का बहाना मिले। बोधगया मठ की दस हजार एकड़ जमीन पर नौ वर्षों के शांतिपूर्ण संघर्ष की बदौलत सफलता प्राप्त करके युवा संघर्ष वाहिनी एवं मजदूरों ने यह साबित कर दिया कि शांतिपूर्ण संघर्ष में वह ताकत है जो सामंती हिंसा तथा राज्य हिंसा के प्रभाव को ध्वस्त कर सकता है। भूमि मुक्ति से संबंधित हिंसक आंदोलन को इससे ज्यादा सफलता आज तक नहीं मिली है। लेकिन इसके साथ ही भूपतियों को भी अपने लोभ पर अंकुश लगाना चाहिए। उनके पास अपनी उपलब्ध जमीन के होते हुए भी अवैध भूमि का दखल है, यह प्रवृत्ति घातक है। इसके लिए भूमि सुधार का क्रियान्वयन सही ढंग से करते हुए कमजोर वर्ग के लोगों को कानूनी संरक्षण देना होगा। न्यायालय की प्रक्रिया को जटिल व लम्बा न करके शीघ्र निष्पादन की व्यवस्था कराना आज की जरूरत है। भारत के जिन क्षेत्रों में सामाजिक असंतोष कायम है वहां विकास एवं विधि व्यवस्था में सरकारी दखल कमजोर है। इसलिए वहां सरकार की साख व विश्वसनीयता बहाल करने के उपाय जरूरी हैं। वर्तमान प्रशासनिक व्यवस्था की सबसे बड़ी खामी उसमें न्याय प्रणाली का अभाव है। यह बेहद खर्चीली, उलझनपूर्ण तथा समय की बर्बादी करने वाली है। इसलिए ग्राम सभाओं को न्याय पंचायतों में बदला जाना चाहिए। केन्द्रीय ग्रामीण विकास मंत्री जयराम रमेश दलितों–आदिवासियों का झुकाव व अंतर्लिप्तता नक्सली संगठनों से हटाने के मामले में ईमानदारी पूर्वक प्रयासरत हैं। इस बात से कोई इंकार नहीं कर सकता कि दलितों–वंचितों के साथ 'नक्सली' के नाम पर जो कुछ हो रहा है वह समाज के विभिन्न वर्गों का बुनियादी सुविधाओं से वंचित रहने का परिणाम है, जबकि संविधान तथा विभिन्न कानूनी प्रावधानों के तहत उन्हें इन सुविधाओं को पाने का अधिकार था। संविधान की प्रस्तावना में घोषित आदर्शों पर अमल से ही ग्रामीण हिंसा से उबरा जा सकता है।

संदर्भ सूची

1. एस0 एल0 सागर, आरक्षण क्यों, सागर प्रकाशन, मैनपुरी, 1987, पृ. सं.–5।
2. प्रसन्न कुमार चौधरी एवं श्रीकांत, बिहार में दलित आंदोलन, वाणी प्रकाशन, दरियागंज, नई दिल्ली, 2005, पृ. सं.–10।
3. वही, पृ. सं.–11।
4. अशोक कुमार अमर, अदृश्य न्याय का समाज एवं आरक्षण नीति, एस0 के0 पब्लिशिंग कम्पनी, रांची, 2005, पृ. सं.–8।
5. एल0 के0 कुन्दन, नक्सलवाद : उद्भव और विकास, क्लासिकल पब्लिशिंग कम्पनी, नई दिल्ली, 2010, पृ. सं.–185।
6. लालेन्द्र कुमार कुन्दन, बिहार राज्य में नक्सलवाद की राजनीति का एक अनुभूतिपूर्ण अध्यापन (शोध प्रबंध), 1988, पृ. सं.–213।
7. योजना, जुलाई 2008, पृ. सं.–53–55।

20

दलित राजनीति और सोशल इंजीनियरिंग: आशाएँ और आशंकाएँ

नन्दलाल भारती

1932 में ब्रिटिश सरकार साम्प्रदायिक प्रतिनिधित्व के सवाल पर अपना निर्णय दिया। इसमें डॉ अम्बेडकर के दलितों के लिए अलग निर्वाचक मण्डल की मांग को स्वीकार कर लिया गया। इससे गांधी जी और कट्टरपंथी हिन्दू विचलित हो गये। फलस्वरूप गांधी जी और हिन्दुओं ने 'कम्युनल अवार्ड' में मिले दलितों के राजनीतिक प्रतिनिधित्व को अस्वीकार कर दिया। उसके विरूद्ध येरवडा जेल में ही गांधी जी आमरण अनशन पर बैठ गये और अंततः भारी सामाजिक दबावों के बीच गांधी जी और डॉ बी0आर0 अम्बेडकर के मध्य 1932 में पूना पैक्ट हुआ जिसमें पृथक निर्वाचक मण्डल के स्थान पर निर्वाचन क्षेत्रों को आरक्षित करने का निर्णय लिया गया।

सुप्रसिद्ध दलित चिंतक कंवल भारती के अनुसार, "पूना पैक्ट ने दलित राजनीति की दिशा ही बदल दी। डॉ अम्बेडकर ने वर्गीय प्रतिनिधित्व का सवाल उठाया था। गांधी और हिंदुओं ने आरक्षण व्यवस्था लागू कर भविष्य की पूरी राजनीति को जाति पर खड़ा कर दिया। पूना पैक्ट कांग्रेस के लिए वरदान साबित हुआ। कांग्रेस ने दलित जातियों में अशिक्षित और सबसे कम योग्यता वाले व्यक्तियों को संसद और विधानमण्डलों में भेजा।

सत्ता स्वार्थ ने उन्हें कांग्रेस हाईकमान और शासक वर्ग का 'यसमैन' बना दिया और वे अपने वर्ग के प्रति दायित्वों को भूल गये।''

कंवल भारती का मानना है कि, ''पूना पैक्ट के परिणाम ने डॉ अम्बेडकर के मन में असंतोष पैदा कर दिया और वे इस निष्कर्ष पर पहुंचे कि आरक्षण और प्रतिनिधित्व की व्यवस्था से सामाजिक परिवर्तन नहीं लाया जा सकता है। उनके अनुसार यह व्यवस्था ब्राह्मणवाद और पूंजीवाद को मजबूत करने वाली है। उन्होंने देखा कि असमानता पर आधारित ब्राह्मणवाद दलितों में भी सिर चढ़कर बोलने लगा था। शिक्षित और नौकरी पेशा दलितों का एक बड़ा हिस्सा अवसरवादी होता जा रहा था जो अपने निजी स्वार्थों के लिए शोषक वर्ग की भांति अपने ही भाई–बहनों का शोषण करने लगा था। इस बीच डॉ अम्बेडकर ने साम्राज्यवाद, ब्राह्मणवाद एवं पूंजीवाद का सामना करने के लिए इंडिपेंडेण्ट लेबर पार्टी ऑफ इण्डिया (1936) का गठन किया। लेकिन वह अपने उद्देश्य में सफल नहीं हुए। इसलिए उन्होंने इंडिपेंडेण्ट लेबर पार्टी ऑफ इण्डिया को भंग कर शेड्यूल्ड कास्ट फेडरेशन (1942) का गठन किया, जिसका प्रमुख उद्देश्य सामाजिक गतिविधियों के माध्यम से राजनीतिक का संचालन करना था। लेकिन कांग्रेस के साम, दाम, दण्ड, भेद के आगे उनके सारे प्रयास निरर्थक साबित हुए। आगे चलकर उनके द्वारा चयनित लेटिनेंटों ने एन0 शिवराज की अध्यक्षता में रिपब्लिकन पार्टी ऑफ इण्डिया (1957) का गठन किया। लोग शुरू में इससे भावनात्मक रूप से जुड़ते गये क्योंकि इसका गठन डॉ अम्बेडकर की इच्छाओं के अनुरूप हुआ था। लेकिन बहुत जल्दी ही यह दिशाहीनता एवं विचारहीनता की शिकार हो गयी। इस खालीपन को भरने के लिए दलित युवाओं ने महाराष्ट्र में सिविल अधिकारों और न्याय हेतु 1972 में दलित पैंथर्स मूवमेण्ट्स का गठन किया। यद्यपि यह कोई राजनीतिक दल नहीं था, लेकिन बहुत जल्दी ही इसमें अर्न्तविरोध शुरू हो गई अंततः इसका विभाजन हो गया। फलस्वरूप दिशाहीन दलितों को कांग्रेस पुनः अपने साथ जोड़ने में कामयाब हो गई और 1971 में इंदिरा गांधी ने जगजीवन राम को कांग्रेस का अध्यक्ष बना दिया। उसी वर्ष मध्यावधि चुनाव हुये और कांग्रेस 'गरीबी हटाओ' नारे के साथ पुनः सत्ता में आयी।

जिन दलितों, वंचितों एवं पिछडे वर्गों के लिए डॉ अम्बेडकर ने संविधान के माध्यम से सामाजिक, आर्थिक एवं राजनीतिक धरातल तैयार किया, उसे मजबूत करने के बजाय उनके समर्थकों ने केवल राजनीतिक

नेतृत्व एवं वर्चस्व की लड़ाई लड़ी और दलितों का सच्चा नेता या रहनुमा होने का दावा करते रहे। बाबा साहब द्वारा बनाये गये विभिन्न संगठनों को आगे बढ़ाने के बजाय ज्यादातर दलित नेताओं ने अपने–अपने दल अथवा संगठन बनाये और उसके सुप्रीमों बनकर प्रत्यक्ष या अप्रत्यक्ष रूप से अन्य राजनीतिक दलों को सहयोग करते रहे और आज भी दूसरे दलों या संगठनों के मोहरा बने हुए हैं तथा अवसर मिलने पर दलित हितों की सौदेबाजी करते हैं, जैसे–उदितराज, रामबिलास पासवान और रामदास अठावले आदि। इन्हें सवर्ण दलितों के नाम से जाना जाता है जो कि क्षणिक निजी स्वार्थ हेतु किसी भी दल के पाले या गोदी में जा बैठते हैं।

1980 तक दलित राजनीति का कोई प्रभावकारी वजूद नहीं दिखायी देता है। दलित वर्ग कांग्रेस का मूक समर्थक और वोट बैंक बनकर रह गया था और यह स्थिति मान्यवर कांशीराम के आगमन तक बनी रही। 1980 में दलित आंदोलन के नायक के रूप में कांशीराम का उदय हुआ। उन्होंने 1978 में बामसेफ (बैकवर्ड एण्ड मॉइनारिटी कम्युनिटीज इम्प्लाईज फेडरेशन) की स्थापना की जो मुख्यतः दलित, पिछड़े और अल्पसंख्यक समुदाय के कर्मचारियों का एक मजबूत संगठन था। इसी से अभिप्रेरित होकर उन्होंने 1981 में राजनीतिक उद्देश्य को पूरा करने हेतु दलित शोषित समाज संघर्ष समिति (डी.एस.–4) का गठन किया, जो आगे चलकर बहुजन समाज पार्टी (1984) के रूप में उभर कर सामने आया। इस प्रकार दिशाहीन दलित राजनीति को बी.एस.पी. ने एक दिशा प्रदान किया।

बाबा साहेब के प्रतिनिधित्व एवं भागीदारी के संघर्ष को आगे बढ़ाते हुए मान्यवर कांशीराम ने राजनीतिक तौर पर 'जितनी जिसकी संख्या भारी, उतनी उसकी हिस्सेदारी' और महात्मा बुद्ध के 'बहुजन हिताय, बहुजन सुखाय' के उपदेश को सुश्री मायावती ने दार्शनिक अंदाज में 'सर्वजन हिताय, सर्वजन सुखाय' के रूप में प्रस्तुत किया जो सभी जातियों के लिए सर्वमान्य और फायदे का सौदा लगा। वास्तव में यही बी.एस.पी. की सोशल इंजीनियरिंग है। उत्तर प्रदेश में कुछ समय से सत्ता से दूर रहीं कुछ प्रमुख जातियाँ जैसे– ब्राह्मण, क्षत्रिय, अल्पसंख्यक आदि ने सोचा कि यहाँ कम से कम संख्या के अनुपात में हिस्सेदारी की बात तो की जा रही है। हिस्सेदारी के इस रहस्य को सबसे पहले ब्राह्मणों ने समझा और पहली बार बी.एस.पी. के आरक्षित उम्मीदवारों को बड़ी संख्या में चुनकर विधानसभा में भेजा। फलस्वरूप सुश्री मायावती के नेतृत्व में चौथी बार स्पष्ट बहुमत

की सरकार बनी और सोशल इंजीनियरिंग के सिद्धांत के अनुरूप मंत्रिपरिषद् में सभी जातियों को उचित प्रतिनिधित्व प्रदान किया गया। बी.एस.पी. की इस सोशल इंजीनियरिंग ने सामाजिक एवं राजनीतिक पंडितों को सोचने पर मजबूर किया कि आखिर सुश्री मायावती ने कौन सा फार्मूला अपनाया, जिससे उन्हें आश्चर्यजनक सफलता मिली। आशाओं एवं आशंकाओं पर बुद्धिजीवियों ने चिन्तन–मनन शुरू किया। दलितों के प्रति सदैव संवेदनशील रहने वाले विद्वान एवं विचारक श्री एच.एल.दुसाद ने इन आशाओं एवं आशंकाओं पर कुछ विद्वानों के साक्षात्कार द्वारा अपनी संपादित पुस्तक 'उत्तर प्रदेश में बी0एस0पी0 की सफलता–सोशल इंजीनियरिंग का कमाल या कुछ और (एक चुनावी अध्ययन)' में जानने की कोशिश की है जो इस प्रकार है–

कुछ विद्वानों का मानना है कि सोशल इंजीनियरिंग शब्द ब्राह्मणों की देन है, जिसे इतिहास के पन्नों में देखा जा सकता है। जबकि गिरिराज किशोर के अनुसार, ''समाजशास्त्रीय शब्दावली के अन्तर्गत यह सोशल इंजीनियरिंग भले ही हो लेकिन इसका प्रयोग सर्वप्रथम गौतम बुद्ध ने किया था। गणिका से लेकर साम्राज्ञी तक और अंगुलिमाल से लेकर अशोक तक उनकी सोशल इंजीनियरिंग के उपकरण या हिस्सा बन गये थे। उसके बाद गांधी जी ने यह प्रयोग किया, जिसमें दलित से लेकर मालवीय जैसे कट्टर ब्राह्मण शामिल हुए, बाद में सोहरावर्दी जैसे कट्टरवादी भी इस इंजीनियरिंग से बच नहीं पाये। मायावती के हाथ में यह इंजीनियरिंग नये सन्दर्भ में आयी है। वह इस इंजीनियरिंग का प्रयोग जितनी सावधानी से करेंगी उतनी जल्दी वह समाज का विश्वास अर्जित कर पायेंगी। इसके लिए जनता को विश्वास दिलाना और पाना दोनों जरूरी है। कांग्रेस इस निधि को पाकर छोड़ चुकी है। अब यह पारसमणि मायावती के हाथ लगी है। किस सीमा तक वे इसे संभाल सकती हैं, यह उन पर निर्भर करेगा कि न्याय व समता के प्रति जनविश्वास राजनीति की ललक से मुक्त होकर कहाँ तक अर्जित करने में सफल होती हैं।'' प्रो. तुलसी राम के अनुसार, ''आज दलित नेता पूरी तरह से भटक गयें हैं। अम्बेडकर को कोई नहीं अपनाता है। कोई सत्ता का नारा देता है तो कोई सत्ता में भागीदारी का नारा देता है और इन सबका उद्देश्य केवल राजनीतिक लाभ और उसके जरिए आर्थिक लाभ ही है।'' आज के नेतृत्व में सकारात्मक सोच एवं दूरदृष्टि का अभाव है जो कार्य डा. अम्बेडकर ने बिना राजनीति के कर

दिखाया उस कार्य के लिए आज के दलित नेताओं को राजनीति करनी पड़ती है।

दलित शुभचिंतक डा. विवेक कुमार ने राजनीतिक दृष्टि से दलित नेतृत्व को दो भागो में विभाजित किया है –एक स्वतन्त्र और दूसरा परतन्त्र दलित राजनीतिक नेतृत्व। उनके अनुसार स्वतन्त्र दलित राजनीतिक नेतृत्व और इस पर वर्चस्व दलितों का ही होता है। स्वतन्त्र कार्ययोजना व विशिष्ट रूझान के साथ दलित ही इसकी मुख्य धारा में होते हैं। इसके विपरीत परतन्त्र दलित राजनीतिक नेतृत्व सवर्ण एवं अन्य पिछड़े वर्गों के पार्टियों के अनुसूचति जाति व जनजाति के प्रकोष्ठ में मिलता है। कांग्रेस और भाजपा जैसे दलों के नाम उदाहरण स्वरूप लिये जा सकते हैं। इन दलों के अनूसूचित जाति व जनजाति प्रकोष्ठ में न तो कोई स्वतंत्र एजेन्डा होता है और न ही कोई खास रूझान। इस प्रकार परतन्त्र दलित राजनीतिक नेतृत्व हाशियें पर पड़ा रहता है और उसका पार्टी में कोई खास दखल नहीं होता, अर्थात वह गांधी जी के तीन बन्दर बन कर रह जाते हैं, जिन्हें न तो कुछ दिखायी देता है, न सुनाई देता है और न तो कुछ बोलने दिया जाता है।

सोशल इंजीनियरिंग को स्पष्ट करते हुए खुशी लाल जाटव कहते हैं कि "ब्राह्मण बुद्धिजीवी वर्ग है तथा जाति व्यवस्था से खुद उबरना चाहता है। ऐसे में वह अपने आप सामाजिक व आर्थिक परिवर्तन की बात करेगा। दलित चिंतक श्री चन्द्रभान प्रसाद का मानना है कि, "सोशल इंजीनियरिंग एक ऐतिहासिक घटना है। यह ट्रेंड सामाजिक समरसता को बढायेगा और वैमनस्यता घटायेगा।" योग गुरू स्वामी रामदेव ने आशा व्यक्त की थी कि, "बहन मायावती की सोशल इंजीनियरिंग ने प्रदेश में चमत्कार दिखाते हुए सत्ता हासिल की है। वह सोशल इंजीनियरिंग केवल सत्ता तक ही सीमित नहीं रहेगी अपितु अगडों एवं पिछडों के संघर्ष पर विराम लगाकर आपस में भाईचारा, प्रेम व सद्भावना का वातावरण बनायेगी।"

श्री वाई.एल.भारती के अनुसार, "दलित–ब्राह्मण की सोशल इंजीनियरिंग से दलितों के सामाजिक, धार्मिक आन्दोलन की मारकता मंद पड जायेगी। दलितों में पनप रहा उच्च वर्ग, ब्राह्मणों के समूह में शामिल होने की होड़ में अपने समाज के दुख दर्द से विमुख/उदासीन हो जायेगा, जिसका दुष्परिणाम यह होगा कि दलित विकास की मुख्य धारा से सैकडों वर्ष पीछे हो जायेगा।"

कुछ राजनीतिक विश्लेषकों का मानना है कि दलित राजनीति अपनी दिशा से भटक चुकी है क्योंकि बहुजन से सर्वजन की ओर कदम बढ़ा दिया है जो कि स्वाभाविक नहीं है। स्वाभाविक गठबन्धन दलितों, पिछडों और मुसलमानों का हो सकता है। यह बिगड़ा तो राजनीति का खेल बिगड़ सकता है, जैसा कि किशन पटनायक कहते हैं कि, ''दलित, पिछड़ों और मुसलमानों को मिलाकर राजनीति करने पर स्वाभाविक रूप से क्रांतिकारी राजनीति का जन्म होगा।''

उत्तर प्रदेश विधानसभा (2012) और लोकसभा (2014) के निर्वाचन में बी0एस0पी0 की दलित–ब्राह्मण और दलित–मुस्लिम गठजोड़ रूपी सोशल इंजीनियरिंग आंशिक रूप से सफल हुई। विधानसभा में तो वह प्रमुख विपक्ष की भूमिका में रही लेकिन लोकसभा निर्वाचन में अपने कारवाँ को आगे नहीं बढ़ा पाई और न ही अपने इतिहास को दोहरा पाई। इस प्रकार राजनीतिक पण्डितों का सोशल इंजीनियरिंग के स्थायित्व को लेकर अभिव्यक्त की गई आशंकाएँ सच साबित हुई हैं। जब कोई पार्टी या संगठन अपने मूल विचारों से भटकता है तो सबसे पहले अपने कैडर्स को संशय में डालता है और जो पहले से संशय में होते हैं उसे दूर या दूसरी तरफ जाने का अवसर प्रदान करता है। बी0एस0पी0 का राजनीतिक इतिहास यही बताता है कि वह अगले हर चुनाव में बेहतर प्रदर्शन करती है। लेकिन 2014 के लोकसभा निर्वाचन में एक भी सीट पर उसे विजय नहीं मिली। यहॉ बाबा साहब डॉ बी0आर0 अम्बेडकर की आरक्षितों सीटों के प्रति व्यक्त की गई आशंकाएं सच प्रतीत होती है और मान्यवर कांशीराम का वोट हमारा, राज तुम्हारा नहीं चलेगा के विपरीत सीट (आरक्षित) तुम्हारा, वोट तुम्हारा और राज हमारा खूब चलेगा–खूब चलेगा देखने को मिली है। क्योंकि सोलहवीं लोकसभा में अधिकांश आरक्षित सीटों पर भारतीय जनता पार्टी की विजय ने यह सच साबित किया है। इसे भी बी0जे0पी0 की सोशल इंजीनियरिंग कहा जा रहा है। लेकिन इसके आधारभूत सिद्धांत प्रतिनिधित्व या भागीदारी को केन्द्रीय मंत्रिपरिषद् में नजरअंदाज कर दिया गया है।

आज बहुजन समाज, सर्वसमाज से कन्धा से कन्धा मिलाकर चल रहा है, जिसे सोशल इंजीनियरिंग का नाम दिया गया है। जबकि यह स्वाभाविक गठजोड नहीं है। बल्कि इसे मजबूरी, लाचारी और अवसरवादी गठजोड़ कहा जा रहा है। इसमें किसने कितना कीमत चुकाया है। यह उत्तर प्रदेश की 2012 के विधानसभा निर्वाचन के परिणाम के बाद देखा जा सकता

है। इसमें न जाने कितने दलितों के घर जला दिये गये और कितनों को अपनी जान गंवानी पड़ी। यह हार–जीत की प्रतिक्रिया थी। जिसमें दलितों को कुछ हासिल नहीं हुआ, बल्कि सामाजिक वैमनस्यता और बढ़ती दिखाई दी।

अतः जिसे जोर–शोर से सोशल इंजीनियरिंग का नाम दिया जा रहा है उसकी काट सवर्णों ने निकाल ली है जिसे हमने सहर्ष स्वीकार कर लिया है। सवर्णों द्वारा सभी सरकारी, अर्धसरकारी संगठनों/संस्थाओं में एकल पद का सृजन कर आरक्षण/भागीदारी की मूल भावना को ही समाप्त करने की साजिश की जा रही है क्योंकि वर्तमान आरक्षण व्यवस्था एकल पदों पर लागू नहीं होती है। यही कारण है कि आज एकल पदों के जरिये सभी संगठनों पर सवर्ण अपना वर्चस्व कायम करता जा रहा है और दलित–पिछड़े भागीदारी से वंचित किये जा रहे हैं। तथा सरकारें मूकदर्शक बनी हुई हैं। इसके लिए सरकार को तत्काल सार्थक कदम उठाना चाहिए तथा संस्था/संगठन को एक इकाई मानते हुए आरक्षण की व्यवस्था करनी चाहिए अथवा एकल पदों पर चक्रानुक्रम में आरक्षण लागू किया जाना चाहिए ताकि सभी जातियों को बारी–बारी से महत्वपूर्ण पदों पर पहुंचने का संवैधानिक भावना के अनुरूप समान अवसर मिल सके।

निष्कर्षतः हम ए.आर. जोशी के शब्दों में कह सकते हैं कि "बहुजन हिताय व बहुजन सुखाय के स्थान पर 'सर्वजन हिताय–सर्वजन सुखाय' की संकल्पना ने भाजपा व कांग्रेस जैसे राष्ट्रीय दलों को सोचने पर मजबूर कर दिया है। ये पार्टियाँ भी सोशल इंजीनियरिंग के दवाब में अपने फैसले और कार्य पद्धतियों को बदलने के लिए बाध्य हो गयी हैं। इसके चलते गैर बराबरी और सामाजिक विशमता की खाई निश्चित रूप से कम होगी और देश में एक नई सामाजिक व्यवस्था का शुभारम्भ होगा।"

संदर्भ सूची

1. बाबा साहेब, डॉ बी. आर. अम्बेडकर, सम्पूर्ण वाड.मय, खण्ड–5, डॉ अम्बेडकर प्रतिष्ठान, कल्याण मंत्रालय, भारत सरकार, नई दिल्ली, 1998
2. नानक चंद रत्तू, डॉ बी0आर0अम्बेडकर, संस्करण और स्मृतियॉ, सम्यक प्रकाशन, नई दिल्ली, 2002
3. नानक चंद रत्तू, डॉ अम्बेडकर 'कुछ अनछुए प्रसंग', सम्यक प्रकाशन, नई दिल्ली, 2003

4. वाई.डी.सॉनटकी, थाट्स ऑफ डॉ बाबा साहेब अम्बेडकर (सम्पादित), सम्यक प्रकाशन, नई दिल्ली, 2004
5. रंगनायकम्मा, जाति प्रश्न के समाधान के लिए, राहुल फाउण्डेशन, लखनऊ, 2010
6. अभय कुमार दुबे, आधुनिकता के आयने में दलित (सम्पादित), वाणी प्रकाशन, नई दिल्ली, 2004
7. राजकिशोर, हरिजन से दलित (संपादित), वाणी प्रकाशन, नई दिल्ली, 2005
8. कांशीराम, चमचा युग, सिद्धार्थ बुक्स, दिल्ली, 2006
9. एच. एल. दुसाध, उत्तर प्रदेश में बसपा की सफलता (संपादित), दुसाध प्रकाशन, देवरिया (उ0प्र0), 2008
10. एच. एल. दुसाध, सामाजिक न्याय की राजनीतिक हार, दुसाध प्रकाशन, देवरिया (उ0प्र0), 2009
11. राजकिशोर, दलित राजनीति की समस्यायें, वाणी प्रकाशन, नई दिल्ली, 2006
12. एच. एल. दुसाध, सामाजिक परिवर्तन और बी0एस0पी0, सम्यक प्रकाशन, नई दिल्ली, 2005
13. विवेक कुमार, दलित समाजः पुरानी समस्यायें और नई आकांक्षायें, सम्यक प्रकाशन, नई दिल्ली, 2007
14. हरिकिशन संतोषी, दलितों के दलित, सस्ता साहित्य मण्डल प्रकाशन, नई दिल्ली, 2009
15. रामगोपाल सिंह, सामाजिक न्याय, लोकतंत्र और जाति व्यवस्था, रावत पब्लिकेशन, जयपुर, 1999
16. अजय बोस, बहन जी, वाणी प्रकाशन, नई दिल्ली, 2008
17. कुमारी मायावती एडवोकेट, बहुजन समाज और उसकी राजनीति, इन्द्रपुरी नई दिल्ली, 2000

21

न्यायिक सक्रियता एवं दलित

गोपाल प्रसाद, मीना, राहुल और नागेन्द्र कुमार

यद्यपि 'न्यायिक सक्रियता' विधि विशेषज्ञ, सामाजिक कार्यकर्ता स्वयं सेवी संस्था, राजनीति विज्ञान के अध्येता एवं प्रबुद्ध वर्ग के लिए आसमान से टपका कोई नया जुमला नहीं है, तथापि ग्रामीण आमजन, निरक्षर, महिला, दलितों एवं पिछड़ों आदि के लिए अनबुझ पहेली जैसा ही दिखता है। स्व के आपसी विवाद, अकड़, मकान एवं जमीन से सम्बन्धित समस्या के लिए तुरन्त न्यायालय की शरण लेते हैं परन्तु जहाँ समुदाय हित एवं सार्वजनिक हित होता है, वहाँ हाथ पर हाथ रखकर चुप्पी साध लेते हैं। यहाँ तक कि प्रबुद्ध दलित वर्ग भी 'जनहित याचिका' दाखिल नहीं करता, वहीं साधनसम्पन्न सवर्ण बिरादरी अपने वर्ग के हित के लिए छोटे–छोटे मुद्दों को लेकर न्यायालय में रिट दाखिल करते हैं और सम्बन्धित मामलों को ठण्डे बस्ते में डाल देने हैं। यह विशेषकर सरकारी नौकरी, सरकारी पट्टा, बंजरभूमि, शिक्षा एवं विशेष सुविधा (आरक्षण) से सम्बन्धित मामले होते हैं। उच्च न्यायालय एवं सर्वोच्च न्यायालय में 'जनहित याचिका' के नाम पर दलितों का एक तरह से शोषण का जरिया बनता दिख रहा है। यद्यपि इसमें पर्यावरण, जल प्रदूषण, साफ–सफाई आदि सकारात्मक विषय भी होता है, लेकिन इनकी संख्या कम है।

'न्यायिक सक्रियता' का सीधा–सा अर्थ है, सरकार के तीनों अंगों में कार्यपालिका, व्यवस्थापिका सुस्त और न्यायपालिका चुस्त। जो कार्य

व्यवस्थापिका व कार्यपालिका का है वह सही ढंग से अपने उत्तरदायित्व का पालन नहीं कर रहे हैं तो न्यायपालिका द्वारा वैसा व्यवहार करने हेतु दिशानिर्देश देना ही 'न्यायिक सक्रियता' है। अर्थात् 'जनहित याचिका' के नाम पर व्यवस्थापिका एवं कार्यपालिका के क्षेत्राधिकार में न्यायपालिका द्वारा कार्यपालिका के कार्य में हस्तक्षेप करना ही 'न्यायिक सक्रियता' है। चूँकि व्यक्ति के मौलिक अधिकार एवं संविधान का संरक्षक उच्च एवं उच्चतम न्यायालय ही हैं, इसलिए इससे सम्बन्धित याचिका भी इसी के शरण में जाती है। भारतीय संविधान के अनुच्छेद 32 में 'संवैधानिक उपचारों का अधिकार' (मौलिक अधिकार) के सभी भारतीय नागरिक को अधिकार मिला है कि यदि व्यक्ति के मौलिक अधिकार का हनन व्यक्ति/संस्था/वर्ग/राज्य द्वारा होता है, तो वह सीधे उच्च न्यायालय एवं उच्चतम न्यायालय में याचिका दाखिल कर सकता है ताकि अधिकार का संरक्षण हो सके, तभी तो दलितों के मसीहा, वंचितों के आन–बान–शान को संवैधानिक हथियार देने वाले संविधाान निर्माता, भारत रत्न बाबा साहेब डॉ. भीमराव अम्बेडकर ने 'अनुच्छेद 32' को 'भारतीय संविधान की आत्मा' से संबोधित किया है।

जनहित याचिका का श्रीगणेश उच्चतम न्यायालय के पूर्व मुख्य न्यायाधीश पी.एन. भगवती के उस निर्णय से माना जाता है जिसमें आदेश पारित किया कि पंजाब बनाम भारत सरकार ''सरकार (संसद) संविधान में संशोधन तो कर सकती है लेकिन इसके आधारभूत संरचना में कोई परिवर्तन नहीं कर सकती।'' साथ ही भगवती ने दिशानिर्देश (अन्य मामला) जारी किया कि यदि व्यक्ति, सरकार व संस्था के किसी निर्णय से सार्वजनिक समूह, विशेष वर्ग के हित में ठेस पहुँचता है तो वह सीधे 'जनहित याचिका' (PIL) के माध्यम से रिट दाखिल कर सकता है, जिस पर तत्काल कार्रवाई होगी। ध्यातव्य है कि, 'जनहित याचिका' जरूरी नहीं है कि वह वकील के माध्यम से ही पेश हो, बल्कि सादे कागज अथवा पोस्टकार्ड पर लिखकर सीधे न्यायालय को प्रेषित किया जा सकता है। ग्रामीण जनता, निरक्षर आमजन एवं दलितों में विशेष रूप से जागरूकता उत्पन्न करने की आवश्यकता है ताकि वह भी तीसरी आँख (न्यायालय) से न्याय की गुहार लगा सकें। विशेषकर दलित वर्ग में 'न्यायालय' के नाम पर हौवा (भय/खौफ) बन गया है कि यदि उच्च एवं उच्चतम न्यायालय की शरण लेंगे तो 25.50 हजार रूपये अवश्य चाहिए। इसमें सच्चाई भी है, क्योंकि व्यक्तिगत याचिका दाखिल करने में वकील मनमाने

ढंग से फीस के नाम पर पैसे वसूल करते हैं जिनसे आर्थिक रूप से विपन्न एवं साधनविहीन दलितों की कमर टूट जाती है। परन्तु 'जनहित याचिका' दाखिल करने में एक भी पैसा खर्च नहीं होता है, बशर्ते मामला 'सार्वजनिक हित' से जुड़ा हो।

दलितों को गरिमापूर्ण जीवन जीने एवं सार्वजनिक क्षेत्र में भागीदारी हेतु संवैधानिक आरक्षण का प्रावधान किया गया, जिससे निःसंदेह दलितों–पिछड़ों को फायदा हुआ है। लेकिन स्वतंत्र, निष्पक्ष, योग्यता से युक्त एवं गुणावत्तापरक निर्णय के नाम पर 'न्यायपालिका' में आरक्षण नहीं लागू किया जो वर्तमान तक बरकरार है, जो दलित किसी तरह हाईस्कूल एवं स्नातक की डिग्री लेकर आरक्षित कोटे से ही सरकारी नौकरी पा लेते थे, वे वकालत (एल.एल.बी.) की पढ़ाई की तरफ नजर भी नहीं उठाते हैं, क्योंकि 'असमान शिक्षा पद्धति' के चलते अनारक्षित सीट पर प्रतियोगिता संघर्श में विजयश्री आसानी से नहीं मिल पाती। परन्तु इसके अपवाद भी हैं, क्योंकि बहुत से दलित छात्र आज न्यायधीश पद पर विराजमान हैं, जिन्होंने अपने प्रतिभा का डंका पीटा है, फिर भी इनकी संख्या नाममात्र ही है। इसका जीता–जागता उदाहरण सर्वोच्च न्यायालय के पूर्व मुख्य न्यायधीश के.जी. बालाकृष्णन (2009) हैं, जो दलित वर्ग से ताल्लुक रखते हैं। आज स्थिति यह है कि न्यायपालिका पूरी तरह साधनसम्पन्न सामंती एवं सवर्ण बिरादरी की गिरत में है। वकील से लेकर न्यायधीश तक लगभग 95 प्रतिशत सीट पर सवर्ण वर्ग का कब्जा है। यह स्वाभाविक सी बात है कि जो भी 'निर्णय' होगा उसमें सर्वोच्च (सवर्ण वर्ग) होने की मानसिकता की गंध जरूर होगी, जिसका उदाहरण 'कोलकाता उच्च न्यायालय' में देखने को मिला, जो एक वर्ग–विशेष को लाभ पहुँचाने के लिए 'रिश्वत' लेकर अशोभनीय निर्णय दिया। इसी तरह का प्रतिदिन निर्णय आता है, लेकिन वह बाहर देखने को नहीं मिलता, क्योंकि मीडिया पर भी सवर्ण बिरादरी को एकाधिकार प्राप्त है, जो बहुत चर्चित मामला (बलात्कार एवं राजनेता से सम्बद्ध) होता है, उसी को मीडिया प्रसारित करती है, वहीं सरकार पिछड़ों, दलितों एवं गरीबों से सम्बन्धित मामलों में कोई विशेष कदम उठाती हैं तो उन्हें 'समानता सिद्धांत' का उल्लंघन दिखता है और मीडिया के माध्यम से 'न्यायालय' तक पहुँच जाता है। न्यायालय की स्वतंत्रता एवं निष्पक्षता पर तब अंगुली उठती है, जब समाचार–पत्र/इलेक्ट्रानिक मीडिया के खबर को संज्ञान में लेकर इसे 'जनहित याचिका' में तब्दील कर स्वयं सरकार के विरूद्ध 'निर्णय' देती

है। इसका जीता–जागता उदाहरण, उत्तर प्रदेश सरकार ने निजी महाविद्यालयों में शिक्षा स्नातक (बी.एड. – बैचलर ऑफ एजुकेशन) के नामांकन में पिछड़ों एवं दलितों के लिए (50 प्रतिशत) आरक्षण अनिवार्य रूप से लागू करने का शासनादेश जारी किया। परन्तु निजीकरण एवं स्व स्वामित्व की दुहाई देकर तुरन्त उच्चतम न्यायालय में 'जनहित याचिका' दाखिल हुई और उच्चतम न्यायालय का तत्काल निर्णय आया कि 'निजी शिक्षण संस्थानों' में आरक्षण देना संभव नहीं है, जबकि निजी शिक्षण संस्थान में 50 प्रतिशत अनुदान राज्य सरकार देती है। मीडिया एवं सवर्ण बिरादरी ने इसे 'ऐतिहासिक निर्णय' बताया परन्तु सच्चाई यह है कि इससे दलित एवं पिछड़े वर्ग के छात्रों का शिक्षक बनने का सपना चकनाचूर हो गया। अभी हाल में ही (जून 2009) इलाहाबाद उच्च न्यायालय ने 'उच्च शिक्षा आयोग' के प्रवक्ता पद के 1208 बैकलाग की भर्ती को निरस्त कर दिया है जो सामंती मानसिकता का ही परिचायक है। इसी तरह अन्य विभागों की भर्ती को भी न्यायालय में वाद दाखिल कर रोका गया है। वर्तमान में तो निजीकरण एवं शिक्षा के बाजारीकरण में दलित न तो गुणवत्तापरक शिक्षा ले सकते हैं और न ही रोजगार की संभावना दिखती है। शिक्षा पर गठित सभी समितियों (कोठारी कमीशन, सच्च कमेटी) ने 'समान शिक्षा पद्धति' हेतु सरकार को संस्तुति दी है, लेकिन 'सर्वोच्च न्यायालय' ने एक भी दिशा–निर्देश या निर्णय जारी नहीं किया है कि, सरकार नियम को समय से लागू करे अथवा प्राइवेट विद्यालय में भी दलित छात्रों का नामांकन अनिवार्य हो। दलित वर्ग में जो साधन–सम्पन्न एवं सरकारी नौकरीपेशा वाले हैं वह अपने बच्चों को गुणवत्तापरक शिक्षा दे रहे हैं परन्तु ग्रामीण, निरक्षर, बेरोजगार, दलित के बच्चों को तो गुणवत्तापरक शिक्षा केवल दिवास्वप्न ही लगती है।

यदि सर्वोच्च न्यायालय 'जनहित याचिका' के माध्यम से दलितों की शिक्षा, आवास एवं स्वास्थ्य के विशेष संदर्भ में निर्णय देती है तो न्यायालय की निष्पक्षता पर अंगुली नहीं उठती, लेकिन इनका 'न्यायिक सक्रियता' केवल साधन–सम्पन्न, उद्योगपति एवं सवर्ण समुदाय पर दिखती है। इसका मूल कारण यह है कि 'न्यायपालिका' में दलितों की भागीदारी नहीं है। सुश्री मायावती का यह कथन कि, "राजनीतिक सत्ता वह मास्टर चाबी है जिससे सभी क्षेत्रों (सामाजिक, आर्थिक न्याय) के ताले खुलते हैं।" न्यायपालिका पर लागू नहीं होता, क्योंकि 'न्यायपालिका स्वतंत्र संवैधानिक संस्था' है, जिस पर व्यवस्थापिका एवं कार्यपालिका का प्रभाव नाममात्र

का है। इसलिए आज आवश्यकता आ गयी है कि दलितों को 'न्यायिक सक्रियता' के प्रति जागरूक किया जाए, जिससे अधिक से अधिक संख्या में वकालत (एल.एल.बी.) की डिग्री लेकर न्यायपालिका में प्रवेश करें। जब तक न्यायालय में दलितों की भागीदारी नहीं होगी, तब तक पूर्वाग्रह से ग्रसित भेदभावपूर्ण निर्णय आते रहेंगे और मुरझाए चेहरे काले होते जायेंगे। यदि दलितों का शोषण रोकना है तो अधिक से अधिक वकील एवं न्यायधीश बनने की जरूरत है। जिस प्रकार आरक्षण के बदौलत ही प्रशासनिक सेवा में भागीदारी बढ़ती है, उसी प्रकार अपनी प्रतिभा को निखारकर बिना आरक्षण के ही न्यायालयरूपी चक्रव्यूह को तोड़ना होगा, वरना उसके आगे–पीछे घूमते ही रहेंगे। एक साधारण 'दिवानी/फौजदारी जिला न्यायालय' में रिट दाखिल करने में ज्यादा–से–ज्यादा 100–200 रूपया खर्च होता है लेकिन गरीबों, दलितों से एक–एक मुकदमा दर्ज करने के लिए 5000 से 20000 रूपये या इससे भी ज्यादा लेते हैं, जो खुल्लम–खुल्ला आर्थिक शोषण है। इस शोषण की तरफ मीडिया की नजर नहीं जाती। इस शोषण का मूल कारण है कि, दलित वर्ग के वकील नहीं हैं। इसलिए मनमाने ढंग से पैसा वसूल कर दलितों को हतोत्साहित किया जाता है, ताकि हमेशा जी–हुजूरी करते रहें। एक उदाहरण द्वारा वकालत शिक्षा की महत्ता के बारे में समझा जा सकता है, यदि कोई सवर्ण व्यक्ति को सुप्रीम कोर्ट में रिट दाखिल करना है तो निःसंदेह उसका मित्र, रिश्तेदार या पड़ोसी दिल्ली में वकालत करता होगा, जिससे वह बैठे–बैठे फैक्स कर रिट दाखिल करवा सकता है जिसमें अधिकतम पाँच सौ रूपया खर्च होगा। यदि जनहित याचिका दाखिल करना है तो केवल फोन से ही दाखिल हो जायेगी और यथास्थिति (Stay Order) का आदेश मिल जायेगा। दूसरी ओर वंचित, गरीब, दलित एवं पिछड़े वर्ग के व्यक्ति को दिल्ली में यदि रिट करना है तो दूर–दूर तक मित्र, रिश्तेदार वकील नहीं हैं, मजबूरीवश वह पहले सारे कागजात लेकर वकील के पास जायेगा, फीस पता करेगा, पुनः घर वापस आ जायेगा। वह किसी तरह गहना बेचकर जमीन गिरवी रखकर लगभग 50000 से 100000 रूपये तक व्यवस्था कर पुनः दिल्ली जाकर रिट दाखिल करेगा और यदि वह साधनविहीन एवं गरीब, लाचार है तो 'न्याय पाना' एक सपना रह जायेगा। यदि उसको 'जनहित याचिका' भी दाखिल करना है तो बिना दिल्ली जाए काम नहीं चलने वाला है, क्योंकि शिक्षा एवं जानकारी का अभाव है। इस प्रकार दलितों को अपना अधिकार पाना है, न्याय पाना है, शोषण रोकना

है तो केवल एक ही हथियार है सक्रिय होकर वकील एवं न्यायधीश बनने की।

दलितों की योग्यता पर एक प्रश्न हमेशा उठता है कि 'आरक्षण' के चलते गुणवत्ता प्रभावित होती है, लेकिन 'न्यायालय फैक्ट्री' तो सवर्णों के कब्जे में है, वहाँ फिर कौन प्रभावित करता है कि लाखों मुकदमे लम्बित हैं एवं अन्यायपूर्ण निर्णय आ रहे हैं। सत्तासीन, शक्तिसम्पन्न एवं सामन्ती लोग अपने हिसाब से निर्णय दिलवा रहे हैं। आरोपी बरी हो रहे हैं, ईमानदार, शरीफ लोग जेल में चक्की पीस रहे हैं। न्यायालय के न्यायधीश तक कहते हैं कि न्यायधीश कम हैं, मुकदमे ज्यादा हैं, इसलिए निस्तारण नहीं हो पाता। परन्तु जहाँ तक लम्बित मुकदमों की जो सूची है उसमें लगभग 75 प्रतिशत मुकदमें पिछड़े, दलितों एवं अल्पसंख्यक लोगों के हैं जो एक साजिश के तहत ठण्डे बस्ते में डाल दिये गये हैं ताकि सवर्ण बिरादरी की हानि न हो। वकील एवं पेशकार भी लॉबिंग कर दलितों के मुकदमों का निस्तारण नहीं करते, बल्कि तिथि पर तिथि लेकर आर्थिक शोषण करते हैं। वहीं सवर्ण बिरादरी के मुकदमे का तुरन्त निस्तारण करते हैं। जिस प्रकार राजनीति, मीडिया एवं उच्च शिक्षा में वंशवाद हावी है, उसी प्रकार न्यायालय में भी परिवारवाद हावी है।

अतः दलितों को अपना हक पाना है, दूसरे को दिलाना है तो अपने होनहारों को वकालत शिक्षा (एल.एल.बी.) दिलाना होगा वरना राजनीतिक सत्ता वहाँ जाकर स्थिर हो जायेगी। इसके साथ ही 'जनहित याचिका' एवं 'सूचना अधिकार अधिनियम 2005' का अधिक से अधिक प्रयोग कर न्यायिक सक्रियता को जन–जन तक पहुँचायें। डॉ अम्बेडकर ने जो नारा दिया 'शिक्षित बनो, संगठित हो, संघर्ष करो' आज उसे 'शिक्षित बनो, राजनेता बनो और न्यायधीश बनो' का व्यावहारिक रूप देना होगा।

सन्दर्भ सूची

1. डी.डी. बसु : "भारतीय संविधान – एक परिचय"।
2. श्रीमती सुशीला कौशिक : "भारतीय शासन एवं राजनीति"।
3. सुभाष कश्यप : "भारतीय संसद"।
4. बसु, डी.डी. : "भारतीय संविधान – एक परिचय", 2014।
5. कौशिक, श्रीमती सुशीला : "भारतीय शासन एवं राजनीति", 2012।
6. कश्यप, सुभाष : "भारतीय संसद", 2010।

7. प्रसाद, डॉ. गोपाल : ''लोकतंत्र और सामाजिक न्याय'', यूनिवर्सिटी पब्लिकेशन, नई दिल्ली, 2009।
8. प्रसाद, डॉ. गोपाल : ''भारत में दलितों की सच्ची तस्वीर'', वी.एल.एम.एस. पब्लिकेशन, नई दिल्ली, 2011।
9. सुमन, गोपाल प्रसाद : ''शोषण के विरूद्ध अधिकार का व्यावहारिक पक्ष'', लोक भारती प्रकाशन, गोरखपुर, 1998।
10. डॉ. विवेकानन्द एवं डॉ. गोपाल प्रसाद : ''पंचायती राजव्यवस्था'', वी.एल.एम.एस. पब्लिकेशन, नई दिल्ली, 2014।
11. डॉ. सन्दीप कुमार एवं डॉ. गोपाल प्रसाद : ''सार्क देशों में मौलिक अधिकार'', वी.एल.एम.एस. पब्लिकेशन, नई दिल्ली, 2014।
12. यादव, डॉ. धर्मेन्द्र कुमार एवं डॉ. गोपाल प्रसाद : ''राजनीतिक आधुनिकीकरण'', वी.एल.एम.एस. पब्लिकेशन, नई दिल्ली, 2014।
13. डॉ. नागेन्द्र कुमार एवं डॉ. गोपाल प्रसाद : ''सुश्री मायावती एवं भारतीय राजनीति'', वी.एल.एम.एस. पब्लिकेशन, नई दिल्ली, 2014।
14. प्रो. वर्मा, एस.एल. : ''उच्चतर आधुनिक राजनीतिक सिद्धांत'', नेशनल पब्लिशिंग, जयपुर, 2006।
15. विद्रोही, एम.आर. : ''दलित दस्तावेज'', सम्यक प्रकाशन, नई दिल्ली, 2004।
16. राम, दिनेश : ''समकालीन हिन्दी कहानी और अम्बेडकरवादी आन्दोलन'', अकादमिक एक्सेलेन्स, दिल्ली, 2007।
17. शील, बोधि : ''दलित साहित्य की वैचारिकी और डॉ. जय प्रकाश कर्दम'', अकादमिक प्रतिभा, दिल्ली, 2007।
18. कन्नौजिया, डॉ. अनीता रानी : ''दलित एवं वर्ग चेतना के आलोक में निर्गुण काव्य'', अकादमिक एक्सेलेन्स, दिल्ली, 2005।
19. राय, डॉ. वी.के. : ''प्रारम्भिक सांख्यिकी'', यूनिवर्सिटी पब्लिकेशन, नई दिल्ली, 2008।
20. महापरिनिर्वाण सूक्त।
21. पाण्डेय, डॉ. राजबली : ''गोरखपुर जनपद और उसका इतिहास''।
22. विकास–पुस्तिका गोरखपुर : ''सूचना एवं जनसंपर्क विभाग'', गोरखपुर 2001–2002, पृष्ठ 83।
23. सिंह, डॉ. उजागिर : ''भारत का आर्थिक एवं प्रादेशिक भूगोल'', उत्तर प्रदेश, हिन्दी संस्थान, लखनऊ, 1978।
24. श्रीवास्तव, डॉ. डी.एन. : ''अनुसंधान पद्धति'', आगरा, 2014।
25. प्रगतिका 2007, सूचना एवं जन सम्पर्क विभाग, उत्तर प्रदेश, गोरखपुर, पृष्ठ 9।

26. Hoda, Md. Minhajul :AlimAkhter and Nizamuddin Khan : "Social Research History, Stratigies and Presentation", Academic Excellence, Delhi, 2008.
27. Sharma, Dr C.K. and M.K. Jain : "Research Methodology", Shree Publisher & Distributors, Delhi, 2004.
28. Tripathi, Dr S.M. : "Human Face of Supreme Court of India", Radha Publications, New Delhi.

22

भारत में सामाजिक न्याय की अम्बेडकरीय परिकल्पना

राम बरन और अजय कुमार

भूमिका

पूरी दुनिया के समाजों में कई प्रकार के सामाजिक, सांस्कृतिक, आर्थिक व धार्मिक विभेद मौजूद रहे हैं लेकिन भारत एक ऐसा देश है जिसका समाज जातिरूपी संस्था में इस तरह विभाजित है, जिसकी मिसाल तथा उदाहरण कहीं नहीं मिलेगा। ये जाति व्यवस्था समाज को हजारों–हजार टुकड़ो में बांटे हुए है। अनेको समाज सुधार कार्यक्रमो तथा समाज सुधार सामाजिक आन्दोलनों, संघर्षो के बावजूद 21वीं सदी में भी ये जातीय विभाजन बरकरार ही नहीं, बल्कि इसके नये–नये रूप रंग सामने आ रहे हैं, आजादी के आंदोलन के दौर में जहाँ एक ओर ब्रिटिश सत्ता से मुक्ति हेतु संघर्ष जारी था, वही इस देश का उत्पीड़ित तथा शोषित (दलित, पिछड़ा, अधीनस्थ समूह) बहिष्कृत समाज जाति व्यवस्था के शोषण से अपने को मुक्त करने हेतु छटपटा रहा था एवं संघर्ष कर रहा था। स्वतन्त्रता प्राप्ति के बाद स्वाधीन भारत के संविधान में अनुसूचित जातियों, जनजातियों एवं पिछड़े वर्ग (अधीनस्थो) के उत्थान के लिये आर्थिक, सामाजिक एवं राजनीतिक, न्याय, विचार, अभिव्यक्ति, विश्वास, मान्यता एवं धर्म की स्वतन्त्रता और प्रतिष्ठा, आरक्षण, शैक्षिक अधिकार

आदि का तथा संविधान में मूल अधिकारो का उल्लेख किया गया, जिसके द्वारा नागरिको को यह विश्वास दिलाने का प्रयास किया गया कि धर्म, वर्ग, लिंग, जाति–प्रजाति एवं अन्य के आधार पर भेदभाव नहीं किया जायेगा, साथ ही जिससे अधीनस्थो के प्रति अब तक किये गये भेदभाव पर अंकुश लगाने का प्रयास किया गया।

इस प्रकार से किसी समाज में कुछ नागरिकों या नागरिक समूहों के प्रति अन्य नागरिक समूहों या राज्य द्वारा भेदभावपूर्ण घृणास्पद व्यवहार करने की बर्हिवेशन कहते हैं। इसका स्वरूप सांस्कृतिक राजनीतिक–आर्थिक व धार्मिक हो सकता है। जब राज्य या कोई नागरिक समूह संस्कृतिक या भाषा के आधार पर किसी नागरिक या नागरिक समूह को दबाता है, या घृणा करता है, तो सांस्कृतिक बर्हिवेशन कहते हैं, नागरिकता सम्बन्धी किन्ही अधिकारों से वंचित करना राजनीतिक तथा किसी विशेष को रोजगार से वंचित करने को आर्थिक बर्हिवेशन कहते हैं। राज्य द्वारा धर्म के आधार पर स्वतन्त्रता व समानता से वंचित करना धार्मिक बर्हिवेशन कहलाता है।

सामाजिक न्याय : ऐतिहासिक पृष्ठभूमि

सभ्यता के विकास के साथ समाज की बुनियादी मान्यतायें बदली हैं जिससे सामाजिक न्याय के स्वरूप में निखार आया है। समाज में औचित्यपूर्ण संबंधों की खोज और न्यायपूर्ण बर्ताव की मांग में निरन्तर वृद्धि होते रहने से सामाजिक न्याय के अभिज्ञान में बहुत विस्तार हुआ है। इस प्रकार सामाजिक न्याय की अवधारणा बहुत व्यापक है। समाज में न्याय की अनुभूति लोगों को तभी से हुई जब से उन्हें समाज का बोध हुआ किन्तु समय एवं समाज के रूप में परिवर्तन के साथ न्याय की धारणा बदलती रही है। प्राचीन काल के विचारकों ने केवल न्याय की ही बात की। जिसे आज सामाजिक न्याय कहा जाता है वह उन विचारकों की वैचारिक परिधि में नहीं था, क्योंकि उस युग में समाज की व्यवस्था ईश्वरीय नियमों द्वारा संचालित होती थी। न्यायिक नियमों की रचना ईश्वर, पैगम्बर या ईश्वरीय शक्ति से विभूषित व्यक्तियों द्वारा ही होती थी। आम आदमी केवल आँख मूंद कर उनका अनुपालन करता था। मध्य काल में भी बहुत कुछ यही स्थिति रही। आरम्भ में न्यायिक विषय मात्र पुरोहित वर्ग तक सीमित था। आगे चलकर इसके क्षेत्र में विस्तार हुआ क्योंकि अदृश्य ईश्वर के नाम पर समाज में लोगों के व्यवहारों को अधिक समय तक नियंत्रित रख पाना संभव नहीं था। ईश्वर के प्रतिनिधि के रूप में राजा लौकिक जीवन में

न्याय एवं शक्ति का प्रतिरूप बना। जिसका परिणाम यह हुआ कि समाज में न्यायिक अधिकार (अर्थात न्याय संबंधी नियमों की रचना, उनकी व्याख्या और उन्हें लागू करने का अधिकार) केवल पुरोहित वर्ग तक सीमित नहीं रहा बल्कि शनैः शनैः इसमें सामन्त वर्ग की भागेदारी बढ़ी। प्राचीन यूनान में दास प्रथा का चलन था। सुकरात व प्लेटों की वैयक्तिक एवं लोकतांत्रिक अधिकार संबंधी धारणायें भी केवल नागरिकों तक ही सीमित थीं। दास नागरिक अधिकारों से वंचित थे क्योंकि उन्हें नागरिक अधिकारों के सार्थक उपयोग के उपयुक्त नहीं समझा जाता था। प्लेटों ने मजदूर, योद्धा और दार्शनिक के रूप में समाज को तीन वर्गों में विभाजित किया। न्याय से उसका आशय दूसरे वर्गों के कार्यों में किसी प्रकार की बाधा (या हस्तक्षेप) पहुँचाये बिना अपने वर्ग के लिये निर्धारित कार्यों को सम्पन्न करना था। दूसरे शब्दों में, प्लेटो की दृष्टि में यदि विभिन्न वर्ग परस्पर सौहार्द्र पूर्वक अपने–अपने कार्यों को सम्पन्न करते हैं तो समाज में सामाजिक न्याय की कल्पना की जा सकती है। परंपरात्मक समाज पुरोहित, सामतं, कृषक एवं व्यापारी तथा श्रमिक के रूप में चार वर्णों में विभक्त था। इन समूहों के कर्तव्य पूर्व निर्दिष्ट थे। व्यक्ति के लिये न्याय का अर्थ अपने समूह, जिसका कि वह सदस्य है के लिये निर्धारित कर्तव्य का निर्वाह करना था जिससे कि इस चतुवर्णीय व्यवस्था, जिसे तब आदर्श एवं न्यायपूर्ण समझा जाता था, को बनाये रखना संभव हो सके। तात्पर्य यह है कि प्राचीन समाज में न्याय की अवधारणा व्यक्ति के औचित्य पर जोर देती थी। व्यक्ति का औचित्य संपूर्ण व्यवस्था को बनाये रखने में उसके द्वारा वर्गीय दायित्वों के निर्वाह से संबंधित था। आधुनिक समाज में सामाजिक न्याय की अवधारणा औचित्यपूर्ण की कल्पना करती है जिसमें सभी व्यक्तियों के साथ समान बर्ताव होता है। यह वर्गीय कर्तव्य की जगह नागरिक अधिकार पर बल देती है जो समाज में सभी व्यक्तियों को स्वतंत्रता व समानता की प्रत्याभूति प्रदान किये जाने पर बल देता है। प्राचीन चिंतन वस्तुतः संप्रभु–वर्गीय चिन्तन था, जिसकी दो मुख्य परिकल्पनायें थीं। एक तो यह कि सामाजिक संस्तरण ईश्वरीय विधान पर आधारित है और दूसरी यह कि असाधारण व्यक्ति असाधारण व्यक्तियों के घर ही पैदा होते हैं। अतः प्राचीन विचारकों ने चतुर्वर्णीय व्यवस्था को आदर्श निरूपित करते हुए इसकी युक्ति संगतता और औचित्य को ही दर्शाने का प्रयास किया। इसमें परिवर्तन की कल्पना उनके सोच के दायरे में नहीं थी। यद्यपि, भारत में ईसा से पाँच सौ वर्ष पूर्व महावीर और गौतम ने इस ईश्वरीय व्यवस्था

के विरूद्ध सशक्त आवाज उठाई, समाज पर उनका व्यापक प्रभाव भी पड़ा, तथापि उनका यह प्रभाव स्थायी नहीं रह पाया। स्वतंत्रता और समता का बुद्ध का संदेश धार्मिक व आध्यात्मिक सोच तक ही सीमित रहा। यह नवीन भौतिक चिन्तन का आधार नहीं बना। परिणामस्वरूप समाज में वर्ण एवं जाति का भेद सामयिक रूप से कमजोर भले हो गया किन्तु पूर्णतया समाप्त नहीं हुआ, साथ ही निम्न वर्णों की दासता और सामंतशाही भी समाप्त नहीं हो पाई। मध्यकाल में मध्यम और निचली जातियों में अनेक संत पैदा हुये, उन्होंने जात–पाँत और ऊँच–नीच का खुल कर विरोध भी किया, किन्तु उनका प्रभाव बहुत सीमित रहा। यह भक्ति के क्षेत्र को लांघ नहीं पाया। परिणामस्वरूप लौकिक जीवन जैसा का तैसा ही बना रहा।

चिन्तन की स्वतंत्रता के वैज्ञानिक एवं तकनीकी क्षेत्रों में विस्तार के साथ मानव जीवन की भौतिक दशाओं में मौलिक परिवर्तन परिलक्षित हुआ। उसने कानून और व्यवस्था के दैवीय आधार के विरूद्ध गंभीर चुनौती प्रस्तुत की। परिणामस्वरूप फ्राँस, इंगलैण्ड, अमेरिका और रूस में क्रान्तियाँ हुईं। इन क्रान्तियों ने पाश्चात्य समाज से सामंती चिन्तन और व्यवस्था को पूरी तौर पर खत्म कर दिया। जिसके फलस्वरूप श्रेणीबद्ध असमानता पर आधारित न्याय के परम्परागत सिद्धान्त की जगह सामाजिक न्याय की धारणा का जन्म हुआ। यह मध्य युग की समाप्ति और आधुनिक युग का समारंभ था।

फ्रांस की राज्य क्रान्ति ने आधुनिक समाज व्यवस्था के निर्माण की आधारशिला रखी। यह कुलीनवाद के विरूद्ध मानव व्यक्तित्व की गरिमा की स्थापना के लिये जनता का संघर्ष था। यह असमानता और सामंतवाद के विरूद्ध स्वतंत्रता, समानता और भ्रातृत्व पर आधारित लोकतांत्रिक व्यवस्था की स्थापना के लिये जन–संघर्ष था। मानव अधिकार की स्थापना के आरंभिक दौर में यह संघर्ष केवल राजनीतिक क्षेत्र तक सीमित रहा। इस दौर में स्वतंत्रता, मुख्य रूप से राजनैतिक एवं विधिक स्वतंत्रता, पर ही जोर दिया गया। जिससे पूँजीवाद के विकास के लिये आवश्यक पृष्ठभूमि का निर्माण हुआ।

मानव स्वतंत्रता संबंधी घोषणापत्र, जिसमें यह घोषणा की गई कि ''सभी मनुष्य समान पैदा हुये हैं'' और ''जीवन, स्वतंत्रता तथा प्रसन्नता की प्राप्ति मनुष्य के अभिन्न अधिकार हैं'' पर हस्ताक्षर करने वालों ने दास प्रथा के उन्मूलन पर ध्यान नहीं यिा। ''मैग्ना चार्टा'' और ''राइट ऑफ बिल'' बनाने वालों ने भी दास प्रथा की बुराई की ओर ध्यान नहीं दिया। उनके

लिये स्वतंत्रता से आशय संपत्ति संबंधी अधिकार की प्रत्याभूति से अधिक नहीं था

पूँजीवाद विचारकों ने स्वंतत्र बाजार व्यवस्था, प्रतिस्पर्धा एवं मुनाफाखोरी तथा नवाचार, सृजनशीलता एवं जोखिम उठाने का साहस आदि मूल्यों पर बल दिया। इन्हें वे विकास के लिये जरूरी समझते थे। समानता को वे प्रगति के लिये वांछनीय नहीं समझते थे। हर्बर्ट स्पेन्सर ने सामाजिक उद्विकासवाद की नींव डाली। जिससे अस्तित्व के लिये संघर्ष, योग्यतम का चुनाव तथा सामाजिक प्रवरण की धारणाओं को बल मिला। उसने मुक्त प्रतिस्पर्धा को स्वाभाविक निरूपित किया और इसमें राज्य के हस्तक्षेप को आवांछित बताया। स्पेन्सर की दृष्टि में सामाजिक न्याय से तात्पर्य समाज में गुणवत्ता के आधार पर लाभ का वितरण था। उसका कहना था कि राज्य को अक्षम और कमजोर लोगों की सहायता नहीं करनी चाहिए क्योंकि ऐसा करने से समाज में जो सक्षम और सशक्त लोग हैं वे लाभ में अपना उचित हिस्सा पाने से वंचित रह जायेंगे (गउबा, 1983:32)। एडम स्मिथ (1723–1790), डेविड रिकार्डो (1772–1823) तथा थामस राबर्ट माल्थस (1766–1834) आदि शास्त्रीय–उदारवादी, विचारकों ने भी अहस्तक्षेप के सिद्धांत पर आधारित व्यक्तिवाद का प्रतिपादन किया। इस विचारधारा ने व्यक्ति की स्थिति, प्रतिष्ठा और उसके भौतिक अधिकारों के निर्धारण में परम्पराओं की भूमिका को समाप्त किया और स्वतंत्र संविदा को नये सामाजिक संबंधों के निर्धारण का आधार बनाया। इन विचारकों ने यद्यपि स्वतंत्रता को प्रमुखता तो दी तथापि उनके चिन्तन में सामाजिक न्याय से आशय संविदा की स्वंत्रता से अधिक कुछ नहीं था।

पूँजीवादी विचारक स्वतंत्र अर्थ व्यवस्था का समर्थन इसलिये करते हैं क्योंकि इसे वे विकास के लिये आवश्यक मानते हैं। समानता को ये प्रगति में बाधक निरूपित करते हैं। उनकी स्पष्ट मान्यता है कि विगत दो शताब्दियों में जिस तेजी से आर्थिक विकास हुआ है वह बहुत कुछ असमानता का परिणाम है और जो उसके बिना असंभव है। उनका मानना है कि समान धरातल पर तेजी से प्रगति नहीं हो सकती। तीव्र प्रगति तो स्तरीकरण से ही हो सकती है, जिसमें कुछ लोग शेष लोगों से बहुत आगे होते है। अर्थशास्त्री जी.आर. पैपनोक के शब्दों में विकास के लक्ष्यों और समानता के मध्य एक संघर्ष है। आय में विषमता आर्थिक समृद्धि में योगदान करती है जो निम्न आय समूह की आय में वास्तविक सुधार को संभव बनाती है। ये विचारक असमानता को एक प्राकृतिक नियम मानते है कि समाज से वर्ग–भेद यदि पूर्णतया मिटा भी दिया जाए तो भी मनुष्यों

में शक्तिशाली एवं कमजोर, प्रतिभावान एवं पिछड़े तथा भाग्यशाली एवं लाचार रहेंगे ही।

प्राचीन एवं मध्य युगीन चिंतन में सामाजिक न्याय का आधार ईश्वरीय था। यह कुलीन वर्गों के हितों की रक्षा करता था। अठारहवीं सदी के चिंतन में सामाजिक न्याय का आधार लौकिक हो गया। आरंभिक दौर में स्वतंत्र संविदा पर आधारित होने के कारण सामाजिक न्याय पूँजीवादी वर्ग के हितों का परिपोषक बन गया। उन्नीसवीं सदी तक पूँजीवाद समाज में जड़ जमा चुका था। जिसके साथ पूँजीपति के रूप में समाज में कुछ लोगों की आर्थिक स्थिति तो बहुत मजबूत हो गई जबकि अधिकांश लोग श्रमिक के रूप में अर्ध–मानवीय दशाओं में जीवन–यापन करने के लिये मजबूर हुये। किन्तु पूँजीवाद के विकास का एक परिणाम यह हुआ कि इससे श्रमिक वर्ग की न केवल संख्या अपितु उनके केन्द्रीयकरण में भी तेजी से वृद्धि हुई। इससे श्रमिकों को अपनी शक्ति का अहसास हुआ और वे अपने हितों की रक्षा के प्रति जागरूक हुये। पूँजीवाद से उपजी श्रमिकों की समस्याओं के निराकरण को लेकर समाजवादी चिंतन का विकास हुआ। शोषित व पीड़ित श्रमिक समाजवादी आंदोलन के साथ जुड़ गये। समाजवाद ने स्वतंत्रता की जगह समानता को बुनियादी सिद्धांत के रूप में अपनाया और राजनैतिक समानता के साथ आर्थिक एवं सामाजिक समानता की स्थापना पर जो दिया। अठारहवीं सदी (1789) में जहाँ कानून के समक्ष समानता संबंधी सामाजिक न्याय की अवधारणा के माध्यम से सामंत वर्ग के वैधानिक विशेषाधिकारों व सुविधाओं को समाप्त किये जाने के लिये पहल की गई वहीं उन्नीसवीं सदी में सामाजिक न्याय की समाजवादी सोच ने समाज से आर्थिक व सामाजिक विषमता के उन्मूलन पर जोर दिया। विलासिता और शोषण पर आधारित पूँजीवादी सभ्यता के दुष्परिणामों के विरूद्ध उदारवादी विचारकों में एक नया वर्ग विकसित हुआ जिसने पूँजीवाद को उदार बनाते हुये पूँजीवाद और उदारवाद के बीच सेतु स्थापित करने का प्रयास किया। आगे चलकर यह विचारधारा नव उदारवाद के रूप में जानी गई। इस वर्ग ने स्वतंत्रता और समानता के बीच संतुलन स्थापित करने का प्रयास किया। इंग्लैण्ड के जान स्टुअर्ट मिल (1806–1873) इस आंदोलन के अगुआ थे। मिल व्यक्ति–स्वातंत्र्य के प्रबल पक्षधर थे। उन्होंने "आन लिबर्टी" शीर्षक से एक पुस्तक लिखी। इस पुस्तक में उन्होंने विचार और अभिव्यक्ति की स्वतंत्रता का पुरजोर समर्थन किया। इसके साथ उन्होंने उन कार्यों को छोड़कर जिससे दूसरों की हानि पहुंचे शेष सभी कार्यों में व्यक्ति की पूरी स्वतंत्रता प्रदान किये

जाने पर जोर दिया। मिल ने स्पष्ट शब्दों में कहा कि एक व्यक्ति को छोड़कर संपूर्ण मानव जाति का मत यदि एक हो तो भी मानव जाति को उस एक व्यक्ति को चुप करने का अधिकार नहीं है, जैसे कि उस एक व्यक्ति के पास यदि शक्ति होती तो उसे शेष संपूर्ण मानव जाति को चुप कराने का अधिकार नहीं होता। मिल व्यक्तिवादी तो था किन्तु अतिशय व्यक्तिवादी (या अतिवादी) नहीं था। उसने व्यक्तिवाद का समर्थन तो किया किन्तु वह समाजवाद से भी प्रभावित था और उसकी उपेक्षा करना नहीं चाहता था। इस दृष्टि से उसने एडम स्मिथ, रिकार्डो और माल्थस के सिद्धांतों की पुर्नव्याख्या की। मिल ने बेंथम के उपयोगितावाद और सुखवाद का भी आंशिक रूप से ही समर्थन किया। उसका कहना था कि व्यक्ति के हित और समाज के हित में एक कार्यकारी संतुलन का होना जरूरी है। उसके अनुसार न तो व्यक्ति के हितों की बलिवेदी पर समाज के हितों का महल बनाया जा सकता है और न ही समाज के हितों की कुर्बानी कर व्यक्ति के स्वार्थों के विलास का भवन निर्मित किया जा सकता है। उसने मुक्त व्यापार एवं मुक्त प्रतिस्पर्धा का समर्थन तो किया किन्तु श्रमिकों के हितों की रक्षा किये जाने पर भी जोर दिया। मार्क्स ने पूँजीवाद और समाजवाद के बीच समन्वय स्थापित करने के मिल के प्रयास को असंयोज्य के बीच संयोजन स्थापित करने की गुस्ताखी तथा चिन्तन का दिवालियापन निरूपित किया। मार्क्स ने समानता के विचार को बुर्जुआ विचार बताया और कहा कि श्रमिकों की मांगों और उद्देश्यों में इसे कोई स्थान प्राप्त नहीं है। उसने एक ऐसी समाज व्यवस्था की कल्पना की जिसमें समानता और असमानता के बीच कोई विवाद नहीं होगा यद्यपि इस व्यवस्था के आरंभिक चरण में असमानता की अनुभूति रहेगी।

एक समतावादी सामाजिक तथा राजनैतिक व्यवस्था की स्थापना के लिए सच्चे सामाजिक न्याय का विचार एवं समानता का दृष्टिकोण दो महत्वपूर्ण शर्ते हैं। उत्तर–औपनिवेशिक भारतीय राज्य के उदय के साथ भारतीय राजनीति तथा नेतृत्व में भी भारत को एक समतावादी सामाजिक व्यवस्था के रूप में देखने की चाहत थी। उनकी यह इच्छा समय–समय पर सामाजिक न्याय एवं समानता पर चलने वाले वाद–विवाद एवं विचार–विमर्शो में खुलकर दिखाई दे रही थी। इस संदर्भ में संविधान सभा में डॉ भीमराव अम्बेडकर के द्वारा बताए गए आदर्श हमेशा ही प्रासंगिक रहे एवं पथप्रदर्शक के रूप में कार्य किया। हालांकि 'सामाजिक–न्याय'

की शब्दावली का प्रयोग तो 1850 से ही होने लगा था पर यदि हम वर्तमान समय में अध्ययन करें तो पाते हैं कि 'सामाजिक–न्याय' का विचार अपेक्षाकृत नया ही है। इसने एक ऐसा दर्शन प्रस्तुत किया जिसने नैतिक एवं राजनीतिक अवशेषण के लिए एक विषय के रूप में समाज के प्रमुख सामाजिक एवं आर्थिक संस्थाओं को सामने लाया जो सुविधाओं एवं समस्याओं के वितरण को निर्णायक रूप से सुनिश्चित कर रहे थे। अधिकांश राजनीतिक दार्शनिकों के अनुसार सामाजिक न्याय की अवधारणा प्रसिद्ध अमेरिकी दार्शनिक जॉन रॉल्स की किताब "ए थ्योरी ऑफ जस्टिस" (1971) के प्रकाशन के साथ अस्तित्व में आयी। इन्होंने एक ओर दर्शन की विद्या के स्वरूप को बदलकर उसमें एक नयी जान डाल दी एवं दूसरी तरफ सामाजिक न्याय के विचार की संज्ञा दी। उनके अनुसार यह विचार कि समाज कुछ इस प्रकार का होता है कि वह न्यायपूर्ण या अन्यायपूर्ण हो सकता है,। न्याय का तात्पर्य है– निष्पक्ष, उचित व भेदभावरहित निर्णय, कार्य या व्यवहार। न्याय की कसौटी है, नियम, कानून और व्यवस्था। समाज में न्याय के लिए विधायिका, न्यायपालिका, कार्यपालिका और मीडिया का यानी लोकतंत्र के चारों स्तम्भों का आचरण सत्य, यथार्थपरक और निष्पक्ष होना जरूरी हैं समाज का अपने सभी वर्गो, उपवर्गों और व्यक्तियों के साथ भेदभाव रहित बर्ताव सामाजिक न्याय है। यह अवधारणा है, लेकिन सत्य कुछ और हैं वस्तुतः आर्थिक न्याय के बिना सामाजिक न्याय मात्र कल्पना है। न्याय से आशय पक्षपात रहित व्यवहार से है। जब कोई समाज अपने सभी वर्गो, उप वर्गों के साथ पक्षपात रहित व्यवहार करता है तो उसे सामाजिक न्याय कहते हैं। इस दृष्टि से न्याय के दो पक्ष हैं–वैयक्तिक न्याय और सामाजिक न्याय। किसी समय विशेष पर राज्य या समाज के स्वीकृत नियमों को व्यक्ति पर निष्पक्ष रूप से लागू करने का अर्थ है उसके साथ न्याय संगत व्यवहार करना। यह कार्य न्याय पालिका का होता है जो यह सुनिश्चित करती है कि प्रचलित नियम अथवा कानून के तहत व्यक्ति के साथ न्यायपूर्ण बर्ताव हो रहा है अथवा नहीं। सामाजिक न्याय व्यक्ति के हितों की अवहेलना तो नहीं करता, किन्तु यह सेवाओं और संसाधनों के न्यायोचित विभाजन, समतामूलक वितरण तथा नियमों की सामूहिक उपयोगिता पर अधिक ध्यान देता है। इस दृष्टि से सामाजिक न्याय का परिप्रेक्ष्य व्यापक है। यह नियमों के निर्माण, उनकी व्याख्या और उन्हें लागू करने में सामूहिक हितों की पूर्ति के साथ वैयक्तिक हितों के समायोजन पर बल देता है।

सामाजिक न्याय के विभिन्न पक्ष

सामाजिक न्याय के आधारभूत तत्व हैं—स्वतंत्रता एवं समानता। स्वतंत्रता से आशय ''अवरोध की अनुपस्थिति'' है, जबकि समानता से तात्पर्य ''भेदभाव की अनुपस्थिति'' है। सामाजिक न्याय के ढाँचे में स्वतंत्रता और समानता के तत्व निरपेक्ष न होकर सापेक्ष हो जाते हैं। तात्पर्य यह है कि सामाजिक न्याय के संदर्भ में व्यक्ति अथवा समूह के लिये स्वतंत्रता से आशय वहीं तक है कि जहाँ तक कि यह दूसरे व्यक्ति की स्वतंत्रता में बाधक न बने।

सामाजिक न्याय के दो पक्ष हैं—विकासात्मक एवं वितरणात्मक। उदारवादी एवं पूँजीवादी विचारक विकास को महत्व देते हैं और इसके लिये वे स्वतंत्रता को आधारभूत एवं अपरिहार्य निरूपित करते हैं। पूँजीवादी समाज में न्यायपूर्ण वितरण का आधार व्यक्ति की योग्यता है क्योंकि योग्यता विकास की बुनियाद है। समाजवादी एवं साम्यवादी विचारक वितरण पर अधिक जोर देते हैं। उनके वितरण का आधार समानता है। उनका कहना है कि पूँजीवादी व्यवस्था में स्वतंत्रता एवं विकास के नाम पर आर्थिक संसाधन एवं लाभ का अधिकांश भाग उन थोड़े लोगों के हाथ में सिमटता जाता है, जो साधन सम्पन्न होते हैं। श्रमिकों एवं सामान्य लोगों को लाभ का बहुत ही कम हिस्सा मिलता है। उनके हिस्से में तो बोझ और दायित्व ही होता है। इसलिये समाजवादी विचारधारा के लोग वितरण में समानता पर जोर देते हैं और योग्यता की जगह आवश्यकता को वितरण का आधारभूत तत्व निरूपित करते हैं।

नव उदारवादी एवं कल्याणकारी राज्य की धारणाओं ने सामाजिक न्याय के विकासात्मक एवं वितरणात्मक पक्षों में उपयोगी सामंजस्य स्थापित करने का प्रयास किया है। विकास की प्रक्रिया यदि ठप्प हो जाये तो वितरण अर्थहीन हो जाता है। विकास की गति बनाये रखने से ही वितरण के उद्देश्य की सार्थक पूर्ति हो सकती है। किन्तु योग्यता, गुणवत्ता और उपादेयता की अवहेलना करके विकास को गतिमान रख पाना संभव नहीं होता क्योंकि ऐसा करने से व्यक्ति की सृजनशीलता कुण्ठित होती है, नवोन्मेष की क्षमता दब जाती है और श्रम करने की लालसा मर जाती है। इसके विपरीत स्वतंत्रता पर प्रभावकारी नियंत्रण के अभाव में कुछ लोग समाज में इतने शक्तिशाली हो जाते हैं कि दूसरों के लिये जीवन का कोई अर्थ नहीं रह जाता। इसलिये नव उदारवादी एवं कल्याणकारी राज्य की अवधारणा के समर्थक, व्यक्ति की योग्यता और आवश्यकता में कार्यकारी सामंजस्य स्थापित किये जाने पर देते हैं।

भारतीय समाज एवं सामाजिक न्याय

प्राचीन एवं मध्यकालीन समाजों की रचना ऊंच–नीच और भेदभाव पर आधारित थी, किन्तु भारतीय समाज में भेदभाव का स्वरूप जन्मगत होने के कारण अधिक कठोर था। शिक्षा और व्यवसाय चुनने की स्वतंत्रता समाज में बहुत सीमित लोगों को ही थी। समाज जातीय आधार पर असमान श्रेणियों में विभक्त था। जातिगत रचना के कारण समाज में असमानता, जन्मगत, श्रेणीबद्ध और अपरिवर्तनीय थी। शास्त्रीय विधान के चलते कुछ जातियों को तो विशेषाधिकार प्राप्त थे, जबकि अधिकांश जातियाँ निर्योग्यताओं से पीड़ित थीं। ऐसे में सामाजिक न्याय की स्थापना का कार्य सरल नहीं था। विदेशी शासन के विरूद्ध संघर्ष में सफलता मिलते ही देश में सामाजिक अन्याय और भेदभाव के उन्मूलन के लिये समेकित प्रयास आरंभ हुआ। यह कार्य एक साथ दो मोर्चों पर शुरू किया गया। एक ओर न्यायपूर्ण समाज की रचना के लिये आवश्यक संवैधानिक और वैधानिक पहल की गई और दूसरी ओर दरिद्रता, भूख और बेकारी से लड़ने के लिये योजनाबद्ध रीति से सामाजिक, आर्थिक विकास संबंधी कार्यक्रम आरंभ किये गये। जब हम भारतीय संदर्भ में देखते हैं तो पाते हैं कि भारत में सामाजिक न्याय की अवधारणा यहाँ के समाज में व्याप्त भेदभाव एवं पक्षपात के प्रतिक्रिया स्वरूप उभरकर सामने आयी। इस भेदभाव से युक्त सामाजिक व्यवस्था के अंदर समाज के चंद लोगों को ही सभी सुविधाएँ उपलब्ध कराने पर ध्यान दिया जाता था। वस्तुतः ब्राह्मणवादी हिंदू जो कि मूलतः आर्य थे, ने एक असमान सामाजिक व्यवस्था का प्रसार किया जो मानवता की विरोधी थी।

इसलिए भारतीय राज्य ने सामाजिक व्यवस्था के दोषों एवं खतरों से निजात पाने के लिए कुछ निश्चित कदम उठाए है। यह सामाजिक व्यवस्था समाज के कुछ खास वर्गों या समूहों के प्रति एक विरोधी रवैया का धारण किए हुए थी जिसकी वजह से ये लोग सामाजिक, आर्थिक एवं राजनीतिक रूप से पिछड़ते चले गए। इन समूहों में अनुसूचित जाति, अनुसूचित जनजाति एवं अन्य पिछड़े वर्ग (एस.सी., एस.टी. एवं ओबीसी) आते हैं। ये समूह सामाजिक रूप से समाज के वंचित समूह के अंतर्गत आते हैं जो अब तक समाज के सुख–सुविधाओं से वंचित ही रहे हैं। अतः इन्हें ऊपर उठाकर समाज की मुख्य धारा से जोड़ने के लिए संविधान में कुछ विशेष प्रावधानों की व्यवस्था की गई है तथा सरकार ने भी इस दिशा में कुछ प्रभावी कदम उठाए हैं। उदाहरण के लिए इनके लिए आरक्षण

की नीति एवं सकारात्मक कार्यवाहियों को एक महत्वपूर्ण कदम के रूप में देखा जा सकता है। इस प्रकार एक समतावादी सामाजिक व्यवस्था की स्थापना की इच्छा के साथ सामाजिक न्याय एवं समानता का विचार घनिष्ठता स जुड़ गया है औरं भारत में उत्तर–औपनिवेशिक आधुनिक राज्य के निर्माण के लिए सामाजिक परिवर्तन एवं सामाजिक न्याय का विचार दो महत्वपूर्ण शर्तें बन गई हैं। भारतीय नेताओं के सामने 1950 के दशक में ही सामाजिक परिवर्तन का मुद्दा एक बड़ी चुनौती थी जो आज भी बनी हुई है। सामाजिक परिवर्तन का सीधा–सा तात्पर्य उन परंपरागत कार्यप्रणालियों को त्यागना है जो सामाजिक, आर्थिक एवं राजनीतिक क्षेत्र में भेदभाव एवं पक्षपात को उत्पन्न करने के भाव से युक्त होते हैं। भारतीय समाज में जाति प्रथा, वर्गीय प्रवृत्तियाँ, लैंगिक असमानता एवं नृजातीय संघर्ष जैसी सामाजिक कुरीतियाँ काफी गहराई से जड़ जमाए हुए हैं। अतः भारत में सामाजिक परिवर्तन पर होने वाले सारे वाद–विवाद इन्हीं चारों मुद्दों पर केन्द्रित हैं तथा इसी के फलस्वरूप यहाँ सामाजिक न्याय का विचार भी सामने आया। स्वतंत्रता आंदोलन में सभी जातियों वर्गों, व्यक्तियों की भागीदारी इस बात का प्रमाण थी कि आजादी के बाद जन्म, जाति, धर्म, क्षेत्र भाषा आदि के आधार पर कोई भेदभाव नहीं होगा। सामाजिक न्याय की स्थापना, संविधान का प्राथमिक उद्देश्य है। संविधान का मूल लक्ष्य है। स्वतंत्रता, समानता और भ्रातृत्व पर आधारित व्यक्ति की गरिमा सुनिश्चित करने वाली न्यायपूर्ण समाज व्यवस्था की स्थापना। इसके लिए संविधान में कल्याणकारी राज्य की परिकल्पना है। नीति निर्देशक तत्वों मे राज्य को सामाजिक न्याय की दिशा में आवश्यक वैधानिक व प्रशासनिक पहल करने को कहा गया। लोकतंत्र की मजबूती भी प्रभावी सामाजिक न्याय पर निर्भर है। लेकिन यह भी सच्चाई है कि राजनीति के जातीय कुचक्र के चलते यह कारगर ढंग से स्थापित नहीं हो गया। हमारी विकास प्रक्रिया असंतुलित हुई, परिणामतः अमीर–गरीब की खाई बढ़ी, जातीय पहचान कमजोर होने की बजाय मजबूत हुई, बहुलतायुक्त समाज में सामाजिक बराबरी व सामाजिक न्याय की बजाय नफरत बढ़ी।

समाजिक न्याय की स्थापना का सीधा अर्थ है– अन्याय के विरूद्ध संघर्ष। भारत में इसके लिए मन, वचन और कर्म से संघर्ष करने वालों में हैं – गौतम बुद्ध, रैदास, कबीर, नानक, ज्योतिबा फुले, नारायण गुरू, अच्युतानन्द, रामास्वामी नायकर, डॉ भीमराव अम्बेडकर। शूद्र, अतिशूद्र दलित, महिला, अल्पसंख्यक आदि वर्गों की मुक्ति के लिए इनका संघर्ष

ऐतिहासिक व पुनः स्मरणीय है। आज फिर सामाजिक न्याय की अवधारणा और सच्चाई में फर्क जानना और करना जरूरी है। आजादी मिलने के बाद जब संविधान की रचना की जा रही थी तब इस बात पर चर्चा जारी थी कि ऐसे कौन से रास्ते निकाले जाये जिससे भारतीय समाज में (दलितों, व पिछड़े को जो भारतीय सामाजिक व्यवस्था में पहले से ही बहुत पीछे रह गये थे) को बराबरी और सम्मान का दर्जा दिलाया जा सकें। चर्चाओं, बहसों, और सामाजिक आंदोलन की प्रक्रियाओं से देश के संविधान में समाज के कमजोर व पिछड़े रह गये लोगों खासकर दलितों व पिछड़ों के लिये आरक्षण का प्रविधान किया गया। संविधान में आरक्षण का प्राविधान इस उद्देश्य से किया गया था, कि समाज का जो उत्पीड़ित पिछड़ा व शोषित समाज है, उसे समाज के विभिन्न क्षेत्रों में आगे बढ़ने के मौके नही मिले, वो आरक्षण के माध्यम से मिले, जिससे उनकी शैक्षिक, सामाजिक, सांस्कृतिक, आर्थिक परिस्थितियों में बदलाव आये। आरक्षण का प्राविधान विशेषकर, नौकरियों, और विधायिका में किया गया। ये प्राविधान बहुत सीमित रूप में समाज के शोषित व पिछड़े वर्गो को आगे बढ़ाने के मौके देता हैं, बावजूद इसके ये मौके एक सकारात्मक कदम हैं, लेकिन आजतक किसी भी श्रेणी की नौकरियों में आरक्षण को पूरी तरह लागू नहीं किया गया। 1990–91 में भारत में शुरु हुई आर्थिक नीतियों के फलस्वरूप भूमण्डलीकरण की प्रक्रिया ने देश के सार्वजनिक क्षेत्र को काफी कमजोर किया हैं, पिछले 15 सालों में निजीकरण की तेज प्रक्रिया ने सरकारी क्षेत्र की नौकरियों को बहुत कम कर दिया हैं, ऐसे में आरक्षण सामाजिक न्याय व सामाजिक बराबरी के प्राविधानों को भारी धक्का लगा है। इस प्रकार से स्वतन्त्रता प्राप्ति के बाद स्वाधीन भारत के संविधान में जनजातियों एवं पिछड़े वर्ग के उत्थान के लिये आर्थिक, सामाजिक एवं राजनीतिक, न्याय, विचार अभिव्यक्ति विश्वास, मान्यता एवं धर्म की स्वतन्त्रता और प्रतिष्ठा, एवं संविधान में मूल अधिकारो का उल्लेख किया गया है, जो नागरिको को यह विश्वास दिलाते हैं, कि धर्म ,वर्ग, लिंग, जाति–प्रजाति एवं अन्य के आधार पर भेदभाव नही बरता जायेगा। इससे जनजातियों के प्रति अब तक बरते गये भेदभाव की समाप्ति होती हैं संविधान में नीति निर्देशक तत्वों का उल्लेख किया गया हैं जिनमें कहाँ गया है कि राज्य कमजोर वर्ग के लोगों को विशेषकर अनुसूचित जातियों एवं जन जातियों के शैक्षणिक व आर्थिक हितों को बढ़ावा देगा, तथा उन्हें सामाजिक अन्याय एवं शोषण से सुरक्षा प्रदान करेगा। इस प्रकार हमारे देश में दलित, स्त्रियाँ, आदिवासी, अल्पसंख्यक तथा वे तमाम गरीब और पिछड़े हुए लोग जो

ऐतिहासिक कारणों से उच्च वर्गो और वर्णो के वर्चस्व वाली समाज व्यवस्था में निचले स्तरों पर जीते रहे हैं। (यह दमन और शोषण की प्रक्रिया लगातार जारी है) ये तब आर्थिक शोषण, राजनीतिक दमन, सांस्कृतिक उत्पीड़न और सामाजिक अन्याय व बहिष्करण के शिकार हैं। इस प्रकार से इसी सामाजिक अन्याय के सवाल को हल करने के उत्तर के रूप में सामाजिक बराबरी व सामाजिक न्याय की बात की जा रही है।

लेकिन सामाजिक बराबरी वास्तव में क्या है, यह अभी तक भी बहुत स्पष्ट नहीं हैं? बहुत से लोग यह समझते हैं कि दलितों, पिछड़ी स्त्रियों, आदिवासियों (दमन व शोषण के शिकार) बहिष्कृत समाज में सामाजिक रूप से बहिष्कृतों को विभिन्न प्रकार के आरक्षण देकर उन्हें सामाजिक अन्याय से बचाया जा सकता हैं। लेकिन वास्तव में क्या यह समझ सहीं है? क्या वास्तव में सामाजिक बराबरी व सामाजिक न्याय की माँग तब तक पूरी हों सकती हैं, जब तक वर्ण, जाति, लिंग धर्म, संम्प्रदाय इत्यादि के आधार पर किये जाने वाले भेदभाव को समाप्त न किया जाये? क्या वर्तमान समाज व्यवस्था को यथावत बनाये रखते हुए सामाजिक अन्याय के शिकार लोगों को सामजिक बराबरी व सामाजिक न्याय उपलब्ध कराया जा सकता हैं ? क्या यह आवश्यक नहीं कि वर्तमान समाज व्यवस्था को बदलकर बराबरी और भाईचारे वाली ऐसी न्यायपूर्ण समाज व्यवस्था कायम की जाये, जिसमें किसी के द्वारा किसी को शोषण, दमन और उत्पीड़न न हो। अन्याय का विरोध और बराबरी की माँग वास्तव में वही कर सकता हैं। जो यह जानता हो कि बराबरी क्या हैं? अतः प्रश्न उठता है कि सामाजिक बराबरी वास्तव में क्या है? जहाँ एक ओर सामाजिक बराबरी का प्रश्न एक ओर देश की सभ्यता और संस्कृति से जुड़ा हुआ हैं, तो दूसरी ओर अर्थव्यवस्था और संवैधानिक व्यवस्था से। अतः इस प्रश्न पर विचार करते समय इन चारों आयामों को ध्यान में रखा जाना चाहिये। लेकिन सवाल वही है कि इन सब चीजों को ध्यान में रखते हुए क्या हम सामाजिक बराबरी की कोई स्पष्ट अवधारणा बना पाये हैं।

क्या दलितों को सर्वणों के विरूद्व, पिछड़ो को अगड़ों के विरूद्व, स्त्रियों को पुरूषों के विरूद्व या किसी एक धर्म सम्प्रदाय के लोगों को दूसरे धर्म सम्प्रदाय के विरूद्व लड़ाकर किसी न्यायपूर्ण समाज व्यवस्था की स्थापना की जा सकती हैं? यदि नहीं तो क्या वर्तमान व्यवस्था को बदला नही जाना चाहिये? और यदि बदला जाना चाहिये, तो इसकी जगह किसी

नयी अथवा वैकल्पिक व्यवस्था की परिकल्पना क्या हो सकती है और उसे कैसे साकार किया जा सकता हैं?

न्यायपूर्ण व्यवस्था की अम्बेडकरवादी परिकल्पना

सामाजिक न्याय के बुनियादी सिद्धान्तों–, समानता और भ्रातृत्व, के आधार पर अम्बेडकर ने एक ऐसी न्यायपूर्ण व्यवस्था की परिकल्पना की जिसमें व्यक्ति और समाज के हितों में कार्यकारी संतुलन हो। यह व्यवस्था और कुछ नहीं वस्तुतः सामाजिक, आर्थिक और राजनैतिक प्रजातंत्र है। अम्बेडकर के अनुसार एक व्यक्ति एक मत के सिद्धान्त को स्वीकार करके हमने राजनैतिक क्षेत्र में व्यक्ति को समानता तो प्रदान कर दी, किन्तु सामाजिक और आर्थिक क्षेत्रों में असमानता अभी बनी हुई है। उन्होंने राजनैतिक और सामाजिक जीवन के बीच इस अन्तर्विरोध के प्रति लोगों को आगाह किया और कहा कि इसे शीघ्रातिशीघ्र समाप्त किया जाना चाहिए। अम्बेडकर धर्म को जीवन में बहुत महत्व देते तो थे किन्तु वे लौकिक आधार को धर्म से पृथक रखते थे। उनका मानना था कि विश्व में जब और जहां कहीं भी धर्म का समाज पर नियंत्रण रहा वहां सामाजिक न्याय का अभाव हो गया। उनका यह भी मानना था कि न्यायपूर्ण समाज की रचना केवल न्यायपूर्ण विधान के माध्यम से ही हो सकती है। क्योंकि यदि कभी कोई अन्याय की स्थिति इसमें पैदा हुई तो उसे दूर किया जा सकता है। इसलिए स्वतंत्र भारत को धार्मिक राष्ट्र के स्थान पर धर्मनिरपेक्ष राष्ट्र बनाये जाने के मत का

उन्होंने समर्थन किया और संविधान के अनुच्छेद 25 से 28 के अन्तर्गत उन्होंने नागरिकों को अन्तयकरण की स्वतंत्रता तथा किसी धर्म को मानने उस पर आचरण करने और उसका प्रसार करने की स्वतंत्रता प्रदान की। सामाजिक न्याय की स्थापना में राज्य और कानून की भूमिका को अम्बेडकर ने स्वीकार तो किया किन्तु वे इनकी सीमाओं से भी परिचित थे। उनका मानना था कि कानून के द्वारा स्वतंत्रता और समानता की स्थापना तो की जा सकती है किन्तु इन्हें लोगों के व्यवहार का सहज अंग नहीं बनाया जा सकता और न ही कानून के माध्यम से लोगों में भ्रातृत्व भाव पैदा किया जा सकता है। अम्बेडकर की दृष्टि में यह कार्य धर्म के द्वारा संभव हो सकता है किन्तु धर्म से अम्बेडकर का अभिप्राय मजहब से नहीं अपितु वास्तविक धर्म से था जो सामाजिक न्याय अर्थात् स्वतंत्रता, समता और भ्रातृत्व की कसौटियों पर खरा उतरता है। अम्बेडकर की एक मान्यता यह भी थी कि संविधान के तहत उन्हें अपनी परम्परात्मक

निर्योग्यताओं से मुक्ति मिल सकती है। इसके साथ स्वतंत्रता और समानता भी हासिल हो सकती है किन्तु शास्त्रों की दासता से उन्हें मुक्ति नहीं मिल सकती। उनका विश्वास था कि मानसिक दासता से मुक्ति के बिना दलितों की पूर्ण मुक्ति सीाव नहीं है और पूर्ण मुक्ति के बिना सामाजिक न्याय की प्राप्ति बेमानी है।

सामाजिक न्याय की स्थापना की दृष्टि से डा. अम्बेडकर ने समाज में समानता की स्थापना पर जोर तो दिया किन्तु समानता के नाम पर वे किसी भी व्यवस्था को लोगों पर थोपने के पक्ष में नही थे। सन् 1947 में शेडयूल्ड कास्ट्स फेडरेशन ऑफ इंडिया के प्रतिनिधि के रूप में उन्होंने संविधान सभा को एक ज्ञापन दिया जो बाद में ''स्टेट्स एण्ड माइनारिटीज'' शीर्षक से प्रकाशित हुआ। उसमें उन्होंने राज्य समाजवाद की जोरदार शब्दों में मांग रखी और कहा कि अब समय आ गया है कि संविधान के माध्यम से केवल राजनैतिक ही नहीं अपितु सामाजिक और आर्थिक समानता की स्थापना भी की जानी चाहिए।

भारतीय संविधान एवं सामाजिक न्याय

स्वतंत्रता प्राप्ति के समय यूं तो समाज का अधिकांश भाग गरीबी, अशिक्षा और पिछड़ेपन का शिकार था किन्तु अनुसूचित जातियों तथा अनुसूचित जनजातियों की स्थिति अत्यधिक शोचनीय थी। अनुसूचित जातियाँ जहाँ सामाजिक दासता का दुःख भोग रही थीं वहीं जनजातियाँ सभ्यता से दूर जंगली अवस्था में जी रही थीं। इन जातियों की संकटपूर्ण स्थिति नवोदित लोकतंत्र के सामने बहुत बड़ी समस्या थी जिसे देखते हुये भावी समाज की रूपरेखा निर्धारित करने वाली संविधान सभा ने सामाजिक न्याय की स्थापना को राष्ट्र का अपने सभी नागरिकों के लिये सामाजिक, आर्थिक और राजनैतिक न्याय तथा विचार, अभिव्यक्ति, विश्वास और उपासना की स्वतंत्रता और प्रतिष्ठा एवं अवसर की समानता तथा व्यक्ति की गरिमा एवं राष्ट्र की एकता सुनिश्चित करने वाली बन्धुता का विकास करना है। यहाँ ध्यान देने योग्य बात यह है कि संविधान की उद्देशिका में न्याय को स्वतंत्रता समानता और भ्रातृत्व से पहले रखा गया है। इसके अतिरिक्त, न्याय की व्याख्या करते समय सामाजिक एवं आर्थिक न्याय को राजनैतिक न्याय की तुलना में प्राथमिकता दी गई है। ऐसा मुख्य रूप से इसलिये किया गया है क्योंकि राजनैतिक न्याय (अर्थात् प्रत्येक नागरिक को मतदाता के रूप में पंजीकृत होने एवं मत देने का समान अधिकार) का कोई अर्थ नहीं जब तक कि समाज में नागरिकों को सामाजिक आर्थिक

न्याय प्राप्त नहीं होता। अनुच्छेद 19 में नागरिकों को स्वतंत्रता संबंधी विभिन्न अधिकार प्रदान किये गये, जिनमें बोलने, अभिव्यक्त करने, शांतिपूर्वक सम्मेलन करने, संगम व संघ बनाने, निर्बाध संचरण करने, देश के किसी भी भाग में बसने एवं निवास करने, कोई भी वृत्ति एवं जीविका अपनाने और कारोबार करने की स्वतंत्रतायें सम्मिलित है। इससे निम्न जातियों के गमनागमन, बसने एवं निवास करने संबंधी निर्योग्यतायें तथा जातिगत व्यवसायिक प्रतिबन्धों का पूरी तौर पर उन्मूलन हो गया है। इसके अतिरिक्त अनुच्छेद 21 में यह प्रावधान किया गया कि राज्य किसी व्यक्ति को उसके जीवन (या प्राण) और दैहिक स्वतंत्रता से विधि द्वारा स्थापित किसी प्रक्रिया के अतिरिक्त अन्य किसी प्रकार से वंचित नहीं कर सकेगा। आगे चल कर उच्चतम न्यायालय ने अपनी व्यवस्था में इसके आशय में विस्तार किया। तद्नुसार जीवित रहने के अधिकार से तात्पर्य अब सम्मानपूर्वक जीने का अधिकार हो गया है। अनुच्छेद 25, 26, 27 एवं 28 लोक व्यवस्था, सदाचार और स्वास्थ्य तथा इस भाग के अन्य उपबन्धों के अधीन रहते हुये व्यक्तियों को अन्तःकरण, विश्वास, धार्मिक आचरण तथा धार्मिक कार्यों के प्रबंध, प्रचार एवं प्रसार संबंधी स्वतंत्रतायें प्रदान करते हैं।

अनुच्छेद 14, 15, 16, 29 तथा 325 एवं 326 समानता संबंधी अधिकारों का प्रावधान करते हैं। अनुच्छेद 14 व्यक्ति को विधि के समक्ष समानता प्रदान करता है। अनुच्छेद 15 धर्म, मूलवंश, जाति, लिंग तथा जन्म स्थान के आधार पर राज्य द्वारा किसी प्रकार के भेद का प्रतिषेध करता है। अनुच्छेद 16 राज्य को लोक नियोजन या नियुक्ति के संबंध में सभी नागरिकों को समान अवसर प्रदान किये जाने का प्रावधान करता है। अनुच्छेद 29(2) राज्य द्वारा घोषित या राज्य निधि से सहायता पाने वाली किसी शिक्षा संस्था में प्रवेश पाने से किसी भी नागरिक को केवल धर्म, मूलवंश, जाति, भाषा या इनमें से किसी के आधार पर वंचित नहीं किये जाने की व्यवस्था करता है। अनुच्छेद 325 एवं 326 सभी नागरिकों को समान राजनैतिक अधिकार प्रदान किये जाने का प्रावधान करते हैं।

अनुच्छेद 23(1) के द्वारा बेगार या बलपूर्वक श्रम कराना निषिद्ध एवं इसका उल्लंघन दण्डनीय अपराध घोषित किया गया। अनुच्छेद 24 के माध्यम से 14 वर्ष से कम आयु के बच्चों को कारखाना या खान में नियोजित करने या संकटमय कार्य में लगाने से मना किया गया।

संविधान के भाग 4 में नीति निर्देशक सिद्धान्तों का उल्लेख है, जिनके द्वारा राज्य को निर्देशित किया गया है कि वह नागरिकों को

सामाजिक–आर्थिक न्याय प्रदान करने के लिये आवश्यक वैधानिक एवं प्रशासकीय पहले करे। सामाजिक–आर्थिक न्याय संबंधी लक्ष्यों की बेहतर पूर्ति को दृष्टिगत रखते हुये संविधान में राज्य की कल्पना एक कल्याणकारी राज्य के रूप में की गई है जो समाज के सभी वर्गों के लोगों को सामाजिक न्याय सुनिश्चित करेगा, उनकी शिक्षा, स्वास्थ्य, रोजगार एवं जीविकोपार्जन के लिये तथा उन्हें निर्वाह योग्य मजदूरी प्रदान कराने के लिये आवश्यक पहल करेगा। साथ ही कमजोर वर्गों विशेष रूप से श्रमिकों, बच्चों, वृद्धों एवं शारीरिक रूप से अशक्त लोगों के लिये सामाजिक सुरक्षा व कल्याण कार्यक्रमों को लागू करेगा।

संविधान के अनुच्छेद 38 में ऐसी व्यवस्था करने के लिये राज्य को निर्देशित किया गया जिससे कि सामाजिक, आर्थिक और राजनैतिक न्याय की स्थापना हो और आय की असमानताओं को कम किया जा सके। अनुच्छेद 39 में राज्य से जहाँ यह अपेक्षा की गई कि वह नागरिकों को जीविका के पर्याप्त साधन उपलब्ध कराने का प्रयास करेगा वहीं इस बात पर भी जोर दिया गया कि राज्य उत्पादन के साधनों का सर्वसाधारण के लिये अहितकारी सकेन्द्रण को रोकने तथा सामूहिक हित के सर्वोत्तम उपयोग की दृष्टि से भौतिक संसाधनों के स्वामित्व व नियंत्रण को नियमित करने का प्रयास भी करेगा।

अनुच्छेद 41, 42, 43 एवं 45 राज्य के कल्याणकारी कार्यों से संबंधित हैं। अनुच्छेद 41 के अन्तर्गत राज्य को निर्देशित किया गया है कि वह अपनी आर्थिक क्षमता व सीमा के अनुरूप लोगों को बेरोजगारी, बीमारी, असमर्थता व अन्य प्रकार की अशक्तता की अवस्था में काम–काज तथा शिक्षा एवं सार्वजनिक सहायता का अधिकार मुहैय्या कराने का प्रावधान करे। अनुच्छेद 42 कार्य की उपयुक्त मानवोचित दशा तथा मातृत्व लाभ सुनिश्चित करने से सम्बन्धित है। अनुच्छेद 43 में निर्देशित किया गया है कि राज्य उपयुक्त विधान, आर्थिक संगठन या अन्य किन्हीं माध्यमों से सभी श्रमिकों चाहे वे कृषि श्रमिक, औद्योगिक या अन्य किसी प्रकार के श्रमिक हों, के लिये कार्य, निर्वाह योग्य मजदूरी तथा कार्य के लिये समुचित दशायें उपलब्ध कराने का प्रयास करेगा जिससे कि उनके लिये उत्तम जीवन स्तर, अवकाश के पूर्ण उपयोग तथा सामाजिक व सांस्कृतिक अवसर सुनिश्चित हो सकें। अनुच्छेद 45 बालकों के लिये निःशुल्क और अनिवार्य शिक्षा का प्रबंध किये जाने से संबंधित है।

भारतीय समाज के कमजोर वर्ग एवं सामाजिक न्याय

समाज के दुर्बल वर्गों के हितों की अभिवृद्धि के संदर्भ में संविधान का अनुच्छेद 46 अत्यधिक महत्वपूर्ण है। यह अनुच्छेद राज्य को निर्देशित करता है कि वह समाज के कमजोर वर्गों विशेष रूप से अनुसूचित जातियों एव अनुसूचित जनजातियों के शिक्षा व आर्थिक हितों की विशेष सावधानी से अभिवृद्धि करेगा और सामाजिक अन्याय व सभी प्रकार के शोषण से उनकी रक्षा करेगा।

यद्यपि, अनुच्छेद 15 में नागरिकों के बीच किसी प्रकार के भेदभाव का प्रतिषेध किया गया, तथापि स्त्रियों एवं बालकों के हितों के संवर्धन को दृष्टिगत रखते हुये 15(3) के अंतर्गत यह व्यवस्था की गई कि इस अनुच्छेद की कोई बात राज्य को स्त्रियों एवं बालकों के लिये कोई विशेष उपबन्ध करने से निवारित नहीं करेगी। आगे चलकर 1951 में संविधान में पहली बार संशोधन किया गया। जिसके अनुसार इस अनुच्छेद में एक धारा जोड़ी गई, जिसमें, अर्थात् 15(4) में, यह कहा गया कि इस अनुच्छेद 29(2) की कोई बात राज्य को सामाजिक व शैक्षिक दृष्टि से पिछड़े हुए नागरिकों के किन्हीं वर्गों की उन्नति के लिये या अनुसूचित जातियों या अनुसूचित जनजातियों के लिये कोई विशेष उपबन्ध करने से निवारित नहीं करेगी

अनुच्छेद 16(1) में लोक नियोजन में अवसर की समानता का प्रावधान किया गया है और (2) में इस बाबत किसी प्रकार के भेद का निषेध किया गया है तथापि नियोजन में कमजोर वर्गों के हितों को सुरक्षित रखने के उद्देश्य से इस अनुच्छेद की उपधारा (4) में इस बात का प्रावधान किया गया कि अनुच्छेद की कोई बात राज्य को पिछड़े हुये नागरिकों के किसी वर्ग के पक्ष में जिसका प्रतिनिधित्व राज्य की राय में राज्य की सेवाओं में पर्याप्त नहीं है, नियुक्तियों या पदों के आरक्षण के लिये उपबन्ध करने से निवारित नहीं करेगी।

विधान मण्डलों में अनुसूचित जातियों एवं अनुसूचित जनजातियों का प्रतिनिधित्व सुनिश्चित करने के उद्देश्य से अनुच्छेद 330 एवं 332 के अन्तर्गत इन जातियों के लिये क्रमशः लोकसभा एवं विधान सभाओं में स्थान आरक्षित किये गये हैं। इसी प्रकार विभिन्न स्तरों पर पंचायतों में महिलाओं सहित इन जातियों का प्रतिनिधित्व सुनिश्चित करने के लिये राज्य पंचायत अधिनियम के अन्तर्गत आवश्यक प्रावधान किये गये हैं। अनुच्छेद 338 के अंतर्गत अनुसूचित जातियों एवं अनुसूचित जनजातियों

की समस्याओं एवं उन्हें संविधान द्वारा प्रदत्त रक्षोपायों से संबंधित विषयों का अध्ययन कर उनकी उन्नति हेतु आवश्यक सुझाव प्रदान करने की दृष्टि से राष्ट्रपति द्वारा एक आयोग की नियुक्ति का प्रावधान किया गया है। संप्रति इस आयोग को वैधानिक दर्जा भी प्रदान कर दिया गया है। इस प्रकार महिलाओं एवं अल्प संख्यकों के हितों की रक्षा से संबंधित कार्यों पर नजर रखने की दृष्टि से राष्ट्रीय एवं राज्य स्तरों पर महिला, अल्प संख्यक एवं मानव अधिकार आयोगों का भी गठन किया गया है।

अनुसूचित जातियों एवं अनुसूचित जनजातियों के अतिरिक्त सामाजिक व शैक्षिक दृष्टि से अन्य पिछड़े वर्गों की समस्याओं का अध्ययन करने एवं उनकी दशा में सुधार लाने की दृष्टि से आवश्यक उपाय सुझाने के लिये संविधान के अनुच्छेद 340 के अन्तर्गत राष्ट्रपति ने पिछड़ा वर्ग आयोग का गठन किया। प्रथम पिछड़ा वर्ग आयोग का काका कालेलकर की अध्यक्षता में 1955 में बना था। इसके लगभग दो दशक पश्चात बी.पी. मण्डल की अध्यक्षता में द्वितीय पिछड़ा वर्ग आयोग (1978–80) का गठन हुआ। इन आयोगों की सिफारिशों को दृष्टिगत रखते हुये केन्द्र व राज्य की नौकरियों में पिछड़े वर्गों के लोगों के लिये आरक्षण का प्रावधान किया गया है।

सामाजिक न्याय संविधान संबंधी विधान

समाज के कमजोर वर्ग, विशेष रूप से महिलायें एवं अनुसूचित जातियों के लोग, सदियों से शास्त्रीय निर्योग्यताओं से पीड़ित थे। संविधान के माध्यम से इनकी निर्योग्यताओं का उन्मूलन कर दिया गया तथा इन निर्योग्यताओं को लागू करना अपराध घोषित किया गया। संविधान में राज्य को इन अपराधों के लिय दण्ड विहित करने हेतु आवश्यक कानून बनाने के लिये कहा गया। संविधान के अनुच्छेद 35(अ)(11) के तहत संसद द्वारा अस्पृश्यता अपराध अधिनियम 1955 पारित किया गया। आगे चल कर इस अधिनियम को अधिक प्रभावकारी बनाने की दृष्टि से 19 नवम्बर, 1976 से नागरिक अधिकार संरक्षण अधिनियम 1955 लागू किया गया। इसी कड़ी में अनुसूचित जातियों एवं अनुसूचित जनजातियों के विरूद्ध भेदभाव व अत्याचार संबंधी प्रकरणों में अधिक सख्ती बरतने के उद्देश्य से अनुसूचित जाति व अनुसूचित जनजाति अत्याचार निवारण कानून 1989 के रूप में एक और कानून पारित किया गया। इस कानून के अनतर्गत अस्पृश्यता संबंधी अपराधों के विरूद्ध दण्ड में वृद्धि की गई तथां इन जातियों के विरूद्ध अत्याचार के प्रकरणों में अधिक कठोर दण्ड का प्रावधान किया गया।

महिलाओं की स्थिति में सुधार और उन्हें पुरूषों की तुलना में समानता प्रदान करने की दृष्टि से कई विधान पारित किये गये जिनमें हिन्दू विवाह एवं विवाह विच्छेद अधिनियम, 1955, हिन्दू उत्तराधिकार अधिनियम 1956, हिन्दू नाबालिगी तथा संरक्षकता अधिनियम, 1956, सप्रेशन ऑफ इम्मारत्न ट्राफिक इन बूमने एण्ड गर्ल्स एक्ट, 1956 तथा दहेज निरोधक अधिनियम, 1961 मुख्य हैं। कारखानों एवं खदानों में कार्यरत श्रमिकों को शोषणसे बचाने, उनकी छटनी रोकने, कार्य की दशाओं में सुधार लाने, काम के घंटे निर्धारित करने तथा वेतन, बोनस, फण्ड, बीमा, दुर्घटना के विरूद्ध क्षतिपूर्ति प्रदान करने तथा मातृत्व लाभ प्रदान किये जाने आदि से संबंधित विषयों पर श्रम सन्नियमों का निर्माण किया गया है। इससे संगठित क्षेत्रों में कार्यरत श्रमिकों को न्याय मिल पाया है। असंगठित क्षेत्रों में कार्यरत श्रमिकों को उनके नियोक्ताओं द्वारा किये जा रहे शोषण से मुक्ति दिलाने के लिये आवश्यक नियमों का निर्माण किया जा रहा है। श्रमिकों के हितों की रक्षा की दृष्टि से न्यूनतम वेतन कानून, 1948, बाण्डेड लेबर एक्ट, 1976 तथा बाल श्रम उन्मूलन अधिनियम, 1986 भी उल्लेखनीय हैं।

वैश्वीकरण के दौर में सामाजिक न्याय की प्रासंगिकता

आज की दुनिया में भूमंडलीकरण, उदारीकरण तथा निजीकरण की पूँजीवादी प्रक्रियाओं के चलते हमारे देश पर एक तरफ पुर्नउपनिवेशीकरण का खतरा मंडरा रहा है तो दूसरी तरफ धर्म और संस्कृति के नाम पर सामाजिक अन्याय की पुरानी व्यवस्थाओं को मजबूत बनाने वाली सांप्रदायिक शक्तियां लगातार मजबूत हो रही हैं। भूमंडलीकरण और अंधराष्ट्रवाद के विरूद्व एक स्वस्थ, प्रगतिशील, धर्मनिरपेक्ष तथा जनतांत्रिक राष्ट्रवाद को अपनाना हमारे लिये जरूरी हो गया हैं, क्योंकि नवसाम्राज्यवादी और नवफासीवादी–शक्तियों की मार अततः उन्हीं लोगों पर पड़ती हैं, जो सामाजिक अन्याय व बहिष्करण के शिकार है। मगर ये शक्तियाँ धर्म, संप्रदाय, वर्ण, जाति, रंग, लिंग, नस्ल, भाषा और क्षेत्रों के आधार पर लोगों को बाँटने और जनता को एकजुट न होने देने में सफल हो रही हैं। ऐसी स्थिति में सामाजिक बराबरी के लिये किये जाने वाले संघर्ष का ऐसा कौन सा रूप हो सकता हैं, जो देश को बाहरी गुलामी से और जनता को भीतरी अन्याय से बचा सके। लेकिन हमारा मानना है कि इन सभी पर व्यापक विचार विमर्श की आवश्यकता है, और गुंजाइश भी है। अम्बेडकर ने जिन अर्न्तविरोधों को दूर करने के लिए कहा था वे सामाजिक स्तर पर चाहे कुछ कम हुए हों, लेकिन भूमण्डलीकरण के वर्तमान दौर में आर्थिक स्तर

पर पहले से कहीं ज्यादा बढ़ गये है। इस प्रकार से आज भारतीय लोकतंत्र के विषय में डॉ भीमराव अम्बेडकर के कहे वे शब्द याद आते हैं जो उन्होंने भारत का संविधान प्रस्तुत करते हुए संसद में कहे थे, उनका कहना था : "जनवरी की 26 तारीख को हम अंतर्विरोधों के युग में प्रवेश करेंगे। राजनीति में समता और सामाजिक– आर्थिक जीवन में विषमता होगी। राजनीति में हम एक व्यक्ति की कीमत एक वोट के आधार पर आंकेगे। लेकिन सामाजिक और आर्थिक जगत में विषमतामूलक संरचनाओं के कारण हम एक व्यक्ति–एक मूल्य के उसूल को नकारना जारी रखेंगे। अंतर्विरोधों की इस गिरत में हम कब तक फंसे रहेंगे? सामाजिक और आर्थिक क्षेत्र में हम समता को कब तक ठुकराते रहेंगे? अगर हमने लंबे अरसे तक समता को अस्वीकार करना जारी रखा तो इसका नतीजा हमारे राजनीतिक लोकतंत्र के संकटग्रस्त होने में ही निकलेगा। (कांस्टीटुएंट एसेंबली डिबेट खण्ड दस, ऑफीशियल रिर्पोट) आज जाति व्यवस्था को बनाये रखने में सभी वर्गों को अपना हित दिखाई दे रहा है लेकिन यह स्थिति सर्वदा बनी रहेगी ऐसी बात नहीं है। जाति व्यवस्था और सामाजिक न्याय के बीच काँटे का विरोध है। देश का संविधान सामाजिक न्याय की स्थापना के लिये प्रतिबद्ध हैं। ऐसी स्थिति में लोकतंत्र, जो सामाजिक न्याय की प्राप्ति का एक संवैधानिक संयंत्र है, और जाति व्यवस्था के बीच निर्णायक संघर्ष होना ही है। इसे टाला नहीं जा सकता। जो लोग सामाजिक न्याय के प्रति, एक नये समाज की रचना के प्रति, एक नये भारत के निर्माण के प्रति, प्रतिबद्ध हैं, उन्हें अपनी परम्परात्मक निर्योग्यताओं से उत्पन्न दुर्भावनाओं अथवा अभिजात्य विशेषाधिकारों के छिन जाने से उत्पन्न खीज से ऊपर उठकर इस निर्णायक संघर्ष में अपनी आहुति देनी होगी। डॉ. अम्बेडकर के सम्पूर्ण चिन्तन और न्यायपूर्ण समाज की रचना के समस्त प्रयासों का सार तत्व है, जाति व्यवस्था का उन्मूलन। इसमें दो मत नहीं है कि इक्कीसवीं सदी जाति के विरूद्ध निर्णायक संघर्ष की सदी होगी। इसलिये यदि इस सदी को डॉ. अम्बेडकर, जो भारत में सामाजिक न्याय के संघर्ष के प्रतीक थे, के नाम अर्पित किया जाता है तो यह गलत नहीं होगा।

निष्कर्ष

मानवीय सम्यता का एक सुनहरा सपना है कि एक समतावादी समाज का निर्माण हो जहाँ सभी की प्रतिष्ठा समान हो। वस्तुतः हर समाज के अंदर चाहे वह अति साधारण हो या सबसे अधिक जटिल हो, सबके अंदर

सामाजिक विषमता किसी न किसी रूप में विद्यमान रहती है। भारत में तो स्थिति और भी जटिल है। यहाँ की सामाजिक हकीकत को देखें तो जाति, वर्ग, जेंडर एवं नृजातीयता के आधार पर असमानता की उपस्थिति चिरस्थायी रूप से स्वयंसिद्ध बनी हुई है। इसका एक प्रमुख कारण समाज में शक्ति, प्रतिष्ठा, संपत्ति आदि का असमान वितरण है। यहाँ हमें सामाजिक विषमता एवं सामाजिक स्तरण में अंतर कर देना चाहिए। सामाजिक विषमता को यदि निचोड़ में कहें तो यह समाज द्वारा निर्मित असमानता की पद्धति को कायम रखने से संबंधित है जबकि सामाजिक स्तरण एक अलग तरह की सामाजिक विषमता के रूप को दर्शाता है। उदाहरण के लिए भारत में जाति व्यवस्था सामाजिक समूहों के एक पदानुक्रमता को समाविष्ट करता है। कभी–कभी भारतीय समाज की जटिलता को सझने के लिए जाति, वर्ग, जेंडर एवं नृजातीयता के अंतर्संबंधों की पड़ताल करना भी महत्वपूर्ण हो जाता है। हालांकि ये सभी श्रेणियाँ वर्ग की श्रेणी को दर्शाती हैं तथापि विशिष्ट रूप में वर्ग से तात्पर्य आर्थिक वर्ग से है जातीय–वर्ग हाल के अतीत की एक नवीन सच्चाई है जो जाति के 'सेकुलरीकरण' के शीर्षक के अंतर्गत 'वर्गीकरण' की प्रक्रिया को दर्शाता है। यह भारत में जाति को 'कर्मकाण्ड से बाहर निकालने' एवं इसके राजनीतिकरण के दो आयामों के साथ देखी जा रही है। इसी प्रकार लैंगिक भिन्नता एवं नृजातीय संघर्षों के जैसी भी कई सामाजिक समस्याएँ भारतीय समाज में अन्दर तक जड़ जमाए हुए हैं। लैंगिक असमानता की समूची प्रक्रिया में भी एक वर्गीय विशेषता दिखाई देती है जेंडर की श्रेणी के अंदर भी निम्न जाति की महिलाएँ एवं सुविधाओं से वंचित महिलाएँ सुविधा सम्पन्न ऊँची जाति की महिलाओं की तुलना में कहीं अधिक दयनीय स्थिति में हैं। इस प्रकार यदि जेंडर को एक अलग नृजातीय समूह के रूप में भी देखा जाय तो इसमें भी भिन्नताएँ मौजूद हैं। अतः भारतीय समाज की सच्चाई को समझने के लिए जाति, वर्ग, जेंडर, नृजातीयता आदि सभी को एक विशिष्ट श्रेणी मानते हुए इसके अंतर्सबंधों को जानना अपरिहार्य हो जाता है और शायद तभी भारत की एक सच्ची तस्वीर भी उभरकर सामने आ पाती है। इस प्रकार डॉ अम्बेडकर सामाजिक एवं आर्थिक अन्याय से मुक्त समाज की स्थापना करना चाहते थे जिसका जरिया उनके अनुसार, सांस्कृतिक क्रांति ही थी। उन्होंने महात्मा फुले की तरह पाश्चात्य देशों की विकास–प्रणाली एवं क्रांतिकारी परिवर्तनों की राह पर चल कर स्वतंत्रता, समानता एवं भ्रातृत्व के आदर्शो की प्राप्ति करनी

चाही। उन्होंने बहिष्कृत जनों को शिक्षित एवं संगठित हो कर आंदोलन की राह पर चलने का आह्वान किया।

Notes

53 एस0 एल0 सागर, आरक्षण क्यों, सागर प्रकाशन, मैनपुरी, 1987, पृ. सं.–5

54 प्रसन्न कुमार चौधरी एवं श्रीकांत, बिहार में दलित आंदोलन, वाणी प्रकाशन, दरियागंज, नई दिल्ली, 2005, पृ. सं.–10।

55 वही, पृ. सं.–11।

56 अशोक कुमार अमर, अद श्य न्याय का समाज एवं आरक्षण नीति, एस0 के0 पब्लिशिंग कम्पनी, रांची, 2005, पृ. सं.–8।

57 एल0 के0 कुन्दन, नक्सलवाद : उद्भव और विकास, क्लासिकल पब्लिशिंग कम्पनी, नई दिल्ली, 2010, पृ. सं.–185।

58 लालेन्द्र कुमार कुन्दन, बिहार राज्य में नक्सलवाद की राजनीति का एक अनुभूतिपूर्ण अध्यापन (शोध प्रबंध), 1988, पृ. सं.–213।

59 योजना, जुलाई 2008, पृ. सं.–53–55।

संदर्भ

1. सिंह, आर.जी., 1987, भारत में सामाजिक परिवर्तन एवं सामाजिक समस्यायें भोपाल, मध्य प्रदेश हिन्दी ग्रंथ अकादमी।
2. रा.गो.सिंह, डॉ भीमराव अम्बेडकर के सामाजिक विचार, म. प्र. हिन्दी ग्रन्थ अकादमी, 1991 पृ. 127।
3. धनन्जय कीर, डॉ अम्बेडकर लाइफ एण्ड मिशन्स, मुम्बई, पापुलर प्रकाशन 1981।
4. आर.जी. सिंह, भारतीय दलितों की समस्यायें एवं समाधान, मध्यप्रदेश हिन्दी ग्रन्थ अकादमी, भोपाल, 1986 (पृ. 14–16)।
5. कश्यप, एस.पी., 1990, आनेस्ट एफर्ट नीडेड फॉर सोशल जस्टिस कुरूक्षेत्र 39(1): 37–41।
6. बिसवाल, तपन : (2009) मानवाधिकार जेण्डर एवं पर्यावरण, प्रकाशक बीवा बुक्स, नई दिल्ली।
7. दुबे, अभय कुमार (2007) आधुनिकता के आईने में दलित, प्रकाशक वाणी प्रकाशन, नई दिल्ली।
8. सिंह, आर.जी. 1999, सामाजिक न्याय लोकतंत्र और जाति व्यवस्था, रावत पब्लिकेशन्स, नई दिल्ली।
9. शोद्यार्थी पेनम छव.8.2006 CSDSè लोकनीतिः नई दिल्ली।

10. डी. आर. जारव' 2004, डॉ अम्बेडकर एक प्रखर विद्रोही, एबीडी पब्लिशर्स जयपुर।
11. डॉ विवेक कुमार, दलित समाज पुरानी समस्याएं नई आकांक्षाएं एक समाजशास्त्रीय अवलोकन, सम्यक प्रकाशन, नई दिल्ली।
12. चौधरी, डी.पी. 1990, की शेप डिवलपमेन्ट स्ट्रेटैजी फॉर सोशल जस्टिस कुरूक्षेत्र 30(1): 67–71
13. रा.गो. सिंह, सामाजिक न्याय एवं दलित संघर्ष जयपुर, राजस्थान हिन्दी ग्रंथ अकादमी।

23

दलित समाज के परिप्रेक्ष्य में– डॉ बी. आर. अम्बेडकर का नारीवादी चिन्तन

अरविन्द कुमार पटेल

दलित समाज ने कितनी प्रगति की है, इसे डॉ अम्बेडकर दलित स्त्री जाति के परिप्रेक्ष्य में देखते हैं। डॉ अम्बेडकर की स्त्रियों के पक्ष में की गई गम्भीर टिप्पणी का अक्सर ऊपरी तौर पर दलित और गैर–दलित साहित्यकारों द्वारा केवल वर्णन मात्र कर दिया जाता है, परन्तु उनमें यह गंभीर नारी चेतना कहाँ से आयी, उनके जीवन के इस सबसे महत्वपूर्ण पहलू को चर्चारहित छोड़ दिया जाता है। डॉ अम्बेडकर के सम्पूर्ण जीवन दर्शन पर बात करें तो यह अतिश्योक्तिपूर्ण कथन नहीं माना जा सकता है कि स्त्री और दलित स्त्री उनके व्यक्तित्व व उनके दर्शन का अभिन्न हिस्सा है और यह स्त्री चेतना उनके परिवार, उनके आसपास व विदेश में किये गये अध्ययन व तरह–तरह के आन्दोलनों से जुड़ने से आयी है। निस्संदेह उनमें स्त्री सम्बन्धी चेतना के विकसित होने का मूल आधार परिवार की महिलाओं की उनके ऊपर पड़ने वाली अमिट छाप भी है।

डॉ अम्बेडकर जब मात्र छः वर्ष के थे तब उनकी माँ गुजर गयी। माँ के अभाव में आये दिन उनके मन में स्त्री समाज के लिए हमेशा–हमेशा के लिए महत्वपूर्ण स्थान बना गये। माँ की मृत्यु के बाद भीमराव का पालन–पोषण उनकी अपंग बुआ ने बड़े मनोयोग से किया। हालाँकि वह

शारीरिक अपंगता के चलते घर का कुछ भी कार्य नहीं कर सकती थीं, परन्तु भीमराव को प्यार से गोद में छिपाकर वह उसे भरपूर दुलार देती थीं।

भीमराव बचपन से अपनी बुआ के साथ ही सोते थे। वे अपनी बुआ से साये की तरह चिपके रहते थे। उधर भीमराव की पढ़ाई के बढ़ते खर्चे के चलते पिता बार–बार अपनी बेटियों को दहेज में दिये गहनों को गिरवी रख जैसे–तैसे भीमराव की पढ़ाई करवाते रहे। इतना ही नहीं ''अपनी पुत्रियों के जेवर जो उन्होंने विवाह में दिये थे लेकर गिरवी रख देते और उस पैसे से भीमराव के लिए पुस्तक खरीदते। पेन्शन मिलने पर वे धीरे–धीरे सारा पैसा पुत्रियों को वापस कर देते।''

डॉ अम्बेडकर के स्त्री–चिन्तन को प्रखर बनाने में सबसे अधिक योगदान अगर किसी का कहा जा सकता है तो वह नाम उनके पिता, बुआ और बहनों के बाद केवल उनकी पत्नी रमाबाई का ही हो सकता है। अक्सर दलित लेखक बाबा साहब का जीवन वर्णन करते समय, उनके संघर्षों को बताते समय, उनको भीमराव से बाबा साहब बनाने वाली रमाबाई के योगदान की चर्चा करना भूल जाते हैं।

रमाबाई दलितों के महानायक डॉ अम्बेडकर नामक विशाल वृक्ष की मजबूत जड़ थीं, जो आंधी–तूफानों से भरे संघर्षपूर्ण दिनों में अविरल रूप में थामे मजबूती से खड़ी रहीं। रमाबाई के मूक बलिदान ने दलित आन्दोलन में रक्त प्रवाह का कार्य किया। रमाबाई और डॉ अम्बेडकर का जीवन आदर्श दाम्पत्य जीवन तो नहीं पर समझदार पति–पत्नी का जीवन तो अवश्य ही कहा जा सकता है। डॉ अम्बेडकर के पढ़ने की क्षुधा को अपने खून–पसीने से एक कर दिन–रात कमाकर एकांकी जीवन जीते हुए उपले पाथते हुए, रात–दिन घर में रहते हुए रमाबाई ने डॉ अम्बेडकर के अन्दर ज्ञान की कभी न मिटने वाली प्यास को धनाभाव के कारण बुझने नहीं दिया। जिस समय रमाबाई का विवाह हुआ उस समय रमाबाई को पढ़ना–लिखना नहीं आता था। डॉ अम्बेडकर ने जिस तल्लीनता से रमाबाई को पढ़ाया रमाबाई ने भी उतनी ही लगन, ईमानदारी से पढ़ना–लिखना सीखा। बहुत कम ही लोग जानते हैं कि जब बाबा साहब विदेश में होते थे तो रमाबाई उनको बराबर पत्र लिखा करती थीं, डॉ अम्बेडकर भी उनको पढ़ाई की भारी व्यस्तता और धनाभाव के बावजूद उन्हें तुरन्त उत्तर दिया करते थे। रमाबाई अपने अथक प्रयासों एवं परिश्रम से डॉ अम्बेडकर के मुक्ति संघर्ष से जुड़ी रही। अधिकतर लोग यह समझते थे कि वह केवल

आज्ञाकारी पतिव्रता स्त्री और कुशल परिवार चालक थी परन्तु उनके बारे में बहुत कम लोग ये जानते है कि उन्होंने डॉ अम्बेडकर के साथ दलित आन्दोलन तथा दलित हितों के लिए कंधे से कंधा मिलाकर काम किया है। रमाबाई अक्सर डॉ अम्बेडकर द्वारा किये जा रहे कार्यों पर बातचीत करती व अपनी उचित सलाह दिया करती थी। बाबा साहब उन्हें दलित समाज की सभाओं खासकर दलित महिलाओं की सभा में अवश्य ले जाया करते थे। 29 जनवरी 1926 मुंबई में रमाबाई को दलित महिला परिषद् का अध्यक्ष चुना गया और उन्होंने अध्यक्ष पद को बड़ी कुशल बखूबी से संभाला। दलित वर्ग की बैठकों में आये दलित स्त्री–पुरुषों का उत्साह दुगना हो जाता। इस परिवर्तन को डॉ अम्बेडकर भी महसूस करते थे।

डॉ अम्बेडकर जब विदेश मे पढ़ने गये तो वहाँ के स्वतंत्र जीवन में उन्होंने स्त्रियों को चहुंमुखी विकास करते देखा तब उन्हें समझ में आया कि बिना स्त्री शिक्षा के बिना कोई भी प्रगति अधूरी है। विदेश में होते हुए वहाँ की स्त्रियों को स्वतंत्रता पूर्वक जीवन जीते हुए, चिन्तन मनन करते हुए उनकी प्रगति देख उनकी स्त्री चेतना को धार मिली। 1913 में न्यूयार्क में पढ़ते हुए डॉ अम्बेडकर ने अपने पिता के मित्र को जबाब देते हुए पत्र में लिखा "यह गलत है कि माँ बाप बच्चों को जन्म देते हैं कर्म नहीं देते। माँ बाप बच्चों के जीवन को उचित मोड़ दे सकते हैं, यह बात अपने मन पर अंकित कर यदि हम लोग अपने लड़कों की शिक्षा के साथ ही लड़कियों की शिक्षा के लिए भी प्रयास करें तो हमारे समाज की उन्नति तीव्र होगी। इसलिए आपकों नजदीक रिश्तेदारों में यह विचार तेजी से फैलाने चाहिए।"

समाज में दलित महिलाओं की स्थिति

डॉ अम्बेडकर एकमात्र ऐसे विश्वस्तरीय चिन्तक है जिन्होंने परिवार और समाज में स्त्री की स्थिति कैसी होनी चाहिए, इस पर गहन चिन्तन मनन किया। पुरुषों के साथ स्त्री को भी समानता एवं स्वतंत्रता मिले, उसे सामाजिक आजादी के साथ आर्थिक आजादी प्राप्त हो समाज में उसका दर्जा पुरुष के समान हो, इसके लिए उन्होंने दलित, गैर दलित स्त्रियों को समाज परिवर्तन के आन्दोलन में सक्रिय रूप से जुड़ने का आह्वान किया। दोनों जगत यानि घर और समाज में नारी की हीनतर स्थिति को देखकर उन्होंने इस विषय पर खूब सोचा कि भारतीय स्त्री की स्थिति में क्रान्तिकारी परिवर्तन कैसे आये। यह क्रान्तिकारी परिवर्तन परिवार तथा समाज मे नारी को विशेषाधिकार देकर ही किया जा सकता हैं।

डॉ अम्बेडकर का मानना था कि स्त्री और समाज की उन्नति, शिक्षा के बिना नहीं हो सकती। सुन्दर और सुशिक्षित व सभ्य परिवार के लिए आवश्यक है कि पुरुषों के साथ–साथ घर की स्त्रियाँ भी पढ़ी लिखी हो ताकि वे समाज परिवर्तन की प्रक्रिया से सक्रिय ढंग से शामिल हों सके। समाज के परिवर्तन द्वारा ही स्त्रियों की मुक्ति संभव है। डॉ अम्बेडकर का अनुभव देश एवं विदेश दोनों का था। दोनों जगत में स्त्रियों ने कितनी प्रगति की इसकी तुलना करने पर वह जमीन आसमान का अन्तर पाते थे और उन्होंने विदेश में शिक्षित व खुशहाल स्त्री को देखा तो उन्हें उनकी खुशहाली का महत्व शिक्षा में निहित नजर आया। डॉ अम्बेडकर को विश्वास था कि शिक्षित होकर ही स्त्री अपने अधिकारों को छीन सकती है। डॉ अम्बेडकर का मानना था कि परिवार में स्त्री शिक्षा ही वास्तविक प्रगति की धुरी है। स्त्री शिक्षा को डॉ अम्बेडकर अत्यधिक महत्व देते हुए कहते है–अगर घर में एक पुरुष पढ़ता है तो केवल वही पढ़ता है और यदि घर में स्त्री पढ़ती है तो पूरा परिवार पढ़ता है। डॉ अम्बेडकर ने भारतीय साहित्य में प्राचीन से लेकर आधुनिक साहित्य के साथ–साथ विदेशी साहित्य का भी अच्छी प्रकार से अध्ययन मनन किया था। उन्होंने दलित परिवारों से अनुरोध किया कि वे अपने बच्चों की खासकर लड़कियों की शादी बचपन में न करें। ''माता–पिता अपनी सन्तान की शादी कम उम्र में करके उनके जीवन को नर्क न बनायें। डॉ अम्बेडकर ने विवाह जैसे सवाल पर भी बातचीत की। पत्नी कैसी होनी चाहिए इस बारे में परूषों का विचार जाना जाता है। वैसे ही पति कैसा हो इस बारे में पत्नी का मन जान लेना जरूरी है। स्त्री भी एक मानव है और उसे भी मानव स्वतंत्रता की सुविधा होनी चाहिए।''

स्त्रियों की समानता और स्वतंत्रता के संदर्भ में डॉ अम्बेडकर अन्यत्र चिन्तकों एवं समाज सुधारकों से काफी आगे की समझ रखते थे। समाज सुधारक जहाँ नारी शिक्षा को परिवार की उन्नति व आदर्श मातृत्व को संभालने या नारी की स्त्रियोचित गुणों के कारण ही उसकी उपयोगिता पर बल देते थे परन्तु नारी भी मानव है, उसके भी अन्य मानवों के समान अधिकार हैं, इस बात को स्वीकार करने में हिचकिचाते थे। उन्होंने लड़कों के समान लड़कियों को पढ़ाने के साथ–साथ उसका विवाह भी उचित आयु में हो, इस बात पर बार–बार बल दिया है। इस विषय पर बोलते हुए डॉ अम्बेडकर कहते है– ''शादी एक महत्वपूर्ण जबावदारी है और शादी करने वाली हर औरत को उसके पक्ष में खड़ा रहना चाहिए लेकिन उसको

दासी नहीं बल्कि बराबरी के नाते या मित्र के तौर पर। यदि ऐसा करोगी तो अपने साथ समाज का भी अभ्युदय करोगी और अपना सम्मान बढ़ाओगी। इस हेतु सभी स्त्रियों को पुरुषों के बाराबर हिस्सेदारी कर खुद को शासक की जमात बनाने हेतु प्रयास करना चाहिए।'' डॉ अम्बेडकर महिलाओं को उसके समाज द्वारा दी गयी भूमिकाएँ माँ, पत्नी, बहन एवं उसके स्त्रियोचित गुणों से इतर उसको पूर्ण स्वतंत्र, स्वस्थ एवं प्रगतिशील कर्मठ मानवी के रूप में देखते थे।

डॉ अम्बेडकर का समय दलित महिलाओं की अपनी व समाज की स्वतंत्रता, समानता को लेकर की गई सक्रिय व संघर्षपूर्ण भागीदारी का स्वर्ण काल है। डॉ अम्बेडकर के समय मे चले दलित आन्दोलन में लाखों शिक्षित, अशिक्षित, घरेलू, गरीब, मजदूर, किसान व दलित–शोषित महिलाऐं जुडी। उन्होंने जिस निर्भीकता, बेबाकी और उत्साह से दलित आन्दोलन में भागीदारी निभाई वह अभूतपूर्ण थी दलित महिला आन्दोलन और अम्बेडकर के साथ महिला आन्दोलन की सुसंगत शुरूआत 1920 से मान सकते हैं हालांकि सुगबुगाहट सन् 1913 से ही हो गयी थी। 1920 में 'भारतीय बहिष्कृत परिषद' की सभा कोल्हापुर नरेश छत्रपति शाहू जी महाराज की अध्यक्षता में सम्पन्न हुई। इस सभा में पहली बार दलित महिलाओं ने भाग लेकर अपनी सक्रिय भूमिका निभाई। पहली बार दलित स्त्रियों ने शिक्षा के महत्व को समझते हुए इस सभा में तुलसाबाई बनसोडे, और रूकमणि बाई ने घरेलू भाषा में लड़कियों की शिक्षा पर बात रखी। उन्होंने अपने विचार रखते हुए कहा कि लड़कियों की उसकी शक्ति शिक्षा ही है। इस परिषद में लड़कियों के लिए अनिवार्य और मुक्त शिक्षा का प्रस्ताव पारित किया गया।

देश भर मे चल रहे दलित आन्दोलन के साथ दलित महिला आन्दोलन भी अपना आकार ले रहा था। 1920 से प्रारम्भ हुए दलित महिला आन्दोलन में दलित महिलाओं की सक्रिय भगीदारी बढ़ती जा रही थी। 20 जुलाई 1924 में मुंबई में आयोजित ''बहिष्कृत हितकारिणी सभा'' की स्थापना की गयी। इस सभा की स्थापना का मुख्य उद्देश्य अस्पृश्यता के खिलाफ जंग छेड़ने के अलावा दलित वस्तियों में स्कूल व छात्रावास खोलने सम्बन्धी प्रयास कर दलित समाज की जागृति व चेतना पैदा करना था। ''बहिष्कृत हितकारिणी सभा'' की अधिसंख्य सभाएं जो जगह–जगह गांव, देहातों, में आयोजित की जाती थी उनमें दलित महिलाएं लगातार उपस्थित रहती थीं। इस समय दलित महिलायें अपने समाज और परिवार

जनित पीड़ा को सार्वजनिक रूप से अभिव्यक्ति कर रही थीं पर उनकी अभिव्यक्ति अधिकतर गानों व स्वागत गान के रूप में ही होती थी।

"बहिष्कृत हितकारिणी सभा" की सभाओं में वेणुबाई पाटकर और रंगबाई सुभरकर अपने मधुर कंठ से दलित पीड़ा की मार्मिक और संघर्षपूर्ण अभिव्यक्ति को गीतों में ढालकर मनमोहक स्वर में गाकर सबका मन मोह लेती थी।

1924 में ही एक अत्यन्त क्रान्तिकारी घटना घटी जिसने दलित महिला आन्दोलन की सक्रियता एवं उसके विचारात्मक पक्ष को उभारने का भरपूर मौका दिया। इस क्रान्तिकारी घटना के द्वारा दलित महिलाओं ने दलित बच्चियों के लिए विद्यालय स्थापित करने का प्रयास किया उच्च शिक्षित दलित महिला जाईबाई चौधरी जो बाद में सशक्त दलित महिला नेता के रूप में उभर कर सामने आयी। उन्होंने 1924 में चोखा मेला कन्या पाठशाला आरम्भ किया। जाईबाई चौधरी स्वयं बहुत मुसीबतों से पढ़ लिख पाईं थीं। जाईबाई चौधरी घर व समाज का तीव्र विरोध सहकर शिक्षिका बनी थी। शिक्षिका के बावजूद एक जागरूक लेखिका एवं अच्छी वक्ता थी। जाईबाई चौधरी बाबा साहब के विचारों से पूर्ण प्रभावित होकर उनकी पक्की अनुयायी बनी। जाईबाई चौधरी ने स्त्री शिक्षा को अत्यधिक महत्वपूर्ण मानते हुए सर्वप्रथम नारी को शिक्षित करने पर बल दिया। जाई बाई चौधरी के अथक प्रयासों से दलित महिला आन्दोलन की माला में सघर्ष का एक मोती और जुड़ गया।

1920 लेकर 1924 तक दलित महिला आन्दोलन मन्दगति से चलता हुआ स्त्री–शिक्षा और अस्पृश्यता के मुद्दों पर समाज का ध्यान खींचता रहा। 1927 का एक दलित आन्दोलन के साथ–साथ दलित महिला आन्दोलन के लिए भी अत्यन्त महत्वपूर्ण है। सन् 1927 के अन्त में बाबा साहब द्वारा चलाये गये महाड़ सत्याग्रह की परिणति "मनुस्मृति दहन" और "चावदार तालाब का पानी पीने" से हुई है। 25 दिसम्बर 1927 को चावदार तनाव के महाड़ सत्याग्रह के ऐतिहासिक सम्मेलन में ढ़ाई हजार दलित औरतों ने "मनुस्मृति दहन" में शामिल होकर हिन्दू धर्म के स्त्री–विरोध कानून को मानने से इन्कार कर दिया। इसी सभा में दलित महिलाओं की भारी संख्या में उपस्थिति देखकर डॉ अम्बेडकर ने उनके पक्ष में अपना ऐतिहासिक भाषण दिया। बाबा साहब ने कहा "स्त्रियों को गृहलक्ष्मी ही क्यों होना चाहिए? मन में ऊँची महत्वाकांक्षा रखो। ज्ञान और विद्या पर केवल पुरुषों का ही अधिकार नहीं है, वह स्त्रियों के लिए भी अति

आवश्यक है। यदि तुम्हें आगे की पीढ़ी सुधारनी है तो तुम्हें लड़कों के साथ–साथ लड़कियों की शिक्षा पर बल देना होगा। घर में पति अगर मरे हुए जानवर का मांस लाये तो उससे कहो कि ये सब मेरे घर में नहीं चलेगा। गले में इतनी वजनी मालायें और हाथों में कोहनी तक के कड़े और कंगन यह सब तुम्हें अश्पृश्य करके पहचानने की निशानी है।'' इस ऐतिहासिक भाषण का दलित महिलाओं पर इतनी तीव्रता से असर पड़ा कि उन्होंने उसी सभा में हाथ में कोहनी तक भरे कड़े, गले में बड़ी बजनी मालाऐं उतार दी और सभा में उपस्थित सौभाग्य सहस्र बुद्धे, व रमाबाई अम्बेडकर से दलित महिलाओं ने समाज की अन्य वर्ग की महिलाओं की तरह साड़ी पहनना सीख लिया। 1927 तक अम्बेडकर वादी दलित महिला आन्दोलन का मुख्य मुद्दा शिक्षा, सफाई, संगठन और संघर्ष था।

दलित महिलाओं की स्थिति केवल अपने घरों में ही खराब नहीं थी अपितु फैक्ट्रियों और खेत–खलिहानों में उनको वर्कर तक नहीं माना जाता था। गर्भावस्था की हालत में उन्हें नौकरी से निकाल दिया जाता था। उनको पूरा वेतन नहीं मिलता था उनके काम के घंटे निश्चित नहीं थे। मुंबई विधान परिषद में कारखाना व अन्य सरकारी/गैरसरकारी संस्थानों में कार्यरत मजदूर महिलाओं के पक्ष में प्रसूति अवकाश सुविधा सम्बन्धी विल पर अपने सशक्त विचार रखते हुए डॉ अम्बेडकर ने कहा कि ''महिलाओ को प्रसूति अवकाश व पूरा वेतन प्राप्त करना राष्ट्रीय हित में एक महत्वपूर्ण कदम है। मैं इस बात से सहमत हूँ कि इससे सरकार पर भारी बोझ पड़ेगा, लेकिन फिर भी मैं वेतन कटौती का पक्षधर नहीं हूँ। यह महिलाओं का उनका अपना अधिकार है जिसकी प्राप्ति उन्हें होनी चाहिए।'' इस तरह दलित महिलाओं ने अपने अस्मिता संघर्ष के साथ–साथ मजदूर आन्दोलन के संघर्ष और उनके मुद्दों को अपने आन्दोलन का अहम हिस्सा बना लिया।

1928 में ही मुंबई में ''महिला मंडल'' की स्थापना की गयी और महिला मंडल की प्रथम अध्यक्षा डॉ अम्बेडकर की पत्नी रमाबाई को चुना गया। 1928 में बने ''महिला मंडल'' ने आगे चलकर दलित महिलाओं की सामाजिक, आर्थिक, राजनीतिक स्थिति संभालने व उसको आगे ले जाने की दिशा में अमूल योगदान दिया।

1930 से 1934 तक का काल बाबा साहब और दलित महिला आन्दोलन के लिए उपलब्धि भरा काल कहा जा सकता है। इस काल अवधि में कई अभूतपूर्व घटनायें घटी। एक तरफ तो नासिक के कालाराम

मन्दिर प्रवेश का आन्दोलन 02 मार्च 1930 से लेकर 1934 तक पूरे चार वर्ष लगातार चला। इस आन्दोलन में महाराष्ट्र, गुजरात, कर्नाटक और अन्य राज्यों व देश के विभिन्न भागों से 10 हजार से अधिक महिला पुरुष सत्याग्राही शामिल हुए, दूसरे इन सत्याग्राहियों की पूरी देखभाल जैसे खाने पीने ठहरने आदि का इन्तजाम पहली बार दलित महिलाओं ने जिस निष्ठा और मेहनत से किया वह अपने आप में एक मिसाल है। इस आन्दोलन द्वारा दलित महिलओं की चेतना कितनी प्रखर रूप में विकसित हो गयी थी इस बात को समझने के लिए केवल एक उदाहरण ही काफी है कि जब ''01 अप्रैल 1930 में मन्दिर प्रवेश के दौरान पुजारी द्वारा दलित महिलाओं को पीछे धक्का मार दिया तब एक दलित महिला ने उस पुजारी के मुँह पर सनसनाता थप्पड़ रसीद कर दिया।''

कालाराम मन्दिर सत्याग्रह में महिलाओं की सभा में भाग लेते हुए राधा बाई बड़ाले सत्याग्रही ने अपने ओजस्वी भाषण में कहा ''हमें मन्दिरों में जाने का, पनघट से पानी पीने का एवं भरने का अधिकार मिलना चाहिए। यह हमारा सामाजिक हक है। शासन करने का राजनीतिक अधिकार भी मिलना चाहिए। हम कठोर सजा की चिन्ता नहीं करती। हम देश भर की जेलों को भर देगें। हम लाठी गोली खायेगे। हमें हमारा हक चाहिए। योद्धा कभी अपनी जान की चिन्ता नहीं करता। गुलामी की जिन्दगी से मृत्यु बेहतर है। हम अपनी जान दे देगें। मगर अधिकार छीन कर रहेगें।'' कालाराम मन्दिर प्रवेश आन्दोलन में रमाबाई अम्बेडकर, सीताबाई, गीताबाई गायकवाड, रमाबाई गायकवाड, रमाबाई जाधव, तुलसी रामजी काले की माता जी, अमृत राव शरण खावें की माता जी ताराबाई, यमुनाबाई, भिकूबाई, सरूबाई भालेराव, और अनेक अनाम अज्ञात औरतों ने भाग लिया जिसमें अन्ततः डॉ अम्बेडकर और उनकी सहयोगी महिला साथियों की जीत हुई। 1930 में ही बाबा साहब ने नागपुर में 'अखिल भारतीय शेड्यूल्स कास्ट फेडरेशन' की स्थापना के साथ ही 'दलित महिला परिषद' भी आयोजित की। इस सभा में दस हजार से अधिक महिलाओं ने भाग लिया। इस सभा की अध्यक्षा सुलोचना डोगरे तथा स्वागताध्यक्ष कीर्ति पाटिल और मुख्य सचिव इन्दिरा पाटिल थी यह सभा पूर्णतया सफल रही। नागपुर में 08 से 10 अगस्त 1930 में अखिल भारतीय दलित कांग्रेस के प्रथम अधिवेशन में दलित महिलाओं का प्रतिनिधित्व करते हुए जाईबाई चौधरी ने कहा– ''लड़कियों को भी लड़कों के समान पढ़ने के पूरे–पूरे अवसर उपलब्ध कराने चाहिए। एक लड़की की शिक्षा से पूरा परिवार शिक्षित हो जाता है।

30 दिसम्बर 1933 नागपुर में राष्ट्रीय परिषद में ''अस्पृश्यता और अस्पृथ्यता निवारण'' विषय पर गोष्ठी आयोजित की गई। इस गोष्ठी में कृष्ण बोस जैसे राष्ट्रीय नेता भी उपस्थित थे। इस सभा में वेणुबाई भटकर ने जाति प्रथा की विडंबना पर भाषण देते हुए कहा– ''मैं वैसे तो अनपढ़ हूँ लेकिन मुझे ऐसा लगता हैं कि जब तक अस्पृश्यों को स्पृश्य नहीं किया जाता तब तक स्वराज्य मिलना कठिन है स्कूल में लड़की के जाते ही पूछा जाता है कि जाति कौन है? ज्यों ही महार कहा जाता है तो अनर्थ हो जाता है यह स्थिति नागपुर की है। नागपुर में महारों को हाजिरी देनी पड़ती है। गांव में तो महारों की स्थिति और भी बदतर है। ऐसी स्थिति में महार कैसे जिन्दा रहें? कैसे अपना स्वाभिमान रखें? मै नर्स हूँ पर मुझे क्रिश्चियन होने को कहा जाता है और क्रिश्चियन होने पर ही नौकरी मिलेगी ऐसा कहते हैं। लेकिन जब में जात–पात छोड़ूंगी नहीं। नाम चुराना, जात चुराना, यह बात मैं बिल्कुल नहीं करूंगी। मैं जाति में रहकर जाति को सुधारना चाहती हूँ इसके लिए मैं जी जान से प्रयत्न करूंगी।'' बेणुबाई भटकर सक्रिय दलित कार्यकर्ता थी। वह अत्यन्त स्वाभिमानी और दलित गरिमा से पूर्ण दलित महिला आन्दोलन के इतिहास का एक चमकता सितारा थी।

08 अप्रैल 1934 में मुंबई के बोरगांव जिला बर्धा में ''अस्पृश्य परिषद सम्पन्न हुई। इस परिषद की खासियत थी कि इसकी अध्यक्षता दलित कार्यकर्ता सुभद्राबाई ने की तथा इस परिषद में विस्तार से स्त्री–शिक्षण व्यवस्था, और दलित समाज में लड़कियों को शिक्षित करने और अल्पायु में विवाह कर देने की कुप्रथा पर चिन्ता प्रकट की गई। इस सभा में शिक्षा को प्रोत्साहन देने के लिए लड़के लड़कियों के लिए वाचनालय, रात्रि कक्षाओं की सुविधा कराने के साथ–साथ दलित छात्र–छात्राओं को भाषण लेख आदि लिखने की प्रेरणा देने के साथ–साथ पुरस्कार व स्कालरशिप आदि की व्यवस्था कर शिक्षा को आगे बढ़ाने के महत्व की पुरजोर वकालत की गई। दलित बालिकाओं की शिक्षा में चिन्ताजनक स्थिति को मद्देनजर रखते हुए पुनः 1935 में बोरगांव, वर्धा में ''अस्पृश्य परिषद'' द्वारा आयोजित सभा में दलित बच्चियों की पढ़ाई पर ध्यान देने के लिए विशेष प्रस्ताव पारित किया गया। इस सभा की अध्यक्षता इस बार श्रीमती कमलाबाई ने की।

16 जून 1936 में धर्म परिवर्तन पर व्याख्यानों की श्रृंखला में बम्बई के दामोदर हाल में बाबा साहब के व्याख्यानों को सुनने के लिए लोगों

का हुजूम का हुजूम उमड़ पड़ा। इस सभा में काफी संख्या में जोगिनी और वैश्याओं ने भी भाग लिया। वे भी हिन्दू धर्म की गन्दगी से मुक्ति की इच्छुक थीं। डॉ अम्बेडकर ने उनसे स्वेच्छा से स्त्री मुक्ति आन्दोलन में जुड़ने की अपील की। डॉ अम्बेडकर ने कहा– ''अपनी गृहणी अच्छे परिवार से आये ऐसी आशा सभी रखते हैं किन्तु जब तक उनके लिए स्वस्थ परिवारों का निर्माण नहीं होगा तब तक अच्छी गृहणी का निर्माण नहीं हो सकता। नारी की उन्नति के साथ–साथ परिवार की उन्नति का प्रश्न जुडा हुआ है। अतः नारी के महत्व को स्वीकारा जाना चाहिए।'' इस सभा में बाबा साहेब ने जोगिनों और वेश्याओं को साफ सुथरी जिन्दगी जीने की प्रेरणा दी फलस्वरूप बाबा साहब की प्रेरणा से कई दलित संगठनों ने अनेक जोगिनी और वेश्याओं के विवाह सम्पन्न कराये और उनके परिवार बसाने का अहम कार्य किया।

23 जून 1938 में बुम्बई में डिलाइट रोड पर दलित महिलाएं दलित आन्दोलन में सक्रिय भागीदारी कैसे निभायें इसको लेकर विशाल सभा हुई जिसमें दलित महिला कार्यकर्ताओं की उन समस्याओं पर बात की गई जो उनके सामाजिक कार्य करने के दौरान आ रही थी। इस सभा में यह प्रस्ताव पारित किया गया कि समाज कार्य के वढ़ाने व दलित कार्यकर्ताओं के मार्ग में अवरोध खड़ा करने वाली वृद्ध महिला पुरुषों को भी जागृत किया जायेगा तथा उनमें भी दलित चेतना पैदा की जायेगी। दलित महिलाओं में व्याप्त शार्मिलापन, संकोच, हीनभावना, व उनके अन्दर व्याप्त संकीर्णताओं और कुरीतियों को खत्म करने के लिए उन्हें घरेलू उद्योग, हाथ के हुनर जैसे कशीदाकारी कार्यों को प्रशिक्षण दिया जायेगा और उनको अक्षर ज्ञान देकर शिक्षित करने का कुपोषण और सफाई की कमी के कारण बीमारियाँ घर बना लेती थी इन मुद्दों पर दलित महिलाओं में साफ–सफाई और सम्मान के साथ रहने की शिक्षा दी जायेगी। गरीब दलित व उत्साहित लड़कियों को शिक्षा के लिए आर्थिक सहायता प्रदान की जायेगी। इस प्रकार हम देखते हैं कि 1936 में तब दलित महिला आन्दोलन ने अपने मुख्य मुद्दों में अनिवार्य शिक्षा, सम्मान से जीने का अधिकार दलित महिलाओं में स्वास्थ्य के प्रति जागरूकता, दलित महिला आन्दोलन से जुड़ने में उसके परिवारों द्वारा लगाई गयी रूकावटों का समाधान, उनकों सम्मान से अपने पैरों पर खड़ा होने को अपने मुख्य मुद्दों में शमिल कर लिया था।

29 जुलाई 1942 को आयोजित ''अखिल भारतीय दलित महिला सम्मेलन'' में 25 हजार महिलाओं ने भाग लिया। इस सम्मेलन में स्वयं डॉ अम्बेडकर भी उपस्थित थे। इस सम्मेलन की विशेष बात यह थी कि इस सम्मेलन में पूरे भारत वर्ष से आई दलित महिला प्रतिनिधियों ने भाग लिया। इस सम्मेलन की अध्यक्षता सुलोचना डोगरे ने की और सभा की मुख्य सचिव इन्दिरा पाटिल तथा स्वागताध्यक्ष कीर्ति पाटिल थीं। 1942 में ही ''अखिल भारतीय दलित महिला फेडरेशन'' ने दलित स्त्रियों की राजनीतिक एवं सामाजिक स्थिति पर अधिवेशन रखा जिसमें फेडरेशन की सचिव इन्दिरा पाटिल ने समाज में दलित महिलाओं की शोचनीय स्थिति पर प्रकाश डालते हुए अपने जोशीले भाषण में कहा– ''अपने पुरुष साथियों द्वारा अधिकारों की लड़ाई में हमें पीछे नहीं रहना है। हमें उनके साथ रहना है। सामान्यतः घर के कामकाज महिलाओं के हिस्से में आते हैं पर हमें उससे नहीं चिपके रहना चाहिए। पुरुषों जैसी स्वतंत्रता पाने के लिए हम बेचैन हैं और वह हमारा अधिकार है। इस अधिकार को हम आन्दोलन और अपने प्रयास से ही पा सकते हैं। जो दुःखों से पीड़ित हैं उन्हें ही स्वतंत्रता की जरूरत है। हमारी दलित महिलाओं में साक्षरता की दर बहुत कम है। उन्हें शिक्षा के प्रति जागृत करना हमारा कर्तव्य है। साथ ही हम अपनी अनपढ़, अनाड़ी बहनों की मदद से अस्पृश्यों के हक के लिए हमारे नेता बाबा साहब अम्बेडकर के नेतृत्व में हम अपने प्राणों का बलिदान देकर लड़ाई के लिए तैयार रहेंगी। हमें अपना पिछड़ापन नष्ट करने के लिए संगठित होकर कार्य करना है। इन कार्यों को करने के लिए मैं एक केन्द्रीय संस्था तथा उसके सभी प्रान्तों में शाखा खोलने का प्रस्ताव रखती हूँ।'' इन्दिरा पाटिल ने दलित महिलाओं की शिक्षा पर विशेष जोर दिया। महिलाओं की शोचनीय स्थिति के लिए जिम्मेदार हिन्दू धर्म की भर्त्सना करते हुए कहा– ''हिन्दू धर्म के पालन की वजह से ही हम पतियों के सामने सिर झुकाना, घर और बच्चों की देखभाल करने को ही हम अपना काम समझते हैं। हमारे सामने सबसे महत्वपूर्ण कार्य है अपनी बहनों के दिमाग से हिन्दू धर्म गुलामी भरी सोच को बाहर निकाल देना है।'' इसी सभा में सुलोचना डोगरे ने कहा कि हम बाबा साहब के साथ अस्पृश्यता के राक्षस को नष्ट कर देंगे।

इसी सभा में डॉ अम्बेडकर ने दलित महिलाओं से अपनी बच्चियों की शादी कम उम्र में न करने की अपील करते हुए उनको शिक्षित कर अपने पैरों पर खड़े होने पर बल दिया तथा कम बच्चे पैदा करने व साफ सफाई से रहने का सन्देश देते हुए महिलाओं का परिवारों में समानता

का स्तर हो। महिलाओं में स्वाभिमान जगाते हुए कहा कि आप घर में पति की दासी बनकर नहीं पति की दोस्त बनकर बराबरी के रिश्ते से जियें। नागपुर में 1942 में शेड्यूल्ड कास्ट फेडरेशन की स्थापना होने के बाद नासिक में शेड्यूल्ड कास्ट फेडरेशन की मीटिंग में शान्ताबाई दाणी को पार्टी का जिला अध्यक्ष बनाया गया। 1944 में कानपुर में दलित फेडरेशन के दूसरे अधिवेशन में भी महिलाओं ने अपना स्वतंत्र अधिवेशन किया। इसकी अध्यक्षता कु0 शान्ताबाई दाणी ने की। इस अधिवेशन में बाबा साहब ने भाग लेते हुए कहा– "आप आगे बढ़ें, आपके जीवन में सुनहरी सुबह का पदार्पण हुआ है।" 06 मई 1945 में तीसरा 'अखिल भारतीय अस्पृश्य महिला परिषद' का अधिवेशन मुम्बई में आयोजित किया गया जिसमें हजारों दलित महिलाओं ने भाग लिया।

इस प्रकार दलित महिला आन्दोलन में स्वागत गीत के माध्यम से, ज्ञान शिक्षा के प्रयास द्वारा, मन्दिर प्रवेश, पानी, समान वेतन, अस्पृश्यता निवारण, विधायिका में अधिकार, पुरुषों की गुलामी से मुक्ति आदि मुद्दों को प्रतीक बनाकर डॉ अम्बेडकर का हाथ धीरे–धीरे समानता, अस्पृश्यता व गरीबी तीनों स्तर पर शोषण से संघर्ष करते हुए अपनी वैचारिक समझ बनाते हुए मुक्ति की राह पर चलकर दलित आन्दोलन का प्राण व अन्य आन्दोलनों का प्रेरणास्रोत बन गया। आजादी, अस्मिता, संघर्ष के उबड़–खाबड़ संघर्ष भरे रास्ते से गुजरते हुए दलित महिला आन्दोलन दलित नारीवाद की सीमा में प्रवेश कर गया भारत में जगह'जगह चले इस आन्दोलन में हजारों की संख्या में दलित महिलाएं जुड़ी व जेल गयीं। दिन–रात धरनों पर भूखी–प्यासी बैठी और हिम्मत, बहादुरी, धैर्य व लगन से अपनी माँगें पूरी करने के लिए संघर्षशील रहीं। अम्बेडकर कालीन दलित महिला आन्दोलन में सैकड़ों दलित महिलाएं निकलकर बाहर आयीं जिन्होंने दलित मुक्ति के संघर्ष की कमान अपने हाथों में सम्भाल ली, इनमें प्रमुख रूप से रमाबाई अम्बेडकर, गीताबाई गायकवाड़, अंजनीबाई गायकवाड़, इन्दिरा पाटिल, कीर्ति पाटिल, सुलोचना डोगरे, राधाबाई लक्ष्मी नायक, रंगबाई शुभकर, मीनाबल शिवराम और न जाने कितनी अनाम–अज्ञात दलित महिलाएं जो इतिहास की गर्त में छिप गईं, इन सभी ने घर–परिवार, फैक्ट्रियों, खेतों–खलिहानों से निकलकर दलित महिला मुक्ति का परचम चहुँ दिशा में फहराया।

संदर्भ सूची

1. डॉ व जलाल वर्मा, सामाजिक न्याय के पुरस्कर्ता डॉ अम्बेडकर 2010, पृ. 12।
2. धनंजय कीर की पुस्तक, डॉ अम्बेडकर, लाईफ एण्ड मिशन।
3. वही।
4. वही।
5. मोहनदास नैमिशराय, महिला आन्दोलन में दलित महिलाओं का योगदान
6. पंडित फडके की पुस्तक काला मन्दिर सत्याग्रह।
7. डॉ कुसुम मेघवाल, डॉ अम्बेडकर और महिला जागरण, पृ. 91।
8. डॉ अम्बेडकर, भारतीय नारी के उद्धारक, पृ. 91।
9. वसन्त मून, बाबा साहब अम्बेडकर, नेशनल ट्रस्ट, नई दिल्ली 2008, पृ. 250।
10. शरद पाटिल, ब्राह्मण और दलित, ब्लैक स्टोन पब्लिकेशन, कोलकाता, 2003, पृ. 203।
11. डॉ अम्बेडकर नारीवादी चिन्तन के स्वर, समता प्रकाशन नई दिल्ली, 2005, पृ. 308।
12. डॉ शिवराम चौबे, नारी अस्मिता और समाज, दीप पब्लिकेशन, मद्रास 2003, पृ. 302।
13. डॉ अरूण कुमार वर्मा, नारी साहित्य की आधुनिक विवेचना, नेशनल पब्लिकेशन, नई दिल्ली 2008, पृ. 41।
14. कौशल्या वैसन्त्री, दलित महिला की पहली आत्मकथाः दोहरा अभिशाप, हंस पब्लिकेशन नई दिल्ली 199, पृ. 84।
15. काशीराम, चमचा युगः दि ऐरा ऑफ स्टूजिस, समता प्रकाशन, नागरपुर 1998, पृ. 214।
16. डॉ कुशुम मेघवाल, डॉ अम्बेडकर और महिला जागरण, 2007, पृ. 91।
17. रामवीर उपाध्याय, दलित महिलाओं की पहचान, भारत पब्लिकेशन, वाराणसी, 2009, पृ. 109।

24

स्वतंत्रता परवर्ती भारत में जनजातीय समुदायों की स्थिति का अवलोकन

दीप्ती श्रीवास्तव

निरंतर विकास किसी भी समाज के अस्तित्व हेतु एक आधारभूत आवश्यकता है, जो कि सामाजिक इकाईयों के बीच स्पर्धा को जन्म देकर पारंपरिक समाज को जटिल समाज की ओर ले जाता है। कुछ समाजों में विकास की गति अति मंद होती है और कुछ में अत्यधिक तीव्र। जनजातीय समाज मंद गति से विकसित समाजों का ही स्वरूप है। जनजातीय विकास को संस्कृति के संदर्भ में देखा जाए तो जनजातीय संस्कृति इस समाज के लोगों के जीवन जीने का ढ़ग है और विकास इस जीवन जीने के तरीके में परिवर्तन लाने का एक प्रयास है।

जनजाति, व्यक्तियों का वह समूह है जो निश्चित भौगोलिक क्षेत्र में निवास करती हैं। आदि पूर्व से उनका उद्‌गम हुआ है। जिसकी एक सामान्य संस्कृति है तथा जो आज भी आधुनिक सभ्यता के प्रभावों से सरपेक्षिक रूप से वंचित है। जनजातियों को समाज के हाशिये पर रखे जाने का इतिहास बहुत पुराना है। औपनिवेशिक काल में ऐसे अनेक कानून बनाए गए जो जनजातीय लोगों को भूमि, वन और अन्य प्राकृतिक संसाधनों से वंचित करते थे। औपनिवेशिक शासन के उद्‌भव ने जनजातियों और गैर–जनजातियों को एकल राजनीतिक और प्रशासनिक ढ़ाचे के

अन्तर्गत खड़ा किया। अतः स्वतंत्रता परवर्ती भारत में जनजातीय समुदायों की स्थिति में सुधार लाने पर विशेष ध्यान दिया गया। स्वतंत्र भारत के नागरिकों के रूप में जनजातीय लोगों को अन्य नागरिकों के समान सिविल, राजनीतिक और सामाजिक अधिकार प्रदान किए गए। भारतीय संविधान की पाँचवी और छठी अनुसूची में ऐसे प्रावधान किए गए हैं जो आदिवासियों को उनकी भूमि पर ऐतिहासिक गारंटी देते हैं। जनजातीय लोगों को प्राकृतिक संसाधन प्रबंधन और स्व–शासन के बारे में व्यापक अधिकार प्रदान करते हैं। जनजातियों के विकास के लिए जनजातीय उपयोजना में इस तथ्य की पहचान की गई कि जनजातीय क्षेत्रों और जनजातीय समुदायों की विविध समस्याओं का एक समान समाधान नहीं हो सकता इसलिए अलग–अलग स्थिति के अनुसार नीतियां, कार्यक्रम और योजनाएं बनाने की आवश्यकता है। इसमें विकास के लिए एक उपयुक्त दायरा तय किया गया जिसमें राष्ट्रीय एवं राज्य–स्तरीय उपयोजना के माध्यम से जनजातीय लोगों पर ध्यान केन्द्रित किया गया। जनजातीय उपयोजना में जनजातीय लोगों का शोषण समाप्त करने के लिए संरक्षणात्मक उपायों को उच्च प्राथमिकता दी गई। प्रशासनिक और संस्थागत तंत्र का पुनर्गठन किया गया ताकि उसे स्थानीय लोगों की आवश्यकताओं एवं आकांक्षाओं के अनुकूल बनाया जा सके।

भारत के संविधान की धारा 366 (25) के उन अन्तर्गत समुदायों को अनुसूचित जाति का दर्जा दिए जाने का प्रावधान किया गया है जो अनुच्छेद 342 के तहत अनुसूचित हैं। अनुच्छेद 342 के अनुसार 'राष्ट्रपति किसी राज्य या संघ राज्य क्षेत्र के संबंध में और जहां वह राज्य है उसके राज्यपाल से परामर्श करने के पश्चात लोक अधिसूचना द्वारा उन जनजातियों या जनजाति समुदायों अथवा जनजातियों या जनजाति समुदायों के भागों या उनमें से यूथों को विनिर्दिष्ट कर सकेगा, जिन्हें इस संविधान के प्रयोजनों के लिए यथास्थिति उस राज्य या संघ क्षेत्र के संबंध में अनुसूचित जनजातियां समझा जाएगा। वर्ष 2011 की जनगणना के अनुसार भारत की कुल जनसंख्या में जनजातियों का भाग 8.6 प्रतिशत है। इनमें से 58 प्रतिशत लोग गरीबी रेखा के नीचे जीवन यापन करते हैं। जनजाति एवं जनजातीय क्षेत्रों का विकास एक चुनौतीपूर्ण कार्य है क्योंकि वे विविधतापूर्ण भौगोलिक, सामाजिक, आर्थिक तथा राजनीतिक, सांस्कृतिक परिवेशों में निवास करते हैं। इसके अतिरिक्त वे दूरस्थ क्षेत्रों में निवास करते हैं, जहां आवागमन की पर्याप्त सुविधा उपलब्ध नहीं है। जनजातीय लोगों का उल्लेख भारतीय संविधान के पांचवीं एवं छठी अनुसूची में है।

उत्तर–पूर्व की जनजाति छठी अनुसूची में हैं तथा शेष भारत की जनजातियां पांचवीं अनुसूची में हैं। उत्तर–पूर्व के कई राज्य जनजाति बहुल हैं। इन राज्यों में जनजातियों की अपनी शासन व्यवस्था के साथ–साथ क्षेत्रीय, जिला एवं इसके नीचे स्तर पर प्रशासनिक व्यवस्था है। जनजातियों के लिए संविधानिक प्रावधान विशय वस्तु के आधार पर दो समूहों में विभाजित किए जा सकते हैं–

- संरक्षण संबंधी उपबंध
- विकास संबंधी उपबंध

संरक्षण संबंधी उपबंध

- अनु0 15(4)के अनुसार राज्य को अनुसूचित जनजातियों की उन्नति एवं प्रगति के लिए कोई भी उपबंध बनााने का अधिकार है।
- अनु0 16(4) पदों और सरकारी नौकरियों में आरक्षण की व्यवस्था।
- अनु0 19(5) के अन्तर्गत राज्य अनुसूचित जनजाति के लोगों के रक्षार्थ किसी भाग में बसने या निवास करने और संपत्ति के क्रय–विक्रय के अधिकार पर विशेष प्रतिबंध लगा सकता है।
- अनु0 23 मानव के दुर्व्यवहार और बलात श्रम का प्रतिरोध करता है।
- अनु0 29 अनुसूचित जनजातियों को अपनी भाषाओं और संस्कृतियों को बनाए रखने के लिए संरक्षण प्रदान करता है।
- अनु0 46 अनुसूचित जातियों व अनुसूचित जनजातियों और अन्य दुर्बल वर्गों की शिक्षा और आर्थिक हितों की अभिवृद्धि का प्रावधान करता है।
- अनु0 164 जनजातीय बहुल राज्यों में जनजातियों के कल्याण के भार साधक मंत्री की नियुक्ति का प्रावधान करता है।
- अनु0 330, 332 और 334 में लोक सभा और विधान सभाओं में आरक्षण का उल्लेख है।
- अनु0 335 आरक्षण के दावे से संबंधित है।
- अनु0 338 में विशेष अधिकारी संबंधी उपबंध है।
- अनु0 339(1) में अनुसूचित जनजाति आयोग की नियुक्ति का प्रावधान है।

विकास संबंधी उपबंधः–

- अनु0 275 और 339 के अन्तर्गत जनजातियों के आर्थिक विकास के लिए व्यवस्थाएं की गई हैं।

- पांचवीं अनुसूची के अनु0 244(1) के अन्तर्गत संसद द्वारा बनाए गए विधान के अधीन रहते हुए राष्ट्रपति को यह शक्ति दी गई है कि वह किसी क्षेत्र को 'अनुसूचित क्षेत्र' घोषित कर दे।
- छठी अनुसूची के अनु. 244(2) में असम, मेघालय, त्रिपुरा एवं मिजोरम में जनजाति क्षेत्रों के बारे में पृथक व्यवस्था की गई है और उनके प्रशासन के लिए उपबंध किए गए हैं। संविधान के अनु. 371–क, 371–ख, 371–ग में क्रमशः नागालैण्ड, असम और मणिपुर के जनजाति क्षेत्रों व पर्वतीय क्षेत्रों से संबंधित विशेष उपबंध हैं।

इसके अतिरिक्त अनुसूचित जनजातियों के विकास पर और अधिक ध्यान केन्द्रित करने के उद्देश्य से अक्टूबर 1999 में एक अलग जनजातीय कार्य मंत्रालय का गठन किया गया। यह मंत्रालय अनुसूचित जनजातियों के बारे में नीति निर्धारित करने, योजनाओं में समन्वय स्थापित करने वाला शीर्ष मंत्रालय है।

जनजातीय शोध संस्थान

आन्ध्र प्रदेश, असम, बिहार, गुजरात, केरल, मध्य प्रदेश, महाराष्ट्र, उड़ीसा, राजस्थान, तमिलनाडु, पश्चिम बंगाल, उत्तर प्रदेश, मणिपुर और त्रिपुरा में 14 जनजातीय शोध संस्थान स्थापित किए गए हैं, जहां जनजातीय वस्तुएं प्रदर्शित की गई हैं।

वन अधिनियम 2006

वनों पर आश्रित जनजातीय समुदायों की समस्याओं का समाधान करने और परम्परागत रूप से किए जा रहे अन्याय से बचाने के लिए जनजातीय और अन्य पारम्परिक वन निवासी (वन अधिकारों को मान्यता) विधेयक 2006 बनाया गया है। इसके तहत वनवासियों को खेती करने के व्यवसाय के लिए भूमि पर वन अधिकारों, लघु वन उपज पर अधिकारों तथा पारम्परिक अधिकारों को मान्यता दी गई है। इस अधिनियम को सरकार ने लागू करने की अधिसूचना जनवरी 2008 में जारी कर दी।

राष्ट्रीय अनुसूचित जनजाति आयोग

भारत में 65वें संविधान संशोधन अधिनियम 1990 के द्वारा राष्ट्रीय अनुसूचित जाति और जनजाति आयोग का गठन किया गया था। पुनः 89वें संविधान संशोधन अधिनियम, 2003 के द्वारा अनुसूचित जाति और अनुसूचित जनजाति आयोग को अलग–अलग कर दिया गया और नया

राष्ट्रीय अनुसूचित जनजाति आयोग का गठन 2004 में किया गया। इस आयोग का मुख्य कार्य भारतीय संविधान के अन्तर्गत अनुसूचित जनजातियों को प्राप्त रक्षापायों का संरक्षण और निगरानी करना है।

भारतीय जनजाति सहकारी विपणन विकास परिसंघ (ट्राइफेड)

जनजातीय लोगों को व्यापारियों और बिचौलियों के शोषण से बचाने और उन्हें छिट–पुट वन उत्पादों एवं अतिरिक्त कृषि उपज के लाभ मूल्य दिलाने के लिए सरकार द्वारा अगस्त, 1987 में एक भारतीय जनजातीय सहकारी विपणन विकास परिसंघ का गठन किया गया था। यह परिसंघ राष्ट्रीय स्तर की एक शीर्ष सहकारी संस्था है। इसकी प्राधिकृत शेयर पूंजी 20 करोड़ रूपये है। अप्रैल 1988 से यह प्रभावी ढ़ग से कार्य कर रहा है।

राष्ट्रीय अनुसूचित जनजाति वित्त विकास निगम

सरकार ने राष्ट्रीय अनुसूचित जाति एवं अनुसूचित जनजाति वित्तीय विकास निगम से अलग करके अप्रैल 2001 में 'राष्ट्रीय अनुसूचित जनजाति वित्त विकास निगम' का गठन किया है। यह भारत सरकार के स्वामित्व वाली कंपनी है, जिसकी प्रधिकृत शेयर पूंजी 500 करोड़ रूपये है। निगम प्रति इकाई 10 लाख रूपये तक की लागत वाली योजनाओं के लिए अनुसूचित जनजातियों को रियायती दर पर वित्तीय सहायता उपलब्ध कराता है। इसके अतिरिक्त इस विकास निगम द्वारा निम्नलिखित योजनाएं संचालित की जा रहीं हैं–

- कृषि एवं समवर्गी क्षेत्र से संबंधित योजनाएं
- यातायात क्षेत्र से संबंधित योजनाएं
- सेवा क्षेत्र से संबंधित योजनाएं
- उद्योग क्षेत्र से संबंधित योजनाएं
- नाबार्ड योजना

सरकारी, अर्द्धसरकारी संगठनों में, नौकरियों में और संस्थानों में अनुसूचित जनजाति को 7/5 प्रतिशत आरक्षण प्रदान किया गया है। इसके अतिरिक्त जनजातियों के शैक्षिक, आर्थिक व स्वास्थ्य सम्बन्धी विकास के लिए समय–समय पर सरकार द्वारा अनेक योजनाओं का निर्माण तथा क्रियान्वयन किया जाता रहा है। वर्तमान में जब तकनीकी परिवर्तन के चलते जनजातियों का अस्तित्व ही खतरे में पड़ गया है, ऐसे में अनुसूचित

जनजातियों के सामाजिक, आर्थिक और शैक्षणिक विकास का बीड़ा उठाना कोई कम चुनौतीपूर्ण कार्य नहीं है।

वर्तमान समय में तकनीकी परिवर्तन से जनजातियों के समक्ष अस्तित्वगत चुनौती खड़ी हो चुकी है। आज उनका परम्परागत आजीविका का साधन छिन गया है। इससे सबसे बड़ी समस्या रोजगार की उत्पन्न हो गई है। इसके अतिरिक्त गुणवत्तापरक शिक्षण व प्रशिक्षण संस्थाओं का अभाव, स्वास्थ्य सेवाओं का अभाव, कच्चा माल व उत्पादित वस्तुओं हेतु बाजार की दिक्कत, सरकारी कल्याण कार्यक्रमों में अव्यवस्था, भ्रष्टाचार व लापरवाही, जनजातीय समुदायों में अंधविश्वास व सामाजिक कुरीतियां, शराब का अत्यधिक सेवन, वन क्षेत्र में बसे गांवों को वन विभाग द्वारा हटाने की समस्या, घर निर्माण एवं रसोई हेतु वन उत्पादन का अभाव आदि मुख्य समस्याएं हैं। दूरस्थ क्षेत्रों में होने के कारण जनजातीय समुदाय आज भी पिछड़ा हुआ है। आदिवासी समुदाय आज भी अपनी पुरानी ढ़ांचागत व्यवस्था एवं संसाधनों पर निर्भर है। जनजातीय क्षेत्रों में विद्यालय हैं तो शिक्षक नहीं, सड़क है तो मरम्मत नहीं, अस्पताल है तो दवा व डॉक्टर नहीं हैं। जिससे जनजातीय समुदायों में विकास का रथ अवरुद्ध है। इसके अतिरिक्त जनजातियों के लिए चलाए जा रहे सरकारी कल्याण कार्यक्रम दिशाविहीन हैं। ये जिस उद्देश्य से चलाए गए हैं, उन्हें हासिल करने में वे अब तक असफल साबित हुए हैं क्योंकि कार्यक्रम क्रियान्वयन का तरीका लचर व अव्यवस्थित रहा है। जनजाति समुदायों में संक्रामक और गैर–संक्रामक दोनों तरह की बीमारियों का खतरा अधिक पाया जाता है। बाल और शिशु मृत्यु दर, एनीमिया जैसी बीमारियां अभी भी जनजातीय समाज के लिए बड़ा अभिशाप साबित हो रही है। अधिक प्रजनन दर भी एक प्रमुख समस्या है। अभी भी अनुसूचित जनजाति में साक्षरता का स्तर कम है। 37/38 फीसदी जनजाति आबादी की सूचना के माध्यम तक स्थायी पहुँच नहीं है। महिलाओं की स्थिति दयनीय बनी हुई है। इन सबके अतिरिक्त पेय जल समस्या, वनों की कमी, अधिक खनन आदि आदिवासियों के लिए समस्या का मुख्य कारण है। विकास के नाम पर डैम का निर्माण, खानों की खुदाई, सेन्चुरी पार्क का निर्माण आदि कारणों से सम्पूर्ण भारत में बहुत बड़ी संख्या में जनजातियों का विस्थापन हुआ है, जिससे निश्चित तौर पर जल, जंगल और जमीन पर परम्परागत हक समाप्त हो रहा है। परन्तु वन अधिकार कानून के आने से जनजातीय समुदायों को अपने हक और अधिकारों की सुरक्षा का अस्त्र मिल गया है। इससे जनजातियों का विस्थापन रोकने तथा इन्हें अपना हक पाना आसान हो गया है। बस जरूरत है इन्हें वनाधिकार कानून, 2005 के बारे में संगठित व जागरूक

करने की। परम्परागत रूप से जनजाति समुदाय का झाड़–फूंक, टोना–टोटका एवं जंगली बूटियों से इलाज में अधिक विश्वास रहा है, इसके कारण स्वास्थ्य सम्बंधी अनेक समस्याएं उत्पन्न होती हैं। परन्तु इसका एक अन्य कारण यह भी है कि दूसरी दवाएं और इलाज इतना महंगा है तथा बेहतर सरकारी स्वास्थ्य सुविधाओं की बेहद कमी है जिससे कि धनाभाव के कारण ये परम्परागत इलाज पर ही निर्भर हैं। अतः इन्हें बीमारियों से बचाव हेतु बेहतर स्वास्थ्य शिक्षा तथा चिकित्सा उपलब्ध कराने की आवश्यकता है।

जनजातीय समुदाय को ऊंचा उठाने में सरकार ने अनेक प्रयत्न किए किन्तु आज भी जनजातीय समुदाय अपने परम्परागत रहन–सहन, संस्कृति, बोलचाल आदि को अपनाए हुए है तथा आज भी वो जागरूक नहीं हैं। सरकार द्वारा उनके लिए चलाई गई विभिन्न योजनाओं की जानकारी उन तक पहुंच नहीं पा रही है। जिन योजनाओं की जानकारी उनके पास है, उनका लाभ लेने के लिए जटिल प्रक्रियाओं का सामना करना पड़ता है, जिससे वे योजनाओं में रुचि नहीं लेते हैं। शासन द्वारा अनेक अनेक शैक्षणिक कार्यक्रम चलाने के बावजूद आज भी वे न तो पूर्ण रूप से शिक्षित हैं और न ही वे अपने बच्चों को शिक्षा–दीक्षा ग्रहण कराने में रुचि लेते हैं। इन सभी परिस्थितियों को ध्यान में रखते हुए यह आवश्यक है कि उनके लिए सरकार द्वारा जो भी योजनाएं बनाई जाएं उनकी प्रक्रिया इतनी सरल हो कि वे आसानी से पूरी की जा सकें और उनकी भाषाशैली में उन तक पहुंचाई जा सकें। इसके अतिरिक्त उनकी समितियों का गठन कर योजनाओं का क्रियान्वयन किया जाए। वैसे इस क्षेत्र में कार्यरत स्वैच्छिक संस्थानों की भूमिका कई मायने में अत्यन्त ही रचनात्मक एवं समुदाय को विकास की ओर प्रेरित करने वाली रही है। जनजाति समुदायों में शिक्षा एवं जनजीवन में बदलाव का श्रेय मुख्यता स्वैच्छिक संस्थानों को ही जाता है। विगत 25–30 वर्षों से सेवारत स्वैच्छिक संस्थानों की वजह से ही आज इस क्षेत्र में अधिकांश युवक–युवतियां पढ़–लिखकर सरकारी एवं गैर–सरकारी संस्थाओं में सेवारत हैं जिससे इनका जीवन–स्तर, रहन–सहन एवं सोचने–समझने के तौर–तरीकों में व्यापक बदलाव आया है। इस दिशा में उत्तर प्रदेश के लखीमपुर खीरी ज़िले में 'उत्तर प्रदेश बनवासी सेवा संस्थान' नामक संस्था महत्वपूर्ण भूमिका निभा रही है। यह संस्था पिछले तीन दशकों से 'पूज्य ठक्कर बापा सेवा संस्थान' नामक संस्था के साथ मिलकर जनजातियों के विकास के लिए उत्तर प्रदेश के तराई क्षेत्र में कार्यरत है। इस संस्था का मुख्य उद्देश्य जनजातियों एवं

समाज के पिछड़े वर्ग का सामाजिक, आर्थिक और शैक्षिक विकास कर राष्ट्र की मुख्य धारा से जोड़ना है। संस्था द्वारा इस समय राजीव गांधी राष्ट्रीय क्रेश कार्यक्रम 128 गावों में, आदिवासी आवासीय बालिका विद्यालय 42 आदिवासी गांवों में, पूज्य ठक्कर बापा शिक्षण पाठशाला 42 आदिवासी गांवों में, 350 स्वयं सहायता समूह लखीमपुर खीरी के 6 विकासखण्डों आदि में संचालित हैं।

अतः आज 21वीं सदी में जब दुनिया के नये स्वरुप, नयी प्रतिस्पर्धा, विकास के नये–नये आयामों और प्रभावों पर लम्बे–चौड़े विमर्श हो रहें हैं तब यह बात महत्वपूर्ण हो जाती है यह विकास समावेशी विकास है कि नहीं, जो समाज के सभी वर्गों विशेषकर जनजातीय समुदायों के विकास की ओर अग्रसर है कि नहीं। इस बात से इंकार नहीं किया जा सकता है कि सरकार ने जनजातियों के लिए विभिन्न विकास कार्यक्रमों को रणनीति के तौर पर स्वीकार कर उनके जीवन स्तर को ऊपर उठाने का प्रयास किया है, किन्तु अभी भी जनजातीय समुदाय समाज के वंचित वर्ग में ही आते हैं। अतः आवश्यकता इस बात की है कि इस समुदाय के लोगों को वंचितों की श्रेणी से निकाल कर क्रियाशील समुदाय में परिवर्तित किया जाए तथा समाज की मुख्य धारा में शामिल किया जाए। आम जन की तरह इन्हें भी मूलभूत सुविधाएं प्राप्त हों। जल, जंगल व ज़मीन पर इनका परम्परागत अधिकार बना रहे, इनके बच्चों को भी आधुनिक उच्च शिक्षा उपलब्ध हो और इनके क्षेत्र में नियुक्त होने वाले विभिन्न विभागों के अधिकारी अभावों के बीच जीवनयापन करने वाली जनजातियों के प्रति संवेदनशीलता दिखाएं। लोकतंत्र का चतुर्थ स्तम्भ माना जाने वाला मीडिया जनजातीय समुदायों की समस्याओं को सामने लाकर उनका समाधान करने में अपना रचनात्मक योगदान दे सकता है। तभी समावेशी विकास का सपना यथार्थ हो सकेगा।

सन्दर्भ सूची

- सामाजिक कल्याण प्रशासन : एस0 एल0 गोयल
- योजना पत्रिका : जनवरी 2014
- क्रानिकल पत्रिका : नवम्बर 2014
- विवास मनोरमा पत्रिका : जून 2014

25

भारत में अनुसूचित जातियों में सामाजिक परिवर्तनः अपर्याप्त सरकारी तथा सामाजिक प्रयास

नूर फातिमा अन्सारी

आज की अनुसूचित जातियों के लिए ऋग्वेद के पुरुष सूक्त में शूद्र शब्द का उल्लेख हुआ है –

ब्राह्मणोऽस्य मुखमासीद् बाहू राजन्यः कृतः।
उरूतदस्य यद् वैश्यः पद्भ्यां सूदो अजायत।।

अर्थात् ब्राह्मण लोग ब्रह्मा के मुख से, क्षत्रिय उसकी भुजाओं से, वैश्य उसके जंघे से और शूद्र उसके पैरों से उत्पन्न हुए थे।

अनुसूचित जातियों या दलितों को दबाकर रखने वाली जाति प्रथा के बारे में कोई इंकार नहीं कर सकता कि जाति व्यवस्था पुरातन और जटिल संस्था है। जाति व्यवस्था के कठोर स्वरूप को न सिर्फ हिन्दू धर्मशास्त्रों में देखा जा सकता है, वरन् उनसे सामाजिक व्यवस्था के अन्र्तसम्बन्धों के विभिन्न स्तरों पर जघन्यतम, क्रूर प्रणाली के रूप में अनुभव किया जा सकता है। जाति प्रथा ने ही अस्पृश्यता को जन्म दिया। अनुसूचित जातियों के सामाजिक–आर्थिक अधिकार छीनकर उन्हें दलित–सामाजिक व्यवस्था में निस्सहाय बनाया। वेद से पुराणों की रचना

तक और उसके बाद भी दलित, शूद्र–अस्पृश्यों के साथ वर्ण व्यवस्था के अन्तर्गत सामाजिक भेदभाव और अस्पृश्यता, जाति भेद और सामाजिक बहिष्कार, आर्थिक–शोषण और जीवन के हर कार्य–व्यापार में धर्म सम्मत उत्पीड़न को सनातन और अन्यायपूर्ण बना दिया गया। भारतीय समाज एक सोपानवादी समाज बन गया, जिसके शीर्ष पर ब्राह्मणवादी स्वर्ण बैठे। उन्होंने सदियों से दलितों को मानसिक तथा सामाजिक रूप से अपना दास बना रखा है। दरअसल भारतीय समाज में अनुसूचित जाति सदियों से शोषित–पीड़ित और उपेक्षित बनकर हाशिए पर पड़ी रही है। शिक्षा, ज्ञान, सुविधा एवं सम्मान से वंचित इस वर्ग को मुख्यधारा से जोड़ने के लिए स्वतंत्रता से अब तक कई प्रयास किये गए पर वर्ण, वर्ग, लिंग भेद के विरूद्ध समता तथा सामाजिक न्याय की संवैधानिक अवधारणा के बावजूद इनकी स्थिति में बहुत कुछ परिवर्तन नहीं हुआ है।

अनुसूचित जातियों के संरक्षण के लिए भारतीय संविधान के निर्माताओं ने संविधान में विशेष प्रावधान करने का निश्चय किया। संविधान निर्माताओं के विचारों के अनुरूप सामाजिक न्याय के लक्ष्य को प्रोत्साहित करने के उद्देश्य से संवैधानिक प्रावधानों के साथ–साथ कुछ विशेष कानूनी उपाय भी किए गए हैं। भारतीय संविधान की प्रस्तावना में राजनीतिक और आर्थिक न्याय के साथ–साथ सामाजिक न्याय का जो आदर्श प्रतिपादित किया गया है, उससे ही ये प्रावधान और कानून प्रेरणा ग्रहण करते हैं।

संविधान का अनुच्छेद 14 सभी व्यक्तियों को कानून के सामने समानता और कानून की समान सुरक्षा की गारण्टी देता है। इसी अधिकार का थोड़े विस्तार से अनुच्छेद 15(1) में उल्लेख किया गया है, जिसमें राज्य को अन्य बातों के साथ–साथ जाति के आधार पर किसी नागरिक के साथ भेदभाव करने से रोका गया है। लेकिन अनुच्छेद 15(4) में राज्य को अन्य बातों के साथ अनुसूचित जातियों के लिए विशेष प्रावधान करने की अनुमति दी गई है। यह संरक्षणात्मक भेदभाव का एक उदाहरण है। अनुच्छेद 15(2) में कहा गया है कि अन्य बातों के साथ–साथ किसी भी नागरिक को केवल जाति के आधार पर अक्षमता या किसी दायित्व का पात्र नहीं ठहराया जाएगा। केवल इसी आधार पर दुकानों रेस्त्राओं, होटलों और सार्वजनिक मनोरंजन के स्थलों पर प्रवेश या कुएँ आदि के इस्तेमाल पर कोई रोक या शर्त नहीं लगायी जायगी। साथ ही ऐसी सड़को और सार्वजनिक आवागमन के ऐसे स्थलों जिनका रखरखाव पूरे या आंशिक रूप में राज्य कोष से किया जाता है या जिन्हें जन उपयोग के लिए

समर्पित किया गया हो, के इस्तेमाल पर भी अन्य चीज़ो के साथ–साथ केवल जाति के आधार पर रोक नहीं लगाई जाएगी।

एक अन्य सन्दर्भ में भी संरक्षणात्मक भेदभाव की जरूरत महसूस की गई। संविधान का अनुच्छेद 15(4) इस आम निषेध का अपवाद प्रस्तुत करता है, जिसमें अनुसूचित जातियों के लिए राज्य को विशेष प्रावधान करने की अनुमति दी गई है।

सरकारी नौकरियों के सिलसिले में जहाँ अनुच्छेद 16(1) और 16(2) अन्य बातों के अलावा केवल जाति के आधार पर भेदभाव करने पर रोक लगाते हैं, वहीं अनुच्छेद 16(4) राज्य को अन्य चीजो के अतिरिक्त किसी भी 'ऐसे पिछड़े वर्ग के नागरिकों के लिए नियुक्तियों या पदों में आरक्षण की अनुमति देता है जिनका राज्य की दृष्टि में सरकारी सेवाओं में पर्याप्त प्रतिनिधित्व नहीं है।' हालांकि अनुसूचित जातियों का इसमें अलग से उल्लेख नहीं है, लेकिन उच्चतम न्यायालय ने यह स्पष्ट किया कि वे एक पिछड़े वर्ग के रूप में माने जाएंगे (जानकी प्रसाद बनाम जम्मू और कश्मीर राज्य, ए0आई0आर0 1973, सु0 को. 930, 937)। इसी आधार पर आरक्षण के निर्धारित कोटे के तहत उनके पक्ष में पदों का आरक्षण और सेवा शर्तों में छूट तथा अन्य चीजें बहाल रखी गई हैं। (ए0बी0एस0 के संघ बनाम भारत सरकार, ए0आइ0आर0 1981, सु0को0 298)।

ऊपर वर्णित मौलिक अधिकारों और उनमें परिवर्तन के अतिरिक्त संविधान में राज्य के नीति निदेशक सिद्धान्तों का एक अध्याय है। अनुच्छेद 37 में कहा गया कि इन प्रावधानों को किसी अदालत के जरिए लागू नहीं करवाया जा सकेगा, लेकिन यहां उल्लिखित सिद्धान्त देश के शासन का आधार है और यह राज्य का कर्तव्य है कि वह कानून बनानें में इन सिद्धान्तों को अमल में लाये।' राज्य के नीति निदेशक सिद्धान्तों में से एक, अनुच्छेद 46 अनुसूचित जातियों के लिए प्रासंगिक है। इसमें कहा गया है कि 'राज्य जनता के कमजोर तबकों और विशेष तौर पर अनुसूचित जातियों और जनजातियों के शैक्षणिक और आर्थिक हितों को विशेष ध्यान देते हुए प्रोत्साहित करेगा और सामाजिक अन्याय तथा शोषण के सभी दूसरे प्रकारों से उनकी रक्षा करेगा।'

संविधान में अनुसूचित जातियों से सम्बन्धित लक्ष्यों के कार्यान्वयन की समीक्षा के लिए विशेष प्रावधान भी किए गए हैं। किसी जाति को अनुसूचित जाति घोषित करने का कार्य अनुच्छेद 341(1) के अन्तर्गत

राष्ट्रपति करता है और इससे संबंधित दूसरे प्रावधान अनुच्छेद 314(2) के तहत संसदीय कानून बना कर किया जाता है। भारत के राष्ट्रपति ने अनुच्छेद 341(1) के अंतर्गत संविधान (अनुसूचित जाति) आदेश, 1950 जारी किया, जिसमें तदनुसार संसदीय कानूनों के जरिए संशोधन किया जाता रहा है। उच्चतम न्यायालय ने एक फैसले में कहा कि अदालतें राष्ट्रपति की अधिसूचना के परे नहीं जा सकती (परसराम बनाम शिवचंद, ए0आइ0आर0 1969, सु0 को0 550) अनुच्छेद 338, जिसमें 1990 में 65वाँ संशोधन किया गया के तहत अनुसूचित जातियों और जनजातियों के लिए राष्ट्रीय स्तर पर एक आयोग बनाया गया है। मंडल आयोग से सम्बन्धित फैसले में इस आयोग के कार्यों का हवाला दिया गया है इंदिरा साहनी बनाम भारत सरकार (1992), पूरक (3), अ.जा.आ. 217)। संविधान के अनुच्छेद 335 में कहा गया है कि संघ या राज्य के मामलों से सम्बन्धित सेवाओं और पदों के लिए नियुक्ति करते वक्त अनुसूचित जातियों और अनुसूचित जनजातियों के सदस्यों के दावों पर विचार 'प्रशासन की कार्यकुशलता के निर्वाह के अनुरूप' किया जाना चाहिए।

मौलिक अधिकारों से सम्बन्धित अनुच्छेद 17 अस्पृश्यता को खत्म कर किसी भी रूप में इसके व्यवहार पर रोक लगाता है। इसमें यह भी प्रावधान है कि अस्पृश्यता के परिणाम स्वरूप किसी अक्षमता पर अमल कानून के मुताविक दण्डनीय अपराध होगा। अनुच्छेद 35(ए) संसद को मौलिक अधिकारों से जुड़े संवैधानिक प्रावधानों के तहत अपराध करार दिये गए कृत्यों के लिए ऐसे कानून बनाने का पूरा अधिकार देता है, जिनमें दण्ड निर्धारित किए गये हों।

1955 में संसद ने अस्पृश्यता (अपराध) अधिनियम बनाया। 1976 में उसी वर्ष के अधिनियम 106 के जरिए इस कानून का नाम बदल कर नागरिक अधिकार सुरक्षा कानून, 1955 कर दिया गया। इस कानून की धारा 3 और 4 के तहत अस्पृश्यता के आधार पर किसी व्यक्ति को धार्मिक या सामाजिक रूप से अयोग्य करार देने के लिए दण्ड का प्रावधान किया गया है। विशेष रूप से किसी सार्वजनिक धार्मिक स्थल में अगर किसी व्यक्ति को प्रवेश से रोका जाता है जबकि वहाँ उसी धर्म को मानने वाले दूसरे व्यक्तियों को जाने की इजाजत होती है, तो व्यक्ति विशेष के प्रवेश पर रोक दण्डनीय होगी। धारा 5 में आम जनता या उसके किसी भी वर्ग के लाभ के लिए चलाए जा रहे संस्थानों–मसलन अस्पताल, शिक्षण संस्थान आदि में अगर अस्पृश्यता के आधार पर किसी व्यक्ति को दाखिला देने

से मना किया जाता है तो यह दण्डनीय होगा। इसी तरह धारा 6 में अस्पृश्यता के आधार पर किसी व्यक्ति को वस्तु बेंचने से मना करने या उसे सेवा मुहैया न करना भी दण्डनीय होगा। धारा 7 में व्यवस्था की गयी है कि अस्पृश्यता को समाप्त करने वाले संवैधानिक अनुच्छेद 17 के तहत मिलने वाले अधिकारों के प्रयोग से अगर किसी को किया जाता है, तो दण्डनीय अपराध होगा। इसी धारा में संविधान के अनुच्छेद 17 के तहत प्रदत्त अधिकारियों के प्रयोग की वजह से किसी व्यक्ति को सताने, बाधा पहुँचाने या बहिष्कृत करने या अस्पृश्यता के पालन के लिए दूसरों को उकसाने अथवा अस्पृश्यता के आधार पर अनुसूचित जाति के किसी सदस्य का अपमान करने को अपराध माना गया है। धारा 7(ए) के तहत अस्पृश्यता के आधार पर किसी व्यक्ति को गैर कानूनी ढंग से मजदूरी करने के लिए विवश करना दण्डनीय है। धारा 10(ए) के जरिए राज्य सरकार विशेष मामलों में कानून का उल्लंघन न करने के लिए सामूहिक जुर्माना कर सकती है। इस अधिनियम की धारा 15 में इन अपराधों को संज्ञेय घोषित किया गया है। धारा 15(ए) में राज्य सरकार से कहा गया है कि वह जरूरी उपाय कर यह सुनिश्चित करे कि अस्पृश्यता के आधार पर अयोग्यता के पात्र बनाए गये व्यक्ति इन अधिकारों का उपयोग कर सकें। धारा 16(ए) इस कानून के तहत दोषी करार दिये गए 14 साल से ज्यादा उम्र के व्यक्ति की परिवीक्षोत्तर रिहाई की मनाही करती है।

अनुसूचित जाति और अनुसूचित जनजाति (अत्याचार विरोध) कानून का मकसद अनुसूचित जातियों के सदस्यों पर अत्याचार होने से रोकना है। इस कानून के तहत विशेष अदालतों के गठन का प्रावधान है, जिसमें अपराध करने वालों के खिलाफ मुकदमा चलाने और ऐसे अपराधों के शिकार हुए व्यक्तियों की राहत और पुनर्वास की व्यवस्था है। धारा 3 में ऐसे अपराधों का विस्तृत उल्लेख किया गया है। धारा 4 के अन्तर्गत इस कानून के तहत निर्वाह किये जाने वाले दायित्व की अगर कोई सरकारी सेवक जानबूझकर उपेक्षा करने का दोषी पाया जाता है तो वह दण्ड का भागी होगा। विशेष अदालत के आदेश के तहत धारा 7 में दोषी व्यक्तियों की सम्पत्ति जब्त कर लेने का प्रावधान है। धारा 10 के अनुसार विशेष अदालत किसी व्यक्ति द्वारा इस कानून के तहत निर्धारित अपराध करने की आशंका के मद्देनज़र उसे स्थान विशेष से हटाने का आदेश दे सकती है। धारा 16 राज्य सरकार को सामूहिक जुर्माना लगाने का अधिकार देती है। इस कानून के तहत ऐसे मामलों में अग्रिम जमानत की मनाही है जिसमें

किसी व्यक्ति पर अपराध करने का अभियोग लगाया गया हो और उसकी गिरतारी सम्भव हो। धारा 19 इस कानून के तहत दोषी करार दिये गये 18 साल से ज्यादा उम्र के व्यक्ति की परिवीक्षोत्तर रिहाई की मनाही करती है।

किन्तु हालात ये है कि देश के राजनीतिक, सामाजिक व आर्थिक मानचित्र पर कल जो निम्नतम स्तर पर थे, आज भी उनकी स्थिति में कोई विशेष परिवर्तन नहीं आया है। ये वही अनुसूचित जातियाँ हैं जिनके सामाजिक, आर्थिक व राजनीतिक विकास के लिए तथा अन्य विशेष व्यवस्थाएं की गई थीं और नीति–निदेशक तत्वों में खास हिदायत देकर कहा गया था कि भारत में एक समतामूलक समाज की स्थापना करनी है लेकिन जिनकी यातना दूर करने का कोई ठोस प्रयत्न अभी तक नहीं हुआ है।

सवाल यह उठता है कि क्या 64 साल बाद अनुसूचित जातियों ने बराबरी का स्तर हासिल कर लिया है? जवाब है, 'नहीं'। तो क्या अनुसूचित जातियों की स्थिति में कुछ भी सुधार नहीं हुआ? जवाब 'हाँ' और 'नहीं' दोनों में है। जो कल तक राजनीति में कहीं नहीं थे, आज अगर वे खुद राजनीति कर रहे हैं, तो कैसे कह दें कि वे ताकतवर नहीं हुए? पर जिसका 60 फीसदी हिस्सा आज भी सामंती अर्थव्यवस्था का हिंसा का शिकार हो, जिनके पेशों के नाम पर आज भी समाज में गाली दी जाती हो और जिसके लिए गाँव में कुएँ–बावड़ी, मंदिर सभी वर्जित हों, तो कैसे कह दें कि बाकी समाज ने उसे अपने बराबर मान लिया है? नहीं वह बराबर नहीं है, किसी भी रूप में नहीं, लेकिन इतना फर्क जरूर आया है कि कल तक उसे सामाजिक अत्याचारों का एहसास नहीं था, आज वह उन अत्याचारों को सहने को तैयार नहीं। कल तक उसे अपनी गरीबी के कारणों का पता नहीं था, आज उसे पता लग गया है और वह उनके खिलाफ लड़ने की ताकत बटोर रहा है। राजनीतिक सत्ता हांसिल करना उसकी यही ताकत बटोरने की कोशिश और उसके व उच्च वर्गों के बीच बढ़ती हिंसा रूढ़िवादी ताकतों की ओर से इस कोशिश को नाकाम कर यथा स्थिति को बनाए रखने के संघर्ष का नतीजा है। कुछ साल पहले गैर–सरकारी संगठन हरिजन सेवक संघ ने 13 राज्यों में एक सर्वेक्षण कराया। कर्नाटक के सौ गावों में यह सर्वेक्षण किया गया और पाया गया कि वहाँ सौ के सौ गाँवों में हरिजनों को सार्वजनिक कुएँ से पानी नहीं भरने दिया जाता, वे मंदिरो में नहीं जा सकते और होटलों में उनका प्रवेश

वर्जित है। केरल तो पूरी तरह साक्षरों का राज्य है। वहाँ के 60 गाँवों का सर्वेक्षण हुआ और एक भी गाँव ऐसा नहीं मिला, जिसमें किसी हरिजन को इन तीनों में से कोई छूट हो। आर्थिक और शैक्षणिक दृष्टि से अपेक्षाकृत कमजोर उड़ीसा में भी यही स्थिति थी।

राष्ट्रीय अनुसूचित जाति – जनजाति आयोग ने 1989 में सात राज्यों का सर्वेक्षण किया और पाया कि इनके हरिजन–बहुल इलाकों में छुआछूत किसी न किसी रूप में मौजूद है। 1990 की उनकी रिपोर्ट के मुताबिक उत्तर प्रदेश, तमिलनाडु, केरल, कर्नाटक और राजस्थान में दलित मंदिर व सार्वजनिक पूजा स्थलों पर नहीं जा सकते। सामाजिक समारोहों में उनके भाग लेने के मामले में भी उनसे भेदभाव बरता जाता है। तमिलनाडु में वे पानी के आम स्रोतों से पानी नहीं ले सकते। उत्तर प्रदेश, राजस्थान और केरल में भी कहीं–कहीं ऐसी स्थिति है। उन्हें चाय के स्टालों और होटलों में नहीं बैठने दिया जाता। ग्राम चौपालों और ग्राम सभा की बैठकों में भाग लेने के मामलों में उनसे तमिलनाडु और उत्तर प्रदेश में और कुछ कम मात्रा में राजस्थान में भेदभाव बरता जाता है। राजस्थान में अनु0जा0 के एक वर्ग के साथ शिक्षा संस्थाओं, लोक स्वास्थ्य केन्द्र जैसी संस्थाओं में भी भेदभाव बरता जाता है। उत्तर प्रदेश, महाराष्ट्र, तमिलनाडु और राजस्थान में आम जनता के प्रयोग के लिए रखे गए बरतनों का इस्तेमाल वे नहीं कर सकते। तमिलनाडु और कुछ कम मात्रा में महाराष्ट्र और उत्तर प्रदेश में सार्वजनिक श्मशान, कब्रिस्तान और सार्वजनिक मार्गों का इस्तेमाल उन्हें नहीं करने दिया जाता। तमिलनाडु व उत्तर प्रदेश में कहीं–कहीं अपने लिए वे मकान और व्यावसायिक परिसरों का न तो निर्माण कर सकते हैं और न उन्हें खरीद ही सकते हैं। वे धर्मशालाओं और सरायों में भी नहीं जा सकते। बिहार में वे सार्वजनिक समारोहों में भाग नहीं ले सकते। स्पष्ट है कि हर राज्य में छुआछूत किसी न किसी रूप में मौजूद है। तमिलनाडु इसमें सबसे ऊपर है।

जो लोग समझते है कि सरकारी या अर्द्ध सरकारी संस्थाओं में छुआछूत नहीं होती, राजस्थान उनके इस भ्रम को भी तोड़ देता है। गुजरात भी एक उदाहरण है। इण्डियन रिसर्च सोसायटी फॉर बैकवर्ड क्लासेस के एक सर्वेक्षण के अनुसार गुजरात में हरिजनों को सरकारी संस्थाओं का सदस्य नहीं बनाया जाता। सहकारी बैंक और खास तौर से दुग्ध सहकारी संस्थाओं में उन्हें सदस्यता नहीं दी जाती। कारण, पटेल और क्षत्रिय उनका दूध खरीदने से मना करते हैं। भेदसाना, अहमदाबाद, कैरा और सुरेन्द्र नगर

जिलों में जिन हरिजन परिवारों के पास दुधारू जानवर हैं, उनमें से मात्र 8 प्रतिशत को ही दुग्ध सहकारी समिति का सदस्य बनाया गया है। कृषि सहकारी संस्थाओं में भी उनकी सदस्यता मात्र 9 प्रतिशत है। इनमें से भी एडवांस राशि मात्र 3.8 प्रतिशत को ही दी गयी, और वसूली सबसे पहले और सबसे ज्यादा इन्ही से हुई। यह स्थिति उस राज्य की है, जिसमें अनुसूचित जातियों को 'हरिजन' का नाम देने वाले महात्मा गाँधी हुए।

ये सभी उदाहरण यही स्थापित करते हैं कि हम इक्कीसवीं सदी के तकनीकी युग में भले ही प्रवेश कर रहे हों, किन्तु समाज के एक वर्ग को अपने से भिन्न और इसलिए अस्पृश्य समझने की सदियों पुरानी हमारी मानसिकता का अंत नहीं हुआ है। यही नहीं, अपने श्रेष्ठ होने की अवधारणा भी उच्च जातियों में उतनी ही मात्रा में जीवित है और इसलिए जब निम्न समझे जाने वाले इस वर्ग का कोई हिस्सा उन्हें बराबरी पर आता दिखाई देता है तो वे उसे बर्दाश्त नहीं कर पाते। उनकी यह असहिष्णुता कितनी क्रूर है, इसके भी उदाहरण देखिए। तमिलनाडु के तंजावुर जिले में वेद्दामंगलम गाँव में उच्च वर्गीय मुहल्ले के लोगों ने एक महिला की शवयात्रा को घातक हथियार दिखाकर लौटा दिया (11 नवम्बर, 1983) वजह, महिला हरिजन थी। कौन कहता है, मृतक की जाति नहीं होती? बिहार के पलामू जिले के झाँसी गाँव में अनुसूचित जाति के लोगों की खड़ी फसलों को 29 मार्च' 83 को सिर्फ इसलिए आग लगा दी गई कि वे लोग भी होली मना रहे थे। तमिलनाडु के हरिजन–बहुल जिले दक्षिण अकोर के नरियेडु गाँव में 18 सितम्बर 87 को अनुसूचित जातियों के 119 घर जला दिये गए। कारण, उन्होंने आरक्षण की माँग कर रहे बनियारों का साथ देने से मना कर दिया था। उत्तर प्रदेश में कुछ साल पहले एक हरिजन बारात पर लाठियों से हमला किया गया, क्योंकि दूल्हा घोड़ी पर बैठा था। हरिजन दूल्हा घोड़ी पर हो और उसकी बारात स्वर्णों के मुहल्ले में से निकलने की हिम्मत करे, यह उन्हें कैसे बर्दाश्त हो सकता था।

धार्मिक स्तर पर स्थिति और भी खराब है, खासतौर से दक्षिण भारत में और उसमें भी तमिलनाडु और कर्नाटक में। 25 मार्च, 1993 को मैसूर (कर्नाटक) जिले के मंजनगढ़ ताल्लुके के बंदनवाल में तीन हरिजनों की हत्या कर दी गई, क्योंकि वे सिद्धेश्वर मन्दिर में जाने की माँग कर रहे थे। यह वही मंदिर था जिसके पुररूद्धार के लिए गाँव के उच्च वर्ण के लिंगायत समाज ने हरिजनों से आर्थिक व श्रमिक मदद माँगी थी, और मन्दिर में प्रवेश का आश्वासन मिल जाने पर उन्होंने 30 हजार रूपये और

श्रम का दान किया था। लेकिन जब उद्‌घाटन का समय आया, तो दो तीन हरिजन विद्यायकों को दाखिला देकर बाकी किसी को मन्दिर के पास भी नहीं फटकने दिया। तमिलनाडु में, 25 मई 1993 को एक दलित संस्था के 33 सदस्यों ने श्रीरंगम मन्दिर में घुसने की कोशिश की, पर पुजारियों ने उन्हें आगे नहीं बढ़ने दिया। बाकी राज्यों में भी स्थिति कोई बेहतर नहीं है। हरिजन सेवक संघ के सर्वेक्षण के अनुसार आन्ध्र प्रदेश के 60 में से 16, गुजरात के 141 में से 130, महाराष्ट्र के 61 में से 26, मध्य प्रदेश में 199 में से 95, उड़ीसा के 50 में से सभी 50, राजस्थान के 75 में से 63, तमिलनाडु के 148 में से 131, उत्तरप्रदेश के 170 में से 78 और हिमांचल प्रदेश के 51 में से सभी 51 गाँवों में हरिजनों को मन्दिरों में जाने की छूट नहीं थी। हरियाणा में भी, जहाँ अस्पृश्यता कम मानी जाती है, 47 गाँवों में से 23 गांवों में अनुसूचित जातियों के लोग मन्दिरों में नहीं जा सकते थे। पंजाब में भी कई जगह हरिजनों पर मंदिरों में जाने पर रोक है।

इन आकड़ो से साफ है कि छुआछूत आज भी हमारे समाज में, खास तौर से ग्रामीण समाज में मौजूद है, जबकि सरकार ने 1955 में ही इसे कानूनन एक अपराध घोषित कर दिया था। सवाल उठना स्वाभाविक है कि क्या कभी इस कानून के तहत किसी को सजा हुई? यदि हाँ तो यह इतने बड़े पैमाने पर कैसे मौजूद है? मौजूद है तो इसलिए कि यह एक मानसिकता है जिसे सिर्फ कानून से बदला नहीं जा सकता। हमारे कानून को लागू करने वाली दो एजेंसियों पुलिस व प्रशासन में बैठे ज्यादातर लोग खुद इसी मानसिकता के हैं। अपराधी और उनकी जाति एक ही होती है। जाति अलग हो भी, तो स्वार्थ एक होते हें। अनुसूचित जाति–जनजाति आयोग की 1990 की रिपोर्ट कहती है, अस्पृश्यता के ज्यादातर मामले इसके खिलाफ कानून के तहत दर्ज किये ही नहीं जाते। पहली बार 1955 में अस्पृश्यता विरोधी अधिनियम लागू किया गया। 1975 यानी 20 वर्षों में इसके तहत देश भर में मात्र 6778 मामले ही दर्ज हुए और इनमें से भी 1779 मामलों में ही कार्यवाही की गई और उनमें मात्र 26 प्रतिशत को ही सजा दी गई। 1975 में लगा कि कानून लाचार है, इसलिए खामियों को दूर करने के लिए संशोधन किया गया। सजा थोड़ी कड़ी बनाई गई। अधिनियम का नाम भी बदलकर नागरिक अधिकार संरक्षण अधिनियम कर दिया गया और तय किया गया कि पाँच साल में देश में अस्पृश्यता का अन्त कर दिया जाएगा। पर हुआ क्या? सिर्फ

इतना कि पहले जो मामले दर्ज नहीं होते थे या दर्ज कराये ही नहीं जाते थे, वे अब कराये भी जाने लगे और संभवत दर्ज (हालांकि सभी नहीं) भी होने लगे। समाज कल्याण विभाग के अनुसूचित जाति–जनजाति आयुक्त कार्यालय की रिपोर्ट के मुताबिक 1975 से' 85 के बीच देश भर में इस कानून के तहत हर साल औसतन 14,334 मामले दर्ज किये गए। इनमें से मात्र 62 प्रतिशत में चालान पेश किया गया। अदालतों में उनमें से भी मात्र 31 प्रतिशत में से भी मात्र 20 प्रतिशत में दोषियों को सजा हुई। यानी कुल मामलों के दस प्रतिशत से भी कम में अपराधी को दण्डित किया जा सका।

आयोग ने 1989 में विभिन्न राज्यों में दस मामलों का अध्ययन करने के बाद कहा–इन मामलों में हिंसात्मक घटनाएं धार्मिक सामाजिक मामलों पर जोर देने, सार्वजनिक स्थलों में भेदभाव बरतने, अपमानजनक व्यवहार किये जाने और बेगार कराने के कारण हुई। ये सभी मामले नागरिक अधिकार संरक्षण अधिनियम के तहत दण्डनीय अपराध है। पर अध्ययन किये गये अधिकांश मामलों में इस कानून का सहारा नहीं लिया गया। आयोग की टिप्पणी थी, ''35 साल से चले आ रहे ऐसे महत्वपूर्ण कानून की थानों को जानकारी न होना अक्षम्य है।'' रिपोर्ट के अनुसार 1986 में देश भर में (बिहार को छोड़कर) 8179 मामले इस अधिनियम के तहत लम्बित थे, इनमें से 2337 पर विचार किया गया और उनमें 81 प्रतिशत मामलों में आरोपियों को दोषमुक्त कर दिया गया। दोषमुक्ति भी उल्लंघन की तरह सबसे ज्यादा 93 प्रतिशत तमिलनाडु में, 90 प्रतिशत आंध्रप्रदेश में और 74 प्रतिशत राजस्थान में थी।

अनुसूचित जातियों के प्रति अस्पृश्यता के बीज हिन्दू समाज की वर्ण व्यवस्था और उससे उपजी जाति व्यवस्था में है, जिसमें अनुसूचित जातियों को न केवल सबसे नीचा ठहराया गया बल्कि अमनुष्य मानते हुए बाकी समाज से अलग भी कर दिया गया। आज भी ज्यादातर गाँवो में मेहतर, चमार, ढोली आदि के मुहल्ले अलग और गाँव से बाहर हैं। सरकारी मशीनरी द्वारा उनकी उपेक्षा का कारण जाति के साथ–साथ सामंती व्यवस्था है जिसमें भूमि का स्वामित्व कुछ लोगों तक सीमित होता है। इसलिए डॉ भीमराव अम्बेडकर कहा करते थे कि अगर दलितों को बाकी समाज के बराबर लाना है तो जाति व सामंती दोनो व्यवस्थाओं को खत्म करना जरूरी है। पिछले 60 वर्षों में जाति व्यवस्था और सामन्तवाद दोनों जटिल हुए हैं।

तकनीकी विकास और उसके साथ बदलते अर्थव्यवस्था के स्वरूप ने सामन्ती व्यवस्था के स्वरूप को भी बदला है और वह ज्यादा ताकतवर तथा क्रूर रूप में सामने आयी है, जिससे गाँवों में अनुसूचित जातियों की स्थिति और भी खराब हुई है। आज सीमांत किसान को उसकी जमीन से धकेला जा रहा है और खेतिहर मजदूर पर भूस्वामियों की निर्भरता कम हो रही है। यह निर्भरता किस हद तक कम हुई है, इसका पता इसी से लग जाता है कि 1981 में जहाँ 48.2 फीसदी हरिजन खेतिहर मजदूर थे, 1991 में उनकी संख्या घटकर मात्र 18 प्रतिशत रह गयी, जबकि 1971 में यह संख्या 51.7 प्रतिशत थी। इसका मुख्य कारण यह माना जा रहा है कि भूमि जोतने व अन्य कृषि कार्यों में आधुनिक उपकरणों को इस्तेमाल ज्यादा से ज्यादा किया जा रहा है, जिसमें कम, पर प्रतिक्षित मजदूरों की आवश्यकता होती है। ऐसे में छँटनी तो हो ही रही है, प्रतिक्षित न होने के कारण जमीन से वर्षों पुराना अपना रिश्ता उसे तोड़ना पड़ रहा है। बड़े–बड़े बाँधो, उद्योगों और कारखानों के नाम पर भी उनसे जमीन छीनी जा रही है। वैकल्पिक खेती का एक दुष्परिणाम यह हुआ है कि 'बंजर भूमि' के नाम पर अच्छी भूमि भी गैर सरकारी संगठनों व अमीरो को, पहले से ही जिनके पास काफी जमीन है, दी जा रही है। इससे एक ओर वे अधिक बड़ी भूमि के मालिक बन रहे हैं और इसलिए ताकतवर हो रहे हैं, दूसरी ओर गरीब के लिए भूमि का, जो उसकी आजीविका का साधन होती थी, टोटा पड़ता जा रहा है।

ग्रामीण सामंतो के अफसर बेटों और शहर के नवधनाढ़य वर्ग ने भी जमीन के बड़े हिस्से को अपने कब्जे में ले लिया है और उसका उपयोग वह खेती में नहीं कर रहा। उनकी दिलचस्पी भूमि के पूँजीगत मूल्य में बढ़ोत्तरी में है। या फिर वह फार्म हाउस बना रहा है जिसकी उपज में गरीब मजदूर का कोई हिस्सा नहीं होता। यह पूरा वर्ग वह वर्ग है जिसके पास धन–बल के साथ–साथ राजनैतिक सत्ता का भी बल है। प्रशासनिक–प्रबन्धकीय ढाँचे में वह या तो खुद ऊँचे पदों पर बैठा है या फिर उन पदों पर बैठे लोगों तक उनकी पहुँच है। कुल मिलाकर वह एक बेहद ताकतवर वर्ग के रूप में उभरा है, जिसका गाँव और शहर दोनों ही जगह काफी दबदबा है। अपने इस दबदबे के कारण वह हर क्षेत्र के सीमान्त या मझोले किसान से उचित–अनुचित तरीको से जमीन छीनता जा रहा है। चूँकि हरिजन से वह प्रतिरोध की अपेक्षा नहीं करता, इसलिए उसके प्रति उसका व्यवहार बेहद हिंसक व क्रूर हो उठा है।

पिछले कुछ समय से हरिजनों में चेतना के विकास का एक नतीजा यह हुआ है कि उनके प्रति हिंसा बढ़ गयी है। अभी तक भूस्वामी से उनके परंपरागत संबंध जोतदार–बँटाईदार, काश्तकार–मजदूर के थे। वे भूमि मालिक के एहसानमंद थे, कर्जदार थे और थे बँधुआ मजदूर, जिनकी जमीन कभी अपनी नहीं होती थी। अपना शरीर तो खैर उनका अपना होता ही नहीं था। लेकिन दक्षिण भारत और बिहार में चले लम्बे किसान आन्दोलन ने उन्हें संगठित किया और अपने अधिकारों के लिए आवाज उठाने की ताकत दी। शिक्षा और नौकरियों में आरक्षण से उनका आत्म विश्वास बढ़ा। लेकिन संगठित आन्दोलन का जवाब सामंतो ने संगठित हिंसा से दिया।

उच्च वर्ग किस तरह अनुसूचित जातियों के प्रति लगातार हिंसक होता चला गया है, इसका अंदाजा पिछले कुछ साल के आँकड़ो से लग सकता है। देश भर में 1955 में 180, 1956 में 481, 1957 में 492, 1958 में 489, 1968–69 में 1908, 1969–70 में 2522, 1977 में 10, 859, 1978 में 15041, 1979 में 13832, 1980 में 13727, 1981 में 14151, 1982 में 14996, 1983 में 14818, 1984 में 16573, 1985 में 15011, 1986 में 15416, 1989 में 15799, 1990 में 17735 वारदातें दर्ज की गयी थी। स्थिति में गिरावट के मुख्य कारण हैं समाज में अनुसूचित जातियों की निम्न सामाजिक स्थिति, उनका गरीब व अशिक्षित होना और जमीदारों पर उनकी निर्भरता। दोषपूर्ण अर्थव्यवस्था, जिसमें गरीब राष्ट्रीय आय में वृद्धि के लाभ से ज्यादातर वंचित रहा, भूमि सुधारों का लागू न किया जाना और अब विकास की उलट प्रक्रिया जिसमें भूमि से उसका सम्बन्ध खत्म हो रहा है और बेरोजगारों की श्रेणी में खड़ा होना पड़ रहा है। राष्ट्रीय अनुसूचित जाति–जनजाति आयोग ने 1990 में बढ़ते अत्याचारों के कारणों पर लिखा था, "गरीबी, निरक्षरता, आर्थिक निर्भरता और कानून से अनभिज्ञता के कारण उनके विकास की गति अवरूद्ध है। इससे वे पुलिस व न्यायालयों के समक्ष हमेशा कमजोर पड़ जाते है। उनके प्रति पूर्वाग्रह और सामाजिक असमर्थता से जब पुलिस थाना और मजिस्ट्रेट भी प्रभावित हो जाते हैं, तो उन्हें भारतीय दंड संहिता, अपराध दण्ड संहिता, सिविल अधिकार संरक्षण कानून और अत्याचार निवारण अधिनियम, 1989 के संरक्षक और दांडिक उपबन्धों के लाभ नही मिल पाते। यह सुनिश्चित करने के लिए कि अनुसूचित जातियाँ और जनजातियां कानून के अन्तर्गत अपने अधिकारों को प्राप्त कर सकें, एक अनुकूल पुलिस प्रशासन का होना सबसे पहली आवश्यकता है।

आयोग का पूरा विश्वास है, और वह गलत नहीं है, कि हरिजनों पर अत्याचारों का एक बहुत बड़ा कारण पुलिसतंत्र का समर्थवर्ग की जेब में होना है। हरिजन–बहुल इलाकों में पुलिस तंत्र कानून और व्यवस्था का संरक्षक नहीं, खुद अपराध तंत्र का एक हिस्सा बन चुका है। ज्यादा क्रूर व हिंसक वारदातें पुलिस ने ही की हैं। आयोग के मुताबिक पुलिस रिपोर्ट करने में देर करती है। चार्जशीट में भी जहाँ न्यूनतम मजदूरी अधिनियम, बंधित श्रम पद्धति (उत्पादन) अधिनियम, सिविल अधिकार संरक्षण अधिनियम, अत्याचार निवारण आदि के नियम लागू होने चाहिए, वह केवल भारतीय दण्ड संहिता और अपराध दण्ड संहिता की धाराओं को ही लागू करती है। आयोग के सर्वेक्षण के मुताबिक अपराध होने और चार्जशीट लगाने में दो महीने का समय आम बात है। पर बिहार जैसे राज्यों में यह अन्तर एक साल से भी ज्यादा हो जाता है। 750 मामलों का अध्ययन करने के बाद उसने पाया कि 50 प्रतिशत मामलों में रिपोर्ट दर्ज होने के बाद 12 घण्टे तक मौके का निरीक्षण नहीं किया गया और 20 प्रतिशत मामलों में 12 घण्टे के बाद पुलिस पहुँची। विशेष अदालतें भी लगातार अपने उद्देश्य में नाकाम सिद्ध हुई हैं।

अनुसूचित जातियों के साथ बढ़ता जुल्म लेकिन इस बात का भी प्रमाण है कि वे अब अन्याय को बर्दाश्त करना नहीं चाहते। सवाल उठता है कि उनमें चेतना का यह संचार हुआ कैसे? स्वतंत्रता से पहले चले कई समाज सुधार आन्दोलन, तथा गाँधी जी की हरिजन दृष्टि ने समाज में बहुत से ऐसे लोग पैदा कर दिये जो हरिजनों के हितों की रक्षा के लिए आगे चलने को तैयार थे। पर खुद हरिजनों की अपनी स्थिति जिससे मजबूत हुई, वह व्यवस्था थी आरक्षण। संविधान ने उन्हें जन प्रतिनिधि संस्थाओं और सरकारी नौकरियों में जो आरक्षण दिया, उससे कुछ समय बाद ही सही, प्रशासन तंत्र और राजतंत्र दोनों में उनके प्रवेश का मार्ग प्रशस्त हुआ। नियम–कानूनों को उन्होंने जाना। अपने मानवीय अस्तित्व का अनुभव किया। आरक्षण से उन्हें नौकरी मिली, पढ़ाई के लिए सुविधाएँ मिली, जिससे अज्ञान और गरीबी दोनों कम हुए। जमींदार पर निर्भरता घटी और अत्याचारी के सामने खड़े होने की हिम्मत आयी। आरक्षण का ही नतीजा है कि आज केन्द्र व राज्य सरकारों में महत्वपूर्ण पदों पर हरिजन अधिकारी बैठे हैं और सरकार में उन्हें लेना जरूरी समझा जाता है। एक सर्वेक्षण के मुताबिक 1981 में केन्द्र सरकार में प्रथम श्रेणी के 9891, द्वितीय श्रेणी के 1,65,982, तृतीय व चतुर्थ श्रेणी के 1,18282 और सभी श्रेणियों

के 1,94,155 अनुसूचित जाति व जनजाति के कर्मचारी थे। हाँलाकि यह आँकड़ा अन्य वर्गों के अधिकारियों के मुकाबले में नाम मात्र है, फिर भी यह उनकी स्थिति में सुधार का संकेत अवश्य देता है। चेतना का संचार इस क्षेत्र में भी हुआ है कि अनुसूचित जातियां अपने लिए आरक्षित स्थानों को पूरी तरह अपन लिए ही सुरक्षित करने की माँग कर रहे हैं।

नौकरियों में आरक्षण का लाभ हरिजन पूरा नहीं उठा सके तो इसलिए कि उसके लिए जैसी शिक्षा या तकनीकी कौशल की आवश्यकता होती है, वह उनके पास नहीं था। संविधान लागू होने के कुछ साल बाद जब इस बात का एहसास हुआ, तो व्यावसायिक व तकनीकी शिक्षा संस्थानों में उनके लिए सीटें आरक्षित हुई। प्राथमिक स्तर से उच्च स्तर तक कई प्रोत्साहन योजनाएं भी शुरू की गयी। लड़कियों की शिक्षा के लिए विशेष छात्रावास खोले गए। बुक बैंक, प्री–मैट्रिक स्कॉलरशिप योजना, व्यावसायिक प्रशिक्षण योजना, लड़को के लिए हॉस्टल आदि का लाभ छात्रों को मिला भी। फिर भी सरकार की अभी तक की कोशिशों के वांछित प्रभाव इस हद तक नहीं आ सके हैं कि अनुसूचित जातियों व बाकी आबादी के बीच शिक्षा दर का अन्तर कम हो जाए। उलटे हो यह रहा है कि यह अन्तर लगभग बढ़ता ही जा रहा है। अनुसूचित जनजातियों को छोड़ दें तो 1961 में अनुसूचित जाति और बाकी आबादी की शिक्षा में अन्तर 13.3 प्रतिशत, 1971 में 10.67 प्रतिशत, 1981 में 18.58 प्रतिशत और 1991 में 20 प्रतिशत हो गया। दूसरे, निरक्षरों की संख्या में भी लगातार वृद्धि हुई है। 1961 से 1981 के बीच अनुसूचित जातियों के निरक्षरों की संख्या में 40 प्रतिशत बढ़ोत्तरी हुई। बाकी जनसंख्या के निरक्षरों की तुलना में यह बढ़ोत्तरी डेढ़ गुनी थी। इसका एक कारण अनुसूचित जातियों में जनसंख्या की वृद्धि दर ज्यादा होना है, पर उससे भी बड़ा कारण उनके लिए शुरू की गई कल्याणकारी योजनाओं का लाभ उन्हें न मिलना है। शिक्षा संस्थाओं का उनकी पहुँच से परे होना या फिर उनकी अपनी मजबूरियाँ भी उन्हें अक्षर ज्ञान की परिधि से परे रखती हैं। राज्य सरकारों को चाहिए कि हरिजन–बहुल गाँवों में उनकी स्थितियों के मुताबिक ऐसी शिक्षा संस्थाएं खोलें जहाँ वे अपने काम के दौरान या बाद (जैसी भी प्रकृति हो) अध्ययन के लिए जा सकें। अभी तो स्थिति यह है कि पहली से पाँचवी कक्षा के बीच 59.4 प्रतिशत, छठी से आठवीं के बीच 74.70 और माध्यमिक स्तर पर 35.72 प्रतिशत अनुसूचित जातियों के छात्र पढ़ाई छोड़ देते है। महिलाओं की शिक्षा मे भी लगातार बढ़ोत्तरी हुई है, पर बाकी आबादी की महिला साक्षरता दर और हरिजन महिला साक्षरता दर में अंतर बढ़ा है।

शिक्षा के कारण अपने परंपरागत धंधो से भी हरिजनों को मुक्ति मिली है। आज चर्मकार या कसाई के बच्चे पढ़–लिखकर किसी भी दूसरी नौकरी में जा रहे हैं। पर मैला उठाने की प्रथा से अभी तक उन्हें मुक्ति नहीं मिल पाई है। आरक्षण की वजह से संगठित क्षेत्र में तो इस वर्ग को नौकरियाँ मिलगई, पर असंगठित क्षेत्र में उसकी स्थिति खराब हुई है। गाँव में रोजगार समाप्त होने से आजीविका की तलाश में उसे शहरों में नौकरी करनी पड़ रही है। आज ज्यादातर ग्रामीण अनूसूचित जातियों के परिवारों के निरक्षर सदस्य शहरों में निर्माण कार्यों या भट्टों आदि पर दिहाड़ी करते हैं, जहाँ ठेकेदार उनकी गरीबी व अशिक्षा का लाभ उठाते हुए उन्हें न्यूनतम मजदूरी के सवाल पर इन जगहों में कई बार उनकी हत्या कर दी जाती है। 1991 के जनगणना 4,98,74,651 मुख्य मजदूर, 4,37,22,784 सीमांत मजदूर और 8,39,75,842 गैर–मजदूर (नॉन वर्कर) यानी बेरोजगार थे। प्रतिशत की दृष्टि से यह आंकड़ा 31.08 प्रतिशत, 3.16 प्रतिशत और 60.75 प्रतिशत या आज भी स्थिति में कोई उल्लेखनीय परिवर्तन नहीं हो सका है। जिन लोगों के आर्थिक विकास के लिए 60 वर्षों से विशेष योजनाएं चलायी जा रही हैं उनका आधे से भी अधिक हिस्सा बेरोजगार है तो कहने की जरूरत नहीं कि नीति निर्माताओं और विकास योजनाएं बनाने वालों को एक बार फिर विचार करना होगा कि उनके विकास का पैमाना आखिर क्या है?

एक क्रांतिकारी माहौल सभी स्तरों पर बदलाव लाता है। लेकिन अनुसूचित जातियाँ अपनी सामाजिक स्थिति सुधारने के लिए क्रान्ति का इन्तजार नहीं कर सकते। इसके लिए प्रायश्चित की प्रक्रिया शुरू हो। चूँकि संघर्ष और प्रायश्चित एक ही सिक्के के दो पहलू हैं, अतः संघर्ष ऐसा होना चाहिए जो प्रायश्चित को सम्भव बना सके और प्रायश्चित ऐसा जो संघर्ष का सम्मान कर सके। वस्तुतः हमारे समाज में अनुसूचित जातियों की स्थिति एक प्रकार से अल्पसंख्यकों की तरह ही है। अल्पसंख्यकों की भांति उन्हें भी विशेष सुरक्षा चाहिए तथा उन्हें मुख्य धारा के ज्यादा से ज्यादा करीब लाया जाना चाहिए। इस प्रक्रिया में भारत के गैर–दलित समाज की निर्णायक भूमिका है। 3 अप्रैल, 1927 को डॉ अम्बेडकर ने जिस मराठी पाक्षिक की शुरूआत की थी, उसका नाम था 'बहिष्कृत भारत'। अनुसूचित जातियां आज भी बहिष्कृत हैं। लेकिन क्या यह वर्ग लड़कर अपने को मुख्य भारत का अंग बना सकेगा? इस बहिष्कार को समाप्त करना वस्तुतः उन्हीं का कर्त्तव्य है, जिन्होंने बहिष्कृत करने का गंदा काम

किया था। कहने की आवश्यकता नहीं कि इसकी प्रेरणा गैर–दलित समाज में स्वयं पैदा होनी चाहिए। इसमें अनुसूचित–जाति वर्ग भी मदद कर सकता है, किन्तु तब उसका मुख्य स्वर रचनात्मक होगा, जैसा कि दलित वर्ग से आये हुए मध्यकालीन सन्त कवियों का था। अकेले अनुसूचित जाति वर्ग सिर्फ अपने स्वाभिमान की रक्षा कर सकता है, जो उसे करना ही चाहिए। लेकिन अगर वह चाहता है कि व्यापक समाज के साथ उसकी मानवीय हिस्सेदारी हो तथा साझा राष्ट्रीय उद्देश्यों के लिए संघर्ष किया जाए तो एक व्यापक, उदार और प्रगतिशील दलित दर्शन की आवश्यकता होगी। आज देश में लोकतंत्र चल रहा है। केन्द्र सरकार, प्रान्तीय सरकारों और स्थानीय सरकारों के तीनों स्तर पर वोट का राज्य है। राजनीतिक पदों पर सभी लोग प्रत्यक्ष या अप्रत्यक्ष रूप से चुनाव लड़कर ही आते हैं। अनुसूचित जातियों को लोकतंत्र में सभी के समान ही समान मत का अधिकार प्राप्त है। विरोधी वर्ग वोट के अधिकार को तभी तक माना करता है, जब तक वह इस माध्यम से चुना जाता रहता है। लेकिन आज आवश्यकता इस बात की है कि राजनीतिक दल अनुसूचित जातियों–जनजातियों के आरक्षण के नाम पर राजनीतिक रोटियाँ न सेकें अपितु इन जातियों के उत्थान तथा समाज में बराबरी का दर्जा दिलाने के लिए ईमानदार व सार्थक कदम उठायें। अनुसूचित जातियों के लिए चलायी जा रही योजनाओं का सरकार दृढ़ता से निरीक्षण करे तथा यह देखे कि उनका लाभ वास्तविक लाभार्थियों को मिल रहा है या फिर केवल कागज़ी खानापूर्ति ही हो रही है। अनुसूचित जातियों के कल्याण के लिए सरकार तथा समाज को साझा प्रयास करने होगें तभी हमारे समाज का यह महत्वपूर्ण अंग विकसित तथा सम्पन्न बन सकेगा।

सन्दर्भ सूची

1. दलित विमर्श, डॉ धीरज भाई वणकर
2. भारत के अछूतों का इतिहास, सुरेश पाटिल।
3. अम्बेडकर की राजनीतिक सोच एवं विचार, आशुतोष मुखर्जी।
4. आधुनिक भारत का दलित आन्दोलन, कन्हैया लाल चंचरीक।

26

ग्वालियर की सहरिया जनजाति– एक समाज वैज्ञानिक विश्लेषण

ए.के. उपाध्याय

भारत वर्ष में जनजातियों का जो स्वरूप व्याप्त है, वह विश्व के किसी अन्य देश में देखने को नही मिलता। भारतीय संविधान के अनुसार लगभग 667 समूहो को अनुसूचित जनजातियों की सूची में सम्मलित किया गया है जो कुल जनसंख्या का 8.20 प्रतिशत भाग है। इनमे से 75 ऐसी जनजातियां है जिन्हे आदिम जनजाति समूह कहा जाता है। आदिम समूह का दर्ज अबूझ माडिया, बोडो, बादो, विरहोर, वैगा, कमार, और सहरिया जनजातियों को मिला है। इन्हे भारतीय सभ्यता व संस्कति का अमूल्य धरोहर माना जाता है जो भारतीय संस्कृति की विविधता को एक निराली छवि प्रदान करते है। पर इनकी सामाजिक–आर्थिक स्थिति हमेशा से दयनीय रही है। इन्हे अनेक प्रकार के उत्पीडन व शोषण का शिकार होना पडा है। समाज के शुभ चिन्तकों एवं आर्थिक रूप से सम्पन्न लोगो ने सामजिक मान्यतायें इस प्रकार विकसित की जिससे इन लोगो का व्यक्तित्व का विकास नही हो पाया।

स्वतन्त्रता प्राप्ति के बाद सरकार ने इनकी सामजिक आर्थिक दशा सुधारने के लिये विभिन्न प्रयास किये। संवैधानिक व्यवस्था के अर्न्तगत इन्हें विशेष सुविधाये उपलब्ध करायी गयी। इनके उत्थान के लिये केन्द्र

व राज्य सरकार द्वारा अनेको ऐसे कल्याण कार्यक्रम चलाये जा रहे है जिससे जनजातीय लोगो को विकास की मुख्य धारा से जोडा जा सके। इस हेतु सरकारी खजाने से करोडो की धन राशि इनके उत्थान के लिये खर्च कर दी गयी पर जनजातियों की स्थिति में कोई अपेक्षित बदलाव नही आ सका। वे आज भी अशिक्षा, निर्धनता, बेरोजगारी, ऋणग्रस्तता और भूमिहीनता की समस्या से ग्रसित है। इनकी सामाजिक आर्थिक स्थिति आज भी दयनीय बनी हुई है।

प्रस्तुत अध्ययन मध्यप्रदेश में सहरिया जनजातियों के समाजिक आर्थिक विकास के विभिन्न पहलुओं के विश्लेषण से सम्बन्धित है। इस अध्ययन में सहरिया जनजातियों के परम्परागत स्वरूपों का विश्लेषण करने का प्रयास किया गया है वही दूसरी ओर विभिन्न कारकों से घटित हो रहे परिवर्तन एवं उनके बीच कार्य – कारण सम्बन्धों की व्याख्या की गयी है। इस अध्ययन में सहरिया जनजातियों के सामाजिक जीवन एवं गत्याात्मकता के विभिन्न पहलुओं का विश्लेषण किया गया है और यह जानने का प्रयास किया गया कि सहरिया जनजातियों के सामाजिक, सांस्कृतिक व आर्थिक जीवन में घटित परिवर्तनों की दिशा क्या है। विकास की इन जनजातियों की अपनी धारणा क्या है। क्या वे अपने प्रयासों से विकास के इस लक्ष्य को प्राप्त कर सकते है।

इस प्रकार प्रस्तुत अध्ययन का मुख्य उद्देश्य सहरिया जनजातियों की सामाजिक, आर्थिक व राजनीतिक जीवन में होने वाले परिवर्तनों के कारणों एवं परिणामों का विश्लेषण करना है।

सहरिया जनजातियों के समाजिक आर्थिक विकास से सम्बन्धित यह प्रपत्र मेंरे द्वारा किये गये एक शोध अध्ययन पर आधारित है जो मध्यप्रदेश के ग्वालियर सम्भाग में सम्पादित किया गया। समय व साधन की सीमा को ध्यान में रखते हुए ग्वालियर सम्भाग के दो जिलों ग्वालियर व शिवपुरी जिलों में सहरिया बाहुल्य क्षेत्र को चुना गया। ग्वालियर जिले के चार विकास खण्ड–घाटीगाँव, मुरार, डबरा व भीतरवार को तथा शिवपुरी जिलें के चार विकास खण्डो शिवपुरी, कोलारस, पोहरी एवं पिछोर को अध्ययन क्षेत्र के रूप में चुना गया। दोनो जिलो के आठ विकास खण्डों से आठ गांव– घाटीगाँव, हस्तिनापुर, करहिया, छीमकव, शिवपुरी, सुनोज, बीलवर माता एवं मानपुरा का चयन किया गया। ये एसे गावं है जहां सहरिया जनजातियों की संख्या सर्वाधिक थी। इन आठ गावं में से सबसे पहले कुल सहरिया परिवार की संख्या ज्ञात की गयी और दैव निदर्शन विधि

से 300 सूचनादाताओ का चयन किया गया। अध्ययन की इकाई परिवार की मुखिया को माना गया। इनका चुनाव करते समय इस बात का ध्यान रखा गया कि वे समग्र का प्रतिनिधित्व करने वाले हो। तथ्य संकलन हेतु साक्षात्कार अनुसूची एवं अवलोकन विधि का प्रयोग किया गया। साक्षात्कार अनुसूची को विभिन्न उपखण्डों में विभक्त किया गया और समस्या से सम्बन्धित विभिन्न पक्षों पर प्रश्नो का निर्माण किया गया। अधिकांशतः प्रतिबन्धित स्वरूप के थे और उत्तरदाताओं को सकारात्मक व नकारात्मक दोनो ढंग से उत्तर देने की स्वतन्त्रता थी। साक्षात्कार अनुसूची में सहरिया जनजीवन के विभिन्न पहलुओं यथा उनका सामाजिक संगठन, जीवन निर्वाह के साधन, परम्परागत राजनीतिक जीवन, उनकी मुख्य समस्याये व उनमें पायी जाने वाली गत्यात्मकता से सम्बन्धित विन्दुओं को सम्मलित किया गया और उनसे सम्बन्धित जानकारी प्राप्त की गयी। स्वतन्त्र रूप से उन्हे अपनी बात कहने का अवसर दिया गया ताकि वे अपनी भावनाओं को स्वच्छन्दतापूर्वक व्यक्त कर सके और प्राप्त तथ्य विश्वससनीय व प्रमाणिक हो सके।

अध्ययन की उपलब्धियां

सहरिया अत्यन्त पिछडी एव कोलारियन परिवार की जनजाति है। यह जनजाति मुख्यतः ग्वालियर, भिन्ड, मुरैना, दतिया, शिवपुरी ,गुना, अशोकनगर, विदिशा, रायसेन व सिहोर जिले में रहती है। सहरिया भीलो की एक उपशाखा के रूप में पायी जाती है। ये अपने आप को भीलो के छोटा भाई मानते है तथा रामायण कालीन शबरी के वंशज बताते है। सौरी से उत्पन्न होने के कारण ये शबर, सबर, सौर और सहरिया कहलाये।

सहरिया अपनी अलग कतार बद्ध मकानो की श्रीखला बना कर समूह में रहते हैं जिसे सहराना कहा जाता है। सहराना का मुखिया पटेल होता है। इसकी नियुक्ति जाति परम्परा के अनुसार होती है जो पीढी दर पीढी हस्तांतरित होती रहती है।

सहरिया जनजातियों का रहन सहन खान पान वेश–भूषा सरल व आडम्बर हीन है। इन लोगो में साफ सफाई पर विशेष ध्यान नही दिया जाता है। नियमित रूप से ये न तो स्नान करते और न ही कपड़े धोते हैं जिससे इनकी स्वास्थ की समस्या बनी रहती है। ज्वार, बाजरा, चना व चावल इनका मुख्य भोजन है। गेहू की रोटी केवल पर्वों व त्यौहारों पर ही बनायी जाती हैं। सहरिया जीवन पूर्णत प्रकृति और उसके उत्पादो पर ही निर्भर हैं। जंगल में मिलने वाले खाद्य फल बेर बिला आम जामुन कन्द मूल और हरी साग–भाजी इनके शरीर के खनिज तत्वों की पूर्ति

करते है। इनके खान पान में पौष्टिक तत्व न के बराबर रहता है। आर्थिक विसंगतियों के कारण इनको पौष्टिक भोजन नही मिल पाता।

सहरिया जनजातियो का वेशभूषा पर राजस्थानी प्रभाव ज्यादा देखने को मिलता है। इनकी स्त्रियां लहगां घाघरा व सलूका पहनती है जबकि पुरूष रंगीन कमीज व साफा पहनते है। इनके वस्त्रो का रंग गहरा चटकदार हरे पीले नीले व लाल रंग के होते हैं। आभूषण पहनने की परम्परा स्त्री व पुरूष दोनो में हैं।

सहरिया जनजाति मद्यपान के भी शौकीन है। परिणामत उनमें निर्धनता निम्न जीवन स्तर पारिवारिक कलह असमय मत्यु आदि समस्याये व्याप्त हो गयी। इन समस्याओ से मुक्ति दिलाने के लिये शासन प्रशासन व स्वयसेवी संगठनों का ध्यान इस ओर अपेक्षित है।

सामाजिक संगठन के पारम्परिक स्वरूप एवं परिवर्तन

प्रस्तुत अध्ययन में सहरिया जनजातियों के सामाजिक संगठन के पारम्परिक स्वरूपों एवं तदजनित घटित परिवर्तनों का विश्लेषण किया गया। सामाजिक संगठन के पारम्परिक स्वरूपो के विश्लेषण के लिये जिन विन्दुओं को लिया गया उनमे पारिवारिक संरचना विवाह परम्परा, परिवार में महिलाओं की स्थिति, गोत्र एवं धार्मिक व सांस्कृतिक गतिविधियां मुख्य है।

परिवार सार्वभौमिक एवं सर्वकालिक संस्था के रूप में समाज की निरन्तरता को बनाये रखने वाली समाज की एक आधारभूत संस्था है। सहरिया जनजाति में परिवार एक संरचनात्मक –प्रकार्यात्मक इकाई होता है जिसे ये कुटुम्ब कहते है। ये परिवार पितृवंशीय पितृस्थानीय एवं पितृसत्तात्मक परिवार के रूप में पाये जाते है। बच्चे पिता के कुल या वंश का नाम ग्रहण करते हैं।

सहरिया समाज में संयुक्त परिवार प्रथा का प्रचलन है। हमारे आधे से अधिक उत्तरदाता संयुक्त परिवार में रहते है। संयुक्त परिवार के प्रकार्यात्मकता के सम्बन्ध में उत्तरदाताओ का विचार सकारात्मक है। हमारे आधे से अधिक उत्तरदाता यह मानते है कि संयुक्त परिवार में धन का समुचित उपयोग होता है और इसी के द्वारा संस्कृति की रक्षा होती है। साथ ही यह राष्ट्रीय एकता में भी सहायक है। परिस्थितियों में परिवर्तन के कारण इसके अकार्यात्मकता को हमारे उत्तरदाताओं ने नजर अन्दाज नही किया। उत्तरदाताओ का मानना है कि मकान छोटे होने और मजदूरी पर आश्रित होने के कारण जितना एकाकी परिवार अच्छे हैं उतने संयुक्त

परिवार नही। यही कारण है कि एक तिहाई उत्तरदाता एकाकी परिवार में रह रहे है। सर्वेक्षित गाँव ग्वालियर व शिवपुरी जिले से जुडे है अतए विकास के आधुनिक संसाधन परिवार के स्वरूप को प्रभावित कर रहा है। के.एम. कपाड़िया (1959) का मत है कि औधोगिकरण नगरीकरण एवं पश्चिमीकण की प्रक्रिया के फलस्वरूप परिवारिक संरचना में तीव्र परिवर्तन हो रहा है। फिर भी ग्रामीण व जनजातियो समुदायों में संयुक्ता के तत्व अभी भी विद्यामान है।

आजीविका के प्रकार एवं परिवार के स्वरूप में गहरा सम्बन्ध है। जो लोग मजदूरी से आय प्राप्त करते हैं उनके यहां एकाकी परिवारों का प्रचलन अधिक है। अध्ययन की प्रवृति यह है कि जीवन निर्वाह के साधन संघर्ष कठिन होने के साथ साथ संयुक्त परिवार का विघटन होता है। इससे एक ओर तथ्य जुडा है कि आय कम होने की स्थिति में संयुक्त परिवार के विघटन की दशायें उत्पन्न होती है।

सभी मामलो में सहरिया परिवार का एक मात्र मुखिया पिता होता है। हालांकि एकाधिक कारणों से उसकी स्थिति में परिवर्तन आ रहा है। तथापि बच्चों के विवाह सम्बन्धों का निर्धारण, उसका आयोजन परिवार के सदस्यो पर नियंत्रण सामाजिक एवं धार्मिक कार्यो का नेतृत्व आज भी परिवार का मुखिया ही करता है। लेकिन परिवार का शासक होना परिवार पर पूर्णतया अधिकार होना और आय व्यय के पूर्ण नियंत्रण पर विरोध के स्वर उभरने लगे हैं। इस प्रकार अध्ययन में देखा गया कि परिवार के पारम्परिक सम्बन्धों के स्वरूप में आज बदलाव आ रहा है। इस बदलाव का मुख्य कारण मकानों की कमी, अपने आय पर अपनी अधिकार की भावना, महिलाओं द्वारा अर्जित आय, युवा वर्ग का नगरीय सम्पर्क, सास बहू में कलह आदि मुख्य है।

सामाजिक संगठन का दूसरा मुख्य आधार गोत्र व्यवस्था है। सहरिया जनजाति में गोत्र की अवधारणा गोत्र के नाम से ही जानी जाती है। यह जनजाति अनेक गोत्र में बटी हुई है। एक गोत्र के लोग कुटुम्बी सगोती या भाईबन्धु कहलाते हैं। गोत्र जनजातीय इतिहास के पहचान का प्रतीक है। सहरिया जनजाति के गोत्र वनस्पति जगत जीवजगत और भौतिक पदार्थो से मिलकर बने होते हैं। गोत्र बर्हिविवाही होते हैं। गोत्र के सदस्य भ्रातृत्व भाव से जुड़े होने के कारण परस्पर सम्मान रखते हुए एक दूसरे के साथ सहयोग करते हैं और सुख दुख के सहभागी बनते हैं। गोत्र का मुख्य कार्य निकटाभिगमन को रोकना समाज के सदस्यों को एकता के

सूत्र में बाधे रखना व्यक्तियों के व्यवहारो पर नियंत्रण रखना तथा सामाजिक व धार्मिक कार्यों को सुचारू रूप से संचालित करना है।

सामाजिक संगठन का तीसरा प्रमुख आधार विवाह सम्बन्ध है। जनजातियों में विवाह प्रथा उतनी ही महत्वपूर्ण है जितना अन्य समाजों में। सहरिया समाज में विवाह एक धार्मिक कार्य है जिसे फूफा सम्पन्न कराता है। पर अब नगरीय प्रभावों के कारण अब ब्राम्हण द्वारा विवाह सम्पन्न कराये जाने लगे है। विवाह में लगुन टीका भेट भावर आदि रस्में अदा की जाती हैं। सहरिया जनजाति में चार प्रकार के विवाह पद्धति प्रचलित है– सगाई, विवाह, झगड़ा विवाह, विधवा विवाह और झारा फेरा विवाह। इसमें से सगाई, विवाह को सर्वोच्च माना जाता है। हमारे सभी उत्तरदाता विवाहित है और सगाई, विवाह द्वारा इनका विवाह सम्पन्न हुआ है। सगाई विवाह दोनो पक्षों के राजी–बाजी से सम्पन्न होता है।

सहरिया जनजातियों में आरम्भ में बाल विवाह का भी प्रचलन था और कमोवेश मात्रा में आज भी है पर अब अधिकांशतया वय सन्धि पार होने के बाद ही विवाह सम्पन्न होते हैं। इनके यहां बच्चों की विवाह की न्यूनतम आयु 15 वर्ष रखी गयी है जो शासन द्वारा निर्धारित आयु से कम है। इनके यहां अर्न्तविवाह का नियम ही स्वीकृत है और सगोत्र विवाह निषिद्ध है। सामाजिक व्यवस्था को बनाये रखने के लिये और रक्त की पवित्रता को बनाये रखने के लिये तथा पारिवारिक जीवन में शान्ति व सांस्कृतिक विषमता को समाप्त करने के लिये अर्न्तविवाह का नियम ही स्वीकृत है। चूकि सहरिया समाज में सगोत्र विवाह निषिद्ध है। अतः अपवाद स्वरूप उसका उलघंन करने पर उसे समाज से बहिष्कृत कर दिया जाता है। इनके यहां मामा के गोत्र को छोड कर अनयन्त्र कहीं भी विवाह किये जा सकते हैं।

सहरिया जनजातियों में एक विवाह की ही प्रथा प्रचलित है। एक समय में एक पुरूष एक स्त्री के साथ विवाह कर सकता है। किन्तु पत्नी के मत्यु के पश्चात सहरिया पंचायत की अनुमति से दूसरा विवाह कर सकता है। इनके यहां विधवा विवाह का भी प्रचलन है। पति के मृत्यु के पश्चात् पंचायत की अनुमति से गोत्र सम्बन्धी नियमो का पालन करते हुए किसी दूसरे पुरूष के साथ निवास करने की अनुमति दे दी जाती है। चूकि स्त्री को एक ही बार हल्दी चढती है। अत वैवाहिक क्रियाकलाप ऐसे में वर्जित रहती है। विधवा स्त्री को इनके यहां खाली कहा जाता

है और स्त्री को खाली नही रखा जा सकता। इसलिये विधवा विवाह अनिवार्य है।

सामाजिक संगठन का एक अन्य आधार धर्म है। धर्म अलौकिक शक्ति में विश्वास के रूप में जाना जाता है। सहरिया जनजाति एक ऐसी जनजाति है जो ईश्वर पर विश्वास के साथ–साथ निर्जीव वस्तुओं में भी अलौकिक शक्ति के निवास करने के तथ्य को स्वीकार करते हैं। हिन्दू समाज में प्रचलित मान्यताओं के अनुरूप सहरिया लोग आत्मवादी हैं और पुर्नजन्म में आस्था रखते हैं। हिन्दू देवी देवता के अतिरिक्त प्राकृतिक आत्माओं वृक्षों आदि में अलौकिक शक्ति के निवास के साथ–साथ मृतात्माओं पर भी काफी विश्वास है। मृतात्माओं को ये अपना कुल देवता मानते हैं और अपने घर में ही मिट्टी का घरौदा बनाकर इन्हें प्रसन्न करने के लिये बलि देते हैं।

सहरिया स्थानीय देवी देवता पर भी अधिक विश्वास करते है। इन देवताओं में तेजा जी महाराज हरीमन देव नाहर देव भैरो देव कारस देव नरसिह देव दरेठ देव परीत देव भूमिया देव आदि मुख्य है। इस जनजाति की सर्वाधिक लोकप्रिय देवी माता कालका है जिनकी पूजा अर्चना जनजातीय पर्वो व उत्सवो पर विशेश रूप से की जाती है।

सहरिया समाज में धार्मिक अनुष्ठानों को सम्पन्न कराने के लिये कोई पन्डित या पुजारी नही आता। परिवार का वयोवृद्ध व्यक्ति ही विभिन्न आयोजनो में पुरोहित का कार्य करता है। पर वाहय सम्पर्क के कारण गैर–आदिवासी ब्राह्मण इनके धार्मिक जीवन में प्रवेश कर रहे है। यद्यपि यह अभी आरम्भिक स्तर पर ही है पर धार्मिक अनुष्ठानों को सम्पन्न कराने की मानसिकता विकसित हो रही है।

सहरिया जनजाति समय समय पर आने वाली बीमारियों कष्टों व विपतियों से मुक्ति पाने के लिये बलि दे की अदृश्य शक्ति को प्रसन्न करने की चेष्टा करते है। इनमें नीम पीपल व अन्य वृक्षो की पूजा की जाती है। अज्ञानता व अतार्किक विचारो के कारण पुरातन परम्परा के अनुसार जीवन व्यतीत कर रहे है। डॉ एस सी दूबे (1961) ने कमार जनजातियों के अध्ययन में पाया कि कमार जनजाति के लोग मृत व्यक्ति का शरीर मढिया बनाकर रहने लगता है। उसी प्रकार सहरिया जनजातियों में मृत आत्मा के प्रति आगाध विश्वास है। उनकी पूजा अर्चना समय–समय पर भी की जाती है।

जीवन निर्वाह के उपक्रम परम्परा व परिवर्तन

प्रस्तुत अध्ययन में सहरिया जनजातियों के जीवन निर्वाह के उपक्रमो का विश्लेषण किया गया।इसके अन्तर्गत तीन पक्षो को विष्लेषित किया गया – प्रथम पक्ष के अन्तर्गत सहरिया जनजातियो के परम्परागत व्यावसायो का उल्लेख किया गया वही दूसरे पक्ष में उनके स्वयं का व्यवसाय भूस्वामीत्व प्रवर्जन व उसके कारणो तथा आय के स्रोतो के बारे मे जानकारी प्राप्त की गयी। तीसरे पक्ष के अन्तर्गत सूचनादाताओं परम्परागत व्यावसायों के प्रति दृष्टिकोण व्यावसाकियक गतिशीलता व श्रमविभाजन के विभिन्न स्वरूपो को विष्लेषित किया गया।

सहरिया जनजाति एक भूमिहीन जनजाति है जिसका मौलिक पेशा लकडी बेचना अस्थायी कृषि करना मजदूरी करना शिकार करना बनोत्पाद संग्रह करना है। वनों पर शासकीय नियंत्रण होने के कारण वनोत्पाद का संग्रह व शिकार निषिद्ध हो गया है। वर्तमान मे जीवन निर्वाह हेतु उनके द्वारा किये जाने वाले कार्यो में कृषि कृषि–सहमजदूरी वनोत्पाद संग्रह व कुटीर उद्योग धन्धा मुख्य है। हमारे उत्तरदाताओं के पास कृषि योग्य भूमि न के बराबर है। 95 प्रतिशत उत्तरदाता भूमिहीन है। शेंष 5 प्रतिशत के पास एक से साढे चार बीघा जमीन है वह भी कम उपजाऊ की असीचित भूमि। हमारे 17 प्रतिशत उत्तरदाताओं के पास उतनी ही भूमि थी जितनी उन्हें अपने पूर्वजो से मिली थी पर 83 प्रतिशत उत्तरदाता यह मानते है कि उनके पूर्वजों के द्वारा भूमि का एक बडा हिस्सा या तो औने पौने दामो पर बेच दी गयी या ऋणदाता को हस्तान्तरित कर दी गयी। वह भूमि जिसका इनके पास विधिवत पट्टा नही था वह भी बन्दोबस्त व्यवस्था के अन्तर्गत इनके हाथो से निकल गयी। उनको भूमि से बेदखल करने में बाहय तत्वो का हाथ रहा है जिसमे सहकारी नीतियां साहूकार ठेकेदार और समाज के दबंग लोग मुख्य रूप से जिम्मेदार हैं। इस कारण उनका आर्थिक आधार बहुत कमजोर है।

हमारे सूचनादाताओं का 84 प्रतिशत भाग जीविकोपार्जन के लिये पास के नगरीय इलाको या कस्बों में चले जाते है। ऐसे स्थानान्तरण से उनके घर की समस्या और शारीरिक शोषण का शिकार हो रहे है। उन्हे अपने जीवीकोपार्जन के लिये कृषि सहमजदूरी या अन्य प्रकार की मजदूरी पर निर्भर रहना पड रहा है। अत्यधिक गरीबी के कारण ये साहूकारो ठेकेदारो व जमीदारो से कर्ज लेते है और बदले में बधुआ मजदूरी के रूप में कार्य करते है। मुरम व पत्थर के खदानों में इनका शोषण देखने को मिलता है।

वनोत्पाद सहरिया जनजातियो के जीवन निर्वाह का परम्परागत आधार रहा है। जंगल से मिले उत्पादो को चोरी छिपे इकटठा कर शहर में बेचते है और आवश्यक वस्तुयें क्रय करते है। सहरिया मधुमक्खी के छत्तें से रस निकालने में माहिर होते है। उन्हे यह ज्ञान अपने पुरखो से मिली है। शहद बेचकर वे अच्छी आमदनी कर लेते है।

अध्ययन में यह पाया गया सर्वाधिक उत्तरदाताओ की वार्षिक आय 4000–10000 रूपये के बीच है। केंवल 9.33 प्रतिशत उत्तरदाताओ की आय 10000 से अधिक आय है। अध्ययन में यह भी ज्ञात हुआ कि सहरिया औसत आय से ज्यादा खर्च करते है इसलिये वे आर्थिक तंगी के शिकार व ऋणग्रस्तता के शिकार हो जाते हैं। फलस्वरूप उन्हे बधुआ मजदूरी के लिये बाध्य होना पडता है। इन्हे इस समस्या से मुक्ति दिलाने की आवश्यकता है।

आज सहरिया समाज में अपने परम्परागत व्यवसाय के प्रति उपेक्षा की भावना पैदा हो रही है और वे विकासन्नोमुख व्यवसाय की ओर जाने का प्रयास कर रहे है। इनमें व्यापार व्यावसाय पशुपालन के प्रति अभिरूची देखने को मिली है। अत वैकल्पिक व्यवस्था करने का सार्थक प्रयास आवश्यक है।

परम्परात्मक राजनीतिक व्यवस्था और नवीन पंचायती राज व्यवस्था

प्रस्तुत अध्ययन में सहरिया जनजातियों की पारम्परिक पंचायत जाति पंचायत व नवीन पंचायती राज व्यवस्था से सम्बन्धित तथ्यों का विश्लेषण किया गया। इस अध्ययन में यह देखा गया कि अन्य जनजातियों के समान ही सहरिया जनजातियों में पंचायत व्यवस्था पारम्परिक रूप से विद्यमान रही है। इनकी पथक जाति पंचायत होती है जिसमे तीन पद–माते मुखिया और साना होते है। यह संगठन समय–समय पर आवश्यकतानुसार जाति विशयक किसी भी समस्या के संदर्भ में निर्णय देने का कार्य करता है। उक्त पदो।के गठन की भागीदारी के लिए बारह गांवों के सहरिया आते हैं और इन तीन सहरिया व्यक्तियों का चयन करते है। जब तक ये पद भरे रहते है।तब तक उस पर अन्य का चयन नही होता।

सहरिया पंचायत समुदाय के सदस्यों के जीवन के प्रत्येक पक्ष कों नियंत्रित करती है तथा उनको नियमित व निर्देशित करती है। पारम्परिक पंचायतों का मुख्य कार्य विवाह से संबंधित अधिमान्यताओं व निषेधों का परिपालन,समाज विरोधी कार्यो को रोकना, सामाजिक, सांस्कृतिक व धार्मिक कार्यो का निर्वहन करना है। इसके अतिरिक्त विधवाओं व परित्यक्ताओं

के लिए पुर्नविवाह की अनुमति प्रदान करना, उत्तराधिकार सम्बन्धी विवादों का हल करना, व मजदूरी संबंधी विवादों का निराकरण करने का भी कार्य करती है। हमारे सर्वाधिक 88 प्रतिशत उत्तरदाता यह मानते हैकि परम्परागत पंचायतें उपयोगी है।

वैधानिक प्रावधानों के कारण परम्परागत पंचायतों के अधिकार सीमित हो गये है, फिर भी पारम्परिक विवादों में परम्परागत पंचायतों को ही महत्वपूर्ण माना गया है। सहरिया पंचायम अपनी विशिष्ट परम्पराओं को बनाये रखने का प्रयास कर रही है, पर बाह्रय प्रभावों के कारण आ रहे परिवर्तनों को रोक पाने में कठिनाई का अनुभव कर रही है। अध्ययन से यह विदित हुआ कि सहरिया आज भी परम्परागत पंचायतों के प्रति आस्था रखते है। वैधानिक पंचायतों ने परम्परागत जाति पंचायत के अधिकार, कार्यक्षेत्र व प्रभाव को प्रतिकूल प्रभावित किया है फिर भी परम्परागत पंचायते भविष्य में बनी रहेगी क्योंकि परम्परागत वैधानिक पंचायतों के कार्यो में हस्तक्षेप न करते हुए स्वयं की अनुरक्षा के प्रति जागरूक है।

सहरिया जनजाति केवल अपनी जातिगत पंचायतों के प्रति जागरूक नही है, बल्कि वैधानिक पंचायतों व राजनीतिक क्रियकलापों के प्रति भी जागरूक है। मतदान व्यवहार में इनके परिवार के स्त्री–पुरूष समान रूप से भागीदारी करते है। हमारे उत्तरदाताओं का सर्वाधिक 93.7 प्रतिशत भाग पिछले पंचायत चुनावों में मतदान व्यवहार में भागीदारी किये थे मतदान न करने वालों की संख्या न्यूनतम होती है।

हमारे उत्तरदाताओं का एक न्यूनतम भाग 5.7 प्रतिशत पिछले पंचायत के चुनाव में पंच/सरपंच हेतु प्रत्याशी बने और निर्वाचित भी हुए। शेष प्रत्याशी के लिए चुनाव कार्य मे सहयोग दिया। चुनाव कार्य में सहयोग का तात्पर्य प्रत्याशी को वोट दिलाने के लिए मतदाताओं से सम्पर्क चुनाव प्रचार करना, इश्तहार लगाना, आदि है। हमारे उत्तरदताओं का एक न्यनूतम भाग 20 प्रतिशत चुनाव के समय राजनीतिक विचार विमर्श भी करते है। यह विचार विमर्श परिवार, पडोसी व जातिगत पंचायतों के सदस्यों के बीच की जाती है।

हमारे उत्तरदाताओं का सर्वाधिक भाग 90.3 प्रतिशत यह मानता है कि वैधानिक पंचायते जनजातीय विकास में अधिक प्रभावशाली सिद्ध नही हो पा रही है। पंचायत से जिन लोगो ने जनजातीय क्षेत्रो में लाभ उठाया है वे या तो जनजातियों के निर्वाचित प्रतिनिधि थें या जनजातियों के परम्परागत अभिन्न वर्गो में से थे। अर्थात व्यवस्था परम्परागत हो या

आधुनिक जनसामान्य विकास से हमेशा वंचित रहा है। विकास योजनाओं का लाभ निर्वाचित नेतृत्व ही उठाने में सफल हुआ है।

हमारे सर्वाधिक उत्तरदाता यह मानते है कि जनजातियों का समाजिक आर्थिक विकास केवल जनजातीय संगठन से ही हो सकता है क्योंकि गैर जनजातीय सदस्यों द्वारा उनके प्रति उपेक्षापूर्ण व्यवहार किया जाता है। यह उपेक्षापूर्ण व्यवहार सामाजिक आर्थिक धार्मिक और राजनीतिक क्षेत्रो में ज्यादा किया जाता है। इस कारण जातिगत संगठन का होना आवश्यक है।

सहरिया जनजातियों की मुख्य समस्यायें

प्रस्तुत अध्ययन में सहरिया जनजातियों की मुख्य समस्याओं को विष्लेषित करने का प्रयास किया गया। सहरिया सामाज की समस्याये।तो बहुआयामी है पर विश्लेषण हेतु जिन विन्दुओं को लिया गया है उनमें से समाजिक व धार्मिक कुरीतियां निर्धनता व बेरोजगारी अशिक्षा एव भूमि हस्तानान्तरण आदि मुख्य है। तथ्यों के विश्लेषण के बाद हमने पाया कि अशिक्षा बालविवाह नशाखोरी और अन्धविश्वास की समस्या सहरिया जनजातियों में अधिक है। हमारे सर्वाधिक उत्तरदाता अशिक्षित है और उन्हे इस बात की जानकारी नही है कि शासन द्वारा उनके बच्चों के विवाह की आयु निर्धारित की गयी है। वे आज भी अपने बच्चो का विवाह 15–17 वर्ष के बीच कर देते है। इनके यहां अन्धविश्वासिता भी अधिक मात्रा में पायी जाती है। ये लोग समय समय पर आने वाली बीमारियो कष्टो व विपत्तियों से मुक्ति पाने के लिये अदृश्य शक्ति को प्रसन्न करने का प्रयास करत है। जादू–टोना, झाड़–फूक अनिष्ट के पीछे–मृतात्मा का प्रकोप आज भी ये स्वीकार करते हैं। हमारे तीन चौथाई से अधिक उत्तरदाता मद्यपान का सेवन करते हैं। मद्यपान में कच्ची शराब महुआ का बना हुआ अधिक मात्र सेवन किया जाता है। ये कच्ची शराब स्वयं बनाते है और कुछ सीमा तक क्रय भी करते हैं।

सरकारी आंकड़ो के अनुसार ग्वालियर सम्भाग की सहरिया परिवार गरीबी रेखा के नीचे निवास कर रहे है। इनकी जीविकोपार्जन अर्थव्यवस्था बाजार अर्थव्यवस्था में बदल गयी हैं। इस परिवर्तन ने इन्हे त्रस्त कर दी है। इनमें भूमि हस्तान्तरण की समस्या सर्वाधिक है। इनके पडोसी समुदाय कुर्मी मुस्लिम मारवाड़ी पंजाबियों ने इनकी भूमि पर अक्रिमण कर लिया है जिस कारण अधिकांश सहरिया भूमिहीन हो गये हैं और अब वे जीविकोपार्जन के लिये केवल मजदूरी पर निर्भर हो गये हैं। उत्तरदाताओ

का 92 प्रतिशत भाग मजदूरी कर अपना जीवन निर्वाह कर रहे है। भूमिहीन होने के कारण नगरीय इलाको में प्रवास के लिये बाध्य है। ये ऋणग्रस्तता व कुपोषण की समस्या से भी ग्रसित हैं। ऋणग्रस्तता के कारण उनका शोषण जागीरदारो जमीदारों व साहूकारो ने किया है। उन्हे बंधुआ मजदूर बनकर उनके कर्ज का निपटारा करना पडता है। निर्धनता व ऋणग्रस्तता के कारण इन्हे सन्तुलित आहर नही मिल पा रहा है जिससे वे कुपोषण के शिकार हो गये। निर्धनता ऋणग्रंस्तता साहूकारो महाजनो द्वारा इनके आर्थिक शोषण आर्थिक समस्याओं के विभिन्न स्वरूप है।

भूमि व वनो पर जनजातियों के अधिकार का हनन अपव्यय की प्रवति अशिक्षा भाग्यवादी व संकुचित विचारधारा सहरिया समाज की निर्धनता के प्रमुख कारण है। निर्धनता के कारण तीन चौथाई से अधिक उत्तरदाता सेंठ साहूकारो और महाजनो के ऋणी है। आकस्मिक व्यय की पूर्ति हेतु इन्हे ऋण लेना पड़ता है।

आवास की समस्या इनकी एक मुख्य समस्या है। सर्वाधिक उत्तरदाता कच्ची मिट्टी के बने मकानों में रहते हैं जिसमें केवल एक या दो कमरे बने हुए हैं। ये लोग आपसी सहयोग से मकान बना लेते हैं। मकान बनाने के लिये आवश्यक सामग्री वनो से प्राप्त कर लेते हैं। शासन ने इन्हे कुटीर उपलब्ध कराने की व्यवस्था की है पर शासन द्वारा बनाये गये कुटीरों में ये नही रहना चाहते। इसका मुख्य कारण कुटीर इनके बस्ती से बहुत दूर बनायी जाती है। असुरक्षा एकाकीपन अन्य स्वजातीय लोगो की दिनचर्या में सम्मलित न होने के कारण ये उसे पसन्द नही करते। स्वयं के भवन बनाने या उसमें सुधार के लिये शासन द्वारा सुविधायें उपलध करायी जाती हैं पर जानकारी के अभाव में इन्हे उसका लाभ नही मिल पा रहा है।

सहरिया जनजातियों में गत्यात्मकता का मूल्यांकन

प्रस्तुत अध्ययन में उन कारको विश्लेषण किया गया जो गतिशीलता को बढाने में अपना योगदान देते हैं। इसमें एक ओर गतिशीलता के साधक कारको संस्कृतिकरण एव पश्चिमीकरण औद्योगीकरण और नगरीकरण की प्रक्रिया का सहरिया समाज पर पड़ने वाले प्रभावो का विश्लेषण किया गया तो दूसरी तरफ इनके विकास हेतु संचालित योजनाओं कल्याण कार्यक्रमों एवं उनके क्रियान्यवन को विष्लेषित किया गया।

तथ्यों के विश्लेषण के पश्चात हमने पाया कि गतिशीलता के साधक कारको ने सहरिया जनजीवन को प्रभावित किया है। हमारे एक तिहाई से अधिक उत्तरदाता यह मानते हैं कि उनके रीति रिवाज कर्मकाण्ड विचार

धारा व जीवन पद्धति गैर–जनजातियों से भिन्न है और वे गैर–जनजातियों के रीति रिवाज कर्मकाण्ड विचारधारा व जीवन पद्धति को अपने जीवन में उतारने का प्रयास करते है जिससे उनके सामाजिक स्थिति में सुधार हो सके। हमारे अधिकांश उत्तरदाता धार्मिक कृत्यों भोजन करने महिलाओ को अधिकाधिक स्वतन्त्रता देने व बच्चो के जीवन साथी के चयन में आधुनिकता के उतने हिमायती नही है जितना व्यवसाय व पहनावे में। इससे यह स्पष्ट होता है कि सस्कृति के प्रमुख क्षेत्र धर्म विवाह पारिवारिक मर्यादा व आचार व्यावहार में गतिशीलता की मात्रा कम है जबकि व्यावसाय व पहनावा में अधिक है। हमारे आधे से अधिक उत्तरदाता परम्परागत व्यवासायो के स्थान पर विकासोन्नोमुख पेशो में लगना चाहते है। इसका प्रमुख कारण परम्मपरागत पेशो की अनुपयुक्तता नये व युवा सदस्यों द्वारा परम्परागत व्यवसायो का विरोध श्रमसाध्य व हीनता का सूचक का होना है। वे व्यवसाय रोजगार व मजदूरी के लिये गावं की अपेक्षा नगर को अधिक उपयुक्त मानते है क्योंकि नगर का वातावरण औद्यौगिक है। यातायात व संचार की अधिकता कार्यकुशलता मे वद्धि व अधिक मजदूरी इसका मुख्य कारण है।

परिवर्तन को धरित करने में शिक्षा की महत्वपूर्ण भूमिका है पर हमारे सर्वाधिक उत्तरदाता अशिक्षित है। पुरूषो में नाम मात्र की शिक्षा जबकि महिलाएं शत–प्रतिशत अशिक्षित है। हलांकि जनजातिय क्षेत्रो में शिक्षा का स्तर उॅचा करने के लिए शासन द्वारा पर्याप्त प्रयास किये जा रहे है। आदिमजाति कल्याण विभाग द्वारा आदिवासी बच्चों को शासन द्वारा शैक्षणिक सुविधायें उपलब्ध करायी जा रही है। फिर भी सहरिया जनजातियों मे शिक्षा के प्रति अचिरूची पैदा नही हो पायी। इसका मुख्य कारण यह है कि वे यह समझ पाने मे असमर्थ है कि उन्हे किस प्रकार की शिक्षा उनके जीवन निर्वाह में सहायक सिद्ध हो सकती है। पाठशाला, पाठ्यक्रम, शिक्षक, शाला का समय बच्चों का पारिवारिक दायित्व, घर व परिवार का वातावरण आदि ऐसे अनेक कारक है जो जिससे आदिवासी बालक, पालक व समुदाय शिक्षा के स्थान पर रोजी रोटी में व्यस्त रहते हैं। पढ़ाई के स्थान पर पेट मारना इनका प्राथमिक कार्य होता है। इस समस्या के समाधान हेतु आवश्यक है कि ऐसी शिक्षा योजना बनायी जाचे जो शिक्षा के साथ–साथ निश्चित आय प्रदत्त करें। उनमें स्वरोजगार की क्षमता उत्पन्न करे। उन्हें अपने गाँव या घर पर ही रोजगार के अवसर उपलब्ध हो। उन्हे इस प्रकार की शिक्षा की आवश्यकता है जो आर्थिक सम्बल व रोजगार प्रदत्त कर सके।

अध्ययन के दूसरे भाग मे आदिवासियो के विकास हेतु चलायी जा रही शासकीय योजनाओं एवं उनके क्रियान्वयन का मूल्यांकन किया गया। हमारे सर्वाधिक उत्तरदाता मानते है कि जनजातिया कल्याण हेतु सरकारी योजनायें संचालित हो रही है ओर इन योजनाओ मे लगान माफी, लाभ के बदले अनाज काम ब्याज पन ऋण सुविधा, विभिन्न क्षेत्रो मे आरक्षण, जवाहर रोजगार योजना, कुटीर उधोग धन्धो के लिए प्रोत्साहन, कृषि व पशुपालन के लिये सहायता ग्राम पर इन योजनाओ का क्रियान्वयन इस ढंग से किया जा रहा है कि सहरिया समुदाय को वांछित लाभ नही मिल पा रहा है। अधिकांश उत्तरदाताओं की दृष्टि मे जनजातिया कल्याण हेतु जो प्रयास किये जा रहे है वे कागजी अधिक व्यवाहरिक कम है। हमारे 73 प्रतिशत उत्तरदाता उनके उत्थान हेतु चलायी जा रही योजनाओं के सरकारी प्रयास से असंतुष्ट है। इसका मुख्य कारण योजनाओ का कागजी अधिक होना, अधिकारीयों द्वारा योजनाओ के क्रियान्वयन मे रूचि ना लिया जाना। कमजोर वर्ग के साथ भेदभाव व उपेक्षित पूर्ण व्यवहार जनसंख्या के अनुपात मे मिलने वाली सुविधाये नगण्य होना मुख्य रूप से चिन्हित किये गये, हमारे उत्तरदाताओं ने यह स्पष्ट किया कि कार्यक्रम व योजनाऐं उद्देश्य पूर्ण (लाभप्रद) होने के बावजूद इनके क्रियान्वयन मे ढिलाई व भष्टाचार के कारण सभी कार्यक्रम अर्थहीन हो गये, वांछित लाभ गरीब व कमजोर वर्ग को नही मिल पाय। इसके अतिरिक्त सहरिया समुदाय का अशिक्षित होना व सरकारी कर्मचारियेा मनमानी के कारण सरकारी सुविधाओं का वांछित लाभ नही मिल पा रहा है।

उक्त विवेचना के आधार पर सहरिया जनजातियों के विषय में कुछ सामान्य निष्कर्ष निकाल सकते है उन्हे निम्न बिन्दुओं के रूप में रख रहे है–

1. सहरिया जनजाति ग्वालियर संभाग की प्रमुख है यह अपनी उत्पत्ति राजस्थान के भीलो के छोटे भाई के रूप मे मानते है, यघपि जनजाति संस्कृति एक अखण्ड व्यवस्था है और यह माना जाता है कि इसमे अभिजात लोकसंस्कृति के तत्व सम्मलित नही है। किन्तु सहरिया जनजाति मे हिन्दु संस्कृति के लोकतत्व विधमान है।
2. सहरिया जनजातिय की सामाजिक स्थिति समाज मे अपेक्षाकृत निम्न है। ओर गैर–जनजातियो की अपेक्षा व उत्पीडन का शिकार होना पडा है। यह स्थिति सामाजिक संगठन एवं एकता की दृष्टि

से गंम्भीर मानी जानी चाहिये। समाज कि विभिन्न सदस्यो परस्पर सद्‌भाव की कमी व दूरी सूचक दृष्टि कोण विद्यठनात्मक को बठावा देता है।

3. सहरिया जनजातियो मे समाजिक संगठन का मुख्य आधार संयुक्त परिवार व्यवस्था है इनके यह परिवार पितृ सत्तामक पितृ वंशीय पितृ स्थानीय पाये जाते है। परिवार मे महिलाओ की स्थिति अपेक्षाकृत निम्न है तथपि सामाजिक, धार्मिक, अर्थिक क्षेत्रो मे काफी स्वतंत्रता प्राप्त है घर परिवार के प्रबंधन मे उसकी भूमिका महत्वपूर्ण परिवार का बडा होना य संयुक्ता का मुख्य कारण कृषि था, जैसे –जैसे कृषि योग्य भूमि अन्य लोगो को हस्तातरित होती गयी। सहरिया परिवारो की संयुक्त टूटती गयी।
4. सहरिया जनजातियो अंतर्गविवाही समूह, पर सगोत्र विवाह निषिद् है। अतः अपवाद स्वरूप इनका उल्लघन होने पर जाती पंचायत द्वारा कठोर दण्ड की व्यवस्था है इस प्रकार सांस्कृतिक क्षेत्रो जैसे विवाह, खान–पान, महिलाओ की स्वतंत्रता आदि क्षेत्रो मे अधिकांश लोग पालन करते पाये गये।
5. सहरिया जनजाति धर्म एवं तत्संबधी विश्वास हिन्दू धर्म से प्रभावित है। हिन्दू देवी देवताओ की पूजा की जाती है इसके अतिरिक्त इसके अपने भी देवी देवता है। धार्मिक विश्वासो मे विशेष परिवर्तन दिखाई नही देता है। धार्मिक क्रियाकलाप एवं कर्मकांड स्वंय सम्पन्न करते हैं।
6. सहरिया जनजातियों की अर्थव्यवस्था का प्रमुख आधार परम्परागत रूप से कृषि और पशुपालन था। किन्तु अब यह जनजाति अपनी भूमि को सुरक्षित नही रख पायी। यद्यपि सरकार द्वारा इनके भू–अधिकारों को सुरक्षा के लिये इन्हे भूमिधर श्रेणी प्रदान किया गया और भूमि को बेचने उपहार देने यह गिरवी रखने प्रतिबंध लगा दिया गया फिर भी इनकी अधिकांश भूमि गैर–जनजातियों के पास चली गयी।
7. वर्तमान मे सहरिया जनजाति भूमिहीन जनजाति है जिसका मौलिक पेशा लकड़ी बेचना अस्थायी कृषि करना कृषि मजदूरी करना वनोत्पाद संग्रह करना है। वनो पर शासकीय नियत्रंण होने के कारण वनोपज का संग्रह व शिकार निषिद्ध हो गया। जीविकोर्पजन हेतु कृषि मजदूरी या मजदूरी पर निर्भर है। इनमे व्यपार व्यवसाय

और पशुपालन मे अभिरूची है। अतः वैकल्पि व्यवस्था करने का सार्थक पहल आवश्यक है।

8. दुर्व्यसनो विवाह कर्मकाण व उत्सवो पर आय से अधिक व्यय करने के कारण अधिंकाश परिवार ऋणग्रस्ता की स्थिति मे अपना जीवन व्यतीत करते है फलस्वरूप ये सहुकारो के शोषण के शिकार होते है। धनाभाव व ऋणग्रस्ता भूमि हस्तानान्तरण का मुख्य कारण है।
9. भूमि व वनो पर जनजातियो अधिकारो का हनन विवाह, मत्यु व मेलो उत्सवो आदि पर क्षमता से अधिक व्यय करने की प्रवत्ति सहरिया जनजातियो के आर्थिक स्तर को वदतर बनाया है। सुविधाओ के बाजजूद अशिक्षा सरल स्वभाव व भग्यावादी होने के कारण निम्न जीवन स्तर निर्वाहन कर रहे है।
10. कृषि भूमि के अभाव मे जीविकोपार्जन के लिए इधर – उधर जाने के कारण सहीपायो कीी जीवन शैली प्रभावित हुई है। इसका जनजातीय स्वरूप मूल मान्यताये, प्रथा व परम्पराये खान–पान, रहन–सहन वेश–भूषा परिवर्तिन हो रहा है। जीवन शैली मे परिवर्तन का बनुयादी कारण गैर–जनजातीय लोगों के सम्पर्क मे आना है।
11. संस्कृतिकरण का प्रभाव उत्तरदातओं पर देखा गया। ये गैर–जनजातियो के रहन–सहन, रीति रीवाज, विचार धारा, कर्मकाण, जीवनविधि जाने अनजाने में अधिकांश व्यक्ति स्वीकार करने लगे है।
12. पश्चिमी करण एवं आधुनिकीकरण का प्रभाव भी एक सीमा तक पडता है। आधुनिकीकरण के प्रभाव के कारण इस जनजाति में उन्नत तकनीकि तार्किक व वैज्ञानिक दृष्टिकोण परम्परात्मक मूलों को प्रभावित कर रही है। वाह्रय संस्कृतियों का प्रमुख व सरकारी के कारण आधुनिक परिवर्तन इनमें आरम्भ हो गये है।
13. औधोगीकरण एवं नगरीकरण की प्रक्रिया ने गतिशीलता को बढाया है व्यवसाय व रोजगार के क्षेत्र में गतिशीलता देखने को मिली।
14. विभिन्न सरकारी योजनाओं के परिणाम स्वरूप इनकी भौतिक संस्कृति में परिवर्तन हो रहा है। इनके उत्थान के लिये सरकार द्वारा चलायी जा रही योजनाओं एवं सरकारी प्रयासो को इन्होने महत्वपूर्ण माना। साथ ही इस बात को दृढ़ता से स्वीकार किया गया कि सरकारी प्रायासों से जितना लाभ मिलना चाहिए उतना नही मिल पाया है।

15. अधिकांश लोग यह स्वीकार करते है सरकार द्वारा सहारिया जनजाति के उत्थान के लिये किये जाने वाले कार्यो का अधिकांश लाभ उन्हे इस लिए नही मिल पाया क्योकि उनकी सामाजिक आर्थिक स्थिति कमजोर है। और गैर जनजातियेा द्वारा अधिकाधिक हस्तक्षेप किया जाता है। सरकारी योजनाओ का वांछित लाभ ना मिल पाने का मुख्य कारण सरकारी कर्मचारियों द्वारा किया जाने वाला पक्षपात भी है।
16. गैर जनजातियो के उत्पीडन शोषण और दुर्व्यवहार के कारण उनमे जातिगत चेतना बढ़ी है। और जातिगत संगठन की आवश्यकता महसूस की जाने लगी है।
17. जनजातियो मे शिक्षा का स्तर उचा स्तर करने के लिए शासन द्वारा प्रर्याप्त, प्रयास किये जा रहे है। सहरिया जनजातियों मे शिक्षा के प्रति अभिरूची नही पैदा हो पायी। शिक्षा के प्रति जाग्रति उत्पन्न ना होने का मुख्य कारण यह है कि वे यह समझ पाने असमर्थ है कि किस प्रकार की शिक्षा उनके जीवन निर्वाह के लिए सहायक सिद्ध हो सकती है। पढ़ाई के स्थान पर पेट भरना इनका प्राथमिक कार्य होता है। अतः यह आवश्यक है कि ऐसी शिक्षा योजना बनाई जाये जो शिक्षा के साथ–साथ निश्चित आय दे सके। उनमे स्वरोजगार की क्षमता उत्पन्न करे। तथा आर्थिक सम्बल व रोजगार प्रदान कर सके।
18. अध्ययन यह विधित हुआ कि जनजातियो का समग्र विकास ना होने का एक कारण यह है कि विकास की प्रक्रिया का अवैज्ञानिक रूप से लागू हुई जनजातियो का वर्गी करण अवैज्ञानिक ओर राजनीतिक दृष्टि से प्रेरित होकर किया गया। राजनीतिक स्वांथ की दृष्टि से देखने पर ना तो सही वास्तविकता का आंकलन होता है। और नाही अवलोकन। अतः विकास योजना बनाते समय यह ध्यान रखा जाया कि विकास प्रक्रिया ऐसी हो जिससे उनकी सांस्कृतिक गरिमा नष्ट ना हो, उनकी आत्मनिर्भरता आत्म विश्वास व जातियगर्व बना रहे।